CM00924703

How to Be
One Cool Cat

How to Be
One Cool Cat

And Live the
Endless Summer Life

Robert Kennedy Rodweller
An Autobiography

Copyright © 2024 by Robert Kennedy Rodweller
All rights reserved. No part of this book may be reproduced in any form, except for brief passages quoted within reviews, without the express written consent of the author:

Robert Kennedy Rodweller
bobrodweller@gmail.com

ISBN (hardcover): 979-8-218-52980-2
ISBN (paperback): 979-8-218-52990-1

Cover illustration: Colleen Gnos (www.GnosArt.com)

Cover and book design: H. K. Stewart

The photograph on page 128 of a Chinook helicopter landing is courtesy of Janet and Tony Seahorn from their book Tears of a Warrior (www.tearsofawarrior.com).

WELL TREE BOOKS
FAYETTEVILLE, ARKANSAS

Printed in the United States of America

Dedication

To all the individuals who have helped me with my journey:

To my parents first and foremost, who planted the seeds of ambition, strength, and love in my heart.

To my loving wife Cathy who has been my most profound supportive inspiration and editor throughout this project.

To my family, some of whom have already passed away, taking their stories with them into eternity. Luckily, I've managed to preserve a portion of our heritage, which I now share within the pages that follow.

To my teachers, role models, and mentors, who illuminated my path with their wisdom, pushing me to question, learn, and evolve, always reminding me that the pinnacle of success is not a destination, but an ongoing quest.

To my friends, both old and new, who infused my world with laughter, lessons, and love, and who have been my anchors in the stormiest of seas.

To those who doubted me, for you showed me the importance of self-belief and provided fuel for my determination.

And lastly, to all the books, stories, and figures that inspired and shaped my perspective from afar, thank you for showing me the endless possibilities life offers.

This autobiography is a tapestry woven from the threads of all your influences. It stands as a testament to the greatness of life and humanity. Herein lies not just my journey, but a piece of yours. Thank you for helping me become who I am today.

But by the grace of God, I am what I am, and his grace toward me was not in vain. On the contrary, I worked harder than any of them, though it was not I, but the grace of God which is with me.

— Corinthians 15:10

Contents

Preface

When we think of autobiographies, we often associate them with famous personalities from entertainment, sports, or wealth. However, I firmly believe that each of us has a remarkable story to tell and share. An autobiography is an opportunity to recount the journey of a life, with its ups and downs, triumphs, and challenges.

In writing this autobiography, I aimed to provide a firsthand account of my incredibly blessed life and the transformative process that shaped me into the person I am today. It required deep introspection and reflection on how I have lived my life thus far. I have had numerous blessings and thrilling experiences worth sharing and undertaking this endeavor to chronicle my life felt worthwhile and deserving. Moreover, as you read, I hope you will also recognize the profound influence of a force greater than myself that has guided and blessed my life in countless ways.

A family's legacy extends far beyond the mere distribution of assets upon our passing. It encompasses the emotions and values that inspire many and is perpetuated through the stories we tell. The true wealth of a family lies not in financial assets left for our children, but in the growth of intellectual, social, and spiritual wealth. Our legacy is a continuum of virtues passed down through generations, shaping our collective heritage. Building a legacy is not a one-time event but an ongoing lifelong process.

This work serves as a gift to the Rodweller family and anyone intrigued by the story of my family and me. Hopefully, my autobiography will entertain and encourage readers while inspiring those hesitant to embark on their storytelling journeys. Throughout the writing process, I experienced moments of profound clarity and joy as I delved into the depths of my inner landscape, reclaiming forgotten or discarded fragments of my life. Much of the material presented here is based on memory, tinged with a touch of imagination. At times, it may be difficult to discern the two, but I have endeavored to make that distinction clear. This undertaking has been challenging, filled with emotions and moments of pain, confusion, fear, frustration, and yet, it has also been refreshingly inspiring. I have strived to be a fair and impartial witness, offering context and perspective to the story of "One Cool Cat" and his endless summer life.

Acknowledgments

I would like to extend my heartfelt gratitude to the following individuals who played pivotal roles in bringing my autobiography to life:

Cathy A. Case, my wife, deserves special recognition for her unwavering support. Cathy meticulously reviewed each version of my autobiography and provided invaluable editing and encouragement throughout the entire writing process. Her constant presence was both comforting and inspiring.

Denele Campbell deserves credit for sparking the transformation of my initial manuscript draft into a logical journey.

Coleen Gnos created a stunning painting that beautifully captures a specific moment from my high school years when I was lost in thought about my future while I was at Ocean City, Maryland.

Les Hines, a companion from our military days, particularly during the Vietnam War, has been an invaluable resource. His profound knowledge and expertise regarding the Vietnam War, along with his dedication and unwavering support, have helped ensure the historical accuracy of my memories of combat.

H. K. Stewart has been the linchpin of this project. H. K.'s meticulous formatting and preparation of my manuscript for printing have been indispensable. Thanks to H. K.'s efforts, this book is now ready to shine on the mainstream stage, ensuring optimal readability.

Janet and Tony Seahorn provided a copy of *Tears of a Warrior*, a family story of combat and life with post-traumatic stress disorder (PTSD), which helped me in writing a portion of this autobiography. I also want to thank them for their words of encouragement and for allowing me to use one of Tony's pictures from his personal collection from his time in the Vietnam War.

Angela Belford for her excellent observations and suggestions. Without her assistance this book would not be what it is today.

Introduction

What defines someone as "One Cool Cat"? Over many generations, the concept of "cool" persists, but those who truly stand out and captivate us often defy societal norms. They possess an allure described as charismatic, stylish, trendy, fascinating, or inspiring. But how does one become "One Cool Cat"?

For me, the journey to becoming "One Cool Cat" started with a seemingly insignificant event during my high school years. In my junior yearbook, a classmate wrote a message that began with "To One Cool Cat." Surprisingly, more classmates echoed this phrase in my senior yearbook the following year. The uniqueness and enjoyment of this description became even more evident when our daughter, in college at the time, came upon the phrase years later while reviewing my high school yearbooks. As she read it aloud, it led to a shared moment of family laughter. Since then, she has affectionately referred to me as "One Cool Cat," a nickname that has endured.

However, this autobiography is not just a recounting of high school memories or the adventures of "One Cool Cat" living an endless summer. It's a reflection on the theme of growth and transformation as I navigated the path to maturity. I grew up in Dundalk, Maryland (MD), a small town nestled between the Chesapeake Bay and Baltimore City. It was home to hardworking individuals who had moved there searching for employment at various industries like Bethlehem Steel, Lever Brothers, General Motors, AT&T, Black and Decker, Thompson, and Armco Steel Companies. During the 1950s, 60s, and 70s, Dundalk was a vibrant and nurturing place to grow up and live.

Shortly after high school, I was drafted into the Army and served in the Vietnam War. My experiences in the military and the war played a pivotal role in shaping my mind and body, a journey that is also an integral part of my autobiography. Upon returning home, I used those experiences as a foundation to pursue higher education in computer technology and business, eventually earning both undergraduate and graduate degrees.

This autobiography is a testament to the transformative power of life's experiences and the importance of embracing growth and change. It's a story that delves into my personal evolution, influenced by the forces of war, education, and the unique circumstances of my upbringing.

In sharing my autobiography, my intention is to present a collection of memories that reflect the beauty and blessings I've experienced throughout my life. This writing process has prompted me to look back and reflect on significant moments and periods of growth, but it's not an attempt to dwell in the past. Instead, my goal is to create a written legacy for my family and relatives, ensuring that the richness of our shared history is preserved.

It's important that this autobiography not be a platform for complaints or grievances, but rather, an expression of joy for the countless wonderful memories I've treasured. I've always believed that every new day carries the promise of greatness, transforming it into a "Good Old Day," and that each tomorrow has the potential to be the "Best Day Ever." This perspective has guided me to lose myself in causes greater than my own self-interest, particularly in my pursuit of education and career. With a clear vision for the direction of my life, I believed that returning home from Vietnam meant embracing the goals and plans that God had in store for me.

However, I've always been cautious about dwelling excessively on the past. I feared that immersing myself too deeply in memories might hinder my ability to fully embrace the present moment. I didn't want my sentimental memories to outweigh my aspirations and hinder my progress toward the goals I had set for myself. Living solely in the past would have meant missing out on countless possibilities and opportunities that lay ahead.

Throughout my life, I've learned the profound impact that decision making can have, both positively and negatively. During my time in high school, I faced the consequences of poor choices and decision-making, and those experiences played a pivotal role in shaping my ability to make sound judgments.

These lessons enabled me to steer clear of troublesome situations that had the potential to harm me, cause distress to my parents, and jeopardize my future.

Making decisions in life is not always easy. While it might have been simpler to make carefree choices, I understood that applying my talents without aligning them with my values and principles would be like accelerating my car without touching the steering wheel. Hence, I often chose the more challenging path, knowing that these decisions, rooted in my core beliefs, would yield the most favorable outcomes. Through experience, I've realized that life inevitably presents us with situations that demand the best decision-making skills. We must summon strength and decisiveness, even in the face of uncertainty. After all, the road of life is strewn with the unfortunate fate of those who hesitated to act.

Reflecting on my most significant blessings, several stand out as pivotal in shaping the course of my life:

- The unwavering love of my parents and the immeasurable impact of their DNA upon my existence.
- Being drafted into the Army immediately after high school, an experience that positively and profoundly shaped and transformed me.
- Surviving the harrowing realities of combat during the Vietnam War.
- Successfully completing my undergraduate and graduate education, equipping me with knowledge and skills for the future.
- Meeting the most remarkable individual, whose presence in my life has been an unparalleled gift.
- Embarking on a lifelong journey with Cathy, my wife and partner in countless extraordinary adventures.
- Above all, God bestowed upon us the ultimate blessing: the precious gift of our daughter, Casey.

Over the years, I've realized that external forces beyond our control influence our lives, regardless of our origins or destinations. However, it is through our individual autonomy that we derive our sense of identity, worth, and self-esteem. Despite this, many of us often ponder the direction our lives are taking.

When I reflect on my early years and the friends I had as a teenager, I understand that the course of any life is unpredictable. We all begin our journey in similar ways, born into the interplay of our parents' genetics and the environments we encounter. Yet, as we grow, we each uniquely harness the influences of heredity and environment. We work, play, yearn, strive, and experience love and longing. Our individual growth becomes intertwined with the lives of others, contributing to our collective journey. Some may briefly impact us, while others leave lasting imprints over a lifetime.

Occasionally, our selfish impulses can influence our actions. Many individuals live solely in the present, pursuing immediate gratification without considering the consequences for others or their responsibilities.

Have we ever considered whether our life path is part of a greater plan? Could it be that a higher power, in their wisdom, carefully crafted these plans for each of us? Plans that encompass both achievements and setbacks, including painful experiences like divorce or the regret of not completing a Ph.D., juxtaposed with a life filled with physical activity, creativity, and inventiveness.

In summary, the tapestry of my life, each thread—from the laughter echoing through the high school corridors to the jungles of Vietnam—has woven the fabric of who I am today. This autobiography is not merely a collection of memories; it is a chronicle of transformation, a journey from a youthful Cool Cat to a seasoned soul sculpted by time, war, and wisdom. I am the culmination of every experience, every sight, scent, word, and even forgotten moments. Each encounter has played a role in shaping my identity.

My path has been anything but ordinary. It has been a voyage of self-creation, constantly evolving through the choices I made, the challenges I faced, and the joys I embraced. The lessons learned in the crucible of war, the triumphs of academic pursuits, and the love that has graced my life have all played a part in shaping me. Each experience, whether it be a test of resilience in combat of Vietnam or the gentle love and laughter of my family, has contributed to this wonderful life.

As you turn these pages, you'll embark on a journey with me—not just through the past but through the ideals and decisions that have guided my steps. It's a story of not just surviving but thriving, of not just living but truly being "One Cool Cat."

So, let the story unfold, and may you find in it reflections of your own journey and inspirations for your path. As I share my tale, remember, life is not just about where you've been, but where you're going and how you choose to get there. Welcome to the world of One Cool Cat—where every day is an endless summer, every moment a step towards achieving who I was meant to be. Those steps are written within the following pages, awaiting to be revealed as you read. **ENJOY!**

I. In the Beginning

Family and Early Years

Moving from Princeton, New Jersey, to Baltimore, Maryland

My father, Alexander William Rodweller, met and married my mother, Margaret Kathleen Kennedy, in Princeton, New Jersey. They moved to Baltimore, MD, after 1940. My father's grandfather built many homes and much of Princeton Junction. My ancestral lineage, through my father's maternal family, is intricately connected to a notable figure of the 18th century, John Berrien. Berrien, originally a surveyor and land agent from Long Island, ventured into the Millstone River valley of New Jersey in the 1730s. His business endeavors in this region led him to purchase a quaint house in 1735, positioned with a scenic view overlooking the river.

John Berrien's career was marked by significant advancements. He first made his mark as a judge in Somerset County and later achieved the esteemed position of justice on the Supreme Court of New Jersey in 1764, a testament to his legal acumen and standing in the community.

His personal life, however, was touched by both joy and tragedy. In 1758, his first wife, Sis Leonard from Perth Amboy, passed away without having children. The following year, Berrien's life took a hopeful turn as he married Margaret Eaton, daughter of the founder of Eatontown, New Jersey. Together, John and Margaret were blessed with a large family, consisting of six children—four sons and two daughters.

Tragically, John Berrien's life came to a sudden end in 1772 when he drowned in the Millstone River. His untimely death left his wife, Margaret, to manage their estate. He was laid to rest in Princeton Cemetery, leaving behind a legacy etched in both family history and the broader tapestry of New Jersey's past.

Notably, John Berrien also has a connection to a significant historical landmark. He built and resided in the Rockingham house, which later gained historical prominence as George Washington's headquarters near the end of the Revolutionary War. Beyond his judicial and real estate accomplishments, Berrien was also a dedicated trustee of the College of New Jersey, now known as Princeton University, for 11 years. His contributions to the state and his community were substantial, making him a notable ancestor in my family's history.

My mother's family was from Trenton, New Jersey, about 12 miles south of Princeton. They were first generation Irish and their ancestors were from Tipperary County Ireland. I don't have much information about my mother's family other than she had a brother and a sister.

I often find myself pondering the reasons behind my parents' decision to leave Princeton and relocate to Baltimore, 11 years into their marriage. The true motives have remained somewhat elusive, leaving me with mere fragments of understanding. Perhaps the allure of Baltimore was rooted in its abundance of employment opportunities, offering a better chance for my parents to provide for their growing family. Alternatively, it is plausible that family complexities and difficulties arose, prompting the need for a fresh start in a new city. I have reason to believe that tensions arose between my father and his father following the passing of his mother and his father's subsequent remarriage. However, these tidbits of information are based on accounts from my siblings and the fragmentary discoveries I have made through my ventures on Ancestry.com. As for my mother's family, their story remains a mystery yet to be unraveled, except for the presence of Uncle James, my mother's younger brother.

I entered this world at Sinai Hospital in Baltimore, MD, marking the beginning of my life's journey on: Thursday, July 8, 1948. It was there, that my mother, in the throes of labor, was transported to deliver her sixth child. Her obstetrician-gynecologist who she spoke highly of had offices in Baltimore but performed most childbirths at Sinai Hospital. Throughout my upbringing, my mother would recount the tale of my birth, etching it into my memory. She shared the incident of her inadvertently falling off a gurney and onto her stomach while trying to get on to it. The obstetrician attending to her was understandably concerned about both her well-being and the welfare of the unborn baby. While the name of this compassionate physician eludes me, my mother held him in high regard. In fact, she was so impressed by him that she had initially intended to name me after him. After engaging in a conversation with my mother, discussing his first and last name, he suggested, "Name your son Robert and utilize your maiden name Kennedy as his middle name, along with Rodweller." Uttering these words twice, he concluded, "It's a pleasant-sounding name." And so, I became known as Robert Kennedy Rodweller, shaped by this serendipitous encounter.

Childhood and Family Memories

My mother was by herself that day in the hospital because my family was in New Jersey to reinter my mother's brother from a grave in France. His name was James L. Kennedy, and he died in France on Monday, August 28, 1944.

I remember my parents talking about how my entire family feared what the Germans were doing to the Jewish population throughout

My childhood home

Europe before World War II. So much so that Uncle James Kennedy enlisted in the Canadian Army in 1937, hoping to stop Germany's world domination campaign. When the United States entered World War II, he returned home and enlisted in the United States Army. I believe the U.S. Army commissioned him as a lieutenant because of his experience and training in the Canadian Army.

My oldest brother Bill mentioned that Uncle James was at Fort Benning and was a Ranger. After spending time with our family in Baltimore, he departed from Fort Meade, MD, for combat in Europe. According to Bill, Uncle James was in many significant battles throughout Europe, and I believe he took part in the invasion of Normandy on June 6, 1944. My brothers often told me that our mother took her brother's death extremely hard. My father and Uncle James were best friends and would exercise and box together. Bill developed a relationship with Uncle James and would write letters to Uncle James while he was in the Canadian and United States Armies.

I was the last of six children, the baby of the family. In order of birth, there was Ruth, William "Bill," Mary "Sis," James "Jimmy," Patrick, and me. My brother Patrick would have been four years older than me, but he died from an intestinal blockage when he was eight weeks old. That happened in 1944, and later that year, my mother's brother was killed on a battlefield in France. I cannot imagine my parents' pain and suffering that year, especially my mother.

When the Korean War began, my brother Bill enlisted in the Army. He told me frequently that Uncle James received the Combat Infantryman Badge (CIB), and he also wanted to earn one. Unfortunately, that wasn't to happen. I remember my parents having a large crucifix on our living room wall for daily prayer to keep Bill from being sent to Korea.

My first-grade picture when I was six years old

Bill enlisted in the Army, entered the infantry, and requested to serve in the Korean War. While Bill and other infantrymen were waiting to board an airplane to Korea, a colonel called everyone to attention. He asked for a volunteer but didn't say what the person was volunteering to do. He then said I will pick a person if I don't get a volunteer. No one volunteered, and the colonel picked someone. He walked up and down the lines and stopped in front of Bill. He then ordered Bill to step out of line and asked if he brushed his teeth daily, and Bill said, yes, sir. The colonel said, good, because you will be a dental hygienist technician. Bill was off to dental hygienist school. He spent the remaining three years in the Army as a dental hygienist. One could assume our family prayers were answered, keeping Bill from being sent to Korea. I now question why he didn't pursue a dental hygienist career after the Army. The Army trained him well and provided lots of necessary experience.

My brother James (Jimmy) enlisted in the U. S. Navy and naval aviation and completed several carrier deployments. When he returned home, he would tell me how much fun he had on a carrier. He described them as floating cities operating 24 hours a day, seven days a week. Being in a giant floating city, a sailor could get a cup of coffee and a sandwich at all hours of the day. On his last carrier deployment, he had spent nine months on the aircraft carrier, USS *Forrestal*, sailing around and visiting ports in the Mediterranean Sea. Jimmy loved the Navy and probably would have made it his career. However, while walking across the flight deck after a flight operation, he was injured by something striking his ankle. He nearly lost his foot. A flight boot made of heavy leather covered his ankle and saved his foot. They sent him to Germany for medical care and then back to Pensacola, Florida.

I was about seven years old when my parents drove to Florida to visit Jimmy in the Pensacola Naval Air Station hospital during his rehabilitation. It was a multi-day drive, and we went through several southern states. My parents would stop our car along the road where people were picking cotton. My parents would share our food and water with the people working in the fields. Entire families were working in those cotton fields. A boy, maybe my age, took me into the cotton plants and showed me how to pick the cotton. He told me to keep the cotton I picked, and for years I prized that cotton. It was just a moment in time, but a moment that was imprinted in my heart and mind. I still remember so many years later.

I remember little about Pensacola except seeing Jimmy with his bandaged foot, walking with crutches, and visiting the white sand beaches. We met a family from New York at one beach who were also visiting a relative at the Naval hospital, and they had a baby boy and a girl about two years older than me. We would return to that beach for several days, and my new girlfriend taught me how to swim in the Gulf of Mexico. The waters of the

Me on my father's lap with my mother and brother Jimmy after changing out of our church clothes on a Sunday afternoon. Jimmy would eventually enlist in the Navy.

Gulf of Mexico changed colors as I looked out over the water thinking how beautiful it appeared. I asked my parents and Jimmy to go to the waterline so I could show them its beauty.

Jimmy continued to improve after we left, and he returned home three times over the next two years. Not long after his last trip home, the Navy medically discharged him. I believe that his medical discharge from the Navy negatively impacted the rest of his life. He constantly searched for the Navy environment in every job he held over his life.

He encouraged me to think about joining the Navy after high school. He said I could fly jets off carriers, and I countered that I needed a college education. He responded that I could enter the Navy without a college education, and he could coach me on how to pass all the tests to become a warrant officer. I would join the Navy as a warrant officer and then attend flight school. It sounded exciting, but he couldn't persuade me. After high school, I wanted to attend Essex Community College and then attend a four-year school.

My early life unfolded like a rich tapestry, vibrant with joy, challenges, and growth. Now, I enter a quieter next chapter, marked by goodbyes and memories settling like dust. Each step forward amplifies the weight of absence. My parents, the pillars of my childhood, and siblings have all passed away, leaving me the last of my immediate family. This profound loss has reshaped me, forcing a new reality upon my life.

Yet, this journey through grief isn't solely about loss. It's a testament to life's impermanence and the enduring strength of love's embrace. Even in death, their love remains a guiding light. As you turn these pages, join me on a gentle walk down memory lane. We'll explore the lives of my immediate family members, where the shadows of their absence mingle with the enduring light of their legacy.

Deaths of My Father and Mother, Sisters, and Brothers

My Father: April 20, 1909–October 5, 1974

Dealing with the loss of family members, dear friends and loving pets has presented me with some of the most intricate challenges in life. While I recognize that loss is an inherent part of our human journey, coming to terms with the shock and bewilderment that accompanies such losses has proven to be an arduous task. Early on, I understood that nurturing my emotional well-being hinged upon my ability to effectively navigate the depths of grief. I realized that responding to grief and sorrow with nothing, but anger left me embittered and cynical. This exacerbated the pain already ingrained in the experience of loss itself. This poignant realization compelled me to acknowledge the innate resilience with which we are all born and to summon the strength necessary to overcome the weight of my losses and to forge ahead on the path of life.

Shortly after my father's retirement, he made the decision to purchase a small boat specifically for fishing on Friday evenings. Intrigued by his choice, I inquired about his reasoning behind it. His response struck me with a sense of thoughtfulness and consideration. He explained that the purpose of the boat was to provide my mother with much-needed time alone. Concerned that they might spend an excessive amount of time together in their newfound retirement, he wanted to ensure that she had opportunities to indulge in her solitary hobbies, particularly her passion for crafting. Thus, boating and fishing on Friday evenings became a cherished routine for my father, granting my mother the solitude she desired and the chance to engage in her beloved crafts.

Approximately six months later, my father made another purchase that reflected his commitment to improving their home. He acquired a cement mixer with the intention of redoing their concrete driveway and driveway apron. One evening, I visited my parents for dinner and stayed a few hours afterward visiting. As the evening came to a close and I prepared to leave for my apartment, they both walked me to my car. I mentioned that I would come by on Saturday morning to assist with the concrete work for the driveway. My father smiled warmly and expressed his gratitude, saying he could use my help. It was yet another opportunity for us to bond and spend quality time together. I bid them farewell, telling them I loved them both, and headed back to my apartment.

The following day, as was his routine, my father went boating and fishing, enjoying his Friday pastime. He always made sure to return home before dark, knowing it would ease my mother's worries. She often praised him, remarking how reliably he would be back well before nightfall. This aspect of their Friday alone time was something my father approached matter-of-factly, prioritizing my mother's peace of mind.

But this Friday evening was different because he didn't return home before dark. As the night progressed and Dad didn't return home, my mother called the police. The police came to my parent's home, took a statement from my mother, and then went to Hart-Miller Island, where my father kept his boat. It wasn't long before they contacted the Coast Guard to assist in searching for my father throughout the night and into the following day.

My mother had provided the police with my name and address if they needed additional information or help locating my father. At approximately 5:30 a.m. Saturday morning, I was sound asleep in my apartment. I lived on the second floor of an apartment building. The guy who lived below me was always stoned when I saw or spoke to him. I believe he sold drugs from his apartment. I had often thought, what if the police raid his apartment and mistake mine for his? This 5:30 a.m., I woke to a banging and beating on my apartment door. At first, I thought someone was trying to break in.

I ran to the door in my underwear and opened it immediately when I saw the police through the security peep hole in the door.

Startled and caught off guard, I found myself standing in my underwear, the door wide open, as two police officers pushed me backward and entered my apartment. They wasted no time in questioning me, asking if I was Robert Kennedy Rodweller, and confirming the identity of my father, Alexander William Rodweller. Still processing the situation, I hastily replied, "Yes sir," my mind racing with thoughts of what this could possibly mean and whether my father was safe.

Amidst the whirlwind of emotions and confusion, one of the officers kindly suggested that I put on some clothes. Although the exact details of that moment escape me now, the gravity of the situation became increasingly apparent. The uncertainty and concern for my father's well-being weighed heavily on my mind, leaving me anxious and desperate for answers.

After quickly getting dressed, I rejoined the police officers who were waiting to share the devastating news with me. It seemed as though they had intentionally waited for me to be fully awake and composed before delivering the information. With a grave expression, one of the officers proceeded to recount the series of events that had unfolded since my mother's initial call, detailing the extensive search efforts conducted by the police and Coast Guard in an attempt to locate my father. Regrettably, their efforts transitioned into a recovery operation when they discovered only his boat adrift without him. In the early hours of the morning, a body believed to be my fathers was found floating not far from Hart-Miller Island in the Chesapeake Bay.

The officer then presented me with a difficult choice, asking if I would accompany them or follow in my car to identify the body. My emotions were in turmoil, and I could not bear the thought of breaking down and crying in the presence of the officers while confined within their vehicle.

As I trailed behind the police cars, an overwhelming sense of dread washed over me, and I couldn't shake the dreadful premonition that this would indeed be my father. My anxiety reached its peak, and I knew I had to summon immense courage and fortitude from the depths of my soul.

Drawing upon my experiences in Vietnam, I understood that courage was not the absence of fear, but rather the ability to confront and conquer it, refusing to allow fear to dictate my actions. I acknowledged that this situation was distinct from my time in Vietnam. I couldn't afford to lose control and succumb to despair if it turned out to be my father. It would require an extraordinary level of bravery to remain composed, demonstrating strength and thoughtfulness. I knew that my mother would be looking to me for solace and courage if the body indeed belonged to my father.

As we reached the Coast Guard boat dock, I was directed towards a group of police and Coast Guard officers who were awaiting my arrival. With their guidance, I made my way onto the ship, where they led me to the side where my father's lifeless body lay. Time seemed to stand still as I stood there, unable to comprehend the reality before me. It was as if my mind refused to accept that this lifeless figure was my father. His body appeared discolored, swollen, and devoid of the vitality that had defined him just two days earlier. The sight evoked a profound sense of anguish within me, overwhelming every fiber of my being.

Having witnessed the brutality and horrors of war in Vietnam, I had never fathomed that I would be confronted with such a scene again. Yet, in those early morning hours, I stood face to face with the lifeless body of my father, and the weight of grief consumed me. Every ounce of strength I thought I possessed seemed inadequate to withstand the surge of emotions coursing through me. Despite my attempts to summon courage, I found myself unable to maintain composure, and the floodgates of sorrow burst open, tears streaming down my face like a torrent. In that moment, I felt utterly vulnerable, my emotions overpowering any semblance of control.

Amidst the overwhelming turmoil, I knew that I had to search within myself to find the inner strength necessary to be a source of solace and support for my mother. It was my responsibility to be strong, thoughtful, and composed in my responses, despite the fog of uncertainty that enveloped me. However, the weight of the loss and the void left by my father's absence made me feel powerless, anxious, and deeply saddened. He had been my hero, my role model, and the anchor that grounded my identity. The enormity of the void left in his absence was almost too much to bear.

Experiencing the loss of my father in such a devastating manner was undoubtedly the most arduous challenge I had ever faced. Returning home to deliver the heart-wrenching news to my mother, his beloved wife, was an experience that etched deep pain and suffering into my soul. The anguish in my mother's eyes and the weight of her grief pierced through me, amplifying the magnitude of our shared loss. Despite the overwhelming sorrow that engulfed me, I knew that I had to gather every ounce of strength and composure. I would need this to support my mother through the difficult months ahead, until my brother could assume the role of assisting her.

Taking on the responsibility of arranging my father's funeral and burial added another layer of emotional weight to my already burdened shoulders. During the viewing, a compassionate neighbor commented on the beautiful casket I had chosen, attempting to offer solace amidst my pain. Little did I realize at the time that I had inadvertently purchased multiple burial plots next to one another, unknowingly preparing for the future resting places of other loved ones in years to come.

In moments of solitude, the weight of grief would wash over me once again, and I would find myself questioning why this tragic fate had befallen my father. The existential "why" questions that had accompanied my reflections on life, war, and the interconnectedness of all things now extended to include my father's untimely demise. I sought solace and answers, grappling with the incomprehensibility of it all, turning to a higher power in search of understanding and peace.

The weight of my father's death had a profound impact on my life, and I found myself struggling with confusion and disorientation in my daily routines. For more than a month, I persistently tried to return my paycheck to the Department of the Army, unable to comprehend why they were still paying me. Though I carried on with my regular tasks of attending school and working full-time, my mind was consumed by a sense of numbness and bewilderment.

It was during this challenging time that a coworker, a systems programmer with a master's degree in theology and counseling, reached out to me in a gesture of quiet understanding. She patiently sat down with me and compassionately explained the reasons behind my irrational and erratic behavior. This encounter marked the beginning of a valuable friendship, as she continued to provide guidance and support to me throughout the years, sharing her wisdom and lending me her helpful textbooks during tough times.

Amidst the confusion and grief, I held dear memories of my father. Early mornings before my father left for work we would play catch and engage in heartfelt conversations. These are lasting memories of moments of pure joy. While I may not recall the exact topics we discussed, I cherished every moment spent with him, believing wholeheartedly in the wisdom and guidance he imparted. Additionally, I have fond recollections of my mother's special treat for my father—sunny-side-up eggs cooked in bacon grease. These delectable eggs were reserved for Saturdays, but on occasion, I would join my father in savoring their deliciousness. The taste lingers in my memory to this day, evoking a sense of warmth and comfort.

My father had a special way of speaking to my mother, using endearing and affectionate names to express his love for her. Among his favorites was "Angel Baby Gal." I would often hear him call out to her when he arrived home from work, saying, "Angel Baby Gal, I'm home." Their love for each other was evident in the way they treated one another, as if they were each other's world.

Years after my father's passing, my mother visited me at my home for dinner, and we engaged in heartfelt conversation. It was during this intimate moment that she expressed the depth of her longing for my father. She shared with me the profound impact his absence had on her life, saying, "Bobby, it has been an incredibly long and lonely 18 years without your father by my side." Her words carried the weight of her enduring love for him, and it was a reminder of the profound bond they shared throughout their lives.

My Mother: April 16, 1909–April 25, 1989

When my father drowned, I lost my hero, role model, and the anchor to my identity, as I previously wrote. But I must add what my mother was to me.

Men are what their mothers made them.
— Ralph Waldo Emerson

My mother played a crucial role in shaping and guiding me throughout my dynamic and eventful childhood. Her presence was a constant source of support and encouragement, guiding me through all the ups and downs. She provided invaluable assistance and coaching. Her influence on my life was profound, acting as my daily mentor and positively impacting my subsequent relationships in later years. While my father provided stability, it was my mother who truly understood and connected with me in my small world.

From the moment of my birth until the day I embarked on my journey to serve in the Army, my mother dedicated herself to instilling in me enduring qualities and habits that would contribute to my growth. A significant

I discovered ties and sports coats in the fourth grade when I was nine years old.

part of this maturation process involved learning to recognize and empathize with my emotions and those of others. It also entailed developing self-control to regulate my emotional responses. There were instances where words alone were insufficient, prompting my mother to assume the role of a disciplinarian, resorting to a gentle slap or two.

Undoubtedly, helping me understand and manage my emotions presented my mother with her most formidable challenge, given that I was an expressive and emotionally driven child. I possessed an abundance of energy and found it difficult to remain still. Perhaps the source of this high energy level could be attributed to the cups of coffee my mother would prepare and share with me each morning. She would make a cup of coffee and allow it to overflow on purpose with warm, sugary goodness. To my delight several times in the mornings, she would hand me the saucer to drink the sugary coffee overflow. To channel my excess energy, she often took me to Eastpoint Bowling Alley for rounds of tenpin bowling.

My mother performed her role admirably by nurturing my emotional well-being and providing me with avenues to release my energy. Her dedication and efforts resonated with me, influencing my character and relationships as I navigated through life.

Furthermore, my mother emphasized that cultivating a kind and genuine heart couldn't be achieved solely through formal education. She imparted the wisdom that true kindness, care, goodness, and introspection can heal our wounds and overcome disappointments. She emphasized that her guidance could only pave the way. Ultimately, it was my responsibility to delve into the depths of my heart and address the pain caused by hurt and disappointment. According to her, a wise person must be prepared to work diligently, as life is bound to present numerous instances of heartache. As I reflect on those intimate conversations between mother and son, I believe she was, in her own way, sharing many of her own life experiences.

Those valuable lessons have remained imprinted in my memory. As my initial teachers, my parents made it clear that there would be other instructors in life who would contribute to my growth. My mother specifically emphasized that I should never cease my efforts in nurturing a compassionate heart. I vividly recall a bitter winter day when I was home from school due to a severe cold. On that day, a gentleman who could not speak or hear came to our house selling handmade brooms. Welcoming him into our living room, my mother offered him a cup of warm coffee while purchasing two of his brooms. At that point in my development, I came to realize that my parents were always striving to assist those who were less fortunate. After the gentleman departed, she prepared another cup of Irish coffee for me. (*The Irish coffee contained Irish whiskey, sugar and topped with thick cream to lessen the effects of my cold.*)

The compassion and empathy demonstrated by my mother on that wintry day left an indelible impression on me. It reinforced the importance of extending kindness and support to others, regardless of their circumstances. My parents' unwavering commitment to helping those in need serves as a constant reminder to me, urging me to contribute positively to the world and embrace the values they instilled in me.

Through my mother's teachings, I realized that life extended far beyond the boundaries of my young world. During those cherished moments with her, she sowed the seeds of knowledge, nurtured the growth of a compassionate heart and instilled in me the desire to help others. These seeds enabled me to recognize the intricate moral framework where my actions and their consequences were intertwined, inspiring me to constantly strive for improvement through acts of kindness. During life's most painful and bewildering moments, such as my time in Vietnam and the painful aftermath of a bitter divorce, I truly grasped the significance of these lessons.

Amidst the turbulence of life, my mother remained a consistent source of affection. Together, we would craft home decorations using cattails we had gathered. She taught me practical skills like making my bed, doing laundry and ironing, cooking meals, and shining my shoes. She took pride in raising two other self-reliant sons and aspired for me to follow in their footsteps. Thanks to her teachings, I have always strived to present myself decently, not only as an exercise in self-discipline but also as an expression of self-respect. I am forever grateful to my mother, who played an integral role in shaping my character.

During those instructional moments, she often quoted fragments from the poem "Invictus," a short poem by the Victorian era British poet William Ernest Henley (1849–1903) It was only years later that I discovered the meaning of the word "Invictus" as "unconquered." She would emphasize the final two lines: "I am the master of my fate. I am the captain of my soul." Instead of using the word "soul," she would substitute it with "destiny." This poem held significance for my two brothers as well.

Curiously, I never questioned my mother about the poem's origins or her frequent reasons for quoting it. Was it influenced by her Irish heritage or her outlook on life, shaped by the adversities her family had endured? As an adult, when I read the poem myself, I recognized parallels between its verses and her teachings. It became evident that she sought to instill in me a sense of perseverance and determination, reminding me that others face even greater challenges in life.

As her youngest son, I believe she aimed to cultivate in me an unwavering strength and fortitude, emphasizing the importance of nurturing my inner resilience and spirit to endure the inevitable difficulties that life presents. Her intention, perhaps, was to offer a perspective that would inspire me to face life's hardships with courage and compassion.

Gratitude for the blessings we had, such as a home, nourishment, and the ability to relish life while others faced struggles, was a value my mother emphasized. As I navigated through life, I came to understand that achieving success required unwavering consistency and persistence in the face of adversity. My mother instilled in me the virtues of kindness, care, and a good heart, emphasizing that enduring setbacks and persisting despite meager results were among the most potent keys to success. Approaching emotions optimistically, with hope and a constructive mindset, became integral to my outlook. Little did I know the challenges that awaited me after graduating high school.

Years later, my mother was diagnosed with breast cancer and underwent surgery. Despite being 78 years old, she continued to smoke. I approached her oncologist, requesting that he urge her to quit smoking. He suggested that it was her choice if she wished to enjoy her remaining years while smoking. It took me a brief but meaningful conversation with him to grasp his point, even though I still believed quitting would benefit her overall health.

After my mother was discharged from the hospital, I would check in on her periodically. My brother Bill had moved in to provide care when needed. One evening, after a day of work, my mother expressed her exhaustion. We discussed her medications and how they might be contributing to her fatigue. I suggested she call her oncologist at Franklin Square Hospital, and she assured me she would. I also informed my brother about this to ensure they would follow through with the call. The following day, Saturday, I departed for a short trip to Florida. On Monday, I received a call from my brother, informing me that our mother had passed away during the early hours of that day due to toxic shock syndrome. I hurriedly returned home, finding that my brother Bill had already taken care of most of the funeral arrangements. In contrast to my father's passing, my mother appeared peaceful and at rest.

It was difficult to comprehend that this had happened again, following the unexpected departure of my father. I struggled to navigate through the denial and anger phase of grief, particularly during my daily commutes to Washington, D.C., using various modes of transportation like cars, trains, and subways. In those moments, I hid my grief of my mother's death from the notice of others.

In the aftermath of my mother's passing, a wave of complex emotions swept over me. I experienced anger, sadness, guilt, emptiness, regret, and remorse. The pain of not being present during her final moments filled me with regret. I carried the weight of the realization that neither my mother nor my father would be able to witness the joy and happiness I have found in my life today, with my wonderful and beautiful family. This regret remains one of the most significant and painful emotions I grapple with.

My Sister Mary Elizabeth Comegys: August 2, 1932–January 7, 1988

My sister Mary, "Sis," lived through a difficult period in 1987 as she went through divorce of her husband Clarence. During this same period of time, she also developed breast cancer. It wasn't long before the cancer spread to her brain. She began having difficulty making decisions, like following a schedule for medications or therapy sessions. Her condition and irrational behavior also affected her family relationships. Everyone in the family tried to help.

She eventually agreed to be admitted to the hospital. After returning from my work in Washington, D.C., I made it a routine to visit Sis at City Hospital in Baltimore every Tuesday and Thursday. This hospital, situated on the east side of Baltimore City, was quite large and had seen numerous expansions over the years. Navigating my way to her room was often a challenge due to the complex layout.

Whenever I got lost and ended up arriving late for my visit, I would share the mishap with her. We would playfully jest about my lack of directional skills or something similar, and it never failed to bring a smile to her face and even a laugh. I truly believed that making her laugh was a form of therapy for her.

One evening when I arrived, her daughter Christine was there. Before I saw Sis, Christine said the doctors told her there wasn't much more they could do to treat her mom's cancer. It was just a matter of time now. That was another difficult communication to receive.

I did my best to be positive throughout my visit with Sis that evening. I would kiss her and say goodbye or goodnight, then head home. But this drive home was difficult because I knew it wouldn't be long before Sis would be gone. That night I had trouble sleeping. My mind was filled with different emotions and thoughts. I kept thinking about being the baby of the family and having to experience more of my family members' deaths than any of my other siblings.

I continued to visit Sis for the next two weeks. On our last visit, she was exhausted and unable to focus. It was challenging to have a conversation with her, and I found myself talking about various topics only to have her shake her head yes or no. Then I talked about all those times after she was first married. She and her husband, Clarence, would come by our parents' house and pick me up to spend the evening with them. They would buy crabs and several cartons of Pepsi. I said it was so much fun being with her and Clarence before they had children. I thanked her for all those wonderful special times.

She seemed sleepy, and I took her hand and thanked her again. Then I told her she was so kind and wonderful to me. She looked at me, smiled, and then took her last breath. I sat there knowing she had died, and I cried. Still holding her hand, I stood up and kissed her, then sat down with tears running down my face. It wasn't long before a nurse arrived. I put my emotions in check and stopped crying. I wiped my eyes and talked with the nurse about the next steps and family notifications.

When I arrived home that evening, I sat in our kitchen on a side chair and was overtaken by my emotions again. Our little Maltese dog, Biff, sat in front of me and whined and cried. Seeing how he could understand my heartache, pain, and emotions was amazing. Over the next several months, I would think it was time to visit Sis every Tuesday and Thursday. It took almost a year to let go of my thoughts about my Tuesday and Thursday visit schedule with her.

My Brother James Leon "Jim": April 7, 1939–August 11, 2005

Reflecting on my brother James Leon "Jim's" passing in 2005, I recall how this event intersected with a significant transition in my own life—my retirement from the Federal Reserve Board of Governors in Washington, D.C. It was on Monday, August 8, 2005, that I embarked on this new phase of life, filled with a mix of uncertainty and anticipation. As I pondered over my options, from returning to work to finding projects around the house or simply relaxing, I remembered my father's advice about staying active to avoid rusting out before wearing out.

Tragically, on Friday, August 11, our family time was disrupted by unexpected news. A phone call from an unfamiliar number turned out to be

Officer Newland from the Oregon State Police, informing me of my brother Jim's sudden death, likely from a heart attack. This revelation was a shock, especially learning that Jim, who had struggled with breathing issues and was a heavy smoker, was found at his computer with several inhalers and a pack of Camel cigarettes nearby. I mentioned to Officer Newland that the combination of several inhalers impact on Jim's heart could have been his cause of death. The officer mentioned that an autopsy would confirm the exact cause of death.

I immediately reached out to Jim's oldest and remaining son, Willie Rodweller, to inform him of his father's passing. Despite the emotional confusion of the moment, Willie agreed to leave immediately.

Accompanied by Casey, I flew to Medford, Oregon, where Cathy took over the responsibilities of caring for our house, dogs, and her consulting work. In Medford for the first three days of our stay I attempted to attend to Jim's final arrangements. Casey and I visited several Federal and State agencies only to learn that only Willie, as the next of kin could make Jim's final arrangements. To utilize our time awaiting Willie's arrival, Casey and I took a scenic drive to Crescent City, California. This quaint old fishing town on the Pacific Ocean coast offered a brief respite, where I mused about the excellent surfing conditions with Casey. On our return drive through the picturesque Western Cascade mountains, I let Casey, who was 15 at the time, to take the wheel and drive the car back to Medford. I was confident in her driving experience from our trips to Clear Spring, MD where I let her drive home from our evenings of skiing.

Realizing that we had been away from home for nearly five days and knowing Casey needed to return to school, I contacted Willie to say that he was the only person to handle his father's arrangements. The subsequent flight home was a time of reflection for me, reminiscing about the years of conversations with Jim, especially those that helped me transition from my time in Vietnam. His counsel had been invaluable in preventing my descent into self-pity and fostering a positive outlook. As the youngest sibling, I was fortunate to have had the guidance of an older brother like Jim.

My Sister Ruth: February 14, 1929–October 8, 1990

Ruth, being the oldest among my siblings, held a unique position in our family, old enough to be my mother. Remarkably, she was expecting her first child while our mother was still carrying me. Throughout my life, Ruth was not just a sister but a mentor, guiding me with her wisdom and patience. Her empathy and sensitivity were akin to a nurturing mother, making our bond exceptionally strong.

During my childhood, filled with the typical boyish zeal for play and adventure, I never delved into the deeper, more complex layers of our family dynamics. I was unaware of the strained relationship Ruth had with our mother, a topic that was often whispered about but never fully explained. As a young boy, my world revolved around outdoor games, cycling adventures, and the innocent belief that all was well within our family. This belief was seemingly supported by the festive gatherings where Ruth, along with our other siblings, would come with their families to celebrate holidays and birthdays, creating an atmosphere of harmony and joy.

Ruth's family grew with the addition of two more children, and I found great joy in being an uncle. My nephews and niece were not just family but also my playmates, and I often rode my bike to their home for joyful playdates. Our bond was further strengthened as I formed friendships with their neighborhood friends, many of whom joined me later in high school.

However, life took an unexpected turn when Ruth was diagnosed with cancer. Despite the shock and despair, she faced her illness with incredible bravery and resilience, displaying a courage that left us all in awe. Her fight against cancer was a testament to her strength of character, even as the disease took its toll. The impact of her loss was profound, not just on me but on the entire family and all who knew her. Ruth's legacy, however, continues to live on through her children and the countless lives she touched with her kindness and spirit of guidance. Her journey, though marked by both joy and sorrow, remains a pivotal part of our family's history, shaping the way we view life, resilience, and the bonds of family.

My Brother William "Bill": June 1, 1930–January 27, 2010

After our mother's passing, a profound sense of loss enveloped us, but it also brought a renewed realization of the importance of family connections. I found myself reaching out to Bill more often, not just as a gesture of consolation, but from a deep-seated desire to reinforce the bonds that our mother had so lovingly nurtured throughout our lives.

I began by calling him for regular dinners at our home, extending invitations not just for the sake of formality but to truly reconnect and share our lives. These dinners soon turned into a tradition. During the holidays, I believe our home became a haven for Bill, a place where he was not just a guest, but an integral part of our family festivities. His presence added a familiar warmth, filling a part of the void left by our mother's absence.

Bill's presence in our lives grew after we moved to Allanwood Place. He wasn't just a regular at our family gatherings; he became a cherished part of our broader community for our daughter Casey piano recitals. Neighbors knew him by name, and his stories and jokes became as much a staple of our neighborhood events as the dishes everyone looked forward to.

Our phone calls evolved into meaningful conversations, delving into the mundane aspects of our daily lives. These conversations were not just check-ins but became the threads that further wove our lives together, as our mother would have wanted. In this new chapter of our lives, Bill was no longer just my brother; he became part of my extended family.

Bill had smoked cigarettes for most of his life. One day, he decided to quit and never smoked a cigarette again. He would have yearly physicals and tried to live a healthy life. During his last physical, the physician suggested chest X-rays. The images indicated spots on his lung. The physician requested additional X-rays to ensure the first ones were accurate. Those second sets of images also showed signs of cancer. The physician suggested an aggressive treatment procedure. Bill asked if I would talk with the physician to gather additional information. Once again, the physician described the lung cancer spot as a fast-growing type of cancer and recommended treating it aggressively.

Bill agreed with the physician's recommendation and received his first treatment the following week. The medication made Bill tired and he felt sick to his stomach. In a day and a half after the treatment, he was back to normal. Then the following week, he received his second treatment and again became ill. I repeatedly asked him if he wanted me to take him to the hospital for his treatments. He said it wouldn't be necessary because a lady in his apartment building had offered to take him to the hospital for his cancer treatments. It also helped that he liked the lady; she would visit him and check in to see if he was doing well.

We spoke several times a week during his cancer treatments. The evening before his third treatment, we talked on the phone, and I asked him to have dinner with us the coming weekend. He replied that it would be nice after these treatments. Again, after receiving the third treatment, he felt exhausted, and his stomach was upset again. He had gone home, put on his pajamas, laid on his sofa, and fallen asleep. He never woke from that sleep. Bill received a military funeral and was buried near our parents and sister Sis in Oak Lawn Cemetery on Eastern Avenue in Baltimore, MD.

Being the last member of my family has had a profound impact on my life. It's a journey that intertwines personal loss with the broader context of my experiences, including the indelible memories from my time in the Vietnam War. The losses I faced there, coupled with the passing of my family members, have deeply influenced my understanding and perspectives on life and death.

These experiences have underscored the importance of the love of family and friends. The profound grief from losing my parents, siblings, and those I knew in the war has been a powerful force in shaping my outlook. Each loss brought its own unique pain and lessons, teaching me about the fragility of life and the value of every moment spent with loved ones.

The emotional resonance of these losses has also highlighted the strength and comfort that can be found in relationships with friends and the wider community. These bonds have been a source of support and understanding, helping me navigate the complexities of grief and loss.

In essence, my journey through these multiple losses has not only shaped my views on the impermanence of life but also on the enduring nature of love and connections. It is a reminder of how the relationships we forge and the love we share continue to influence and guide us, even in the absence of our loved ones.

44

Coat of Arms or Family Crest

The Rodweller coat of arms holds deep significance, symbolizing the rich and intertwined legacies of both Rodweller and Case lineages. This emblem originated from a profound act of love by Casey, who designed it as a birthday gift, adding a significant chapter to the family's history.

Traditionally, coats of arms served as unique identifiers for individuals, often passed from

Rodweller family crest, designed by daughter Casey

father to son, with descendants adding personal touches over time. The Rodweller coat of arms, however, is intended to remain unchanged, representing a steadfast family legacy.

In its design, the coat of arms typically includes a shield with various elements like a crest, helmet, motto, crown, wreath, or mantling. The Rodweller crest, crafted by Casey, draws inspiration from combat and warfare, reflecting the valiant service of Cathy's father, Robert Ridgeway Case, in the 8th Army Air Force during World War II. His harrowing experiences, including flying B-17s, being shot down, and enduring as a POW, have profoundly shaped the family's values.

Similarly, my service supporting the U.S. Army Green Berets during the Vietnam War and being a member of the 11th Group Special Forces at Fort Meade also significantly influenced the crest's design. We incorporated the Special Forces Insignia and the gold star and wings emblematic of the 8th Army Air Force. These elements symbolize our family's commitment to generosity, the pursuit of knowledge, and personal growth.

The vibrant red in the crest pays homage to the warrior spirit, denoting military strength and nobility, while the tranquil blue signifies our unwavering dedication to truth and loyalty. The white stripe represents peace and sincerity, highlighting our commitment to peaceful resolutions and genuine intentions.

At the center of the crest, the crossed arrows signify the value we place on friendship and our aspiration to forge and maintain strong relationships. The inclusion of a dagger underscores the importance of defending and safeguarding these connections.

The coat of arms of the Rodweller and Case families, rich in symbolism and history, serves as a bridge from our ancestral past to our present and future. It encapsulates a legacy of resilience and courage that has been passed down through generations. As I transition from this emblem of our family's heritage to my school years, it's evident how these values influenced my upbringing and character.

School Years

Growing up, I was always an active child on my way to becoming One Cool Cat. I loved riding my bicycle, running, and swimming at the local swimming spots along Bear Creek, a tributary to the Chesapeake Bay. During the summer months, I would ride my bike about five miles to Bear Creek. I would spend most of the day in the water because that's what One Cool Cat does when living the Endless Summer life.

I was one of those children who loved all aspects of life. My parents taught me that we live in a country that values all life, where each life is precious. They would give me rabbits, ducks, and animal pets for Christmas or birthdays. I grew up believing all life was sacred and beautiful. I also thought I should allow every creature to live its life to the fullest and its natural end.

While in elementary school, I had fun making things and learning how to paint with watercolors. It was fun to create a watercolor painting, but I never seemed as good as my brothers. Bill and Jimmy were both talented artists. Because of my brothers' abilities, I never thought I possessed an artistic gene in my body. It wasn't until years later that I could overcome this self-doubt. This ah-ha moment occurred when my wife Cathy and I traveled to France on a river cruise and took a watercolor painting lesson. Cathy's encouragement helped me realize I could create a lovely, but elemental watercolor painting.

Growing up, I loved music. My parents purchased small transistor radios for me. I listened to local AM radio stations throughout the day and night. In bed, I would place a radio under my pillow and listen to music through the pillow until I fell asleep.

Those little radios intrigued me, and I thought I could make one. At the Dundalk library, I found a book describing the basics of making an AM radio using an empty wooden sewing spool, a nine-volt battery, and a safety pin with a pencil lead. Constructing those radios took longer than I envisioned because I had to locate lots of copper wire to build an antenna and a tuner for the radio to work. Admittedly, the receiving range of that small hand-built radio was maybe 10 miles, and I could only receive three local AM radio signals within the Dundalk area. Nevertheless, those stations were all I needed! I felt a sense of accomplishment when I listened to my homemade radio.

I loved all types of music and still do. In elementary and junior high school, I would forgo eating my lunch to save money to buy tickets to the Baltimore Symphony or other classical music concerts sponsored by the schools. Listening to classical music allowed my imagination to visualize being somewhere different. It was an extraordinary experience to let the music take me to all those places it represented. I even took trumpet lessons in elementary school because I loved the sound of the trumpet in classical music.

I always loved to play outside. One year in elementary school, my parents bought a nice winter coat for me. It was a stylish bomber-style cloth jacket with a heavy liner and knit cuffs to keep the wind from blowing up my sleeves. In a commanding tone, my mother told me I was to only wear that jacket to and from school. She did not want me to get it dirty. When I played outside with friends, I was to wear one of my older jackets.

But one day I disobeyed her request. I don't remember why I wore my new school jacket and hadn't changed into an older one. Not far from home, my friends and I played on several high mounds of dirt created by dump trucks alongside Northpoint Road. These mounds of earth were great for boys to climb and stand on the top like conquerors. Having too much fun and not thinking of what my mother told me not to do, I rolled around in the dirt wearing my new stylish bomber jacket.

I was atop one of the dirt hills when another boy pushed me down the backside. I tried not to fall, but gravity won. I broke my fall with my right hand, and that's when the trouble began. At the bottom of the dirt pile was a sizable clear broken glass jar. My right thumb landed squarely on a large piece of the broken glass jar. The glass cut through two-thirds of the base of my right thumb, right up to my wrist. I pulled the glass out of my thumb, believing the bleeding would stop, but it only worsened as I ran home. By the time I arrived home, the blood had soaked the entire right sleeve of the coat and had mixed with the dirt covering the jacket. I don't know if I was more worried about the blood-soaked dirty coat or that I had nearly cut off my thumb and was feeling lightheaded.

I cannot imagine what my mother thought, seeing me burst into the house with blood running out of my right hand and my thumb nearly cut off. I was dripping blood all over the floors from the front door to the kitchen sink. Everything was a blur until I realized my mother and I had arrived at Dr. Jacobs' office. Dr. Jacobs was an excellent family doctor who cared for every ailment and injury. He was a short, round man who always wore a suit with his pants halfway up his stomach. I liked Dr. Jacobs because he would talk with me throughout his examination, making for a more pleasant experience. While examining or resolving patient ailments, he usually smoked or chewed on cigars. His office was inside a converted house with wood paneling in the patient waiting area and his office/examination area. He sat behind a large wood oak desk in a wood swivel chair, and from there, he would give shots and examinations.

On that particular day, my mother and I rushed to the doctor's office with a towel wrapped around my hand to slow the bleeding. Fortunately, we arrived in a lull between scheduled patients, and Dr. Jacobs was able to see us immediately.

Upon entering his examination room, Dr. Jacobs pulled a chair close to the left side of his desk and gently placed my hand on the desk's letter writing shelf. Recognizing the severity of the situation, he placed another towel under my hand to address the continued bleeding. Due to the urgency of the situation, there was no time for anesthesia, given the heavy bleeding from my thumb.

Dr. Jacobs promptly and skillfully began to control the bleeding from my severely injured right thumb and began quickly suturing, demonstrating a high level of skill and efficiency. Throughout the procedure, he maintained a reassuring and calm demeanor, which helped alleviate my fear and distress. He spoke to me in a soothing tone, providing frequent assurances that the procedure wouldn't take much longer. Thanks to his comforting words and skilled hands, I eventually stopped crying.

Before long, Dr. Jacobs completed the procedure, and I found myself looking at my right hand, now covered in bandages and splints. His comforting words worked. I don't remember feeling any pain during the cleaning or stitching. I must have been more worried about the pain of what my mother and father would do to me for having gotten my new jacket dirty and nearly cutting off my right thumb. After Dr. Jacobs cleaned up my blood from his work area, he pulled me close and said I should never put my mother through such an ordeal again. "Take good care of your mother because she loves you so much." I interpreted that to mean that I should always do what she tells me. We returned home. Cleaning my new jacket helped Mom calm down after the harrowing ordeal I had just put her through. That evening at dinner, my parents, in calm voices, both said I was not to leave the house or the backyard for a month. That was a minor inconvenience for me after what I had put my mother through earlier that day.

Dr. Jacobs was an excellent family practice physician, and I continued to see him until I left home and entered the Army. After returning home from the Vietnam War, my mother said that some drug addicts lied to Dr. Jacobs to obtain pain medications. They were arrested and the drug addicts told the police that Dr. Jacobs had willingly provided their drug needs. He lost his license to practice medicine in Maryland. I always thought Dr. Jacobs was a trusting and kind man. It's a shame that an outstanding family practice physician like Dr. Jacobs lost his license to practice medicine because he was so professional. I never followed up to find out what he did after leaving the practice of medicine.

Camping with My Father

While growing up, my father and I were involved in Boy Scouts. The Scoutmaster, I remember most is Mr. Lloyd Cavey. He was in the Marine Corps during WWII and served in the Pacific. I was curious about the war as a young boy and had watched movies about it every chance I could. Mr. Cavey taught us many skills. One night camping at Chesterwood Park in Dundalk, a thunder and lightning storm erupted. We had to move our camp into a pavilion to escape the rain. The pavilion was large, with overhead lights and large fireplaces at each end. Once we moved our camp into the pavilion, we built fires in each fireplace for warmth from the damp cold.

For some unknown reason I couldn't sleep. Mr. Cavey was awake and drinking coffee by the fire with other fathers. My father wasn't with us that weekend because of work. I left my sleeping area, walked over to where everyone was sitting and told them I couldn't sleep. Mr. Cavey asked me to sit and join in the group conversations.

Not long after sitting down with Mr. Cavey and the other fathers, I asked him, "How did you not get caught or shot at night while fighting in the Pacific during World War II?" Everyone just looked at me and waited for Mr. Cavey to respond. He smiled and answered my questions matter-of-factly as if I were an adult, not a child.

"I counted sounds," he replied. Now he had everyone's attention. He said he learned how to count the recurring sounds. Those sounds that were out of the ordinary could mean trouble or an enemy approaching. I asked whether he could teach us that skill when we played hide and seek. His response surprised me and others. "Let me think about the best way to show and teach you this." He did think about it. Over the next several camping trips he taught us how to listen and count sounds. This fun skill would eventually become invaluable during my time in the Army.

When not camping with the Boy Scouts, my father would take me camping along Bear Creek's shores, a large tributary feeding into the Chesapeake Bay. Those camping trips took both of us away from our regular daily routines. We would pitch our tent along the water's edge, catch fish, cook our meals, and clean up. In addition, Dad taught me how to clean iron frying pans with sand and how to pack and unpack for a camping trip quickly and effectively. We would talk by the campfire about anything that came to my mind. I remember one time asking him if he ever got in trouble when he was my age. His response was immediate when he stated no because he was afraid of the hurt it would bestow upon his parents. My father always answered my questions matter-of-factly in a direct and matter of fact way. Sometimes his answers about the facts of life were unexpected and surprised me because he was so honest and direct. But nevertheless, he always answered.

My father had a favorite camping spot, Pleasure Island, situated on the eastern edge of the Chesapeake Bay. In its earlier days, this little landmass had been an amusement park with a substantial wooden bridge that allowed cars to access the island. I cherished the rides over that bridge, marveling at the sound of the wooden beams creaking beneath us.

We had a special connection to the island since my father knew the island's caretaker, who generously allowed us to camp and fish there on weekends. The remnants of the old amusement park had vanished, leaving behind only sand dunes and scattered puddles of water across the island. This small, unique island, nestled in the Chesapeake Bay, held a special place in my father's heart, and over time, I grew to share his deep affection for it.

One of the most breathtaking moments was when my father and I would sit on the sandy beach, gazing up at the night sky, and witness the mesmerizing sight of thousands of stars. It was impossible not to smile, and just say "WOW" during those precious moments.

Those father/son camping trips turned into shared experiences I have never forgotten. Reflecting on that time, I wish I had spent more time with my father and mother reliving those memories after returning from the Army. My father helped me enjoy nature by explaining our surroundings and experiences together. These special times deepened my appreciation and awe of nature and created beautiful lifelong memories. Camping with my father was always an incredible bonding experience for both of us. Those camping experiences led to a shared sense of pride in our camping accomplishments and other projects. Being with my father allowed me to learn more about him on a more profound level of life.

Favorite Sports

In addition to riding my bicycle, I also liked to run. In junior high/middle school, my gym teacher was a marathon runner. Because of my gym teacher's love of running, each gym class incorporated running. It was in his class that I discovered the pleasure and benefits of running mini cross-country races through the adjoining elementary school and neighborhoods. We even ran in the rain and snow, wearing only cotton gym shorts and tee shirts. I remember being freezing cold during those events. One would think you would generate enough body heat by running to keep warm, but I never did. I bet my classmates were just as cold as I was.

After school, but before the school buses arrived to take us home, our gym teacher would organize practice races to further develop our speed training and a sense of basic competition. My bus left without me on one occasion because our training lasted longer than expected. Missing my bus meant I could run home. I was thrilled with the extra time to improve my race performance. It was late in the afternoon, and the sun was setting. Taking the long way home meant I would arrive after sunset, causing my parents to worry. I decided to take a shortcut through a big cemetery along German Hill Road. The cemetery route reminded me of all the ghost stories I had ever heard. I became more frightened with every step through the cemetery. At first, I wasn't afraid. But with each following step, I felt like I was risking my life and might get caught by a ghost. Those thoughts caused me to run as fast as possible to get out of the cemetery as quickly as I could. I did make it to German Hill Road without getting caught by a ghost and could breathe a sigh of relief. It would take me another 15 minutes to arrive home.

At dinner that evening, my mother and father asked me why I had missed my school bus and had to walk home. I told them about the after-school races, and they asked me about my performance. I said I felt good about my results and then mentioned my gym teacher had taught us how to belly breathe. It was a way of opening my stomach further and allowing significantly more air into my lungs. My father asked how I did with this new belly breathing. I said it felt awkward initially, but I felt the benefits of developing this breathing method. I would use this technique later in life in the Army and when I participated in sports training, foot races and swimming.

I also told my parents how afraid I was running through the cemetery. My father smiled and said, "Never underestimate the mental fear of the unknown. Use it to gather strength and courage." He also said, "I should not fear those in the grave; instead, fear those above the grave." Those were inspiring words, and in the future, whenever I walked through that cemetery going home, I thought of his words of encouragement. I was still apprehensive about the ghosts but never as afraid as I was going through that cemetery the first time.

Another junior high memory was when I fought with another boy just before we boarded our buses. I don't remember why we were fighting. The teacher who was supervising the bus loading broke up our fight. School policy required the teacher to call my parents and explain I was fighting. I immediately told my parents about it when I arrived home that afternoon.

Sitting in the kitchen, I thought my parents would have strong words with me and possibly punish me for fighting. Instead, my father explained many reasons for avoiding conflict and why I should avoid fist-fighting. We left the kitchen, but the profound words about the damage fist fighting could cause lingered in my mind. Physically, the dangers were apparent—the risk of injury and the toll on one's body. However, the spiritual harm was more profound and often overlooked. Engaging in fist fighting can lead to a corrosion of inner peace and moral integrity. It can foster negative emotions like anger and resentment, distancing one from the principles of empathy and compassion. Such acts of aggression can cloud judgment, leading to a cycle of violence and bitterness that eats away at the soul. Over time, this can cause a deep spiritual void, as continuous involvement in physical altercations contradicts the values of understanding, forgiveness, and human connection. This lesson was a crucial reminder of the importance of resolving conflicts peacefully and nurturing one's spiritual well-being.

Patapsco Senior High School—The Beginning

The following passage from my high school yearbook was written by a fellow classmate. I liked it when I read it in high school and believe it reflects my life today.

I'm still running, but my road has seen many changes. I've strolled eagerly from childhood to adolescence. I've stumbled through a forest of uncertainty, haunted by doubts and fears. I climb the hill of knowledge, strengthened by every foothold obtained. I run with the light of truth across the meadow to the future. My arms outstretched to the winds of fortune. As I look rearward into the past, I see the well-worn path of time.

When I reflect on my high school experiences, a multitude of memories flood my mind. These memories encompass both the positive and the negative moments of triumph, lessons learned, elation, heartache, adversity, joy, drama, and amusement. High school seemed to rush by in a blur, almost too swiftly. Amid those years, I acquired numerous invaluable life lessons and forged friendships that endure to this day.

Through the journey of high school, I grasped the significance of hard work and unwavering commitment. I also honed the ability to differentiate between true friends and mere acquaintances. Though it presented challenges, the experience of evolving into "One Cool Cat" while embracing an "Endless Summer Life" was genuinely rewarding.

On Friday, September 6, 1964, Paul E. Dowling, the first principal, opened Patapsco High School for students. The school enrollment comprised approximately 900 students made up of only the sophomore and junior classes, and there were no seniors in the first year. It was an exciting year for me because I was beginning my sophomore year at a newly constructed high school.

The first official act of the student body was selecting school colors for athletic uniforms. Once colors were chosen, athletic uniforms were ordered. A group of about 20 representatives from Sparrows Point and Dundalk High, the schools which would furnish some of the initial junior students, met at Dundalk Senior High in May of 1963 and selected the colors red and white and navy blue. Rumor had it among the students that Patapsco became the first school in the United States to use three colors for school colors. I remember the colors were selected because of our community's historical heritage. The American flag was always displayed throughout Dundalk on holidays. Therefore, the student body used the American flag colors, red represented hardiness, and valor, as well as courage and readiness to sacrifice on the field of competition. Blue signified justice for all, following school policies, vigilance, and perseverance that the students should remain watchful and strong. Lastly, the color white represented a student body that primarily embraced purity, innocence, and independence.[1]

Two of the first committees organized were the School Name and School Ring committees. After much debate, the school's name committee placed four names before the student body to select for school teams. They were the Patriots, Rebels, Spartans, and Titans. After a vote, an overwhelming majority ruled that the school teams would be known as the Patapsco Patriots. I remember that name had an excellent sound to it. It just sounded and felt right for my high school.

As the school year progressed, so did tradition and history. The student council became known for its leadership in school activities. The athletic teams became respected throughout the county when the wrestling team won

---

[1] https://www.gettysburgflag.com/

their first home game, and the basket-ball team won several victories over other local schools. In the spring of the first year, two trophies entered the scene as the Dramatics Club and the JV track team both won championships. That JV track championship motivated my running group to take our running more seriously. The tradition grew as Patapsco became the first school to name its halls after famous men; Franklin, Jefferson, Kennedy, and Lincoln. The center of the gym floor was painted with a big blue P for Patriots and the school symbolic mascot officially came into existence, a Patriot dressed in full uniform.

My high school senior picture when I was 17 years old

A few of my junior high school friends and I became sophomores at the new Patapsco High School. The rest of my friends went to Dundalk Senior High. My parents explained how school districts were established and gently suggested, "Make new friends, keep the old. One is silver and the other gold." This helped some, but I knew I would still miss my friends, but I had fun making new ones. Over time, I realized that not only did I have my old friends in Dundalk High, but their new friends would eventually become my friends as well.

As One Cool Cat, I usually wore a white or light-colored long-sleeve button-down shirt with dark-colored cuffed pants and penny loafers. Most, if not all, guys dressed alike. The girls dressed alike as well. I remember thinking that even the teachers dressed like the students, but quickly realized the students dressed like the teachers. The only exception was the principal's office staff, who dressed differently. The principal and vice-principal wore suits. I'm unsure if it was a requirement, but I only remember them wearing suits.

Growing up in Baltimore during the 1960s I was exposed to children from many different races, colors, and national heritages. One of my best friends in high school was a boy who lived in Norris Lane. Norris Lane was a black community less than a mile from my house. Some men who lived there knew my father, and on Sundays, my parents would invite their families to afternoon dinner. Having others of different races in our home for dinner was an excellent life experience for me.

Friends

As a teenager, one of my close friends was Arden. He and I raced go karts, rode Vespa scooters, and helped each other work on our cars. Arden was also allowed to drive his parent's car, a 1962 Ford Falcon. Usually, on Saturday nights, after hanging out at Amechi's fast-food restaurant,[2] he would drive us to Ocean City, MD, and sometimes others were invited to contribute money for gas. Because the Ford Falcon got excellent gas mileage, we often had extra money left to buy Fishers French Fries or Popcorn[3] on the boardwalk. Everyone who lived in Maryland knew about Fishers Boardwalk Fries and Popcorn.

We truly lived the "Endless Summer Lifestyle," visiting Ocean City regularly throughout the summer. While driving to the beach, we listened to 60s surfing music and once we arrived immediately jumped in and swam in the ocean. Surfboards were too big to carry in or on a Ford Falcon. After swimming and playing on the beach, we sometimes got a few hours of sleep on the sand before heading home. We didn't have many cares or worries in those days, and our primary interests were girls, the beach, and cars. What could have been better for One Cool Cat, who was living the Life of The Endless Summer?

Arden was a year older and a year ahead of me in high school. After graduation, he had difficulty finding work because of the draft and decided to enlist in the Army. Many companies didn't want to hire draft-age high school graduates because many wouldn't work long before being drafted. When Arden told the Army recruiter of his interest in cars he was told he

---

[2] Ameche's Drive-in was a fast-food restaurant chain based in Baltimore, founded by Alan Ameche. https://en.wikipedia.org/wiki/Alan_Ameche# Business career

[3] Fisher's Popcorn was opened in 1937 by Everett Fisher on the corner of Talbot Street and the Boardwalk in Downtown Ocean City, Maryland. Everett took great pride in choosing quality ingredients to make his secret caramel recipe, and today they still use that secret recipe.

could be trained as a mechanic for trucks and jeeps as well as a truck driver. Arden wasn't sure what he wanted to do at that point in his life. He believed this training would provide work for him after the Army.

After enlistment and training, Arden did become a truck/jeep mechanic and truck driver. After training, he received orders to go to Vietnam and was allowed to take 30 days of leave before heading to Vietnam. Over those 30 days, we had many conversations about being in the service. I learned much about the Army from Arden's perspective. When he left for his 12month tour in Vietnam, I was still a senior in high school. I occasionally thought about our military conversations. Not long after Arden left for Vietnam, I received my pre-induction/draft physical request during my senior year of high school.

Arden completed his Army enlistment and once again faced a very tough time finding a job. Returning home after Vietnam caused depression and despair for many veterans because they could not find work. The war was unpopular at home, and those who returned were treated horribly. Many people and organizations blamed the war on returning Vietnam veterans. Those same organizations would not hire returning veterans, believing the false claims about veterans being drug addicts, killers, or just plain misfits. One source of depression and despair was a topic not often discussed: survivor's guilt. Many of us experienced it and probably to this day still do.

I saw the hurt and frustration on Arden's face. He told me he planned to visit his relatives in West Virginia and hopefully find work there. He did go to West Virginia and stayed with his aunt and uncle until he found a job working in the coal mines. He met and married a local young lady. They had two daughters, and he continued working in the mines for the rest of his life. Years later, I talked with him, and he described the type of work he performed. His descriptions clearly showed that he had a challenging and grim work life.

As I wrote in my introduction, the unfolding of any life is beyond prediction. I was thinking of Arden when I wrote the introduction. Arden has a brother who is three years older. The older brother was ineligible for the military because he had been in trouble with the law many times. While Arden was in the Army and Vietnam, his brother moved to Florida and lived with other troubled friends. None of them worked, resulting in no money. It was then they decided to rob a bank. During the bank robbery, Arden's brother shot and killed an unarmed security guard. Arden told me about the entire incident describing how the unarmed guard was retired and had to work to supplement his income. Somehow, Arden's parents were able to keep his brother from receiving the death penalty. He received a life sentence in prison. I couldn't believe Arden's brother could have been that vicious and cold to take another's life for a few bucks.

Upon learning about Arden's brother, I found myself grappling with the concepts of life and death, a pursuit that gained intensity upon my return from Vietnam. Driven by a quest for insight into my post-war emotions and guilt, I took numerous psychology courses, hoping to unearth explanations to my many questions. It appeared to me that Arden's brother had not encountered any genuinely meaningful or productive experiences in his young life. I had learned in the Army that often, the sense of purpose and fulfillment emerges for individuals after they engage in an activity and discover their passion, rather than the other way around.

Perhaps, Arden's brother hadn't thoroughly explored the spectrum of possibilities available to him. Had he devoted his focus to work or constructive endeavors, idle thoughts might have been replaced with more purposeful actions. It's also plausible that his emotional state or physiological balance faltered, leading him to associate with negative influences, thereby influencing his choices and decisions.[4] My intention wasn't to pass judgment, but rather to deepen my understanding of the intricate tapestry of life's unfolding.

Growing up, I developed many activities I enjoyed. Working on cars was the most attractive. During my junior year in high school, I began working at a gas station after school. On weekends I pumped gas and performed minor repairs. My paycheck went to pay for a car and dating girls. The gas station owner was a middle-aged man with red hair and freckles who trusted me and had confidence in my honesty and abilities. I never saw him drink, but in my opinion, he was always inebriated. His breath reeked of alcohol, and he was unbalanced and stumbled when he walked.

---

[4] www.thindifference.com/2012/06/decisions-vs-choices-is-there-a-distinction/

Thinking about that time in my life, I realize I could have worked fewer hours and studied more. I might have been an A-plus student, but I enjoyed being One Cool Cat and living the Endless Summer Life. Applying myself to school and studies didn't enter my mind at that time! But another high school friend did apply himself in school. His name was Charlie Zaledonis. He was a brilliant guy who applied himself to his studies, and his high grades reflected his efforts. He lived a few doors away from another one of my friends, Marty Murray. Charlie would hang out with us as we worked on our cars but he never offered to help. Charlie always said he didn't want to get dirty working on old cars. Like most of us in high school, he always wore button-down shirts, cuffed pants, and penny loafers. While working on our cars, Marty and I wore old clothes and sometimes coveralls in cold weather.

I'm sure we looked scuzzy to Charlie.

Because of his excellent grades, Charlie's parents gave him a spotless, beautiful 1962 Chevrolet Bel Air painted robin's egg blue with a white top. He never worked on that car, but it was always clean, just like his clothes. I'm willing to bet Charlie's father washed and took care of the maintenance on that car.

After graduating from high school, my friend Charlie enlisted in the Marine Corps, which came as a major shock to me. I had always imagined he would head to college and thrive there. Perhaps his decision to enlist was influenced by his father being a Marine, though I'm not entirely certain. In a twist of fate, I too found myself entering the military soon after my high school graduation when I was drafted.

Interestingly, Charlie and I both ended up serving in Vietnam at the same time. This coincidence brought our families closer; our fathers would often discuss the letters we sent home. My mother mentioned in one of her letters how they would meet for lunch and share their impressions of our experiences. Charlie's letters often described the combat conditions he faced, which led my mother to worry and ask me if I was in danger. To alleviate her fears, I responded with made-up stories of fun activities, hoping to lessen their worries about my safety in Vietnam. I've never regretted sending those fictional cheerful letters.

The most incredible part of this time was discovering that Charlie's Marine artillery firebase was only about 15 miles north of my location in

I-Corps[5]. Years later, over drinks, Charlie mentioned playing football more than engaging in artillery fire, which seemed unbelievable to me given the constant attacks we faced. This led to a humorous exchange about our respective experiences in the Marine Corps and the Army, reminiscing about our time in Vietnam.

Charlie married his high school sweetheart after returning from Vietnam while still in the Marine Corps. They had two daughters in the following years. Interestingly, he never pursued college, being fully immersed in his life as a husband, father, and enjoying life to the fullest.

During this time, he and his wife purchased a white Volkswagen Beetle with a red and white interior. I remember the car reeked of cigarette smoke, and the interior paint had turned a yellow/orange color from the nicotine. Charlie had become a heavy smoker and drinker during and after his time in the Marine Corps.

After completing my undergraduate and graduate studies, I lost touch with Charlie. We reconnected years later, and told me that he and his high school sweetheart had divorced. He appeared to me to have lost his zest for life and didn't appear to be the happy go lucky Charlie of previous years. Nonetheless, I introduced him to Cathy and invited him to our pre-wedding pool party and our wedding. It wasn't long after that I lost contact with him, plus we had moved closer to Washington. Several years later I heard from other high school friends that Charlie had moved out of Dundalk and was working at Aberdeen Proving Grounds. Unfortunately, at a class reunion, I learned that Charlie had passed away from lung cancer. His obituary in the Baltimore Sun confirmed his death on May 2, 2004.

Cars in High School

Back in high school, there were many occasions when my car mechanic friend Marty and I would work together repairing or rebuilding our Ford cars.

---

[5] During the Vietnam War, South Vietnam was divided into four Corps Tactical Zones, also called Military Regions, and the Special Capital Zone (Saigon area) for purposes of military operations. The four Corps Tactical Zones were identified as **I-Corps** (pronounced as "EYE"), **II-Corps**, **III-Corps** and **IV-Corps**. Each Corps was an administrative and command area for tactical operations. I-Corps was located in the region nearest North Vietnam and adjacent to the DMZ.

I had a 1955 Ford Crown Victoria, black with a white top. It had rolled and pleated white-and-pink leather interior and a small V8 engine with not much horsepower. I had the grand idea of replacing the engine with one having more horsepower, but the cost was beyond my meager budget. I found a newer used engine that fit my budget in place of a large horsepower engine.

Another friend owned a 1963 Ford Galaxy 500 two-door hardtop with a 427 425-horsepower engine. It was a good-looking and very fast car. He continuously challenged me to race my car. He thought I had installed my "dream" engine with lots of horsepower. Whenever he saw me at Amechi's, he would ask, "Wanna race for 50 dollars?" Finally, one night I parked next to his car and lifted my car's engine hood. He was surprised to see the more affordable smaller engine. Everyone had a good laugh and our friendship was strengthened.

Everyone with a car would drive through Ameche's during the weekend evening hours. Ameche's had three locations, Glen Burnie, Wise Avenue in Dundalk, and Loch Raven and Taylor Avenues in Towson. The evening car tours included the Circle Bar-B-Que restaurant in Highlandtown and the Thunderbird in Essex. I can remember riding to those fast-food locations several times on the weekends. It was something the cool cats did with their girl and their car. I reflect on that period now and think, "Wow, what a complete waste of time and gas!" But it was fun, especially when a group would drive together. Occasionally, we would even buy something to eat or drink.

There was also weekend drag racing. We wouldn't drag race on regular streets or roads. Instead, we would drive to Peninsula Highway and race there. It was the perfect place for cars to race, away from neighborhoods, people, and traffic. Peninsula Highway was two miles long, resembling a drag strip with a bridge behind the starting line over Humphrey and Bear Creeks. The road was built to be a quick way for employees to travel to and from Bethlehem Steel Corporation. Bethlehem Steel owned this road, and their security force patrolled it. On weekends it became a drag strip, okay an admission: I raced on that highway several times, and in some races, I was the driver for someone who didn't want to get caught participating in a speed contest. Plus, I could shift a manual transmission faster than most of my friends with manual transmissions.

One Saturday night, the fastest Corvette in Maryland was racing the fastest Oldsmobile 442. There must have been 800 to 1,000 of us lining the side of Peninsula Highway, waiting to watch the race. It was the largest race I had ever heard of or seen. I'm sure the local and state police and Bethlehem Steel also knew about it! Upon arriving, I could feel the excitement and anticipation in the air. It was energizing as we waited for the cars to reach the starting line. The winner would receive $3,000, a lot of money in those days. It was cool to see people two and three deep standing alongside the road waiting for the race.

I rode to the race in a friend's car, and we walked up close to the starting line. Wanting to get a better view of the actual start of the race, I left my buddies as I walked to the starting line and talked with the supporters of the Corvette and Oldsmobile. Then when the supporters and drivers were satisfied that everything was ready to race, both cars came up to the starting line. The drivers made final adjustments. It was so exciting. Guys standing alongside the cars with flashlights illuminating the entire starting area made it appear as though it was early evening before it became dark. I looked left and saw a person standing on the bridge at the center, looking for traffic headed toward the race. They gave the all-clear signal and ran toward the starting line to see the beginning of the race. Then just as the engines revved higher and louder and the race was about to begin, police sirens and flashing red lights were heard and seen crossing the bridge and heading in our direction. I looked in the other direction and saw police cars blocking the race cars from escaping at the end of the road or race course. The vehicles on the side of the road were stopped by police cars. Most of us stayed where we were, believing, like me, there wasn't a chance of escaping this dragnet.

Rather than be arrested by the police, many jumped into the water and tried to swim away. I stood there in my white button-down shirt, black cuffed pants, and highly shined penny loafer shoes, looking like One Cool Cat. I decided to stay put. It was amusing to witness people swimming, running, and attempting to drive their cars away. I stood near the starting line and smiled while I waited for the police officers to round us up and lead us into police cars and vans.

I was transported to the Dundalk police station in a police car and given a citation for participating in a speed contest. Fortunately, it was not considered a moving violation, and I only had to pay a $35.00 fine. No points would be added to my driving record. The police officers in patrol boats arrested those who had tried to swim away. Some fortunate ones did manage to get away as the police focused their attention on loading others into the police boats while keeping many from drowning.

This was my only encounter with the police as a teenager, except for one other incident with a local state police officer as a youngster. I had seen this particular state patrolman for years in his cool brown and green car with the Maryland state flag on the sides as I rode my bicycle. I even waved at him every time I saw him. He always had his arm stretched across the back of the front seat. He would place his Smokey the Bear drill sergeant-style hat on the dashboard. After I obtained my driver's license, things changed. When I would see him from my car, I would wave hello. He stopped me as I drove through my neighborhood about two weeks after I began driving. He wanted to ensure my tires were the proper width and fit inside the wheel wells. At the time, I questioned what was going on. My car and my parents' cars were completely stock. Nevertheless, he stopped me at least three times. Each time he explained another aspect of how wheels and tires protruding beyond the wheel well were extremely dangerous.

Maybe he had a negative experience with them or had seen someone hurt or an accident resulting from them. His coaching worked. I've never had tires protruding outside a car's wheel wells. Today when I see a car or truck with monster wheels and tires sticking out well beyond the side of the car or truck speeding along the highway, I think of that trooper.

Fireworks and Boating

Many of us liked being in and around the water in high school. There were many opportunities to swim at a beach, a local swimming hole or quarry. Even a group of guys and girls would drive to Edgemere and Millers Islands to rent small wooden rowboats with small gas engines. We had a great time in those boats, swimming on the reefs and around the islands. On one Fourth of July, we decided to go boating and swimming. A group of us rented six wooden boats. Fireworks were plentiful and readily available during that time.

With our gear in our boats, we motored over to the sand bars near Hart-Miller Island, dropped anchors, and began to swim and play on the sandbars.

My high school friend and classmate, Mike Metallo, had brought along an ample supply of fireworks. They were the big ones, M80s, Hammer Heads, etc. We were out for about two hours when Mike reached into his bag and pulled out some of these powerful fireworks. He lit each and immediately threw them into the water. The fireworks exploding in the water really looked cool. The water would explode and blow upwards like the exploding depth charges that rolled off ships in the movies. I became uncomfortable as he threw those giant fire-crackers into the water while we were swimming. His boat was anchored with the rest of the boats, but his boat was moving around in the water. It wasn't long before I realized sitting in the boat was safer than being in the water. I didn't want to get in the path of wayward fireworks, even though watching the fireworks explode in the water while swimming was fun.

Mike threw one under his boat to see what it would do. There was a delayed blast and an upwards water splash. At this point, we all were cheering him on. As he looked at us smiling, he took another big fire-cracker and threw it under his boat again. This time there was no delay. The massive explosion blew a hole in the bottom of his boat. No one expected that to happen, least of all Mike. A sizable chunk of wood shot up from the bottom of the boat, hitting Mike just at the bottom of his right ear. Immediately, the blood gushed. I could see it from a distance. I jumped into the water and swam over to his boat. Fortunately, several others got to him in time to collect his belongings before his boat sank. As I look back on that adventure, I have no idea how we paid for the damages or the boat rentals. Fear for Mike's safety was our only concern. He had stitches at the base of his right ear and had to wear a big white bandage to cover his wound, making it look even worse. He was one lucky guy. He could have lost his ear, an eye, or much worse. Mike had to wear that big white bandage to school, and it certainly was a conversation starter.

Teachers in High School

I owe thanks and sincere appreciation to several teachers who helped me in high school. Many were excellent judges of character and saw qualities in me that I failed to acknowledge. Those teachers contributed substantially to laying the foundation for my evolution.

I had several exceptional high school teachers who were, in my opinion, saints. My social studies teacher, Miss Barbara Hinkleman, was one of those saints. She was my favorite teacher. She was always breathtakingly beautiful and elegantly dressed. As a 16-year-old, I thought she was the most classy and attractive woman to walk the earth. She was habitually optimistic and encouraging to all her students. Her classes were without exception informative and exciting. She inspired me to learn. Unfortunately, I didn't apply myself and had difficulty turning in my homework assignments on time. I was focused on my work at the gas station and running cross-country. I could have made time for those missed homework assignments, but I didn't. I was living the life of One Cool Cat and the Endless Summer Life. Miss Hinkleman was very kind and lenient about my missed homework assignments.

I vividly recall rushing through the halls after leaving the auto shop classroom because I was running late for Miss Hinkelman's history class. Not only was I tardy, but I was also chewing bubble gum, which I should have discarded before entering her class. When I finally arrived, I found everyone seated and engrossed in Miss Hinkelman's lecture. Hastily, I took my seat, completely forgetting about the gum in my mouth. Unthinkingly, I blew a bubble. To this day, I'm uncertain why I did that, perhaps becoming momentarily lost in her discussion. Instantly, Miss Hinkelman noticed the bubble and reprimanded me verbally. She instructed me to leave her class and immediately go to the principal's office.

During my time in Vietnam, a close brush with death and the lingering rush of adrenaline brought forth memories of profound embarrassment and shame that stemmed from my lack of focus and direction in high school. In that intense moment, I felt a strong desire to reach out to Miss Hinkelman and offer my sincerest apologies for the rudeness and disrespect I had shown her. This near-death experience seemed to serve as a form of atonement for my past shortcomings, mainly my lack of self-direction and failure to apply myself to my studies. Perhaps these thoughts resurfaced subconsciously, floating into my consciousness in the aftermath of combat. This moment of revelation has stayed with me throughout the years, serving as a reminder of the importance of personal growth and the consequences of our actions, even in the face of life-threatening circumstances.

There were other teachers I liked as well. Mr. Phil Retchless was my social studies and problems of democracy teacher. He was the teacher who stimulated my government interest beyond conversations with my parents at the dinner table. It was a subject area that piqued the One Cool Cat's interest. My interest in local, state, and federal politics began when my parents would discuss politics over the dinner table. I became extremely interested in our nation's founding documents along with state and local government structures because of those conversations. Mr. Retchless encouraged my interest in local, state and federal governments and provided a solid foundation to expand my knowledge in these areas. I continued to build on these interests as I matured and saw the world from an adult perspective.

My auto shop teacher, Mr. Norvell, was another teacher who inspired me to learn. My father had provided me with essential mechanical how-to guides, but Mr. Norvell advanced those capabilities to skills I would build upon and use in the Army and all my adult life. Mr. Norvell and his brother owned and operated a successful automobile body and paint shop in Essex. They created beautifully painted cars that were only displayed at car shows. I took an auto shop class as an elective in the 11th and 12th grades. I traveled to several auto shows during those years where Mr. Norvell and his brother had cars on display.

In my senior year, my classmates and I stripped the body off the frame of a car. We cleaned, painted, and polished all the components. Only the steering wheel column remained. We installed one removable bucket seat. Mr. Norvell entered this project at the prestigious Washington, D.C., auto show. We transported the frame project in Mr. Norvell's enclosed auto trailer to the D.C. convention center. The auto show was an exciting event for high school students. It was one of the premier auto events in the nation. After setting up our car project at the convention center, we walked around and viewed the many beautiful automobiles, motorcycles, and trucks.

Before going to the auto show, Mr. Norvell asked for volunteers to spend the night at the convention center with our project. Those who wanted to spend the night needed a signed approval or permission letter from our parents to allow Mr. Norvell to take us to the Washington, D.C., auto show and spend the night. My parents approved and gave me money for food and drinks for my trip.

Mr. Norvell talked with all who were spending the night and told us to be on our best behavior. He explained that we represented our high school and parents at a national event where there would be lots of news coverage. After setting up our frame project, I stepped back and looked at it and thought, we've created a unique and remarkable display. Many cars and truck owners came by and talked with us about our project. Each student thoroughly enjoyed talking with the other car enthusiasts and participants.

Our automobile frame project was awarded several trophies. We were all proud of our accomplishment. Most of us believed that Mr. Norvell was due the most credit because of his guidance and direction in making these efforts a winning project. Mr. Greenberg, a social studies teacher who became a vice-principal, was very proud of our effort. He would bring his Ford Falcon to the shop when it needed repairs. After it was repaired, he was always very complimentary of our work. Plus, it was a wonderful feeling to be well thought of by the vice-principal in case we ever stepped out of line. Thankfully, many "Cool Cat's friends" never went to the principal's office, and the vice principal received free expert car repairs!

In high school, I occasionally thought of those who made it on the honor roll and would say to myself, "I could do that. Wouldn't having my name on the honor roll be great?" But those times were few and far between. I didn't know or realize how important the value of honor roll success could be at that stage of my life. I was so into being One Cool Cat living the Endless Summer life.

Nonetheless, when fleeting moments of self-improvement surfaced, I often brushed them aside in favor of immediate gratification[6]. Back then, I remained oblivious to the fact that each of us harbors latent strengths and capabilities, waiting to be harnessed to realize our true potential. Unfortunately, these potential sources of empowerment remained buried within me, obstructing my progress during my high school years. Little did I know or realize that this significant obstacle would become starkly evident to me shortly after my graduation.

My First Motorcycle

During my junior year of high school, I came across an Army surplus 1945 Harley Davidson motorcycle for sale. Although it didn't run, the seller was eager to make a quick deal, asking a price for it ranging from 35 to 50 dollars. For me at that time, that was a substantial amount of money. However, I asked a friend to accompany me and evaluate its potential for restoration. The motorcycle was large, painted a flat Army green, with an oversized seat with large prominent springs underneath. Positioned next to the gas tank was a left-hand shifter. The tires were nearly deflated. After inspecting it for about 30 minutes and assessing the necessary repairs, I decided to take on the project. I offered the owner 25 dollars for the motorcycle and surprisingly he agreed to my offer.

Working on the Harley proved to be an enjoyable experience, although some repairs were complex and costly. Eventually, I managed to save enough money to have several parts chromed and along with its new red paint enhanced the visual appeal of the bike. The motorcycle had a kick-starter, which posed challenges and dangers during the starting process. In fact, once while I tried to kick start it, a kickback threw me over the handlebars. Needless to say, I took great care to prevent that from happening again.

After all my efforts to get the Harley running smoothly, I began riding it around Dundalk and the surrounding areas. However, I soon noticed that

---

[6] The Meaning of Instant or Immediate Gratification? Instant (or immediate) gratification is a term that refers to the temptation, and resulting tendency, to forego a future benefit in order to obtain a less rewarding but more immediate benefit. https://study.com/learn/lesson/instant-gratification-examples-vs-delayed-gratification.html

my lower back would start to ache after approximately 30 minutes of riding. I was told that this was typical for a Harley, but I couldn't fathom enduring that discomfort during longer rides lasting several hours or even days. The longest ride I embarked on was from Dundalk to Havre de Grace, MD. By the time I returned home, I was exhausted and my back was in pain. Following that experience, I made the decision to avoid long rides without taking breaks. I continued working on the motorcycle, constantly striving to improve it. However, once I was selected for military service, I covered and stored the motorcycle at my parents' home.

I always looked forward to the day when I could once again hop on that beautiful machine and ride it. That day arrived when I returned from Vietnam. Excited to reunite with my motorcycle, I searched for it at my parents' home, but it was nowhere to be found. Curious, I inquired about its location, thinking they might have relocated it to a storage area. To my astonishment, my mother and father stood together and simultaneously said, "WE SOLD IT!"

Initially, their statement caught me off guard, leaving me unsure of how to respond as I contemplated the reasons behind their actions. However, it took only a moment for me to understand what selling the motorcycle symbolized for them. It was merely an object, a machine, and having their son back home from the war was far more important to them. They believed that the motorcycle could lead to my demise, especially after I had survived the perils of Vietnam, and they could not bear the thought of losing me. What I did next surprised both them and me. I walked over to them, embraced my mother and father, and sincerely said, "I love you." In that fleeting moment, I considered the hardships they endured while I was away at war. My mother had lost her only brother in WWII, and my father had lost his best friend. These thoughts lingered deep within my mind as I hugged my parents.

Over the years, I would occasionally borrow my friend's Harley Davidson Sportster motorcycle for rides. I always knew that I would eventually own another motorcycle. What I didn't anticipate was that my next motorcycle wouldn't be a Harley Davidson. Fast forward to my retirement, and as a gift to myself, I bought a striking BMW K1200RS motorcycle in an eye-catching red color that practically screamed "arrest me." The color, combined with the impressive speed, thrilled me, and the comfort provided by the BMW was exceptional.

Excited about my decision, I hurried home to share my plans with Cathy. I was brimming with enthusiasm, but to my surprise, Cathy responded with a simple question, "Are you absolutely certain about your choice and do you intend to ride it frequently?" Without hesitation, I reassured her with a resounding "yes" to both questions. Then, unexpectedly, I asked if she would join me for rides on the motorcycle, and to my delight, she said yes, occasionally I'll go.

Eventually, I sold my first BMW, a 21-year-old model, to a motorcycle mechanic in South Carolina. I replaced it with a newer BMW K1300GT, which enhances safety features and increases comfort for the rider. This model also offers more space for luggage, making it ideal for longer or overnight trips. Although I haven't embarked on any extensive journeys yet, the potential for exciting adventures awaits.

Ameche's and the Circle BBQ

Ameche's and the Circle BBQ were popular hangout spots for high school students with a driver's license. It was common for us to make plans by saying, "I'll meet you at Ameche's." The full slogan was "Meet Cha at Ameche's, Treat Cha at Ameche's, A 'Powerhouse' and a chocolate shake!" It's amusing to think back on the things we used to say. Alan Ameche, a former Baltimore Colts football player, started the Ameche restaurant chain after retiring from professional football. He gained fame for scoring the winning touchdown in the 1958 NFL championship game, known as "The Greatest Football Game Ever Played," against the New York Giants.

During our teenage years, our primary focus was cruising rather than eating. If you pulled into one of the drive-up stalls at Ameche's, you had to order food and drinks. Just ordering a soda wasn't sufficient. We had to purchase food along with the soda. They served classic items like the "Powerhouse" hamburger and the "Cheerleader" hot ham and Swiss cheese sandwich with mustard long before McDonald's became popular. Ameche's was known for their "no charge" carry-out service, but we still felt obligated to give large tips to the waitresses who risked their lives navigating through the inattentive young drivers, as we waved to others and checked out the parked cars.

Once parked in a designated spot, a grating mechanized voice would blast through the speaker integrated in the illuminated menu, demanding

Ameche's Restaurant

your order. If you were indecisive or unable to decipher the menu obscured by condiment splatters, you were out of luck. After a few seconds, the robotic voice would assume you were only there to save gas and insist that you immediately vacate the space or face consequences. This threatening warning was enough to make many drivers hastily pull out into traffic without caring about potential vehicle damage or personal injury.

If I wanted to meet up with my friends on weekends, I would drive my car to one of three locations: Ameche's, the Circle, or the Thunderbird. The Circle Bar-B-Que restaurant, also known as the Circle, was situated on Dundalk Ave, near Highlandtown. For five decades, it served as a drive-in fast-food spot famous for its milkshakes and Cheese E Qs, a delightful combination of barbecue and cheese in sandwich form. The restaurant opened its doors at 6 p.m. every day.

Located across from Steelworkers Hall on Gus Ryan Street, the Circle Bar-B-Que restaurant had a concise menu consisting of only 11 items. Most people would order a barbecue sandwich and a milkshake. We would collect our food at a service window and either enjoy it outside or eat it in our cars. The restaurant lacked air conditioning or screened windows. However, I distinctly remember the interior featuring a sleek and shiny stainless steel soda fountain counter. There were only a few tables with chairs and the soda fountain counter was adorned with four large stools.

True to its name, the Circle had a perfectly round building, a single story measuring 38 feet in diameter, constructed from white-painted concrete. The word "BAR-B-Q" was spelled out with over 1,000 individual orange flashing light bulbs, forming letters that adorned the exterior of the building. Adding to its distinctive appearance, there was a rotating elevated sign shaped like a barbecue sandwich positioned atop the building.

These establishments were the weekend go-to spots for my high school friends with cars. If you did not have a car yourself, you'd find someone who did because you didn't want to miss out on the weekend excitement!

One of our carless friends was John Stanley Mantheiy. We all called him Jackie. Jackie and I were close friends who shared many classes in high school. He owned a Honda 50cc motor scooter that he rode around Dundalk. It was always entertaining to see him zipping through Ameche's, trying to outshine the powerful muscle cars with his little Honda engine. He would park his scooter next to one of our cars, and we would spend hours engaged in the important discussions that only high school students can have.

Circle Barbecue

I recall Jackie's battle with diabetes, requiring him to take daily injections and refrain from drinking alcohol. Nevertheless, on one evening at Ameche's parking lot, a rather inebriated Jackie appeared, struggling to maintain his balance as he walked. Coincidentally, I had parked my car next to a friend's stunning 1965 Corvette convertible, colored a striking deep red. Engaged in our customary high school talk on a Friday or Saturday night at Ameche's, we both decided to purchase lots of coffee for Jackie and then take him home. Jackie had already sat in the Corvette and the decision which car to take him home in was made.

I recall our fifteen-minute drive in the packed Corvette vividly. The passenger door handle kept poking my right side as the three of us squeezed into the loud and bustling two-seater vehicle. We arrived at Jackie's home around midnight and escorted him to his parents' front door. I knocked on the door, and Jackie's father answered. It was immediately apparent to him that his son was intoxicated. He became furious and yelled at us as we helped Jackie inside. He was angry and scared about his son's condition, initially assuming that we had provided the alcohol that caused Jackie's drunkenness. It took us several minutes to explain that we had found Jackie already inebriated at Ameche's and had given him coffee before bringing him home. While our explanation somewhat eased Jackie's father's anger, he remained upset. After leaving Jackie's home we returned to Ameche's and tried to recover from the emotional blow we had just received.

During high school, I became well-acquainted with Jackie's younger sister, Vickie. She was always friendly and pleasant, and we would exchange greetings whenever we crossed paths at school. Vickie was dedicated to her studies and excelled academically, consistently earning A grades. Like many of us in the neighborhood, both Jackie and Vickie were raised in a strict Catholic household.

Before my departure for Vietnam, I visited Vickie and Jackie's house to say goodbye. The three of us shared hugs and exchanged goodbyes. Vickie handed me a Saint Christopher medal to wear and kissed me on the cheek. She explained that the medal would protect me and keep me safe from harm. Jackie later revealed that Vickie had plans to become a nun after graduating from high school. Because of this, I believed the medal held special significance and wore it daily during my time in Vietnam. I still possess the Saint Christopher medal today, alongside my Army memorabilia.

Throughout my entire time in Vietnam, Vickie faithfully wrote letters to me. I had the opportunity to see her again at our 10-year class reunion. I distinctly remember being struck by how remarkably lovely she had become and how grateful I was that she had pursued a different path instead of becoming a nun.

Unfortunately, over the years following my service in the Army, I lost touch with Jackie. Recently, I reached out to Vickie and had a wonderful conversation catching up. During our call, she informed me that Jackie had passed away several years ago after relocating to Pennsylvania and starting a family.

During my high school years, I prioritized having fun while neglecting my grades. I was under the false assumption that I would graduate, attend Essex Community College to earn an Associate of Arts (AA) degree, and then transfer to a prestigious institution like the University of Maryland or Johns Hopkins. It was a dream that I wasn't prepared or ready for. At the time, I was simply living the carefree life of "One Cool Cat," believing that life would be all about fun after graduation, like an endless summer.

Towards the end of my senior year in high school, I was shocked when I received a letter from the local draft board, requesting that I undergo a pre-induction physical for the draft. At just 18 years old, I still felt like an adolescent. That period of growth and development between childhood and adulthood and not old enough to be drafted into the military. This unexpected turn of events left me wondering why I was chosen. What did the future hold for me? What did God have planned for my life? Over the next few days, my parents and I engaged in discussions about personal destiny. They encouraged me to forge my own path, make responsible choices, and be accountable for the decisions I made. They believed that the direction of my life was mine to determine.

After attending the pre-induction physical, I resumed my daily routine and temporarily forgot about the possibility of being drafted. I continued living my life as "One Cool Cat," embracing the carefree spirit of an endless summer. While most of my friends eagerly anticipated graduation and the next phase of their lives, I was reluctant to move forward. I was thoroughly enjoying the thrill and invincibility of youth. As a high school senior, everything seemed within reach and nothing felt permanent. Every moment was an opportunity for excitement and the pure enjoyment of life. It was an era of extreme adventure for me.

Throughout my junior and senior years of high school, the United States was embroiled in the Vietnam War, a time characterized by tumultuous and transformative changes. The nation underwent significant political, social, and economic transformations during the 1960s. The war in Vietnam became a constant presence, with news of it pervading every living room through evening broadcasts. Embedded reporters provided daily updates on the war, further reinforcing its impact on the nation.

As graduation drew near, the looming realities of work, military service, and adult responsibilities served as a stark reminder of how extraordinary our high school lives were. However, once we graduated, we were thrust into adulthood much sooner than anticipated. Little did I know or realize how quickly some of us would be forced to mature.

II. Military Detour

Entering the Army

I must have been number one on my "friends and neighbors" favorite young men lists. The following example of my draft notice and accompanying letter began with, "Greetings, your friends and neighbors have selected you for military service":

> You are hereby ordered to report for induction into the ARMED FORCES of the UNITED STATES and to report at The Selective Service Office in Dundalk, Maryland (Place of reporting) on _____ (date) at _____ (hour) for forwarding to an ARMED FORCES INDUCTION STATION at Fort Holabird.
>
> Signed:
>
> _____
>
> (Member or Clerk of Local Board)

On the day of my induction, my father drove me to the Selective Service Office, while my mother, still deeply upset about the situation, could not bring herself to come along. The weekend prior, I observed the stress and concern weighing heavily on my parents. I worried about how they would manage in my absence.

After bidding farewell to my father, I entered the Selective Service Office, located on the second floor of one of Dundalk's historic buildings. Upon signing in, I was asked if I had ever encountered any trouble with the police, to which I replied in the negative. I soon realized that this was merely a formality, as background checks on each potential inductee had already been conducted. Once all the necessary paperwork was in order, the selective service staff would transport us to Fort Holabird,[7] an Armed Forces Examining & Entrance Station. As the morning progressed, more young men arrived, further heightening my anxiety. I had no idea what awaited me. Would I be joining the Army or not?

By mid-morning, twelve to sixteen additional young men had gathered, and we were taken for physical and psychological examinations. Then the military oath was administered, and I solemnly swore to bear true faith and allegiance to the Constitution of the United States, defending it against all enemies, foreign and domestic, and obeying the orders of the President and superior officers, with the assistance of God.

Following the examinations and the oath-taking, we were directed to another sizable room, where we were informed that some of us would be drafted into the Marine Corps. It was at that moment I recognized one of my female high school friends, Joyce, who had been working part-time at Fort Holabird during her senior year. Joyce was the person responsible for organizing all the completed forms in folders for each of us. An Army Officer requested volunteers to join the Marine Corps before making the final selections.

It's truly remarkable to imagine a group of teenagers being asked to volunteer for the Marines. However, in our case, the Army officer made the decision on our behalf and selected four individuals, including me, the One Cool Cat. Everything became a blur at that point. I didn't know what to do. The last thing I wanted was to be in the Army, let alone the Marine Corps. I didn't have much knowledge about the Marines, except for what Charlie Zaledonis had told me, and it wasn't flattering. He described the Marine Corps as a crazy organization. I wanted no part of that madness.

Amidst the confusion, an older gentleman from the Salvation Army approached me and handed me a shaving/personal hygiene Dopp kit. He shook my hand, looked me in the eyes, and said, "Son, don't worry, God will take

---

[7] Fort Holabird was alive and thriving. I remember when now trendy Canton was a true blue-collar neighborhood of small factories, a can company, waterfront oyster and vegetable packing houses, seed companies, tug boat piers, filthy harbor water, and a few greasy-spoon restaurants.

Fort Holabird, where I entered the Army

care of you; you'll be just fine." I remember feeling a sense of calmness wash over me as he walked away. That little Dopp kit contained a metal razor with blades, shaving cream, toothpaste, a brush, a comb, and other grooming items. I never used any of its contents because it served as a reminder of the man who gave it to me, and I wanted to keep it as a memento. Unfortunately, my Dopp kit, along with all my belongings, was destroyed three months after my arrival in Vietnam when Vietnamese sappers[8] used explosives to blow up my living quarters. Reflecting on the man's words about God taking care of me, perhaps he knew more about how God works than I did.

Several others had joined our larger group of draftees, including Ernie Brown, a fellow high school classmate who was a year ahead of me. I recalled from our junior yearbook that Ernie aspired to obtain a psychology

---

[8] In Vietnam, the term "sapper" was used primarily for North Vietnamese Army and Viet Cong units that broke through defensive lines using tactics more akin to raids by commandos than to the work of engineers. Sappers were specialized in explosives and stealthy infiltration tactics, and reported only to a sapper command, which in turn reported to North Vietnam's Politburo ruling body. They built mockups of each base they targeted and rehearsed every mission down to the tiniest detail. https://www.historynet.com/sapper-attack-the-elite-north-vietnamese-units/

degree and pursue graduate school. When I saw him at the induction center, I wondered what had happened to his college dreams. We had a brief conversation, and I informed him that I was being drafted into the Marine Corps and desperately wanted to avoid it. In a loud and brash manner, Ernie exclaimed, "I'd like to join the Marine Corps."

Joyce, my high school friend who was still handling the inductee folders, caught our attention. Ernie and I approached her, surrounded by stacks of folders. We asked if she could swap our names. She inquired if we were sure about this decision. Ernie grinned and confidently replied, "Hell, yes!" With a smile, Joyce changed our names in the folders. That was the last time I saw Ernie Brown. In my pursuit of writing my autobiography, I sought to find Ernie and compare our memories of the induction process. It took some effort, but I eventually located him. After his service in the Marine Corps, he ventured to Hollywood, California, and began an acting career in various Western movies. In 1979, after getting married, he took his wife's surname and became Ernie Lively. Yes, his daughter is Blake Lively, the actress married to Ryan Reynolds. Sadly, Ernie passed away on June 3, 2021, at the age of 74 due to cardiac complications.

After going through the previous phases of being drafted, we entered the final phase. A military officer, likely the recruiting officer, had us stand on a painted line. He instructed everyone to take one step forward. By taking that step, we were essentially volunteering for the US Army. Our status changed from "registrant" to "inductee."

Once again, the military oath was administered, and I solemnly swore to bear true faith and allegiance to the Constitution of the United States, defending it against all enemies, foreign and domestic, and obeying the orders of the President and superior officers, with the assistance of God.

We were then directed to a waiting area near the exit, where we awaited the bus that would take us to boot camp. Shortly after gathering in the waiting area, an officer approached and selected another recruit and me from the group. For the next two days, we operated mimeograph machines under his guidance. The officer informed us that we could go home and return the following day. While my mimeograph operating buddy went home that night, I made the decision to stay at Fort Holabird and not return home. As a result, I spent my first two nights in the Army sleeping in a two-story

World War II barracks at Fort Holabird. Those two days allowed me to become familiar with that type of barracks, little knowing that it would be my home away from home for the next eight weeks during boot camp.

On the third day of my new life in the Army, when our mimeograph machine operating duties were over, we boarded buses bound for Fort Bragg, North Carolina. Before that day, the name Fort Bragg held no significance for me. Growing up in Dundalk, I wasn't aware of Fort Bragg. As a new draftee, I was going there for basic training. After a long bus ride, we finally reached Fort Bragg sometime after midnight. I remember one of the drill instructors offering cookies and milk. At first, I wanted to laugh because cookies and milk were the furthest things from my mind. Maybe the Army drill instructors were looking to identify recruits who needed to lose weight or were just being kind and thoughtful. I don't remember anyone accepting cookies and milk. We were all too anxious and fearful of what was going to happen next.

After the drill instructor offering cookies and milk left the scene, another instructor took command with a loud, resonant voice, ordering us to promptly get off the bus and stand shoulder to shoulder on the painted lines.

Fear, as an adaptive function, serves to prolong our lives. It signals potential danger, like when we approach the edge of a cliff and suddenly feel a surge of fear. This adaptive fear serves as a warning. It also triggers the

The barracks at Fort Holabird

fight-or-flight response. In those early morning hours, my own fear was in overdrive. I felt an intense readiness to take action and escape the situation immediately. However, I was bound to my seat, only able to endure the piercing shouts of the drill instructors.

The drill instructor assigned to my bus was a physically formidable African American Sergeant First Class (SFC) or E-7. For our information, he yelled out his name in an extremely loud and thunderous voice stating that he was the senior drill instructor in charge of the processing of the recruits in our two buses. As I gazed at Sergeant First Class (SFC) Watson it seemed as if the ground trembled with every step he took. The mere thought of him sent a tremor through me, a primal fear so deeply ingrained it felt like an inherited memory. It wasn't just apprehension; it was a visceral reaction, a tightening of my chest, a cold sweat prickling my skin. His presence wasn't a storm approaching; it was a predator stalking, and every instinct within me screamed run, hide, disappear before he could even notice me. He appeared to be the embodiment of the Drill Sergeant from HELL. Clutching his clipboard with a list of names, I knew that if he called my name, I would be under his command for the next grueling eight weeks. I couldn't help but anticipate eight weeks of absolute torment, an experience that seemed unfathomable for anyone to endure.

As I desperately avoided making eye contact, I hoped that the drill instructor would overlook my presence. He proceeded to call out several names, and I naively believed that I had escaped his attention when he engaged in conversation with another drill instructor. However, my relief was short-lived, shattered by the resounding extremely loud bellow of my name, "RODWELLER!" In that moment all time stopped, I was paralyzed with uncertainty, contemplating whether I should succumb to the overwhelming panic and perhaps even wet my pants.

Caught in a state of PURE panic, I mustered all my courage and screamed at the top of my lungs, "Here!" That single word sealed my fate as I realized that I now belonged to SFC Watson for the next grueling eight weeks of relentless possible life-threatening torment. I passionately believed that those weeks would be the most physically and mentally brutal of my young life. Little did I know then that my initial perceptions of the Army would prove to be incorrect. Over time, I would come to understand the profound and positive impact those eight weeks would have on shaping my character. It was through this experience that I would learn the futility of living a carefree and aimless existence as "One Cool Cat" and embrace the realization that there was far more to life, waiting for me to unlock my full potential and capabilities.

Unbeknownst to me, the drill sergeants would be the best teachers for my Army training. SFC Watson would be the absolute best. A drill sergeant would teach me many things, but the first part of my education included such things as learning how to speak Army, figuring out the rank structure of enlisted and officer personnel, while understanding a vast alphabet of acronyms. As I stood in line shoulder to shoulder waiting to hear SFC Watson give commands, I remember seeing a sign at the reception center at Fort Bragg indicating what a drill sergeant is with words similar to the following:

- He is a cautioning voice, a helpful hand, and a watchful eye that guides the new trainee through eight weeks of strenuous training.
- He may have gained his knowledge in Korea or Vietnam.
- He guides, instructs, and encourages young men to become soldiers.
- He teaches the "fundamentals" of basic training to develop future American Soldiers. He is a seasoned graduate of the Drill Sergeants School and wears the distinctive World War I campaign hat.
- Over 1,000 basic combat trainees enter and leave Fort Bragg's Army Training Center each week, but the Drill Sergeant remains to fulfill his mission of developing combat-ready soldiers.

For some unknown reason reading those words on that sign in the early hours at Fort Bragg left an indelible impression on me, its words echoing the very essence of the drill sergeants I met. Those sergeants were the living embodiment of the traits described on that sign. Despite this, nothing could have prepared me for the reality of their intense and unyielding manner. The initial shock of being in the presence of such forceful personalities was overwhelming. I had never before encountered someone who communicated with such verbal volcanic eruption, unleashing shouts and curses with a passion that left me shaken and unsettled. Over time, however, I came to understand the necessity of this approach.

For many of the inductees, this form of communication was necessary and a crucial part of their basic training. I remember drill instructors singling out recruits who required extreme verbal abuse because they absolutely were not assimilating to the Army. The names and descriptions they used to describe everything about us was shocking. I wondered if drill instructors stayed awake at night creating those words and phrases. As time passed, I would laugh internally at their hilarious form of communication, never wanting one to see a smile on my face when he used those nasty names or language.

SFC Watson had called 24 names that morning and I was one of those names, making up his training company. We spent the next two days processing. My first Army haircut was given by a civilian barber, and I had to pay for it. Can you believe that! I was given lots of shots, provided uniforms, boots, socks, underwear, other gear and took additional aptitude tests. Near the end of the second day, we went to another building for further processing. The clerks inquired about our career aspirations in the Army or the schools we hoped to attend post-basic training. Interested in a comprehensive education, akin to what community college offered, I asked the clerk for the longest available programs. He provided a detailed list of various training opportunities, including medical, military police, ranger school, special operations, interpreter/translator, transportation, general aviation, helicopter crew chief, and flight engineer school. Drawn to the duration and perceived value of the flight engineer program, I requested assignment to that school. Upon assignment, the clerk outlined the challenging yet enjoyable curriculum. Despite expecting to be drafted as an infantryman, the opportunity to choose my path and receive training in a desired field felt like an unexpected blessing.

There was a particular language we were never to use. For example, we were NEVER to call one's rifle a gun. I made that mistake only once. It resulted in me having to do 20 pushups and then holding my rifle over my head in one hand and yelling, "This is my rifle!" then grabbing my private parts with my other hand and yelling, "This is my gun! One is for shooting, and the other is for fun." I was required to say that for ten minutes. I did not make that mistake again. But many others did, and sometimes they were required to get on top of a big parade field stand and yell the same embarrassing chant at the top of their lungs, "This is my rifle, this is my gun, one is for shooting, the other is for fun!"

SFC Watson asked if anyone in the group of 24 had never shot a weapon before. I looked around to see if anyone raised their hand, but no one did. Meekly, I raised my hand, not knowing what to expect next. SFC Watson approached me, got close to my face, and said, "Great Rodweller, I won't have to reteach you the right way to shoot a rifle. I can teach you the right way from the beginning."

We ran or jogged everywhere to get everyone physically fit while singing cadence songs. I enjoyed learning the cadence songs, and some I still remember to this day. Singing while jogging, made running in Army boots somewhat easier.

One of those runs was in the sand and was pivotal for me. It was in the second week of training, when all 24 trainees were running along a sandy path. I was the fourth runner in the group of 24. Running in loose sand and wearing Army boots was beyond difficult. Because of this I was taking it easy not wanting to expend too much energy. Our company commander, a captain, ran up to me and turned around, and began running backwards *in the sand.* He looked into my eyes and yelled, "Rodweller, get your ass in gear! Somebody's life is going to depend upon you. Now pick up the pace and get moving." He turned back around, and away he went. That was Captain Wesley G. Morehead. Little did I know that within the year he would be correct.

After he yelled those words to me, something inside my brain clicked, and I immediately took my training much more seriously. It's not that I hadn't before, but now it was different, profound, and urgent. I realized I was part of a team and wanted to be a valuable and productive member. I approached my training with a different attitude from that point forward. Viewing everything about my training more critically, always asking myself, how could I improve? I didn't want to fail. Failure might mean I would miss out on flight engineer aviation school or jeopardize my safety or the safety of one of my fellow soldiers.

During my weeks of basic training, all trainees were assigned to kitchen patrol, or KP, at least once. My sole assignment to KP involved operating a potato peeling machine, a simple task that required placing potatoes into the machine, ensuring it was running with water, and watching as the sandpaper inside peeled the skins off.

The food in boot camp was neither notably good nor bad. We exercised before each of the three daily meals while waiting to enter a small mess hall.[9] Inside, we had only a few minutes to eat, often so quickly it felt like inhaling the food, before leaving for more exercises outside. During our training sessions, which included activities like rifle range practice, grenade range training, map reading, and learning how to camouflage foxholes, we were given box lunches. These meals were a practical solution, allowing us to stay nourished and focused during the intensive training exercises.

Hydration was extremely important and constantly emphasized, with trainees encouraged to drink from a large green canvas water bag. The only available drinking vessels were large steel ladles. I never hesitated to drink from the communal ladle because it was a great opportunity to share our training experiences. However, several trainees from the South refused to drink from the same ladles as the trainees of color from Philadelphia. The southern trainees said they wouldn't drink after anyone who wasn't white. Their refusal, rooted in racism, seemed childish and deeply troubling to me.

Continuing to drink from the ladle, I faced hostility from these trainees. One night, the southern trainees threatened to attack me after the lights were turned out. Prepared with my bayonet, I waited, but they never came and confronted me.

The next morning, SFC Watson conducted an inspection, asking about the rumored conflict. Despite his inquiries, no one confessed or explained. I believe SFC Watson was already aware of the situation; he always seemed to have a keen sense of events.

The inspection ended dramatically. SFC Watson confronted the main instigator of the racist behavior, physically reprimanding him for his actions. This altercation resulted in the instigator falling down the stairs, an incident reported as an accidental slip. His return from the hospital marked a change; he no longer exhibited racist behavior or used derogatory language as he had before. This experience was my first real

---

[9] A small basic training Army mess hall is a dining facility that provides meals to soldiers during their basic training. According to the U.S. Army Quartermaster Corps, the mess hall is managed by a small team of personnel, including a mess sergeant, two or more cooks, plus dining room orderlies, and other labor. The team divides the responsibilities for breakfast, dinner, and supper by working through the shifts, under the overall supervision of the mess sergeant.

encounter with racism, an eye-opening and unforgettable aspect of my time in basic training.

Before the Army, I had never shot a weapon. I remembered what SFC Watson said to me about learning correctly the first time. I knew that shooting a rifle would be loud, and the rifle's kick against my shoulder could leave a bruise. Yet I gingerly accepted my assigned M14 rifle. SFC Watson said, "don't be afraid of it Rodweller. It won't bite." He taught us to disassemble, clean, and reassemble our rifles expertly and in minimal time. It was essential to keep our rifles clean because a dirty weapon might not fire when needed in combat. After learning the basics of handling and operating the M14, it was time for everyone to go to the rifle ranges for actual shooting. Every soldier is, first and foremost, a RIFLEMAN.

To say I was apprehensive doesn't even begin to describe how afraid I was of shooting that big loud explosive rifle. I had never been around any other weapon before, not even a BB rifle let alone an intimidating M14 rifle. The rifle ranges were extremely loud, deafening and scary, I flinched as every rifle fired. In addition, I wasn't provided ear protection to block the loud explosions from each round being fired. Then it was my turn to fire my M14 rifle. SFC Watson called me over to the last firing position on the right side of the firing range and stayed with me throughout my first experience of firing a rifle. When he was with me, he immediately became a completely different person. As the sign stated in the reception center, he was a cautioning voice, a helpful hand, and a watchful eye that guided the new trainee through training by guiding, instructing, and encouraging me to become an excellent soldier. SFC Watson became like one of my high school teachers or my father. He showed me how to do something straightforwardly and matter-of-factly. He talked me through each step as I prepared to fire my rifle. After each rifle shooting practice, my ears would ring. I would have difficulty hearing for several days. Maybe that was good because I couldn't hear all those funny names and caustic phrases from the drill instructors.

Because of SFC Watson's coaching, rifle shooting became fun, and I wanted to do more. I was competing against myself to attain smaller, more accurate shot groupings on each target. Over the next several weeks, my wish came true. We would regularly go to the rifle ranges, and I continued to improve with each practice. SFC Watson was there by my side, coaching me, suggesting ways to enhance my aim on targets at distances up to 600 yards. He stayed by my side even during rifle qualifications, ensuring I maintained my form and accuracy with each shot. I owe my marksmanship medals to SFC Watson because of his coaching and instructions.

As trained infantrymen or riflemen, we had to learn how to use and be proficient with other implements of war. The next implement was the hand grenade. We had to learn to handle and practice throwing hand grenades before going to the range. We practiced with dummy grenades, which looked and felt like the real ones but without the explosive capabilities. Then it was onto the grenade ranges and throwing pits. How could I not remember the grenade pit where we were learning to throw the real live Mk2 grenade? The Mk2 was a big and heavy fragmentation-type anti-personnel hand grenade. At each grenade range there was a giant white painted concrete wall with thick glass panels to see through. One trainee and a drill instructor would go to the practice area together. Everyone else would stand behind the wall and thick glass windows observing the practice of throwing the real grenades.

It was both thrilling and frightening to watch and hear as each grenade was thrown and exploded. The grenade explosions were so loud I could still hear them standing behind the wall with my fingers in my ears. The explosions made my body and clothes vibrate even though we were 60 yards away and behind the wall. At this point, I was really petrified and even terror-stricken because I could only imagine what one of these exploded grenades would do to a human body.

Each of the 24 trainees was required to pass this course by throwing several grenades and hitting a big pile of truck tires approximately thirty to fifty feet away. We had to lower ourselves into a dirt pit that had several throwing positions. The hole was dug as a circle approximately eight feet deep. There was a three-foot high dirt platform to stand on with several throwing positions that allowed a person to see out of the pit towards the pile of tires. We began practicing from the middle position. The center position was safer if a trainee dropped a real grenade. If this happened from the center position, the grenade fell into a lower dirt trench where it could explode, allowing the trainee and drill instructor an extra few seconds to exit the pit.

90

It seemed easy enough in training, but now those real grenades were heavier and much bigger than I had realized. They were probably the same size, but I saw them as massive because they were real. I was in a state of paralyzing panic, preparing to throw those live grenades.

Nevertheless, I followed my instructions precisely and bounced my grenades off the tires as they exploded, vibrating my clothes and body.

Because I hadn't missed, I didn't have to throw any more grenades. Those who had missed the tires were required to throw additional grenades. We had to stay on the grenade range and watch until everyone qualified.

I understood why not everyone in our class of 24 liked our drill instructors. Some harbored deep contempt toward them due to their tendency to shout loudly, act mean and abrasive, and employ some of the crudest language I had ever heard. Most of us in the trainee group understood their tough approach, and at times I suspect we even laughed at their language. However, there was one trainee from Philadelphia who stood out. His name was Reginald Jackson, and he had a strong contemptible dislike for SFC Watson. He was always clowning around and would frequently mess up tasks, requiring multiple do-overs. Despite the drill instructors' efforts to teach him properly, it appeared to me that he wanted to intentionally fail and be sent home.

On the day we were at the grenade range, Jackson was acting up and trying to be a clown as usual. Eventually, it was his turn to throw the grenades, and both he and SFC Watson lowered themselves into the grenade pit. I stood behind the wall with the other trainees, waiting to see what would happen. It seemed to take longer than usual, with SFC Watson spending more time talking to him than to the other trainees. We watched as SFC Watson took a hand grenade out of its container and handed it to Jackson. Jackson then looked back at us and scanned the entire grenade pit area as he pulled the pin from the grenade and released its handle. Everything seemed to be going as expected, but the next few moments unfolded in slow motion.

Instead of following instructions and throwing the grenade at the designated pile of tires, Jackson looked directly at SFC Watson and dropped the grenade into the pit in front of him. In a split second, Jackson jumped out of the pit, leaving SFC Watson with only seconds to react. Thanks to his superior physical shape, SFC Watson planted one hand on the ground above the grenade pit and the other on the side of the dirt wall, pushing himself up and out. He rolled over and quickly grabbed Jackson, covering him with his body, and rolled further away just as the grenade exploded. Dirt flew everywhere, raining down on everyone present.

I stood there, completely astonished by what I had just witnessed. Jackson's attempt to harm SFC Watson was met with a well-deserved response. SFC Watson got up, yelling at Jackson and pulling him to his feet. He administered a severe thrashing to Jackson, a punishment I believed he would never forget. An ambulance arrived, and Jackson was taken to the hospital, where he spent several days. As the story goes, it was said that Jackson went to the hospital because he slipped and fell down the steps of the barracks. Slipping on the highly polished floors and falling down the steps was a significant hazard for those who attempted to harm others, especially a drill instructor. Not long after this occurred, I heard a second-hand account that Jackson remained in the hospital for some time, and after his release, he was charged with attempting to murder a drill instructor. He was subsequently sent to military jail and dishonorably discharged. While I personally could not verify the truthfulness of this rumor, one thing was certain: I never saw Reginald Jackson again at Fort Bragg.

I just could not fathom the mindset behind wanting to kill someone who had the important task of teaching us vital skills. Despite SFC Watson's occasional fierceness, harshness, and demanding nature, his role was to impart the knowledge necessary for us to defend ourselves, fight the enemy, and ultimately survive in combat.

Bringing It All Together

For several weeks, we had heard about the infamous bivouac, an experience that would put our training to the ultimate test. Bivouac[10] was dreaded by all, as it aimed to simulate the harsh realities of actual combat. The tasks included pitching pup tents and maneuvering by low-crawling under barbed wire while live ammunition whizzed just inches above our heads. The rainy

---

[10] A bivouac is a temporary encampment that is usually set up under little or no shelter. A military encampment made with tents or improvised shelters, usually without shelter or protection from enemy fire.

weather made the infiltration course even more challenging, and unfortunately, it rained persistently throughout our time on bivouac.

To march to the bivouac area, our drill instructors paired us trainees up, expecting each pair to carry half of their gear, like half a tent along with the poles and stakes needed to secure it. To assemble a complete tent, we buttoned the top portions together, which unfortunately leaked during rain, soaking everything inside. I vividly remember spending my birthday in one such wet tent as the rain poured relentlessly. When dinner time came, all of us had to stand in the heavy rain to get our hot meal. Among my 22 companions, I stood in the unyielding downpour, waiting eagerly for dinner. Watching the rain cause my mashed potatoes to overflow from my aluminum mess kit, a feeling of helplessness overwhelmed me, mirroring the relentless rain. Despite the soggy chaos, a strange sense of camaraderie emerged among us. There we stood, all 23, united under the pouring rain, each of us holding our meal plates, finding an unexpected moment of unity in the midst of the storm.

During one evening on bivouac, we were fortunate to have several Green Beret Vietnam veterans join us in our training. Our lesson for the evening focused on survival techniques and how to avoid becoming a target during nighttime operations. Specifically, we were taught to observe the brightness of a lighter, a match, or a lit cigarette from distances ranging from half a mile to a mile.

This exercise highlighted the importance of staying hidden in the dark. We discovered that a simple act like taking a drag from a lit cigarette creates a strong glow on a person's face and head, making them easily visible from up to a mile away. It was truly surprising to see how brightly a single cigarette could illuminate someone's face even at such a distance. Within the darkness of the woods, it looked like a powerful flashlight directly focused on their features.

Another component of our training on bivouac included escape and evasion training from the Green Berets. I thought the training sounded like fun, because of how the instructors described it, it actually sounded like hide and seek. We were sent into the woods and our challenge was not to be discovered and caught.

Because of their experiences in Vietnam these battle-hardened Green Berets thought this would be easy working with trainees. Little did they know, there was an outlier in the group of trainees. I utilized the techniques my Boy Scout Leader, Mr. Cavey, taught me and others on a previous youthful camping trip to listen, to count the sounds. From his experiences in the South Pacific, Mr. Cavey taught us to be extremely quiet and stealthy to avoid danger. Each time they sent me into the woods, the Green Berets couldn't find me, and they eventually had to call my name to return to the group. I enjoyed walking out of the woods from an area they hadn't considered looking.

The SFC drill instructor for this training was a giant Hawaiian. He was carrying one of those large army radios, a PRC 6 walkie talkie type radio. I was so close several times that I could hear him talking to the Green Berets. I was proud of myself for being quiet and stealthy while not being found. The SFC drill instructor was angry because I hadn't gotten caught. He thought I was doing something unauthorized, like going outside the training area and not getting found. As a result, he threw his hand-held radio at me when I walked out of the woods the last time. I picked it up, doubled timed (ran) over to him, and returned the radio. Even in the darkness, I could see his anger and how upset he was with me as he cursed at me. I quickly sat in the bleachers to review the night's training.

At the conclusion of our training review, the SFC drill instructor asked me how I managed to evade detection and capture. I shared that my Scoutmaster from my days in the Boy Scouts had taught me a technique of counting sounds, which he had utilized to stay alive in the South Pacific. The simplicity of the method made the SFC drill instructor skeptical, and he responded with angry curses once again. I became worried about his outbursts and anger, fearing that I might lose my balance and fall down the barracks' second-floor steps like others had previously done. To my dismay, I was informed that I would be accompanying him once more the following evening.

On the second night, there was only a small group that consisted of the Green Berets, the SFC drill instructor, and myself. I felt scared and anxious, doubting that counting sounds would work for me on this particular night. I had no idea what to expect. The SFC drill instructor told me to explain the exact process again. Once more, he expressed strong doubts about the effectiveness of my simple methods, resorting to coarse language as we walked approximately half a mile into the woods and concealed ourselves.

I was filled with fear because getting caught would result in serious trouble for me. I had no clue what the consequences might be or how he would respond. Throughout the entire evening, I stuck close to him, shadowing his every move. I demonstrated how to count sounds and showcased my own ability to remain quiet and stealthy, ensuring we remained undetected.

Then, he proceeded to repeat the counting process. As the other Green Berets walked past us, he experienced a sudden realization. An "a-ha" moment swept over him, and he smiled. However, his subsequent pleased comments were filled with vile, vulgar, and utterly reprehensible language again. I thought how someone could be so pleased yet use such foul language.

From that evening onward, whenever our paths crossed at Fort Bragg, the SFC drill instructor would acknowledge me or say hello. It was a pleasant surprise to see him even smile, which was a rarity considering he had previously relied on using various forms of repugnant language towards me. In his own way, he had inadvertently expanded my vocabulary of the English language by introducing me to new obscene, vulgar, revolting, and repulsive words and phrases.

I understood that his choice of language was a means of communication he employed with many individuals in the Army. It was his way of breaking through to those individuals needing additional encouragement and ensuring they followed orders. Interestingly, to this day, I have yet to encounter such a level of repulsiveness in the use of the English language.

Our last bivouac field exercise was the night infiltration course. It would be the most realistic example of simulating the live-fire conditions of combat. The infiltration course required each trainee to crawl from one end of a path to the other with our M14 rifle. Each crawling path was well over a hundred yards long. Sandbags were stacked around the demolition pits along the required crawl paths to protect the trainees from real explosions. The instructors detonated grenades and claymore mines inside those demolition pits to simulate actual combat. It was terrifying and exhilarating at the same time. The explosions caused sand and dirt to rain down on us as we crawled. The concussions from the deafening explosions were more severe than the grenade range because some sandbag pits were only a few feet away. The instructors also placed obstacles along the crawl, such as strips of wood or barricades of barbed wire to simulate actual combat conditions. All those obstacles had to be negotiated amidst flying sand and deafening explosive concussions in the rain and dark of night.

To pass this portion of our training we were required to successfully crawl close to live explosions and machine gunfire. The bullets would zip overhead a mere 12 inches above our bodies. The instructors and drill instructors told us repeatedly not to panic. If we did, then yell or scream for help. **DO NOT GET UP!** No matter how terrified we were, stay on your stomachs and hug the ground. Do not try to get up. If you do, you will die.

Upon hearing about the course and witnessing its challenges, I was once again overcome with an intense and paralyzing fear, to put it mildly. As if that imminent danger was not enough, I found myself at the front of the line, about to tackle this terrifying infiltration course first. I felt as though I was still adapting to the various aspects of my Army training and now, I had to do this. This dreadful infiltration course felt like an overwhelming ordeal I had to successfully complete.

As I stood on the brink of entering the course, horrifying thoughts raced through my mind. With the United States Army firing actual machine gun rounds overhead, I had to crawl over a hundred yards in the pouring rain and wet sand. Giant and huge explosions would be erupting from the demolition pits along the crawling path, and strategically placed flares illuminated the sky, would also severely impair my night vision.

Positioned at the front of the line, armed with my M14 rifle, I prepared to run and dive under the barbed wire. Looking around, I could barely make out the faces of our drill instructors in the darkness. Their watchful eyes were keenly observing each of us for any signs of abnormal fear. Sargeant Watson stood nearby, ready to give the command to proceed. Before embarking on my run and dive, I locked eyes with him, seeking reassurance or encouragement. To my surprise, he looked directly into my eyes nodded and almost smiled, and with that, I set off on the crawl of my young life.

Crawling on my stomach through the rain-soaked sand, with machine gun bullets and tracer rounds cracking/whizzing overhead, the giant and huge explosions raining down wet dirt and sand all over me. I became acutely aware of the razor's edge I was operating on. This combat simulation marked my first encounter with the precarious nature of life itself that I had

The night infiltration course with live rounds whizzing over our heads

never experienced up to that moment. As I maneuvered through those obstacles, I often had to roll onto my back, and when I looked up, I witnessed tracer rounds streaking across the sky forming a line of orange and yellow lights just inches from my body, intensifying both my fear and excitement. It was a strange mix of emotions, as I felt a childlike thrill of playing Army in the field near my parents' home, yet now here I was in the real Army with real munitions going off all around me.

Turning back onto my stomach, I pressed on, crawling persistently. The rain-soaked sand had saturated my fatigue shirt sleeves, mixing with sweat and further wetting the sand inside. This caused my elbows to throb with pain. The incessant downpour made the sand within my sleeves even wetter, resulting in my elbows scraping against the sandpaper-like texture.

I crawled with my rifle as instructed following the specific instructions to not get it caught in the barbed wire. While crawling a thought flashed through my mind and I was relieved that my M14 rifle didn't have a loaded magazine full of bullets. Without the added weight of a loaded magazine, it was much easier to carry as I crawled in the heavy rain and dim night light. Some of the other trainees failed to follow the instructions, resulting in their rifles getting tangled in the barbed wire. This hindered their progress and made navigating the course incredibly difficult for them. Thankfully, the course turned out to be less complicated and tricky than I had anticipated.

Despite the challenges, I managed to complete the course. My clothes were soaked, my boots were filled with water, and my elbows were painfully throbbing, and blood was staining my shirt sleeves. My ears hurt as they rang from the intense loud and explosive experience. Yet, the excitement and adrenaline still coursed through my veins as I crawled away. I had successfully conquered this grueling course on my own, without any major mishaps. It was an achievement of immense proportions for me, something I would never have imagined experiencing as One Cool Cat living in Dundalk. The Army continued to instill in me many invaluable life skills while nurturing my abilities. I was beginning to truly and fully realize that with determination and focus, I could accomplish anything I set my mind to. That night, I had successfully crawled through the infiltration course, propelled by my training and unwavering desire to achieve.

Many trainees did not complete basic training due to injury or sickness. Others had to repeat portions of their training or leave the Army altogether. Out of the 24 who began basic training with me, only 16 completed the training.

Think for a moment and imagine what it's like to stay awake for 72 hours. Our mission was to guard Post Exchanges (PX), gas stations, and storage facilities around Fort Bragg. We were given a loaded shotgun for this guard duty. The shotguns were not the 2x4's we had previously been provided that replicated guns. At times during my guard duty, I felt like I was sleepwalking. I was so DEAD tired. We were divided into groups and sent to locations throughout the three 24-hour periods of guard duty.

My first guard duty assignment was at a gas station. At the end of our guarding assignment, we went to another location to relieve the previous person. We were transported to other sites to replace other trainees so they could rotate to another location. It was a way to keep each trainee awake and to change the location of our guard duty assignments. The instructors ensured we wouldn't become too familiar with the site and find ways to sleep. After the gas station, I was taken to a clothing storage facility. I knew it was a clothing storage facility because I could smell the strong scent of mothballs. After completing my time at the storage facility, I was taken to a small Post Exchange (PX). After the first day, I rotated to the same exact locations to guard but in a different order. On day two we guarded the same areas again. On day three, my last guard post to watch was a small Post Exchange (PX) in the woods. I couldn't tell where it was on Fort Bragg because I was so exhausted, I didn't recognize any of the surroundings. I took two turns guarding that PX. To say I was sleepy would only trivialize the stupor and lethargy I experienced that night. I couldn't fall asleep because if I did, I would fail, and I wasn't going to fail, not at this stage of my training.

My first watch was uneventful, and I walked one way and turned and danced in the opposite direction to keep awake. Even trying to dance, I felt like I was sleepwalking. Suddenly, I heard a shotgun go off in the distance. That brought me back to being awake immediately as I wondered who had fired their shotgun. Was someone walking on their guard post asleep when they heard something and just pulled the trigger?

I was walking around this little PX in my final hour of watch, probably asleep, just placing one foot in front of the other like I had done all night. Daybreak was beginning, and I continued to walk. Then out of the total silence the air-conditioners for the PX came on with a big rumble. That enormous loud abrupt sound frightened me, and I felt like I jumped several inches off the ground. Moments later I thought about and realized this might have been what happened earlier in the morning when someone fired their shotgun. I was just happy that this was another task accomplished without any adverse incidents.

I successfully emerged from basic training unscathed, a feat I largely attribute to SFC Watson's rigorous guidance and unwavering support. Yes, he was stern, even formidable at times, but I came to understand that his severity was not mere harshness, but a crucible designed to forge my character and skills. As a city kid, I entered the Army with no prior exposure to military life other than stories of my brothers—a blank canvas waiting to be painted with the strokes of discipline and knowledge. SFC Watson didn't have to correct any ingrained habits; every lesson he imparted was etched into a fresh, unmarked surface.

Under his watchful eye, I was transformed. Like silly putty, malleable and shapeless, I was sculpted by the deft hands of the Army and SFC Watson into a soldier of mettle and resolve. I wasn't just trained; I was renewed as a skilled rifleman, a testament to the meticulous and relentless training regimen. This metamorphosis was recognized and rewarded at graduation, where I was elevated to the rank of Private First-Class (E-3), a proud moment that marked the culmination of my transformative basic training journey from a novice to a soldier ready to serve with honor and skill.

My First Love

Ah, the captivating allure of my first love, a force that seized my heart and irrevocably transformed my very existence forever. It was an extraordinary journey, seemingly boundless, a venture into the uncharted territories of raw, unbridled emotion. This inaugural voyage of the heart was euphoric, a memorable fusion of emotional and physical intimacy that imprinted itself indelibly upon my soul. It was an awakening, a revelation that allowed me to experience life with an intensity I had never known previously. Despite my efforts to move on, the echoes of this first love linger, a passionate flame that still and will always flicker in a corner of my heart.

As time marched on, I came to a poignant realization: this monumental first love was just that—the first chapter of many. I understood the necessity to venture forth, yet I often find myself lost in contemplation, wondering about the path not taken. The memories, the vivid tapestry of feelings from that era, are etched into my being, my soul, and are destined to accompany me till my final days on earth.

This first love was a paradoxical blend of blessings and a curse. A blessing, for it gifted me with a treasure trove of thrilling, joyous memories. A curse, because it sparked an obsession, a relentless pursuit to recapture the magic of that initial encounter. My heart became a prisoner to this addiction, yearning for the euphoric high that once filled my being. It was an addiction not easily shaken, for my mind vividly remembered the intoxicating rush of those moments.

My first love took flight in the skies above 8,000 feet, amidst the clouds and the boundless blue. It was an encounter that set my heart racing like never before. My love was larger than life, with an unconventional beauty— bulbous eyes, whimsically shaped lips, and an awkward, wide stance. Cloaked in a hue of Army olive drab, it was an UNCONVENTIONAL PARAMOUR—a CH-47 Chinook helicopter.

Before that first defining flight at Fort Eustis, I had never soared above the earth in any type of aircraft. The moment we ascended, I was hopelessly forever in love with aviation, with the Chinook. It was a revelation, a distinction between mere liking and profound love. That inaugural flight stirred a whirlwind of emotions and sensations—the enormity, the cacophony, the complexity of this majestic flying machine imprinted an indelible mark on my heart.

After a mesmerizing two-hour journey, my curiosity was ignited. I yearned to master this complex craft, to navigate the skies as its pilot. I took flying lessons to become a licensed pilot and lost many hours of sleep because I just couldn't get enough of this love of flying.

This first love's power lay in the accumulation of all those intense, passionate sensations. It embodied the significance of a first love, unforgettable in its impact. Flying in that Chinook was not just an activity; it was a deep-seated passion in my heart, reminiscent of my childhood days watching "Sky King" and dreaming of soaring with Penny and Uncle Sky.

John Hermes Secondari once penned, "Once you have tasted flight, you will forever walk the earth with your eyes turned skyward."[11] How true he was. As a child, I would gaze through windows on my parents' porch at aircraft high above, while building wooden and plastic model airplanes. Dreaming of the many ways that I would take off into the skies in the future. In high school, my friends and I with our dates would watch airliners land and depart at Baltimore's Friendship Airport (later to be renamed Baltimore Washington International Airport), immersing ourselves in the world of aviation with fries and sodas from the local Dairy Queen.

Even as my career shifted into high gear with computer science and technology, the memories of Army aviation remained vivid, a wonderful and cherished chapter of my life. Times of reckless abandonment[12] when flying was my life and saving and supporting others was my sole purpose in life. I may not dwell on those memories daily, but whenever a Chinook passes overhead or the distant hum of an aircraft reaches my ears, I'm trans-

---

[11] The quote is often incorrectly attributed to Leonardo da Vinci. https://airfactsjournal.com/2020/08/the-famous-quote-that-da-vinci-never-said/

[12] I use Reckless Abandon as a phrase that means acting in a very wild and reckless way, without regard for the consequences, the rules, or the opinions of others. I would describe myself back then as a person who gave my total self to the passion and enthusiasm of flying in Vietnam while I ignored all the possible costs or risks.

My last Chinook helicopter

ported back in time to those halcyon days when flying filled me with an unparalleled sense of vitality and joy. It was a time when the sky was not just
a canvas, but a realm of endless possibilities, a sanctuary where I felt most
alive, most true to myself. A feeling of flying in an environment of reckless
abandonment I've never ever in my life been able to capture again.

In those moments today, as I watch an aircraft or helicopter carve its
path across the sky, a nostalgic euphoria envelops me. It's a gentle, yet powerful reminder of the exhilarating days when the roar of engines and the
sweeping of rotor blades created vistas from high above were my world.
These instances of aerial reminiscence are not mere flashbacks; they are
vivid, vibrant recollections that reignite the same passion and happiness I
felt back then. Not to mention the addiction to the drug adrenaline that
coursed through my veins at that time of my life.

My journey with aviation, though rooted in my youth, continues to be
a defining aspect of who I am. It's a testament to the enduring impact of a
first love, a love that not only shaped my past but continues to influence
my daily perspective and aspirations. The Chinook, helicopters in general

and airplanes with the skies they traversed were more than just a fleeting infatuation; they were the architects of my dreams, the kindlers of a lifelong passion that, to this day, continues to soar.

How My First Love Led Me to Technology

Fort Bragg forever holds a special place in my heart, as it's where I unexpectedly encountered my first love during basic training processing. The simple question about my Army interests, posed by the processing clerk, sparked a connection that would forever change my life. When the clerk read the description for the helicopter flight engineer[13] school, I immediately asked if I could be assigned to this training. After basic training, I was assigned to helicopter flight engineer school at Fort Eustis, Virginia. There I began a 20-week rapid and intense training course. The program was composed of two segments. One segment was a four-week introductory class. This class taught the fundamentals of helicopters. The second 16-week segment presented a tremendous amount of information to be learned about the many extraordinarily complex systems of the CH-47 Chinook helicopter.

A classmate with just the engine manual we studied

We had to learn and retain an enormous amount of information in an extremely short period of time. There were several manuals and each described portions of the many systems needed for the Chinook to operate. During one of the many flights in the

---

[13] A flight engineer on a CH-47 Chinook helicopter is a crucial crew member responsible for the safe and efficient operation of the aircraft. They work alongside the pilots to monitor and manage the helicopter's systems, ensuring smooth flight and mission success.

Chinook, I stood in the companionway watching the pilots operate the aircraft. At that moment, everything clicked for me. I understood how the intricate technology and elaborate procedures converged to make such a complex machine function and fly. I was so impressed.

While stationed at Fort Eustis, I took flight lessons in Cessna 150s and 172s to deepen my understanding of aviation, flight physics, while at the same time to become a licensed pilot. On one memorable day, I operated a Cessna 150 in the morning and later experienced a flight in a Chinook helicopter. I was fortunate to be able to afford this flight training independent of my Army duties. This additional training provided a profound grasp of the principles of flight. That pilot training would later prove invaluable during my service in Vietnam, where I frequently had the opportunity to pilot the CH-47 and receive additional flight training by a seasoned combat pilot.

That seasoned pilot, a Captain, played a pivotal role in teaching me the intricate flight characteristics of the CH-47 Chinook. It's important to note that flying the Chinook was a tremendously more complex and challenging endeavor compared to operating a small, fixed-wing Cessna aircraft. This complexity was further amplified by the integration of advanced computer technology in aviation.

Modern aviation technology, particularly in sophisticated aircraft like the CH-47, heavily relies on computers for various functionalities. These systems enhance navigation accuracy, flight stability, and overall safety. The use of flight management systems, autopilot, and advanced navigational aids are prime examples of how computer technology has revolutionized aviation. These technologies reduce the pilot's workload, allowing for more focus on critical decision-making and situational awareness.

In the context of the CH-47, computer systems play a crucial role in managing its dual rotors and the unique aerodynamic challenges they present. This integration of technology demands a deeper understanding and skill set from pilots, who must be adept not only in traditional piloting techniques but also in the operation of complex computer systems. This dual expertise was part of the invaluable training and knowledge I gained from the Captain, underscoring the evolution of aviation into a high-tech field where computer technology is as essential as the pilot's own skills.

My passion for aviation initially introduced me to the world of technology. In those days, the term "computer" encompassed various components related to my love for aviation. I was eager to continue expanding my knowledge and experience in this exciting field. During my time in the Army, I had the privilege of learning about the intricate technical systems of one of the most complex machines ever created: the Boeing Vertol CH-47 Chinook helicopter. As I delved into studying and learning about these systems, I encountered a new term and concept frequently referred to by the instructors "computer technology." This term, akin to how we now use "artificial intelligence," today encompassed the various aspects of technology and its impact on advancing aviation. Although the technology at the time was relatively basic, it piqued my interest and instilled a strong desire to pursue a career in this fascinating field.

CH-47 Helicopter and Advanced Training

There were 24 other guys in my class. We were assigned to live in Officer Candidate School (OCS), Quonset hut barracks with two guys to a cubicle. We were bused all over Fort Eustis. Having transportation provided allowed for additional time to study and keep our barracks brilliantly clean. Occasionally, we would have an inspection in the middle of the night to ensure the barracks were held to the highest standards of order and cleanliness.

Often, we were alerted ahead of time when the inspection would occur. One night we were told about an inspection being conducted at 2am. After studying and getting ready for bed, my cubicle mate and I decided to put a fresh coat of wax on our portion of the floor before the 2am. inspection. Picture two guys with a big floor polisher and a larger can of wax waxing the floor at midnight in their underwear and half asleep. It made for an exciting picture. We wanted the floor to sparkle like transparent glass. To achieve this see-through floor shine, we lit the can of wax on fire, poured the melted wax onto the floor, and immediately began polishing with that big spinning buffing machine. We moved the buffer back and forth over the poured liquid paste wax until it hardened. The floor would look amazing, as if it had a glass covering.

However, this night, our floor polishing became more difficult and challenging. Our exhaustion from studying, working and lack of sleep meant we were not at the top of our floor polishing game. My cubicle mate operated the buffering machine while I poured the melting wax onto the floor. Suddenly, the flaming wax spilled out of the can and burned my hand. I immediately dropped the flaming can and the wax splashed on my legs and feet. I was jumping around from the burning and watched the flaming can of wax roll across and through four cubicles, burning the waxed floors as it rolled. It is difficult to describe how upset our classmates were. I knew they were furious with me because it was after midnight, and everyone was concerned we would fail the inspection and would receive demerits. Due to our significant screwup, my cubicle mate and I had to rewax the entire burnt floor. This meant moving all the furniture out of the four cubicles, waxing the floor and moving everything back before our 2am. inspection.

At 2 a.m., the Duty Officer, a Captain, entered the barracks with a second lieutenant for the inspection. I was sweating profusely. The captain asked me why I was sweating. I immediately replied saying I had just finished using and cleaning the toilet before the Captain arrived, Sir. He looked at me oddly as he thought about my response but then moved on. A half-hour later, the inspection was over, and we passed.

That floor waxing screw-up taught me a powerful lesson about avoiding such mistakes in the future. My tiredness and lack of focus could have negatively affected our inspection, and everyone would have suffered. I realized I would need to stay laser-focused to accomplish my goals in the future. Remembering what SFC Watson would ask me, what was I willing to give up to be better? I wanted to scrap all those unfocused study habits from my earlier years in high school. I was committed to be even more focused on my tasks and studies in the future.

Because we were studying so much material about the Chinook helicopter, we would take a test on the previous day's material at the beginning of each day. It didn't take long before we had developed a routine of studying and reviewing the previous day's materials. The tests were an excellent review process. The tests pointed to areas that needed study and retention improvement for each student. There were also tests at the end of a category, such as flight controls, avionics, or engines. These were much more comprehensive and were a good reflection of our learning. If a teammate had a problem with a category's answers, others would help them to better understand the material. It was a great team effort and contributed to excellent team results. At the end of our 20-week course, everyone graduated.

Studying in the Army was a radical departure from my high school days. It was much more complex, and I had to apply myself like never before. The Army environment taught me to quickly develop exceptional study skills and habits not acquired in my school years. In the Army, I wasn't just One Cool Cat living the life of the Endless Summer. I was a soldier and part of a team and was expected to excel in all aspects I was required to accomplish. My success was the team's success and vice versa.

Early in the Army, I realized I was being trained to be a leader. A leader of myself first and secondly a leader to others, if needed. How could I lead others if I could not lead myself first? Soon, I came to the realization that my knowledge about leadership wasn't as extensive as I had initially believed. I needed an immediate change in my attitude, behavior, and habits. My "One Cool Cat" ego had to be adjusted quickly.

I had to identify those everyday practices that no longer worked and kept me from progressing. I didn't want to go to war with my old mindset and ways of living. Developing new and improved habits allowed me to change and lead my life. I asked myself, what was I willing to sacrifice and give up to gain freedom from my old habits, attitudes, and behaviors? During one of those many thoughtful moments when I was waxing floors or cleaning the bathrooms, the following three thoughts came to mind from SFC Watson:[14]

There is no freedom without sacrifice.
There is no victory without loss.
There is no glory without suffering.

SFC Watson constantly reminded us that these principles apply to the Army, war, and life. Those skills and habits would serve me well in the Army, after returning home, continuing my education, and over my career.

---

[14] I researched SFC Watsons words after leaving the Army and believe he came up with those three phrases from a Frederick Douglass speech given August 4, 1857 titled: The West India Emancipation.

After leaving the Army, I often remembered what SFC Watson taught me about leading myself. He was more than a Sergeant in the Army; he was a molder and developer of young men.

Weekend Passes and an Austin Healey 3000

While I was at Fort Eustis, we were allowed weekend passes to go off post if we hadn't received any demerits. Weekend passes were provided only after we passed our inspections and did well in our studies and tests. Once all the requirements were met, the Company Commander (CO) gave us our weekend passes. We were released on Friday at 5 p.m. and were expected back in our barracks no later than 10 p.m. Sunday for bed check between 10 and 10:30 p.m.

A fellow Fort Eustis classmate, Charles Stones from Baltimore, brought his car on base and would drive Jimmy Wines from Bel Air, MD and me home to Baltimore on weekends. The three of us would share the gas, toll, and food costs. Jimmy's parents or brother would usually pick him up at my parents' house.

On those weekends, I planned to stay close to home, helping my parents around the house, cutting grass, or working on my parents' car, or any task they needed assistance in completing. One of my neighbors and high school classmates was Ann Clark. She lived four houses from my parents' home. Ann and I were good friends growing up, and she began working while I was in the Army. She bought a really nice car before starting college. It was an almost new Austin Healey 3000 roadster, painted British Racing Green with black leather interior. It had a manual transmission with an overdrive system, which was so much fun to shift. WOW, I loved her car and especially loved driving it!

During my first weekend at home visiting my parents, Ann was about to drive by our house in her fantastic-looking car when she stopped to say hello. We talked for a few minutes, and then she asked me if I wanted to go for a ride. I practically jumped into her car. That drive was the beginning of many future weekend get-togethers. At first, she would take me for rides, and I wondered if she was dating anyone. What guy wouldn't want to go out with her? She was a lovely girl with a great car. Over the next 19 weekends, I wanted to race home so we would go out and drive her car. After a few weekend visits, she let me drive, and driving her special car made our visits much more enjoyable. Nothing romantically ever happened between us. I think it was because we both knew I was going to Vietnam. A serious relationship would not have been a good idea for either of us. Nevertheless, we had lots of fun and good times throughout this time, and I met many of her girlfriends.

I believe Ann's parents didn't mind me visiting her on weekends either. It might have been because I was the only neighborhood guy in the military. While growing up, I would always wave to her parents as I rode my bicycle through the neighborhood. When I visited Ann during my military training days, her parents would ask about my week in the Army. I believe they enjoyed hearing about my experiences. My status had changed. I was no longer the boy who rode his bicycle throughout the neighborhood. But now I was considered an adult ready to go off and fight a war our country had conscripted me to serve.

During my time in Vietnam, Ann attended Towson State Teachers College, where she successfully earned her undergraduate degree in teaching. Later, she relocated to Pennsylvania to pursue a teaching career. Upon my return from Vietnam, I learned that Ann had settled in Pennsylvania, married, and had a family.

An Austin Healey

III. Vietnam

Leaving Home for Vietnam

Note to Reader:

This text is not a comprehensive listing like in a memoir. Instead, it is a reflection on a selection of profound moments that significantly shaped my journey and personal growth. These stories are a short sampling and windows into my experiences, each one a pivotal point that contributed to and were a part of my life's evolution. Many are based upon activities from long ago and if you read something you believe to be not factual, it's my history and factual to me. Personal war stories are in many cases observed differently because of the rush of adrenaline and fear. Who can say with absolute certainty what exactly happened fifty years ago.

On the day my father accompanied me to the airport for my journey to Fort Lewis, Washington, I proudly wore a meticulously tailored dress uniform that I had acquired during my time at Fort Eustis. The uniform was freshly dry-cleaned, and I had diligently polished all the brass buttons. It was a uniform I cherished, fitting me perfectly like a second skin. Completing the ensemble were my brand-new leather dress shoes, meticulously spit-shined to a brilliant gloss, not those plastic shoes that some guys wore.

At the departure curb of the airport, emotions ran high as my father embraced me, presenting me with a pint of Pikesville whiskey and a copy of the U.S. Constitution. Our hearts were heavy, and I refrained from questioning him about his gifts, fearing that any exchange of words might dissolve into tears. I hugged him tightly, retrieved my duffel bag from the car, and whispered, "I love you, Dad." With a final wave, I turned away, though a profound sense of unease settled in the pit of my stomach. Attempting to steady myself, I focused on the upcoming journey, a whirlwind of emotions swirling within me.

It was during that moment that I realized the sinking feeling in my stomach stemmed from leaving my previous life behind. The path I had chosen meant there was no going back to the person I once was. SFC Watson's words echoed in my mind, reminding me that this was an opportunity for personal growth that I would not have experienced had I not been in the Army. However, a smile graced my face as I recalled the bottle of whiskey nestled in my bag. With newfound determination, I strode towards the United Airlines counter, ready to check in for my flight bound for Seattle/Tacoma, Washington.

At the United ticket counter, I ran into my two fellow Fort Eustis classmates, who were also bound for Vietnam and joined me on our weekend travels home during training at Fort Eustis. Once we settled into our adjacent seats aboard the Boeing 707 aircraft, I retrieved the bottle of whiskey my father had given me, and the three of us began to indulge. As our flight included a layover in Chicago, it proved fortunate for my companions, who had fallen ill during the descent into O'Hare airport. My own stomach churned uncomfortably. The effects of the Pikesville whiskey had taken their toll on all of us.

During our layover in Chicago, I took the opportunity to disembark and make a call home. My father answered, and I shared with him the unfortunate sickness my friends and I experienced after consuming the questionable Pikesville whiskey. In response, he calmly advised me that I should only drink good whiskey, as cheaper ones like Pikesville tended to cause illness and unpleasant hangovers. To this day, I have never understood why he knew I would never be a drinker of beer or a connoisseur of wine. It was a valuable lesson that stuck with me, and since then, I have only indulged in the finest bourbon whiskey. Our conversation continued for a few more minutes, but it was evident that my mother was not in a good emotional state and did not wish to speak with me. My father explained her feelings and mentioned her tears. Once again, I reassured them of my safety and my intention to return home alive and well. With heartfelt words of "I love you and Mom," we concluded the call. I hurriedly made my way back to the plane. Four hours later, when we arrived at the Seattle-Tacoma airport, my two classmates and I felt somewhat better after the ordeal with the cheap whiskey and a lesson well learned.

During the same flight, I struck up a conversation with a female flight attendant. By the end of the journey, she had shared her address and phone number with me, requesting that I write to her when I could. For nearly three months, I corresponded with her until a devastating incident occurred. My barracks was destroyed by North Vietnamese Sappers resulting in the loss of everything I owned. My papers, address book, personal belongings, and even my cherished private pilot flight hours logbook were all gone. In the accompanying picture, she can be seen sitting in

My stewardess friend

the rear passenger lounge area of the 707 aircraft we traveled in to Seattle-Tacoma, Washington. I can't help but wonder if it was indeed my tailored uniform and highly polished shoes that initially caught her attention and led to the exchange of contact information. Just jesting.

We arrived at Fort Lewis, Washington, on Friday and immediately began transitioning to Vietnam. I received additional shots and another physical examination. I began taking a regular dose of malaria drugs and salt tablets. It rained a cold rain all three days we were there. I'm not sure if it was the rain and damp cold or the shots and drugs we received but I had a good case of the chills.

Unfortunately, I was under the misperception that I would keep my possessions in Vietnam. Sadly, I discovered that the personal possessions I arrived with at Fort Lewis would be taken away and replaced with jungle fatigues and boots. The Army in all probability combined my uniform, shoes, and other personal belongings with different clothing and sold the lot to an Army surplus store. I bet someone got a great deal on an expensive, extremely well-made Army uniform and a nearly new pair of highly polished leather shoes.

On Saturday night, about 40 of us were sent outside to police[15] a parade field for trash and cigarette butts. We walked around in the rain, picking up wet soggy paper and cigarette butts. This was when I truly learned the definition of "make work." We stayed both physically and mentally occupied to divert our thoughts and attention from our impending destination.

That night the field lights shone brightly on the wet parade field grass and surrounding buildings making everything look magical and beautiful. As I sit here typing and reflecting on that night, it's amazing how vividly those memories remain in my mind to this day.

Upon fulfilling my duty of collecting discarded papers and cigarette butts, I found myself drawn to a quaint church nestled near the parade field. It stood as a beacon of tranquility amidst the disciplined chaos of military life. There, in that sacred space, I paused to reflect and pray. My thoughts turned to the uncertain future that lay ahead and to my parents, whose images lingered in my heart. I sought guidance, strength, and a sense of peace in the face of the unknown journey that awaited me.

As I was about to leave the church, my eyes caught a sign that read "Take One" hovering above a stack of small Bibles. It was a simple invitation, yet it felt like a profound calling. I heeded the directive, my hand reached out to claim one of those sacred texts. Little did I know, this small Bible would become my steadfast companion, a source of solace and strength in the days to come.

This little Bible journeyed with me to the distant lands of Vietnam, a constant presence amidst the turmoil and uncertainties of war. It miraculously survived several explosions, its pages bearing witness to the chaos and the miracles of survival. Each scar on its cover, each wrinkle on its pages, told a story of endurance and faith in the face of adversity and po-

---

[15] Army term for picking up something, https://www.thefreedictionary.com/policing

tential death. At this point in my life this humble book was more than a collection of scriptures; it was a symbol of resilience, a testament to the enduring power of faith under the most trying circumstances that provided me strength and courage to march forward with God's grace and survive.

The next day, we were taken to the airport late afternoon and boarded a stretch Boeing 707 contract airliner. It was larger and more significant than the usual Boeing 707 and was owned and operated by World Airways. I sat next to the window on the middle-left side of the plane. While walking to my seat, I thought, what a picture: 189 young men wearing new jungle fatigues with faraway looks on their faces. We were all in the dark about our destination in Vietnam, uncertain if we were heading to a war zone or somewhere else. The lack of information added to the uncertainty and apprehension of our deployment. There wasn't much conversation on the plane. We were just sitting, thinking, and wondering what was in store for us, like so many young men going to previous wars for our country.

The first leg of our flight took us to Anchorage, Alaska. We landed at night for a two-hour stop for refueling, cleaning up, and resupplying food and fuel. In the mid-1960s, there were no passenger jetways like today, only rolling stairs. Everyone entered and exited the aircraft by those steps. When the aircraft doors opened, everyone instantly felt the frigid air. The airport lights illuminated the horizontally blowing snow, which looked like a blizzard. Before leaving the plane, we gave the officer in charge our names and service numbers. Once on the ground, we were to walk along a canvas covered walkway. But because of the extreme temperature, we were double-timing (running) to the terminal building to get out of the cold and blowing snow. We were freezing cold because we were wearing only lightweight jungle fatigues and boots. I was sure we had mistakenly landed in Siberia or the North Pole.

After our stop, we departed Anchorage for the next leg of our flight to Japan. Like many others on that airplane, I couldn't sleep and was exhausted when ultimately, we landed in Japan for a short layover to clean the aircraft and take on additional food and fuel. We were allowed to visit the duty-free shop on this layover, and after the aircraft was ready, everyone boarded the plane for our final destination, Cam Ranh Bay, Vietnam. This last leg of our trip to Vietnam was approximately six hours. On this leg of the flight, I was able to sleep. When the pilots announced we were landing at Cam Ranh Bay, I woke and became anxious. I'm sure the other 189 passengers were nervous as well. Our anxiety increased when our airplane didn't land immediately. Instead, it climbed to a higher altitude and circled the airport in a holding pattern. Thirty minutes passed before we were finally cleared to land. Once the plane landed and came to a stop, the flight crew promptly opened the doors. As soon as they did, an intense blast of heat and humidity engulfed everyone on board. The immediate oppressiveness of the air was astonishing, almost as if the airplane had transformed into a steam room.

The ground crew and welcoming personnel came on board and announced that the airbase had come under a rocket attack just as we were about to land. Incoming rockets exploded on the airfield when our aircraft was cleared to land. They also mentioned that rocket attacks were frequent at Cam Ranh Bay because it was such a vast U.S. military installation. In addition to its two 10,000-foot runways, it had an excellent deep-water port. Large quantities of munitions, petroleum, oil, lubricants, or POL, as the military referred to it, would arrive and be stored at this port. Cam Ranh Bay's vast exposure to the ocean was a perimeter that invited the enemy to continually test the airbase defenses.

I learned later that the Vietnamese would target the materiel at Cam Ranh Bay, but they historically underestimated the vast resources of the United States. The Vietnamese Sappers[16] managed to destroy many areas within Cam Ranh Bay, but their rocket attacks never significantly impacted the U.S. logistical or combat operations. More often than not, those rocket attacks resulted in the attackers' deaths.

After taking a few breaths of the humid Vietnam air, several large Army trucks (called a deuce and half or a 2 ½ ton) drove up and parked close to the airplane. Those big Army trucks would have been our ride to the terminal, but there was a change in plans. We were all given rifles as we climbed up and into the back of those trucks. It didn't matter if you were a cook,

---

[16] Today, "sapper" refers more broadly to combat engineers who handle a variety of construction and demolition duties. In Vietnam, however, American troops used the name primarily for North Vietnamese Army and Viet Cong units that broke through defensive lines using tactics more akin to raids by commandos than to the work of engineers. https://www.historynet.com/sapper-attack-theel-ite-north-vietnamese-units/

clerk, helicopter crew chief, or flight engineer everyone was given a rifle and ammunition. Now all our training as riflemen was about to be put into practical use. We were driven close to the mountains to patrol and hopefully, find the Vietnamese who fired those rockets at the Cam Ranh Bay air base prior to our landing. I don't know how to describe my feelings at that time. I would venture to state I was scared as well as many others on our airplane and couldn't understand why we were required to undertake such a tenacious and dangerous mission. I was issued an M16 rifle and ammunition, but my comfort level lay with the M14 rifle and the 7.62 cartridge, as this was the weapon I had used for the majority of my training. This familiarity made the M14 feel more reliable and comfortable in my hands.

Nevertheless, after several hours of searching and sweating in the heat and humidity, the Vietnamese who fired the rockets hadn't been found. They were long gone. My first takeaways from this brief time in Vietnam were 1.) we went on a wild goose chase and 2.) how resourceful the Vietnamese were. The attackers filled large empty cans with water, then they created a floating weight with a string attached to a North Vietnamese 122mm rocket.[17] As the water evaporated, the heavy line would tighten the rocket firing mechanism, which would fire the missile. By then, the responsible enemy would be long gone. It was an ingenious way of firing rockets and to avoid getting caught or killed.

I also discovered through our talking with Air Force personnel on the base that the Vietnamese made sandals from old tires and inner tubes. One had to admire their creativity and ingenuity even though they were the enemy. After those admiring thoughts were gone, I could only imagine what awaited me at my next location. When we returned from patrol, we turned in our weapons and ammunition to the supply personnel. We were then taken to a processing center where the clerks welcomed us to "The Nam." as they called Vietnam. Then they said if all goes well, you will be coming

---

[17] One of the most used ground-based Rocket (and System), The 122mm Rocket was used by both North Vietnamese Army (NVA) and Viet Cong (VC) Armies. They were fielded in 1966 and would remain dominant until the end of The War in 1975. Many 122mm Rockets were deployed against US Air Bases as well as US Army Base Camps throughout their history. As stated the speed in which a Crew could fire and move to another position ("Shoot and Scoot"), was very effective. https://www.stronghold-nation.com/history/ref/nva-122mm-rocket

through here again on your way back to "The World" in 365 days from now. The clerk who processed my papers said I would be quickly assigned to an aviation company because my MOS (short for military occupational specialty) and training was critical in Vietnam. I was going to ask why, but decided not to because I already had a good idea why. The clerk then told me what hooch[18] I was assigned to spend the night, and then he handed me a set of orders to travel to Nha Trang and then to Qui Nhon (Quin-YON). He smiled and said, "See, you're valuable, and you won't have to wait long to get to your permanent company."

The clerk was correct, I caught a flight in a Huey helicopter to Nha Trang to my assigned replacement company[19] the following day. I was assigned to a replacement company because I was in transit to a permanent location. Replacements are necessary because a company needs additional personnel, a soldier's tour of duty is over, or they are wounded and taken out of combat, or because of their death. The Nha Trang theater or war zone replacement company managed moving replacements within the theater of operations or the war zone of that area in Vietnam. The replacement company was the primary replacement delivery unit on the battlefield. Each company could manage up to 400 replacements per day if needed.

At the replacement company, I was first required to change any of my remaining U.S. dollars into military payment certificate (MPC) money. I was told that using U.S. currency in Vietnam would help the enemy fight against us. I'm still unsure if this was true or whether it was a way to stop the illegal trading of dollars on the world market or a con job. But I exchanged the U.S. money in my wallet for military payment certificates (MPC) as the military called it. The MPC actually looked like monopoly money.

After changing money, I entered another building and received my first in-country briefing. The briefers told me I was a guest in Vietnam and that

---

[18] Our living quarters in Vietnam were called hooches most of the time.

[19] The replacement company is the basic personnel replacement delivery unit on the battlefield. Replacement personnel categories are: Soldiers and civilians arriving in theater. Soldiers and civilians moving from one unit to another within the theater. Soldiers and civilians returning to duty from medical or confinement facilities or on straggler status. Soldiers and civilians in transit to or from rest and recuperation (R&R) areas outside the theater. Soldiers and civilians in transit in- and out-of-theater (for example, emergency leave).

120

the government of South Vietnam had invited me to help secure their country from socialism and communism. After this briefing and completing multiple forms, we were assigned to a barracks. The clerk assisting me said I wouldn't be assigned guard duty because I wouldn't stay more than one night. Once again, he explained that my stay would be brief because my MOS was critical for our military war effort.

I took my time locating my temporary hooch because I wanted to look around and see more of the Nha Trang Army base. After walking around the area and going out to the airfield, I found my assigned hooch and went inside. There was only one other guy in the hooch sitting by himself. He was in the rear, sitting on his bunk. He was keenly focused on sharpening his knife. I walked over and introduced myself and noticed he was wearing what looked like a Hawaiian necklace. He continued honing his knife blade while we talked. Because I was new to Vietnam, I asked how long he had been in-country. To my amazement, he said four years. My immediate thought was, WOW, that's a very long time to be in a war zone and combat and still be alive! But I dared not say it out loud for fear of insulting him.

I asked him if he had just returned from R&R.[20] He said, "No, I'm just being reassigned to another company for my next 12-month tour." That meant this guy was going to be spending five years in Vietnam. I then said I mentioned R&R because of your Hawaiian necklace. He took hold of the necklace and said, "Oh this? No man, this isn't from Hawaii. These are dried-up ears. I cut off the ears of the Vietnamese I kill because of what they do to us Americans when they kill us."

I was left stunned and speechless, unsure of how to respond. I simply looked at him, offering a smile and a nod in agreement before returning to my sleeping area to finish unpacking my gear. It dawned on me that I might have to go out on patrol with him, just as I had to do when leaving the airplane at Cam Ranh Bay upon arriving in Vietnam. Suddenly, an uneasy feeling washed over me, and the hair on my neck and arms stood on end. He would be the first of several individuals I would encounter during my time in Vietnam who had been profoundly affected by the harsh realities of

---

[20] Rest and Recuperation—United States servicemen on a 12-month tour of duty were given seven days R & R outside Vietnam. Sydney, Australia was my choice late in 1969.

combat, inhumanity, brutality, and death. It ultimately became clear to me how such experiences could affect and change a person.

That first night, I struggled to sleep, my mind racing with all the intense stimuli I had encountered since arriving in Vietnam, and the image of my hooch mate with his eerie necklace made of ears. I lay awake for most of the night, reminiscing about home and the conversations I had shared with my parents about life and the skills I had learned so far in the Army. I made a promise to myself not to become like the guy sleeping at the other end of the hooch. His eyes held an emptiness, a lost soul, reflected in his facial expression. That emptiness seemed to seep into my own heart, and the encounter deeply affected me. I had never seen a person who appeared so haunted.

With little sleep, I ate breakfast and then walked around the Nha Trang compound. I saw the hustle and bustle of a very active Army combat base. I met and talked with several Green Berets from the 5th Special Forces Group headquarters and talked about my training at Fort Bragg. Little did I know that I would soon support their efforts across II and III CORPS.

In Nha Trang, the sights and smells were incredibly stimulating. They crystallized the reality of being in Vietnam and a war zone. Years later, I gave a talk about my time in Vietnam. The smells were the first things that came to mind as I prepared my talk. The smells and vapors I experienced were so intense that they are forever imprinted in my memories.

Even to this day, whenever I come across sights or smells that remind me of Vietnam, it immediately triggers my senses, transporting me back in an instant. It's a constant struggle to manage and control these sensations and memories. When they resurface, I find myself needing to consciously remind myself that the war has long ended, and it's important for me to focus on moving forward. Despite the challenges, I cannot help but feel grateful to God for granting me life and the opportunity to live it.

During my time in Nha Trang, I received orders directing me to report to a small helicopter company located in Qui Nhon. This helicopter company primarily specialized in aviation depot maintenance. What this meant was that they were equipped to perform extensive maintenance work on helicopters, including complete overhauls, rebuilding of various parts, assemblies, subassemblies, and even manufacturing parts when needed. This comprehensive service also encompassed modifications, testing, and an important aspect known as "recovery," which was crucial, although I had little knowledge of the specific missions involved in this aspect of depot maintenance.

Additionally, the depot maintenance unit provided support to lower maintenance categories by offering technical assistance when others were faced with tasks beyond their responsibility or capability. They also supplied serviceable parts, equipment, and supplies through their more extensive repair facilities. It became clear to me that my Military Occupational Specialty (MOS) had provided me with the necessary training and experience, which was why the Army had assigned me to this particular company.

However, in my heart and thoughts, I couldn't deny that I had not volunteered to go to Vietnam with the intention of repairing helicopter parts. But I had to acknowledge the reality of my situation: these were official orders, and I had a duty to follow them. Viewing this assignment from a positive perspective, I recognized it as a valuable opportunity to gain insights into various Army units and acquire firsthand experience in how the military functions in a war zone. Importantly, it offered a safer alternative to direct combat, making it a unique chance for growth and learning.

Depot Maintenance and Recovery

With my orders, I walked to the airfield and caught a helicopter ride to Qui Nhon. The aircraft landed in my assigned unit's flight line area, and I saw four Chinook CH-47s, two Huey helicopters, and a Cobra gunship in the company revetments[21]. Off to the side was a large aviation hangar. I didn't think the hangar looked like a depot maintenance facility.

There had to be more.

I grabbed my gear and walked over to check in at the company headquarters. The company clerk was from California and had recently joined

---

[21] A revetment, in military aviation, is a parking area for one or more aircraft that is surrounded by blast walls on three sides. These walls are as much about protecting neighboring aircraft as it is to protect the aircraft within the revetment; if a combat aircraft fully loaded with fuel and munitions was to somehow ignite, by accident or design, then these risks starting a chain reaction as the destruction of an individual aircraft could easily set ablaze its neighbors. The blast walls around a revetment are designed to channel any blast and damage upwards and outwards, away from neighboring aircraft.

the company. I remember him well because he also was a fellow hooch mate of mine for the next several months.

During my first week in the company, our company clerk fell asleep without covering his bunk with mosquito netting. The following day, it was painfully obvious the mosquitos had a good time feeding on him during the night. His skin was swollen and red all over except under his underwear. He was in severe and excruciating pain that caused him to go out on sick call. I never saw anyone bitten like that before. I learned the invaluable lesson of mosquito netting. I never slept without mosquito netting or applying bug repellent!

The unit I was assigned to was quite unique within the Army, as our primary role involved conducting numerous recovery and combat support missions. Depot maintenance work was infrequent and limited to our own company's helicopters. Our regular duties included flying missions in support of the Green Berets stationed at the 5th Special Forces headquarters in Nha Trang. These missions extended beyond that as well, falling under the broader umbrella of Special Forces operations. Many of the people we worked with and supported were dressed in jungle fatigues, which notably lacked any visible indicators of rank, name, or unit affiliation. I came to believe that this anonymity was indicative of their involvement in a broad network of Special Forces and government operations. Nonetheless, in an effort to ease my parents' concerns, I made sure that the letters I sent home were filled with stories of beach outings and enjoyable cookouts with American Red Cross nurses.

I painted vivid pictures of visits to picturesque villages and the meaningful interactions I had with the Vietnamese locals, who graciously shared their history and insights with me. As I crafted each letter, my goal was to infuse them with a sense of positivity, blending real experiences with fictional tales that I hoped would bring joy and relief to my parents' hearts.

Initially, I was puzzled by the purpose behind our missions in support of the Green Berets. Our tasks involved dropping off and picking up small teams of Green Berets, occasionally accompanied by German Shepherd dogs. We also conducted air drops of chemicals and various gasses near their camps or suspected enemy locations. Moreover, we were responsible for delivering *and properly setting in place* big wooden guard towers at Special Forces camps.

Some Red Cross nurses

Additionally, during some of those missions we were frequently tasked with retrieving damaged or crashed helicopters, jets, bulldozers, trucks, and even riverboats. Prior to this assignment, I lacked experience in such operations. However, after a few on-the-job training sessions, I quickly became comfortable with these missions, including being left on the ground to prepare equipment for recovery. It was a stark contrast to my initial expectations of what a depot maintenance company entailed.

A guardtower after placement

Preparing gas cans for a drop. The white-striped 55-gallon drums contained defoliant chemicals we would later be dropping.

The company maintenance officer was a Chief Warrant Officer 4, commonly referred to as a CW4. His name was Robert Remsberg from Frederick, MD. He had served two flying tours in Korea and was a helicopter pilot on his second tour in Vietnam. He was a tall, very matter-of-fact, by-the-book officer. He and I didn't fly together often, but I did join him in some exciting maintenance activities. We performed our own aircraft maintenance and repairs allowing me to put my training to use immediately.

He had served two flying tours in Korea and was a helicopter pilot on his second tour in Vietnam. He was a tall, very matter-of-fact, by-the-book officer. He and I didn't fly together often, but I did join him in some exciting maintenance activities. We performed all our own aircraft maintenance and repairs allowing me to put my training to use immediately.

In the 1960s, replacing helicopter rotor blades was a labor-intensive and potentially hazardous task, especially when done in the field. Due to the urgency of the situation, certain safety protocols were often overlooked during these on-site replacements. The focus was on expediting the process, with only essential manual adjustments being made to ensure the helicopter could safely return to our flight line for further repairs and maintenance.

Once the aircraft was returned and other adjustments made, an additional manual procedure called tracking and balancing was carried out to ensure that the newly replaced rotor blades did not cause unnecessary vibrations. This process involved using a large pole equipped with bungee cords, which held a sizable canvas strap. While the rotors were spinning, the pole with the canvas strap, facing the rotor blades, would be slowly advanced towards the blade ends until three distinct slaps on the canvas were heard.

It is important to note that this procedure was highly dangerous. If the pole accidentally struck the blades, it would be forcefully yanked out of the person's hands, resulting in severe injuries to the individual holding the pole and potential damage to the rotor blade.

During a critical medevac mission, we were tasked with landing in a recently cleared landing zone using grenades and ripcord blasting cord wrapped around tree trunks to create the Landing Zone (LZ). The guesses of clearances from surrounding trees often posed challenges, as there wasn't always enough space cleared for a successful landing. This particular landing site appeared extremely tight, requiring the pilots to exercise precision during

A Chinook descending into a tight landing zone among trees

both landing and takeoff. Moreover, it was considered a hot landing zone due to enemy fire, which made everyone on board anxious as we descended.

As the gunfire intensified, the pilots shifted their attention away from the landing zone, searching for the source of the shooting. In doing so, they momentarily lost focus on the minimal distance between the rotor blades and the nearby trees. Regrettably, the helicopter's front rotor blades collided with a tree. The Vietnamese forces instantly recognized that they had a prime opportunity to bring down a CH-47 helicopter. The subsequent events seemed to unfold in slow motion as bullets struck the aircraft, causing fragments to scatter in all directions. Despite sustaining numerous bullet holes and damage to the rotor blades, we persevered and successfully completed the medevac mission, ultimately saving several lives that day, including our own.

Upon completing the mission, it was necessary to thoroughly inspect various aircraft areas for damage and potential metal fatigue due to the bullet holes and blade strike. The three front rotor blades had to be removed and replaced. To minimize vibrations, it was crucial to perform tracking and balancing on the replacement blades, ensuring that they aligned precisely on the same plane. CW4 Remsberg, aware of my training in this task, requested

128

my assistance, specifically in the dangerous role of holding the pole. While my training experiences had been straightforward and uneventful, I felt a mix of apprehension and determination. CW4 Remsberg stayed close by, providing constant encouragement as I prepared the necessary equipment. When I heard the three slaps on the canvas, I swiftly withdrew the pole from the blades to prevent any potential injury that would result in me being sent to a medevac hospital or becoming another statistic in a cemetery.

Setting the pole down on the ground, we were pleasantly surprised to find that only minor adjustments were required for the blades. Once these adjustments were made, I performed the manual tracking and balancing procedure again to verify that the alignments had been corrected. Remarkably, all three blades tracked together precisely. The sense of accomplishment that washed over me was truly gratifying.

Despite my curiosity, I could not comprehend why one of the two Huey helicopters wasn't utilized for such operations. It seemed that the rationale behind this decision was intentionally kept from me, likely dictated by the individuals in white short-sleeved shirts and skinny black ties who provided the mission parameters. Over time, I came to learn that these individuals

A blade tracking device

were CIA staff members. They maintained a rapport solely with CW4 Remsberg, excluding direct communication about missions with the flight crew members such as me.

Another lingering question remained: why wasn't I engaged in depot maintenance? Despite flying combat missions to numerous dangerous areas without complaint, I couldn't help but wonder why I wasn't assigned to work in an actual depot maintenance facility, involved in the rebuilding of airplane and helicopter components and parts. On the other hand, the activities I was engaged in proved to be unquestionably more intriguing and exhilarating.

During my early months in Vietnam, my role often involved flying into combat zones for essential resupply missions and life-saving medical evacuations. It was a far cry from the sensationalized portrayals of war in Hollywood movies. In Vietnam, the standard tour of duty lasted for 12 months, and as the end of someone's tour approached, they experienced a mix of caution and excitement. Three months into my own deployment, I found myself at an impromptu farewell party for a fellow soldier who had completed his 12-month tour. He was one of those individuals who decided to let loose and live without inhibitions during his final days, resulting in a severe hangover. The atmosphere was filled with revelry and drinks, but as I consumed more alcohol, an uneasy feeling crept over me—homesickness. Though I had only briefly felt such sentiments before, the alcohol seemed to magnify them. I yearned for home, missing my parents, my young niece Irene who was being cared for by my parents because of marital difficulties, and my high school friends. Memories of my previous life before joining the Army flooded my mind. I began to wonder who was playing with Irene after school now that I was gone, a thought that lingered in my thoughts. The more I dwelled on home, the more I sought solace in drinking. Not wanting to get intoxicated, I knew my mind could spiral into a dark place, so I made the conscious decision to stop drinking and retreat to my living quarters. I sought refuge in sleep.

As night fell, the entire airfield suddenly came under attack by North Vietnamese sappers. These surprise assaults conducted by highly skilled Communist units were among the most formidable and feared threats faced by American forces in Vietnam. Sappers[22] possessed exceptional stealth capa-

---

[22] https://en.wikipedia.org/wiki/Sapper

bilities and were virtually invisible in the darkness. They would patiently wait in perimeters around base camps, fire support bases, or airfields, sometimes for days, selecting the perfect moment to strike. Coordinated with NVA mortar fire to divert attention, the sappers would swiftly infiltrate the compound. Armed with grenades and canvas satchels filled with explosives (commonly known as satchel charges), and rifles, they would create chaos by hurling their weapons and initiating automatic gunfire against the surprised troops.

Upon hearing weapons firing and explosions I was immediately awakened. I quickly leapt out of my bunk. My memories of the ensuing moments are fragmented, but I recall instinctively grabbing my Kbar knife and rushing outside, intent on reaching a nearby bunker for safety. In the chaos, I encountered another soldier running towards the same bunker. "Stick together!" he shouted and I nodded in agreement, moving swiftly but cautiously. As we neared the bunker, we saw a group of sappers approaching from the left. We quickly ducked behind a pile of sandbags, barely avoiding their line of sight. The other soldier, whose name I believe was Mitchell, signaled for us to stay low and wait for an opening.

Moments later, a mortar round exploded nearby, creating a plume of smoke and debris. Using the distraction to our advantage, we sprinted the final distance to the bunker and dove inside. Once safely inside, we found a few other soldiers already hunkered down, weapons ready. What's the Status? I asked, trying to gauge the situation.

This one is a heavy attack," a someone replied. "We're holding this position until the Korean soldiers arrive. The Republic of Korea (ROK) soldiers provided security for the entire camp and airfield.

We all nodded and took our positions, ready to defend the bunker in the ongoing battle outside as explosions and gunfire echoed from multiple directions.

Finally, after what seemed like an eternity, we heard the distinct sound of helicopters approaching. Huey and Cobra gunships had arrived and began flying around the entire camp and airfield looking for the sappers. The sappers, realizing their opportunity had passed, began to retreat. The gunfire gradually diminished, and a tense silence fell over the airfield.

Cautiously, we emerged from the bunker, weapons still at the ready. The damage to the airfield was significant, but we were relieved to see that the main structures had held. Medical teams quickly moved in to assist the wounded, and we began to assess the situation at the airfield. None of the aircraft were destroyed, however several sustained damage and could be repaired to fly again.

I took a deep breath, feeling a wave of exhaustion wash over me. Despite the chaos and danger, we had survived the night. As I looked around at my fellow soldiers, a profound sense of camaraderie and relief settled over me. We had faced one of the most formidable threats in Vietnam and lived to tell the tale.

Fears and Self-Doubt

Many times, I felt uncomfortable when my assigned company flew missions to remote locations without gunship support. One of those missions took us near the Cambodian border to resupply a tank and armored personnel carrier (APC) group. The group's job was to stop the constant flow of the North Vietnamese Army into the South. They were close to depleting their ammunition and needed resupply. We delivered necessary fuel, ammunition, food, and water. When we finished our delivery and flew out of the area, we began receiving fire from North Vietnamese soldiers.

As we left the area, the crew chief appeared to be having trouble firing the right-door machine gun. I helped him resolve the problem and turned back to my right when a bullet went through my fatigue shirt pocket. Thankfully, the only harm done was the destruction of a pack of cigarettes I carried to offer smokes to others. That bullet caused me to fall into the heater closet. I hit the crew chief and knocked him off the machine gun. I regained balance and grabbed the machine gun as I pulled myself up and returned fire.

I have written previously about where American virtues stay one's trigger finger. This was one of those times when I hesitated and saw a North Vietnamese soldier within a larger group look directly into my eyes. That split second seemed like an eternity. The North Vietnamese soldier wearing his khaki-colored uniform fired again while running. Squeezing the trigger of the M-60 machine gun, a barrage of bullets flew in that person's direction, hitting him several times. The helicopter made an immediate left banking turn to avoid further damage. I lost sight of the person and his comrades. I had never shot at another human being before and didn't understand my emotions or the adrenaline flowing through me. As a child, I was taught not to hurt others, but soldiers are trained to kill in war. In my opinion, that's what war is, killing and breaking things. No matter how much training one has, taking another human being's life is still painfully difficult. Then the painful guilt surfaced when my mind created imaginary visions of shooting someone wearing a white tee shirt that had several bright red blood spots on it. That vision took many years to be placed back in the deepest recesses of my memory. But the extreme guilt of shooting at another human being has never left.

The experiences I faced created a confusing emotional period in my life. It became imperative for me to embrace the teachings of SFC Watson from my basic training. To strengthen my resolve and commitment to myself and life, I had to let go of my old ways of thinking and living. Allowing fear and guilt to consume me would only hinder my chances of survival and personal growth. It was essential to hold steadfast to my commitment, especially with a whole year of service remaining in Vietnam.

We frequently embarked on missions into Laos and Cambodia, often without the support of gunships. Maybe we were competing for air support with the CIA. The CIA owned the airline Air America and had two dozen twin-engine transports, two dozen STOL aircraft and 30 helicopters dedicated to the operations in Laos. This airline employed more than 300 pilots, copilots, flight mechanics, and airfreight specialists flying in and out of Laos to support the CIA's bombing campaign in Laos[23]. In most instances, I felt confident in my experience and intuition. I recognized the importance of voicing my concerns when something seemed amiss. The Army operated as a cohesive team, where each member played a crucial role in achieving mission success. Throughout my time in Vietnam, I witnessed how self-doubt and the fear of failure paralyzed individuals, preventing them from taking action. Such lapses in self-confidence could lead to catastrophic failures and even death. What was needed in those moments was unwavering self-commitment and courage.

Those observations served as a reminder to never doubt myself or fear failure. Failure is a natural part of life, but it is through failures that we

---

[23] https://en.wikipedia.org/wiki/CIA_activities_in_Laos

gain valuable lessons to propel us towards success. Success is not a mere stroke of luck but a disciplined habit that drives us to excel in every endeavor we undertake.

Throughout my time in Vietnam, I diligently maintained detailed logbook records of every helicopter I flew. These records meticulously documented the hours flown, as well as the times allocated for maintenance and repairs. I had assumed that my official military personnel file would contain accurate and comprehensive records, much like the detailed helicopter logs I methodically maintained. Only Army clerical personnel were authorized to handle and update my flight records. Consequently, my official personnel records did not encompass all the flight times I accrued, as I often flew for others in cases of illness or other unforeseen circumstances.

Years later, when I reviewed my official personnel record, the DD-214,[24] to gather information about my training and experience, I discovered that a significant portion of my Army experience and training was missing. I initially attributed this to a lack of attention to detail by the Army clerical staff, but I found it difficult to comprehend how my meticulously maintained aircraft records did not correspond to my official records.

One notable example of missing information was a mission in which I was assigned and given a new set of dog tags. Each crew member received new dog tags, but the reasons behind this change were never explained to me. Even to this day, I remain uncertain as to why it was necessary. However, the most startling revelation came when I read my brother James' name on the new set of dog tags. This discovery left me restless and troubled, pondering how such an occurrence could have taken place. I contemplated the significance, if any, of my brother's name being imprinted on the metal tags. Was it a random mistake or did it hold deeper meaning?

My brother, Jimmy, served in the Naval Air and was medically discharged from the Navy many years ago. The unexpected sight of his name on my dog tags left me shaken and fearful. Despite my unsettled state, I proceeded with the planned recovery mission, which involved venturing

---

[24] The DD Form-214, Certificate of Release or Discharge from Active Duty, generally referred to as a "DD-214", is a document of the United States Department of Defense, issued upon a military service member's retirement, separation, or discharge from active duty in the Armed Forces of the United States.

into Laos to retrieve the crew's remains or, if necessary, the heads of the bodies if the remains were unattainable. Our objective was also to destroy any remnants of the downed Huey helicopter. It was speculated that the helicopter may have been destined for

My older brother's dogtag

another classified U.S. base located on a mountaintop in Laos, similar to Lima 85,[25] which had been overrun and destroyed. This recovery mission was just one of many operations in which we were tasked with either recovering or eliminating evidence.

The flight to the crash site in Laos took longer than anticipated, as it was situated further inside the country. Surprisingly, we encountered no enemy fire throughout the journey, which struck me as odd given the intelligence assertion that the area served as a staging ground for the North Vietnamese Army. Once we located the crash site, we swiftly landed and shut down the engines to minimize our presence. Half of the crew, including one pilot, the crew chief, and the gunners, immediately began conducting a thorough preflight inspection to expedite our departure once the rotor blades stopped.

While the inspection was underway, the rest of us proceeded to the downed Huey to retrieve the remains of the crew. It was a challenging task, as the front section of the helicopter had been engulfed in fire and destroyed. The bodies of the pilot, copilot, crew chief, and gunner had been burned as a result. We placed their remains in separate body bags and positioned them at the rear of our helicopter's flight control closet, ensuring their safety and preventing any inadvertent damage during the loading of the tail section for the return flight.

We then went back to the wreckage and retrieved the tail section of the Huey. Our orders were to transport this section back to Qui Nhon, al-

---

[25] Lima Site 85 was a secret Air Force radar facility that sat atop one of the highest mountains in Laos, 15 miles away from the border with North Vietnam. The site was defended by a force of 1,000 CIA trained Hmong irregulars in the valley below, but a key element in its security was the mountain itself.

though at the time, I considered it yet another perplexing mission. It was later that I learned the reason behind not destroying or burning the remaining parts of the helicopter. Unbeknownst to us, there were North Vietnamese regular army troops within close proximity to our location, and setting the Huey ablaze would have immediately exposed our position.

Four of us carried the tail section toward the ramp area of our helicopter. As we reached the ramp, the crew chief had just completed the upper portion of the preflight inspection and began descending. It appeared that the North Vietnamese had been lying in wait until the inspection was concluded, for at that precise moment, we came under enemy fire. I took hold of the jagged end of the tail section and hurriedly moved backward up the ramp into the Chinook. While loading the tail section, one of the jagged edges got caught on something and refused to budge. Bullets started penetrating the aircraft, and I urgently yelled, "push, push, push!" In the chaos, I lost my balance and fell backward as the tail section finally broke free. Unfortunately, the sharp edge cut the inside of my right knee, causing immediate, intense pain.

In the midst of the shooting, while I was on my butt nursing my injured knee, I heard the crew chief's desperate cries for help outside the aircraft. He was yelling, "Help me! Help me! Help me, I'm stuck!" Despite the ongoing gunfire, everyone armed themselves and started returning fire. I quickly stood up and went outside to assist the crew chief. To my astonishment, he was hanging from the helicopter by his left-hand wedding ring finger. It was strictly forbidden to wear jewelry or wedding rings while working on or flying the Chinook, without any exceptions. I could not comprehend why he had disregarded this rule on that particular day, knowing full well the risks involved. His wedding band had become wedged between the uppermost step and step cover.

Reacting swiftly, I unsheathed my Kbar knife, and using the pommel end, I struck the step cover while pushing his hand inward. After several attempts, his hand finally came free, much to our relief. Had his finger not dislodged, I would have been forced to amputate one or more of his fingers to save his life and the lives of others.

Due to the crew chief being suspended on the side of the aircraft, the pilots were unable to start the helicopter's engines. As soon as they were certain we were in the aircraft they swiftly initiated engine start-up. The pilots executed a radical and forceful takeoff the moment the rotor blades reached the necessary rotations for flight, not wasting a second more. It was astounding to witness and hear the thunderous and perilous sounds produced as the Chinook pushed beyond its designed limits during this extreme airframe-stressing departure. The helicopter emitted sounds I had never heard before, while the entire airframe contorted under the strain of the severe turns and maneuvers.

On that day, we were extraordinarily fortunate that no lives were lost. Several crew members sustained injuries and minor cuts from fragments of aluminum or bullets, in addition to my injured knee. I attended to my knee wound by providing my own medical care, applying multiple bandages to stop the bleeding and minimize the size of the scar. I also drank a significant amount of water and took four aspirin tablets. Later that night, after consuming several drinks of bourbon along with additional aspirin tablets, my makeshift medicinal concoction helped alleviate the remaining discomfort.

On another mission, we were to rig, and sling load[26] a Chinook helicopter that had been shot down and return it to Qui Nhon. It would then be packed and shipped back to a rebuild facility in the United States. It was damaged beyond the rebuilding capabilities of any depot maintenance facility in Vietnam. Nevertheless, we were to recover it. CW4 Remsberg wanted to be the pilot in command of this mission. Everyone believed he didn't want to fly these complex missions because he was close to retirement. It was perilous to return to the site of a downed helicopter, crashed vehicle, or boat stuck in the water. The Vietnamese would set up firing positions and wait for the recovery teams.

On this recovery flight, there were several extra crew members; a technical sergeant, three other maintenance personnel, and three additional gunners with weapons and ammunition. When we finally landed at the crash site, I quickly rigged the downed Chinook. We used a drogue parachute to stabilize the Chinook sling load underneath us because I expected we would be high tailing it back to Qui Nhon. On high-speed fighter jets,

---

[26] A sling load is an aviation operation of transporting supplies, artillery, ammunition, and vehicles underneath an aircraft usually a large helicopter when ground transportation is not an option.

a drogue chute is a parachute that deploys upon landing from the aircraft's rear and helps to slow the plane while keeping it going straight down the runway. Flying fast with an unstable sling load can cause the above-carrying aircraft to crash, destroying both the carrying aircraft and the cargo beneath it. This was another reason for the drogue chute.

We were supposed to fly faster that day because of the large number of North Vietnamese enemy fighters in the area. That, however, is not how the flight occurred. Once I had everything hooked up and ready for flight, CW4 Remsberg and the copilot checked the rigging to ensure I had not overlooked any aspect of the recovery. I was thankful they checked my work because I had completed the necessary rigging quickly and in record time. With the rigging finished and everyone aboard the aircraft, we took off for Qui Nhon with the damaged Chinook slung underneath.

The flight began as routine and uneventful. Instead of flying over land, we all settled in to enjoy the flight over the South China Sea. We were in the air for some time when CW4 Remsberg began flying toward land at a much slower airspeed. We flew over water roughly a half-mile off the coast to avoid heavy enemy fire. Remsberg, the senior officer and pilot in command, changed course and began flying over land. Because he was the senior officer and oversaw all aspects of this mission, his decision was final.

He flew over an area with reports of substantial enemy troops. Later I learned it was also called no man's land.[27] He continued to slow down and flew at a lower altitude to conserve fuel. I could hear the heated and strained conversations over the intercom about this course change and the concern over running out of fuel.

I was lying on the floor behind the cargo access hatch watching the CH-47 below us, ensuring it was stable and was still tracking forward. The land we flew over was a sizable beach-type area with only sand and vegetation growing in clumps near the beach. As I continued to observe the terrain, it looked like the ideal area for enemy troops to dig a hole and wait in what we called spider holes. Spider holes were hiding places for the Vietcong or North Vietnamese, and they used these locations to hide and wait for a helicopter to fly over and then attempt to shoot it down. I had

---

[27] No man's land is waste or unowned land or an uninhabited or desolate area that is unoccupied out of fear or uncertainty.

138

heard many stories about those incidents but never experienced one. I believed this flight might allow me to experience this firsthand.

Little did I know that my thought would become a reality as I returned to the task at hand, watching the sling-loaded Chinook below us. The aircraft below was approximately 50 feet off the ground. I wanted to say something about how low and slow we were flying but thought better of it because of the angry and anxious conversations occurring over the intercom. Then the co-pilot complained several times about the low, slow flying. When he again repeated it, I stopped looking downward. Based on what I heard over the intercom, I thought the copilot would start arguing heatedly with CW4 Remsberg at any second about his flying over land and possible enemy ground fire.

I lifted my head and looked toward the front of the aircraft and the arguing pilots. Then I saw the first rounds coming through our helicopter's floor and directly toward me. It appeared as a movie playing slowly as the bullets emerged from the floor. I was fixated on them and didn't move. Those bullets were hypnotizing me. A bullet went through the floor an inch in front of the cargo door area, then the next one hit the large metal cross member inside the cargo access hole and ricocheted, almost hitting my head. The bullet fragments hit my lip, left cheek, and lower left jawline.

Now instead of arguing, there was chaos over the intercom. Then I heard one of the pilots yell release the load, release the load over the intercom. I held a control with switches for controlling the cargo hook and other parts of the aircraft, and I pushed the release button allowing the Chinook below us to drop and crash onto the sandy landscape below.

With the damaged helicopter released and, on the ground, we had to land immediately or crash because of the damage from the enemy bullets. After landing, I helped everyone grab weapons and ammunition as they exited the aircraft. Once outside they began returning fire. Even the copilot was out immediately. But CW4 Remsberg remained sitting at the flight controls. I thought he might be wounded then thought he was frozen with fear, I didn't know but I ran forward to help him. Just as I arrived and stood next to him, he took off his flight helmet, hurriedly got up, and we left the aircraft together.

I left the aircraft with an M16 rifle with extra ammunition and magazines, while the crew engaged the Vietnamese in a gunfight. What seemed

The rear of the on-fire Chinook we crash-landed. It was a very hard landing into soft ground. Look at the front wheels on the right deep within the earth.

like less than a minute, helicopter gunships arrived overhead and provided covering fire. Seeing how quickly the gunships arrived, I realized CW4 Remsberg had called for help before leaving the helicopter. Then two Huey helicopters landed allowing us to jump inside as we were evacuated.

Upon reflection, my perspective about CW4 Remsberg had shifted. Initially, I believed he was paralyzed by fear, which explained why he didn't exit the helicopter along with everyone else. However, I understood that his decision to remain inside and call for help was the best course of action. CW4 Remsberg's extensive Army experience and training allowed him to maintain control over his emotions and fear, enabling him to take charge of the situation and think and act logically. In my view, he saved lives that day. Yet, I could never fathom why he chose to fly the helicopter on such a perilous, low-altitude, and slow route over known enemy territory.

Nonetheless, this experience taught me a profound lesson. While I thought I had already grasped this lesson before, that day of battle proved to be another transformative moment. It was a battle for victory in life because every day is essentially a continuous fight. On that day, the objective was to fight and emerge triumphant. CW4 Remsberg demonstrated that we must fight with unwavering determination, even in the face of death. His display of courage inspired me to persist in my own struggle against limitations and outdated perspectives on living and life in general.

After a few hours of downtime and ensuring that the Vietnamese forces had vacated the crash site, we returned to our aircraft. We made the necessary repairs to get our Chinook airborne once more. Unfortunately, the other CH-47 had to be left behind overnight. We lacked the equipment to retrieve it and relocate it to a secure area. The following day, we revisited the crash site to find that the North Vietnamese had taken anything of value from the Chinook during the night. They would repurpose seating and strap materials for backpacks, clothing, or tools, while destroying what they didn't take. They had completely vanished from the area, likely unwilling to risk being targeted by our Cobra gunships. We couldn't ascertain the number of attackers killed as they typically carried away their fallen comrades. The skeletal remains of the helicopter, stripped of weight, posed no difficulty during the flight back to Qui Nhon.

In Qui Nhon, my daily routine returned. I began flying again. Once again, the flights were regular and routine in support of the 5th Special Forces: resupply, transporting heavy artillery, munitions, medevacs, and troop transport to remote areas. During another day, I visited the flight line with the intention of carefully reviewing the maintenance records and flight logs of each helicopter.

My primary objective was to verify their accuracy and ensure that they were up-to-date and correct. While updating the documents and flight logs, a Chinook landed and taxied over to our ramp area. I was the only person on the flight line at that time. I immediately directed the helicopter to a vacant parking space. Once the rotor blades stopped turning, the ramp was lowered, and a jeep backed out with only a driver. I was standing off to one side when the jeep stopped next to me. The driver was a major, with starched and pressed fatigues. I saluted, and he returned the salute and thanked me for the assistance.

During our brief conversation, he mentioned he was Major Sines, the Commanding Officer (CO) of the 178th Assault Support Helicopter Company (ASHC). He described how the 178th provided combat assault troop incursions, troop transport, artillery movement and resupply, and large-scale medevac and troop evacuations.[28] The 178th aircraft flew day and night and needed parts to maintain operational readiness for supporting the entire American/23rd Infantry Division in I-CORPS. There was another unit the 132nd Assault Support Helicopter Company, but later I discovered that their operational readiness was consistently less than the 178th. I appreciated that the CO was on a mission to locate the necessary helicopter parts himself. This task was usually the responsibility of the maintenance officer. I could tell this CO was a very can-do company commander who wanted to participate in this activity with his troops.

He asked for directions to the main parts depot, and I recommended ways of maneuvering to the airfield's other side. Six hours later, Major Sines and his crew returned. He had located many of the needed components, which were transported to the flight line in trucks to be loaded onto his Chinook helicopter. Many of the remaining components and parts were to be transported by truck to the 178th in Chu Lai over the following days. The 178th crew loaded everything they could into the Chinook while Major Sines and his copilot conducted the preflight inspection. Major Sines began conversing with me again during his preflight and asked about my training and experience. I spoke about my Army aviation and Chinook training and experiences. I also told him about my training flying small fixed-wing civilian aircraft back in the United States.

He described the missions of the 178th in more detail and how they supported the 23rd Infantry/American Division in I CORPS, the largest infantry division in Vietnam. He said the 178th didn't have enough qualified and trained flight crews, especially flight engineers. Hearing him say that I blurted out, how does someone transfer to the 178th? He smiled and provided the necessary form number to transfer from one unit to another. After he departed, I thought about this for an hour, walked to my company headquarters, and completed the transfer forms. Once again, my MOS made

---

[28] That was its official mission. While it performed so many other missions in support of the war such as chemical and gas drops, taking food and medical supplies to civilians on coastal islands who were blockaded and couldn't leave their islands. I drove a Jeep to a leprosy colony to deliver food, medicine, and money to help the Vietnamese. I also drove to an orphanage once to deliver supplies and medicine.

this quickly happen because I arrived at the 178th ASHC flight line two weeks later. The 178th ASHC was part of the American or the 23rd Infantry Division located In I CORPS.

History of the 23rd Infantry Division/ American Division

Rather than delving into a comprehensive account of all my Army units, I would like to focus on the Infantry Division where I spent the majority of my time during the Vietnam War. The 23rd Infantry Division, known as The American Division, boasts a rich and esteemed history, and I am honored to have contributed to it. The American Division's roots can be traced back to its establishment during World War II in the Pacific theater, specifically on the island of New Caledonia, positioned approximately 750 miles east of Australia.

During that time, the 164th Infantry Regiment, accompanied by additional artillery assets, joined forces with the existing 132nd and 182nd Infantry Regiments on the island. This amalgamated task force was formally organized into an infantry division named "American" on May 24, 1942. The division derived its name from the abbreviation "Americans in New Caledonia" and uniquely lacked the numerical label common to other American divisions of that period.

Following its return to the United States, the American Division was deactivated on December 12, 1945. Nonetheless, on December 1, 1954, the division was revived and officially designated as the 23rd Infantry Division. While it acquired a numerical identifier, it retained the moniker "American" and was stationed in the Panama Canal Zone until April 10, 1956, when it was once again disbanded.

The division was reactivated on April 20, 1967, in Vietnam. This reactivation emerged from Task Force Oregon, operating throughout the I-Corps or northernmost region of Vietnam. In its initial form, Task Force Oregon comprised the 196th Light Infantry Brigade, the 1st Brigade of the 101st Airborne Division, and the 3rd Brigade of the 25th Infantry Division, which later became known as the 3rd Brigade of the 4th Infantry Division.

Throughout the Vietnam War, the American Division maintained its commitment with distinction and honor. Numerous soldiers from the

Americal Division were recipients of the Medal of Honor, and various units received Presidential Unit Citations, Valorous Unit Citations, as well as multiple valor awards from the Vietnamese government. In the fall of 1969, I also had the privilege to have met Major General Lloyd B. Ramsey, the commander of the American or 23rd Infantry Division in Vietnam. The Americal Division can also count among its ranks several distinguished individuals, including General H. Norman Schwarzkopf, General Colin Powell, former Governor of Pennsylvania, and former Secretary of Homeland Security, Tom Ridge.

After leaving the Army, I found myself shopping at a major retailer in Towson, MD, on a day when I was in search of appliances for my apartment. Interestingly, I happened to be wearing my Army field jacket adorned with the Americal Division shoulder patch. As I entered the store, a gentleman took notice of the patch and approached me. He revealed that he had served in the Americal Division during its formation in the Pacific. Throughout our conversation, it became evident that he had fought valiantly across the Pacific theater as a proud member of this renowned infantry division. His sense of pride in his service was reflective.

Over the years, I have often recollected that encounter and thought of the man I met that day. I regret not having obtained his contact information, as I would have relished the opportunity to engage in further discussions about his experiences. I am certain he would have delighted me with a multitude of captivating and fascinating stories.

Returning to my Vietnam experience, I met Sergeant First Class (SFC) Lee Dorsey, an exceptional leader of young men, at the 178th flight line. He greeted me while waiting in a jeep. After introductions, he shared that he was from Bel Air, MD, and asked about my hometown. I mentioned Baltimore, to which he responded with a smile, there are several others from Baltimore in the 178th. During our drive to the company headquarters, he provided a thorough description of the 178th. This made me confident that my decision to transfer to this unit was the right one.

Upon reaching the company's headquarters building, my conviction was affirmed. SFC Dorsey introduced me to the Executive Officer and company commander, Major Ken Sines. Major Sines expressed his satisfaction with my choice to join and inquired if I was ready for a flight. I enthusiastically said yes. Upon completing the necessary paperwork and officially becoming a 178th flight engineer, SFC Dorsey guided me to my hooch and showed me my assigned bunk. The location, near the entrance of the hooch, proved to be strategic. This convenience allowed me to come and go without disturbing others, irrespective of the time. It also meant a swift exit in case of attacks. However, there were some downsides, such as the inconvenience of navigating the hooch or going outside to access facilities like the latrine or makeshift urinal. The urinal was a cut-in-half 55-gallon drum embedded in the sand and covered with a screen to prevent objects from falling in. The latrine resembled an outdoor shed with adjustable screened windows and wooden panels, usually kept raised for obvious reasons.

Inside the flight platoon hooch, SFC Dorsey introduced me to John LeCates, who he claimed was from Baltimore too. I jokingly inquired about his specific part of Baltimore, and LeCates chuckled, clarifying he was actually from Delmar, Delaware. This humorous exchange lightened the atmosphere. Continuing the introductions, SFC Dorsey presented Robert Bruce Criswell, affectionately known as "Bougie." He, too, was attributed to Baltimore, but Bougie clarified he was from Riverdale, MD.

During my time I was assigned to the 178th ASHC I became good friends with John LeCates, Robert Bruce (Bougie) Criswell, and Robert (Bob) McLaughlin who were also flight engineers and bunked near me in the flight platoon hooch. These guys have been lifelong friends. I have many stories about our time together in the Army and civilian life. To write about those stories would require another book, maybe Volume II of this autobiography or a memoir of my entire military service and the Vietnam war. In addition, I became friends with others who performed maintenance and repairs. Because they usually worked at night the maintenance crews lived in other hooches than the flight platoon crews. Due to their nightly working hours, many maintenance crew members slept during the day. While I would on many occasions work through the night because of my emotions from the day's flights, my time in Vietnam went by quickly.

After connecting with my fellow platoon members, SFC Dorsey and I returned to the jeep and drove to the flight line. Just three hours after my arrival at the 178th, SFC Dorsey assigned me to a CH-47B model aircraft. Together with the pilots, we conducted a preflight inspection.

The pilot in command that day was Captain Larry Self. It was a typical flight, transporting troops, resupplying, and relocating artillery. During the preflight, Captain Self began asking me how many flight hours I had, and then he started asking me questions about the helicopter's flight systems and flight characteristics. I was a little nervous because I didn't want to answer his questions incorrectly. I remember him looking directly into my eyes each time he asked a question. He probably wanted to determine if I was genuinely listening. Near the end of the preflight, we walked to the helicopter's rear when he asked, "Do you know how to fly?" I said, "Yes sir, I am a private pilot and have hours in a 150 and a 172. He looked at me smiling, saying, "That's good." I assumed I was a backup insurance policy if he or his copilot were wounded and could not fly.

Reflecting on that flight afterward, I believe his questions were his way of testing me to determine the depth of my training as a flight engineer. I thought I passed the test because Captain Self wanted me to fly with him for the next several days. Over those days, I would fly with other crew members to determine which ones I wanted to form my crew. I selected two, a crew chief and a gunner. Gunners from the flight platoon would operate the M-60 machine guns and a machine gun at the helicopter's rear on the ramp called the stinger. When required we would have additional flight crew members perform as gunners to man the stinger or one of the forward positions.

The 178th appeared to have enough pilots but lacked enough trained flight crews. With Captain Self's suggestions, we created a solid, well trained flight crew team. Captain Self would often pick us to fly as his crew. Captain Self was an infantry captain who attended Reserve Officers Training Corps (ROTC) in college, received his commission, and immediately went to flight school. He was an excellent pilot, and we became good friends. We would ask each other very technical questions about the CH-47 before each flight, and it became a routine that allowed us to continue advancing our knowledge about the CH-47 and aviation.

After we left the Army, Captain Self and I kept in contact by letter, and telephone. We continued to share our friendship, brotherhood, and bond over the years. While in Vietnam I became friends with many others, and like Captain Self, and we have remained lifelong friends.

One of my lifelong friends is Major Kenneth Sines, the commander of the 178th helicopter company. After our time in Vietnam, Major Sines continued his career in the Army and retired as a Colonel. Throughout the years, we have maintained our friendship and stayed connected. I must say, Major Sines was truly one of the finest leaders I had the privilege of serving under during my time in the Army.

Major Sines possessed a genuine care and concern for his soldiers. He always took a personal interest in everyone under his command, wanting to know how they were doing. His actions spoke volumes about his character as a leader. He never hesitated to undertake tasks himself that he had asked of others to do, setting a strong example of leadership within the 178th. I admired his meticulous approach and attention to detail. Whenever he had the opportunity, he would fly on my aircraft, displaying his commitment to being actively involved. During pre-flight inspections, he would engage with me, asking questions about the aircraft and our mission. His high standards became a benchmark for other pilots in our company.

One remarkable quality that set Major Sines apart as a leader was his genuine concern for the well-being of the troops under his command. There were countless nights when I struggled to sleep and would head to the flight line to assist the maintenance crews. On many of those occasions, I would find Major Sines walking up and down the flightline, engaging in conversations with the personnel working on maintenance or repair tasks. It seemed that he, too, had difficulty sleeping at times. His purpose was clear—to observe and understand the night maintenance and repair operations firsthand, ensuring that each individual was faring well. He aimed to identify and address any challenges that hindered the completion of maintenance or repairs, such as shortages of parts or supplies. This hands-on approach provided him with invaluable insights into the company's overall flight readiness and night operations.

I observed that Major Sines also had a habit of asking questions before every flight he undertook. As I had the opportunity to fly with him, I came to understand that he regarded the soldiers under his command as his most valuable assets. He recognized that their positive attitudes and genuine enjoyment of their work were crucial for the success of the 178th helicopter company. These principles of personnel management made a lasting impression on me. When I later progressed into a management role in my career, I drew upon the principles I learned from Major Sines. I am eternally grateful to him for imparting those valuable lessons.

Major Sines was a remarkable leader, embodying qualities that earned the respect and admiration of those under his command. His genuine care, hands-on involvement, and high standards made him an exceptional commander. I am grateful for the privilege of serving alongside him and I cherish friendship.

In a previous account, I mentioned my friend Jimmy Wines and our training at Fort Eustis. After arriving in Vietnam, Jimmy was assigned to the 228th Aviation, which was part of the 1st Cavalry Division stationed in An Khe. He flew missions in the middle and southern parts of Vietnam. Despite being stationed at different locations, we kept in touch through letters, occasionally sharing details about our experiences. In one of my letters, I mentioned my transfer to the 178th and how I flew every day while working on the flight line at night. To my surprise, Jimmy managed to obtain a three-day pass and took several flights to Chu Lai, eventually hitching a helicopter ride to the 178th's flight line. I couldn't believe that he had been granted a three-day leave pass to visit me in I CORPS. Curious about how

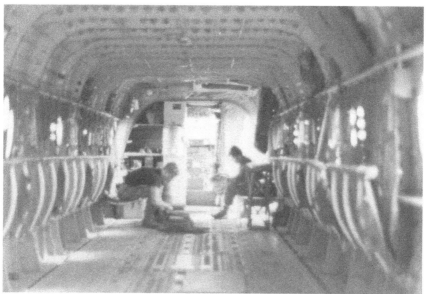

Lyle Keller (left), my crew chief, and Jimmy Wines inside a Chinook in 1969 before we embarked on our flight

148

he managed it, I asked him, and he simply said that he had requested the pass from his company commander to visit me. I was incredibly impressed! I sought permission from my company commander, Major Sines, for Jimmy to stay and visit over the weekend, and he approved, even allowing Jimmy to accompany me on flying missions. I arranged a sleeping bunk for him and took him to the flight line, teasing him about witnessing firsthand what a real combat aviation company did.

I recall a mission with the 178th where both pilots were injured and unable to fly. In that situation, the flight engineer, a Texan, took charge, attended to the pilots' wounds, and safely flew the aircraft back to Chu Lai. The flight engineer and I were good friends because we shared similar experiences and had accumulated many flight hours in the Chinook. We also faced the same issue of hearing loss due to the loud noises of the helicopter's operations and constant machine gun fire. At the time, we never really considered the long-term effects on our hearing because we were too caught up in the excitement of the moment. Furthermore, using hearing protection while shooting in combat during flight would have posed practical challenges. We couldn't simply pause and say, "Hold on, I need to put in my

Another flight engineer returning a Chinook to the flight line with wounded pilots aboard. He was allowed across the runway without clearance because of the pilots.

149

earplugs to protect against the helicopter's loud sounds and gunshots" or predict an explosion before it happened. Absolutely not!

One of the most unpleasant flight missions I encountered was when we had to transport deceased North Vietnamese soldiers from the battlefield. I believe this was a challenging experience for every crew member involved. Each of us could not help but reflect on the fact that those lifeless soldiers could have been Americans or even ourselves. It was a somber reminder that these North Vietnamese soldiers had been alive just hours before, and their remains deserved proper respect and burial.

On another day one of our missions was resupplying and moving artillery pieces to an Americal division fire support base.[29] A second 178th Chinook assisted us because of the amount of materiel supplied that needed to be moved or relocated. The other Chinook was behind us as we hovered and dropped our sling load. Once we had dropped the sling load, we landed and unloaded the internal supplies and ammunition. The pilots of the second aircraft reduced their speed and came to a hover. We weren't aware of any enemy fire that day, but as the second Chinook slowed, it became a big target for the North Vietnamese. The second Chinook received several rounds of enemy fire. Each of those rounds found its mark as they went through the fuselage. No one was injured, and only one flight control hydraulic line in the rear was hit. The damage to the hydraulic line caused the helicopter to make a forced landing within an area where American troops could provide defensive covering fire for the aircraft.

The downed helicopter crew didn't have an extra hydraulic line. They were in a perilous situation. We heard their call for help over our radios. I replied over the intercom we had an additional hydraulic line on board. We landed, an infantry unit and several armored personnel carriers returned .50 caliber fire against the North Vietnamese infantry heavy machine guns. There wasn't much time before one of those large North Vietnamese rounds would hit the huge Chinooks sitting on the ground.

---

[29] A fire support base is a temporary military encampment to provide artillery fire support to infantry operating in areas beyond the normal range of fire support from their own base camps. FSBs follow a number of plans; their shape and construction varying based on the terrain they occupy and the projected garrison.

I jumped out of my aircraft as we landed, still wearing my flight helmet with the hydraulic line in hand and I sprinted across a field with waist-high vegetation. I didn't hear much except my heart beating and heavy breathing. Arriving at the downed helicopter, I gave the flight engineer and crew chief the hydraulic line and turned to run back when one of the pilots yelled, they're shooting .50 calibers at you. (He mistakenly believed they were 50s, but those weapons were a much larger caliber Copter killer firing the 12.7×108mm cartridge)

In the moment's excitement I heard him, but what he said didn't register with me until I was halfway back to my aircraft and saw the vegetation being torn apart as I ran. Realizing what the pilot had said, I ran even faster, what seemed like a sub-four-minute mile back to the helicopter.

After returning to my aircraft, the other Chinook started its engines and took off. Connecting to the intercom, I heard Larry say, "Hold on, boys, here we go, and away we flew at treetop level while making several tight turns before gaining altitude. I believed after that departure and flying at tree top level there would be parts of the top of the trees stuck in our landing gear. To my surprise, upon landing, I found none.

I worked throughout the night, and Captain Self had to locate me. He took this picture before we embarked on a day filled with missions.

When I wasn't flying, you could find me assisting the maintenance crews at the flight line during the day and night. Working at night gave me first-hand knowledge of the essential components required for daily combat flying. As a result, I maintained extra parts on my assigned aircraft and often shared them with other flight crews when needed. I lost all sense of time and would spend the night working at the flight line. Then in the morning, I'd go flying again.

There were moments when I became so engrossed in my work that the boundary between night and day blurred. Sometimes, I worked tirelessly through the night, completely losing track of time, to the point where Captain Self had to personally come and remind me to switch to my day-time duties. I can't pinpoint whether it was my deep immersion in the task at hand or sheer exhaustion that made me oblivious to the passing hours. Yet, there's a saying that time flies when you're having fun, and perhaps that was exactly what happened.

Left Alone

A new pilot had recently joined our company, bringing with him extensive experience flying the CH-47. Although he had served as a pilot in command before, he had not yet flown in combat. As part of his check ride to assess his ability to pilot a Chinook effectively, he completed a few hours of flying on short resupply missions. On his first full day of flying, he expressed a desire to fly with me and my crew. It seemed that Larry Self had briefed him about our crew and me, as he also requested my assistance in the preflight process and wanted to review the maintenance and flight log-books. I admired his thoroughness, which allowed us to showcase our crew, aircraft, and our meticulous record-keeping.

Our missions that day primarily involved resupplying artillery firebases with ammunition, relocating 105 and 155-mm artillery pieces, and delivering water trailers and fuel containers. We were also responsible for providing gasoline and diesel fuel for equipment. As the day progressed, I felt optimistic that it would be a smooth day without any issues. However, we suddenly heard distress calls over the radio from Landing Zone (LZ) Siberia, which was located near the border of Laos. The choice of naming the LZ Siberia stemmed from its remote location, making it the furthest LZ occupied by

Americal Division troops. Additionally, its strategic position allowed a clear view of the Song Tran River, a significant route along the Ho Chi Minh trail.

The intense attack on LZ Siberia by three North Vietnamese Regular troop companies caught everyone by surprise. According to previous intelligence, the North Vietnamese were believed to be near the demilitarized zone (DMZ) and not in the vicinity of this LZ. Furthermore, the North Vietnamese had observed a three-day lull in their attacks following the death of Ho Chi Minh in early September 1969.

Despite the unexpected and intense fighting initiated by the North Vietnamese, we were assigned to provide support to LZ Siberia. Upon approaching the LZ, I vividly recall its bare dirt hill appearance, stripped of vegetation. It stood out like a prominent thumb amidst the lush green mountains and hills. The pilots felt an immense sense of anxiety as we flew in and out of the LZ. Our large, noisy, and slow-moving Chinook presented an easy target for the enemy.

After delivering the artillery and ammunition supplies, we landed on the second or third flight. Inside the helicopter, we carried additional critical supplies and ammunition for the troops stationed at the LZ. Their primary mission was to direct artillery fire at the North Vietnamese Army infiltrating

Landing zone Siberia

153

the southern region through the river and Ho Chi Minh trail. As we touched down with the resupply, several mortar rounds exploded on the opposite end of the LZ.

The chaos seemed to engulf us, with radio chatter escalating to the point where it was challenging to hear the pilots. Our new pilot, who had not previously experienced such a situation, appeared visibly distressed and apprehensive when communicating over the radio. I could empathize with his uncertainty, as I recalled my own early combat missions in Vietnam and the difficulty of deciphering who was speaking to me amidst the barrage of voices. However, with time and more missions under my belt, I learned to discern the crucial voices within the aircraft. Simultaneously, multiple high energy radio conversations on different frequencies (FM, AM, VHF, UHF) occurred alongside mortar explosions and our gunners engaging the enemy with machine guns. The ground personnel speaking over the radios were shouting, making it challenging to grasp clear and concise statements. It sounded like a tower of babel. Nevertheless, I managed to differentiate the voices of the pilots and crew over the various radio channels and intercom system on that eventful day.

In a rushed manner, I leaped off the ramp and joined in the swift unloading of internal supplies, aiming to complete the task as quickly as possible. It was evident that our pilot in command had grown increasingly distressed. Throughout his communications with the ground personnel, he continually yelled over the intercom, urging us to hurry and emphasizing the need to depart swiftly. As the unloading progressed smoothly, I remained connected to my flight helmet through a long communication cord.

Taking a moment to survey the surroundings and ensure the area was clear, I made a remark along the lines of "it's clear in the rear." At that precise moment, several additional mortar rounds detonated on the lower side of the hill, just before I could turn and reenter the aircraft. Suddenly, my helmet was jerked hard by the disconnecting communication line, while the Chinook took off without me. The long communication line dangled from the still-down ramp as the pilot had kept the engines and rotor blades in flight mode, prepared for an immediate departure. Yes, he swiftly took off, leaving me behind as another wave of mortars exploded on the opposite side of the hill.

I found myself standing on the LZ, under intense attack from the North Vietnamese who were ruthlessly trying to kill every American they spotted. Their objective was to swiftly overwhelm and seize control of that patch of ground. Assessing the dire situation, I quickly scanned the area, desperately searching for any available cover as bullets cracked and whizzed dangerously close and explosive mortars continued to rain down upon the LZ. The North Vietnamese were determined to inflict maximum damage on the LZ, pressing on with their assault.

As I rushed towards cover, my gaze remained fixed on the Chinook helicopter rising to a secure altitude, leaving me stranded on the ground. My mind was flooded with countless thoughts, almost overwhelming me. I could envision the crew members onboard frantically communicating over the intercom, alerting the pilot that I had been left behind at the landing zone. However, due to the flight dynamics and characteristics of the Chinook, attempting to abruptly stop the climb and return would have risked stalling the helicopter and potentially causing a crash. Consequently, the pilot had no other option but to continue the climb.

Standing there, observing the Chinook ascending into the sky, I pondered my next move. Without any type of weapon I sought cover and made my way towards the inner perimeter and the bunkers. In the meantime, the unmistakable sounds of other helicopters firing their weapons reverberated through the air.

The helicopters were Huey gunships, effectively suppressing and stopping the advance of the North Vietnamese soldiers across the river. I looked upward, observing the Chinook execute a dramatic turn at its highest altitude as it rapidly descended towards the LZ where it had left me. The helicopter approached from the opposite direction, where the mortars were exploding. Like a person possessed, I raced back to the landing pad. The Chinook hurtled towards me with the ramp still lowered, and without hesitation, I jumped or dove onto the ramp, rolling inside just as the pilot initiated the landing. The voices of everyone connected to the intercom echoed in unison, urging us to go, go, go, and the mighty helicopter never touched the ground. With me safely on board, clutching onto various parts of the aircraft, it immediately veered left and flew away in the opposite direction from which it had arrived for my rescue. The pilot maneuvered the

Chinook with the finesse of a small observation helicopter, swerving left and right, ascending and descending. Once again, I heard the familiar strained sounds emanating from the aircraft's structure, transmissions, and engines, reminding me of the tremendous stress they endured during such maneuvers. While relieved to be back inside the helicopter, I couldn't help but worry about the strain placed on the rotor blades, fearing they might be torn off due to the extreme conditions. Yet, once again, the CH-47 demonstrated its exceptional durability, exceeding its design limitations. The Chinook performed admirably, ready to take flight again the next day. Perhaps it is this remarkable resilience that has allowed the Chinook to continue its service in the Army for over 60 years. That day the Chinook endured such punishment to retrieve me, and here I am, decades later, recounting the story. Kudos to Boeing Vertol for crafting the incredibly hardy and robust helicopter.

When we landed for our next fuel stop, the pilot immediately apologized. I smiled and said, no problem, and still smiling, I said, "What a rush. That was so close, I could see the whites of the North Vietnamese Soldiers' eyes." We all laughed and then moved on with the rest of the day's flying.

I had every reason to be furious with the pilot, but there was simply no time for such an emotional response. The Army had taught me that we are all human and prone to making mistakes. However, it is the strength of the team that supports those who falter and helps them recover from their errors. The pilot, too, was a fallible human being who had made a mistake, and I thanked God that his error hadn't cost me my life that day. From that point on, whenever our paths crossed in the company area or on the flight line, the pilot would always acknowledge me.

Upon arriving in Vietnam, I found myself thankful to God for the privilege of being part of aviation. Despite this gratitude, I could not ignore our stark reality: we were prime targets, constantly at risk of being shot down during combat missions. To the Vietnamese, we might have seemed like easy marks due to our conspicuous presence. Yet, we were more than mere machines of aluminum, brass, and metal; we were living beings, capable of bleeding and experiencing profound pain and death.

This realization led me to a deeper contemplation. I pondered the universal human inclination towards belief in a higher power, spurred by my own brushes with mortality. These experiences made me question the nature of the divine, suggesting it might be beyond our conventional understanding and recognition. This epiphany encouraged me to think about the divine's essence and presence in a more expansive way. I felt God's presence in moments of trauma and beauty alike, in the awe of a starry night or the vibrant colors of a sunset. This ineffable presence, transcending time and space, but seemed to emanate from the depths of my heart.

During my service, my small Bible from Fort Lewis became a source of solace, prompting me to explore how scripture addresses war, suffering, and death. The Bible, to me, was not just a text but a narrative filled with God's voice, carrying profound significance from my childhood prayers for my brother's safety from the Korean War. My upbringing instilled in me that freedom lies in aligning with God's will as expressed in the scriptures, a belief that might seem restrictive to some.

At nine years old, the Bible's depictions of death were daunting. I accepted its stories as absolute truths without understanding their historical context or interpretations. This lack of understanding persisted into my young adulthood.

In Vietnam, seeking reason and answers amidst brutality, my Bible offered no solace. I struggled with the contradiction of a beautiful world marred by suffering and death. Reflecting on God and religion, I initially dismissed religion as a naive response to life's profound questions. However, upon further reflection, I recognized that my perspective was colored by my emotional state. These experiences taught me the importance of confronting grief and mortality head-on.

Years later, Wendell Berry's poem titled, "Rising" resonated with me, offering insights into the interconnectedness of life and death. The poem reflects on the enduring impact of those lost and the "severe gift" of grief, urging us to live truthfully and embrace the lessons of God and our losses.

This journey through grief and transformation instilled in me with resilience and a new sense of purpose, bridging personal and literal battles. It prepared me to face future challenges with a strengthened spirit, acknowledging the precious gift of life. My experiences in war and the lessons learned have shaped and guided me toward a path of focused determination and gratitude for the gift of life.

New Offensive

In 1969, the echoes of conflict resounded not just in the hearts of those mourning, but on the rugged terrains of Vietnam. The battle for Ap Bia Mountain (Hill 937), known as Hamburger Hill, captured the world's attention. Yet, unbeknownst to many, another significant struggle unfolded just over 100 miles south in Quang Tin Province. Operation Lamar Plain became a testament to the resilience and tenacity of the American soldiers training and spirit, marked by fierce combat and significant sacrifices. This operation was hugely different because of its size and how hard-fought, gritty, and costly in both life and material it became.

The North Vietnamese Army (NVA) was unaccustomed to the tactics and sheer numbers of helicopters they would face in the coming days when they began an offensive on May 12th, 1969, and continued it until August 14th, 1969. Over this period, I would log an extraordinary amount of flight time/hours in reckless abandonment[30]. During Operation Lamar Plain, our combat assaults started to pick up momentum. A clerk from the 178th company reported that our helicopters completed over 1,000 missions during the operation.

The American/23rd Infantry Division's Area of Operations (AO) consisted of all I-Corps[31]. This AO was the largest and the most difficult in South Vietnam. The Division had two CH-47 Chinook helicopter companies to support the United States' largest Army division and area of operations in Vietnam. Being the largest U.S. division in Vietnam it was stretched thinly over the AO. It lacked the assets to defend against such a large-scale NVA offensive. Due to the overwhelming attacks by the North Vietnamese Army (NVA) throughout I-CORPS, the American/23rd Infantry Division declared a Tactical Emergency. Consequently, the 1st

---

[30] I again describe myself back then as a person who gave my total self to my first love and the passion and enthusiasm of flying in Vietnam while I ignored all the possible costs or risks.

[31] During the Vietnam War, South Vietnam was divided into four Corps Tactical Zones, also called Military Regions, and the Special Capital Zone (Saigon area) for purposes of military operations. The four Corps Tactical Zones were identified as I-Corps (pronounced as "EYE"), II-Corps, III-Corps and IV-Corps. Each Corps was an administrative and command area for tactical operations. I-Corps was located in the region nearest North Vietnam and adjacent to the DMZ.

Brigade, 101st Airborne Division, was placed under the operational control of the Americal/23rd Infantry Division. The 101st conducted extensive air-mobile and surveillance operations with three large-scale battalions. These battalions were supported by one artillery battalion and one air cavalry troop that provided aerial reconnaissance.

The extreme terrain in northern I-Corps areas offered several advantages to the enemy. The villages with friendly populations were located along the coastal region; therefore, anyone in the mountainous areas was considered the enemy. West of the coastal town of Tam Ky, the terrain became gently rolling with open landscapes and enemy-friendly villages interspersed within the low jungle. Further west were the open mountain areas which allowed the North Vietnamese Army (NVA) rapid movement, easy resupply, and protection around and within friendly villages. This was because their supply routes came from the north and through Laos and then into the mountains.

Ten days after the inauguration of President Richard M. Nixon, the communist leadership in North Vietnam decided to test him and the American people's resolve. The continuous television broadcasts from the United States showed protests and public objections to our involvement in the Vietnam War. The North Vietnamese Government created Directive Number 71, which ordered the North Vietnamese Army and its supporting local Viet Cong forces in the south to cause and create maximum American combat casualties. At the same time, the North Vietnamese wanted to disrupt our lines of communication and disable the pacification programs such as Vietnamization, a program to expand, equip, and train South Vietnamese forces, and village movement and resettlement. I had participated in the movement and relocation of several Vietnamese villages during this time. At the same time, the South Vietnamese troops were assigned ever-increasing combat roles to reduce the number of U.S. troops in combat. This meant that the 178th had to support the South Vietnamese increasing participation in the war. I remember there were times I truly felt sorry for those South Vietnamese troops because they all looked so young and terrified. Nonetheless, the communist leadership planned combat actions and essential battles to destroy as much equipment, vehicles, and aircraft as possible. They believed this would slow our efforts while they could win more significant battles.

Shortly after midnight on May 12, 1969, under cover of a moonless sky, two regiments of the 2nd NVA Division, with the support of local and regional units, a force of more than 2,500 soldiers, launched an offensive in the American Division's area of operations against three major LZ's. The LZ's were Baldy, Center, and Professional. The NVA would also engage smaller tactical targets occupied by American troops. The North Vietnamese successfully overran and captured several key United States military installations in I CORPS, including the provincial headquarters at Tam Ky.

These North Vietnamese attacks came from a highly motivated, and well-coordinated enemy. The NVA forces were reinforced with an anti-aircraft battalion equipped with heavy machine guns firing the 12.7×108mm cartridge. As mentioned previously, these machine guns were considered equivalent to American .50-caliber but were larger, more deadly, and often referred to as Copter Killers.

Our aviation crews would gather at 4:30 a.m. for mission briefings. It wasn't long after our briefing that our CH-47 Chinook helicopters were carrying cargo loads of men and materiel. Operation Lamar Plain was underway. The 178th CH-47 helicopters were part of a combined aviation effort with the 101st Division.

Tam Ky is located approximately 40 miles south of Da Nang and 20 miles north of Chu Lai. Chu Lai is home to the headquarters of the 23rd Infantry Division/American, situated along the coast of the South China Sea. Tam Ky was a market center where the Vietnamese bought and sold fruits, vegetables, and fish. By mid-afternoon on May 15, 1969, the tiny airstrip south of Tam Ky became the focus of all aviation activities. The 178th aircraft from Chu Lai landed to offload men and materiel. I remember flying in and out of Tam Ky through air that was cloudy with red dirt dust, the smell of JP-4,[32] diesel fumes, and lots of smoke. Darkness arrived, but our aircraft continued to fly throughout the night. At the end of the first day of Operation Lamar Plain, we had transported nearly 80 tons of supplies, equipment, and 751 soldiers.

The next day we continued to bring men and equipment to Tam Ky. The American Division forces wasted no time pursuing the enemy. During our efforts, we transported two 105mm howitzer batteries from Tam Ky to

---

[32] JP-4, or JP4 (for "Jet Propellant") was the fuel used in helicopters.

the Young and Professional artillery fire support bases. On May 16, these same artillery units began firing toward the North Vietnamese to clear the enemy off and around LZ Professional by early afternoon. To assist in this clearing operation, we transported a battalion of 500 to 600 infantry soldiers over several flights to LZ Professional during combat assault missions. That same battalion conducted reconnaissance to the south to locate and eliminate additional enemy forces. As the battle continued, the temperature soared over 100 degrees. There were many heat casualties among the American troops who carried over 80 pounds of equipment on their backs. We conducted several air medevac missions to the 91st medevac hospital in Chu Lai for heat casualties and the combat wounded. Many of the wounded were loaded onto our aircraft still wearing their webbing and flak jackets. Most of those wounded required additional medical care in flight. We had to remove their bloody gear and flak jackets to treat their injuries or wounds. After unloading the wounded at the 91st medevac hospital, we had to wash off the aluminum floor to remove the blood to minimize dangerous slips and falls.

The combined infantry units continued their search operations, finding well-established enemy huts, hooches, bunkers, and trenches. Many of these were occupied by North Vietnamese as recently as the night before. Our CH47s and aerial recon teams discovered many enemy installations while facing withering fire from heavy machine-gun positions located in the surrounding area. During the next two weeks, virtually every aircraft assigned to Operation Lamar Plain had received damage from ground fire. I was gaining additional experience with every type of imaginable helicopter field repair.

Infantry contact with the enemy was light during the first days of Operation Lamar Plain. Then, early in the latter part of the first week, the infantry began climbing hills north of LZ Professional. When the Infantry reached the summit and established a command post (CP), the enemy walked exploding mortar rounds up to the command post (CP), resulting in significant American casualties. This action continued with more American forces wounded and casualties. For me, these were some of the most challenging days during my time in Vietnam. We experienced the non-stop raw reality, horror, and brutality of everyday combat. We were in constant fear of being shot down and crashing during those missions.

During this period there were many times when my mind would want to take a break but the war and all its brutality and horror would be front and center. At those brutal times one could not help but gaze upon the unpleasantness of combat and even in the midst of this horror there was a magnificence to it. I would stare at the North Vietnamese heavy machine guns firing the 12.7×108mm caliber tracer rounds the size of basketballs with bright red ribbons attached to them. The red ribbons were the tracer bullets' powder, burning as they came directly at me and my aircraft. I watched the great streams of red and white metal fire flowing from the machine guns on my helicopter or other Huey or Cobra helicopter gunships. At times, I found myself watching the illumination rounds, the white phosphorus, and the vibrant hues of napalm and exploding artillery shells. In those moments, I'd find the displays not pretty, but astonishingly captivating, even beautiful at times. While my eyes took in these scenes, part of me detested what I was seeing, but another part could not look away. Much like a devastating forest fire or cancer cells under a microscope, battles and bombings possess a kind of moral indifference, yet they also have an undeniable visual allure and purity.

Describing war is paradoxical, much like describing peace. Almost everything can be both true and false at the same time. Strangely enough, I felt most alive when I was closest to death. Every moment unfolded on a razor's edge, making me acutely aware of life's value. During those times, it was as if I was experiencing everything that truly mattered for the first time. I discovered a newfound love for the best aspects of myself and the disorderly and chaotic world around me.

I came to understand that everything could be lost in an instant. For a soldier, war feels like an ever-present, ghostly fog that obscures clarity. Everything becomes distorted; it can thin out, grow dense, or swirl unpredictably. The traditional rules of life no longer apply, and previous truths become irrelevant. In those intense moments, I couldn't discern my location or purpose. The only thing that was clear was the overwhelming uncertainty of the situation, especially during the brutal, horrific episodes of the war.

In this battle, I lost all sense of certainty, and as a result, my grasp on truth itself wavered. It's worth noting that in a true war story, nothing is ever completely reliable. Sometimes my own story seemed aimless, or its

162

deeper meaning only revealed itself 50 years later in a moment of late-night reflection. I would wake, wanting to tell my wife Cathy a story that had percolated to the top of my memory during my sleep. I knew that if I woke her and told her my story, I would have forgotten the point by the time I had gotten to the end, just like I had on so many other occasions. I would lie in the dark for a long time, watching that story happen in my head again with crystal clarity. Then I would listen to Cathy's beautiful breathing and think to myself. The war is over, move on. I would close my eyes, smile in the darkness, and say to myself, God, thank you for my life and the life you have allowed me to live.

As we seized Vietnamese positions, we found equipment they had left behind. They had taken only the essentials during their retreat. We loaded this abandoned material onto our helicopters and transported it to a staging area to determine its disposition. Among the items were stacks of new uniforms, sewing machines, and medical supplies, many originating from the United States.

As the fighting gradually subsided, the North Vietnamese resorted to involving every individual in the battle. During one of our missions, we received information that a North Vietnamese regimental commander and several staff members had died while defending their positions towards the end of the battle. Following numerous additional losses, the North Vietnamese came to the realization that their campaign to gain control of I-Corps had failed.

After months of intense warfare, Operation Lamar Plain finally came to a close as the North Vietnamese communists retreated to safer areas along the Laotian border. What I remember most about the after-action statements was that the NVA prisoners later referred to this operation as "the vast fight with many big helicopters." They were surprised at our aggressiveness in utilizing helicopters and our firepower against them. Operation Lamar Plain is not much of a name for a battle, and unlike Tet, Hamburger Hill, and Khe Sanh, it might not be found in history books. But every soldier who participated and fought in Operation Lamar Plain knew he had been in one "helluva" fight.

After Operation Lamar Plain, we continued to receive substantial enemy fire. American intelligence believed there was a sizable number of

North Vietnamese still in our area of operation who wanted to continue to do us harm and shoot down such a big prize as a CH-47 Chinook helicopter. We couldn't let our guard down as we began repositioning troops, artillery, and supplies to other critical areas.

My Rest & Relaxation (R&R), November 1969

After Operation Lamar Plain I realized I had waited over a year to take my R&R. The truth be told, down deep, I loved aviation and the excitement of flying and didn't want to take time away from it. I instinctively knew that I would never again experience the extreme adrenaline rush of flying aircraft on such dangerous mission in my life again. Talking with others about their R&R got me thinking that I should take mine. I applied for R&R and was approved for a seven day, six-night leave to Sydney, Australia. I caught a helicopter flight to Da Nang and then onto Sydney. I sat in the middle of the plane with a CIA/DIA operative from the Da Nang area beside me. We became friends almost immediately while discussing the day's topics. He knew a lot about the 178th and the Depot Maintenance unit I was previously assigned in II CORPS. We talked about what we hoped to do while in Sydney. Our plane landed in Darwin, Australia, for fuel. I remember thinking Darwin looked like a nice place to visit after leaving the Army. I learned from information in the airport that Darwin is in northern Australia and the capital of Australia's Northern Territory.

When we arrived in Sydney, military personnel greeted the airplane and provided each of us with initial information about R&R and Sydney. They indicated that additional information would be provided at the R&R center. Buses took us to the R&R center, where we were instructed how to act during our week's stay. We learned about all the possible hotel options. I was looking forward to sleeping in a real bed in a room by myself. I soon discovered my new CIA/DIA friend, and I were staying at the same hotel. The Chelsea Hotel was one of the highest-ranked hotels in Sydney and was worth the additional cost. The hotel management team were Joan and Brian Smith. They were originally from Auckland, New Zealand, and treated me like family. My hotel room was located at the end of the upstairs hallway and had two large windows. It was nice and quiet and faced the Kings Cross district. I could view nearly all of Sydney from that room. After unpacking, I moved a chair to the middle of the two windows and looked over Sydney. I remember a feeling of calmness and relaxation with a sense of peacefulness. I could have sat there for most of my R&R, but I realized I might never have this opportunity again to visit such a beautiful city in a country halfway around the world from my home.

During my R&R visit to Sydney, Australia, I wanted to surf at Bondi Beach, located just east of Sydney on the eastern coast of Australia. I borrowed a surfboard from the R&R center and took a taxi to the beach. It was quite a sight to see the board protruding from the front passenger side of the cab that took me to the beach.

Upon arrival, I changed into a surf swimsuit I'd bought at a local surf shop, grabbed my board, and headed into the waves. After riding several waves, I took a break on the shore. During this rest, a lifeguard warned me about the frequent sightings of great white sharks near the beach. Given my past experiences surviving helicopter crashes and gunfire in Vietnam, tangling with sharks wasn't on my list of something I wanted to do. I promptly ended my surfing session, showered, changed, and returned the surfboard to the R&R center.

Years later, I read about a safety feature that had been put in place at the beach: a steel net across the bay's entrance, designed to protect swimmers and surfers from sharks. While my surfing adventure was brief due to the shark threat, the experience still resonates with me. Surfing the Australian coast remains a memorable accomplishment.

On my second day in Sydney, I prepared and ate a meal in my room. I wanted to have a quiet peaceful meal by myself. There weren't any supermarkets in Australia, so my taxi driver drove me to a butcher shop and a local grocery store to buy meat and provisions for my evening dinner. While driving back to the hotel, the taxi driver asked me how much money I was carrying. I thought, oh uh-oh, he's going to rob me. To my surprise, he cautioned me to be aware of the many pickpockets roaming the streets of Sydney, looking to prey on young military men like me. He suggested I take my money out of my wallet, divide it into equal amounts, and place those in my other pockets, shoes, and socks. I thanked him for the advice and immediately did what he suggested. I have never forgotten those great words of advice. Needless to say, I also gave him a very generous tip for his help, assistance, and coaching.

Upon returning to the hotel, I knocked on the Smiths' door and asked if I could use their kitchen to cook my dinner. They were surprised at my request and graciously said yes. They helped with my preparations and brought a table, a tablecloth with China, silverware, and a chair to my room. I sat in the quiet room and ate dinner alone while drinking a bottle or two of wine. When I finished dinner, I called home and talked with my parents for over an hour. I didn't know what time it was back in Baltimore, but it was wonderful hearing my parents' voices. When we were about to end the call, I asked them to promise they would not pay for that long-distance call, and they agreed. But they went ahead and paid the bill, but when I returned home, I reimbursed my parents. That phone call in 1969 cost over $300 but it was worth every penny.

The hotel managers, Joan and Brian Smith had lived in Sydney for several years while running the Chelsea Hotel. When I visited them years later in Auckland, New Zealand, they said no one had ever asked to use their kitchen to prepare a meal in all the years of operating the hotel. I made an impression, maybe an odd one, but an impression, nonetheless.

The following morning, at breakfast my CIA/DIA operative friend asked Brian where a guy would find some action, you know, women in Sydney. I was surprised by my friends' boldness. Brian smiled and recommended a few places for him to visit. Then Brian suggested I visit a well-known club in Sydney. He gave me a handwritten note to give to one of the band members. Brian smiled and said George would show me a good time in Sydney. George knew the after-hours city very well.

Later that evening, the CIA/DIA guy and I decided to have a drink while visiting several establishments. We didn't stay together long because he was looking for women and action—his words not mine. I wished him well, and that was the last time I saw him until we boarded the bus to return to the airport for our travel back to Vietnam.

At the club Brian had recommended, I met George during one of the band breaks. We briefly discussed that I was staying at the Chelsea Hotel and how I became friends with Joan and Brian Smith. I handed the handwritten note to him. George read it, smiled, and suggested I come back at 2 a.m., I agreed. But I spent the rest of the night dancing with nurses in training from the teaching hospital across the street. I wanted to dance, and I had plenty of partners. Isn't that part of being "ONE COOL CAT," knowing how and wanting to dance?

After 2 a.m., George took me to a much nicer club a few blocks away. It was the professional musicians' club. The musicians would gather there after work to drink and socialize. George walked to a table and began talking with friends. I walked to the bar, sat beside this beautiful woman. We immediately started a conversation. I thought, Woo Hoo, I might have found my Sydney ambassador to show me the town. I had a wonderful conversation with this beautiful lady and never noticed her wearing a wedding ring. Maybe it was the lighting or the amount of alcohol I had consumed at that point.

I was shocked when George walked over, kissed this beautiful woman and said, "Bob, I'd like you to meet my wife." Oops, I nearly melted into the seat, and my HAPPY balloon popped! I was a big boy and recovered quickly. We moved to a table and discussed my visit to Sydney, my background, the Army, and Vietnam. They even spoke about the many Australians and New Zealanders fighting in the war. As we ate a delicious breakfast, they suggested several places for me to visit while in Sydney. I left the club around 4:30 a.m.

They also had provided a list of Sydney activities, places to avoid, and places American soldiers patronized. They warned me that those places patronized by American soldiers usually had problems, and guys could get in lots of trouble. I appreciated their suggestions and recommendations. They also gave me the address and owner's name of a must-visit ice cream store on Manly Beach. They emphasized the importance of meeting the owner and said I wouldn't regret it.

After getting only two hours of sleep, I quickly showered and pressed my clothes. I dressed and embarked on my day with excitement, ready to explore the recommended attractions in Sydney. The first stop on my list was the Sydney Zoo, which I reached by taking a ferry. Interestingly, during the ferry ride, I found myself seated among a group of nuns who were also headed to the zoo. Perhaps I appeared harmless, as each of them struck up a conversation with me. To my surprise, they graciously invited me to join them on their zoo tour. Eagerly, I accepted their offer, and together we explored every animal enclosure in the zoo. Throughout the tour, I couldn't help but express my awe at the animals' beauty and the well-maintained surroundings. Walking and conversing with the nuns turned out to be a delightful experience for me. The memories of that visit will remain with me forever. Eventually, our lovely time at the zoo came to an end, and we bid farewell as we boarded the ferry back to Sydney. After spending several hours in their company, a profound sense of serenity enveloped me.

It was a different kind of tranquility, one that didn't involve ignoring pain or suppressing my past experiences in Vietnam. This tranquility seemed to emanate from the depths of my soul, long concealed by fear, frustration, and heartache. Somehow, being with those nuns provided me with an overwhelming feeling of safety and peace. It felt as if our encounter on that morning ferry ride was destined to happen. As much as I wanted to return to the nuns and spend more time with them, I realized it would be inappropriate and I had made a promise to visit the ice cream store. Nonetheless, that encounter with the nuns has stayed with me, and I have never forgotten it.

I took a cab to Bondi Beach to visit the recommended ice cream store. The Bondi area was a small but bustling beachfront and surfing destination surrounded by tall trees, various shops and eateries. I enjoyed the scenery and sights as I walked to the ice cream store. On the way, I walked through a large crowd of people protesting the Vietnam War. As I observed their protesting, I said to myself this was the last place I needed to be. Many of these individuals handed flyers to me written by Dr. Spock, a United States pediatrician who adamantly opposed the Vietnam War. I didn't stop but continued walking. I did keep one of the flyers as a souvenir. Little did I know that years later, after Casey was born, Cathy and I would read several of Dr. Spock's excellent parenting books. At my seasoned age, I can relate to why he was against a war. As a matter of fact, I had had similar thoughts about war over the past decades as well.

Upon arriving at the ice cream shop, I approached the lady behind the counter and inquired about the person George had recommended. To my delight, she confirmed that he was present and offered to fetch him. Soon, a man emerged, and I introduced myself, mentioning that George, the guitarist, had suggested I introduce myself. The man then introduced me to his wife, who happened to be the lady serving behind the counter. Interestingly, both spoke without an Australian accent, leading me to believe they were originally from the United States. We found a small table and began conversing. They showed genuine interest in my visit and inquired about my military service. They wanted to know about my time in the Army and Vietnam, including details about my unit and rank. Their extensive questioning regarding my combat experience and duration in Vietnam raised my suspicions and made me apprehensive. Nobody else had been that curious about my Vietnam military time and information during my stay.

Sensing my unease, they swiftly changed the topic and then I asked them about their lives in Sydney and whether they had family there. As they noticed my discomfort, they started sharing more about their decision to sell their home and belongings in Chicago and relocate to Sydney. Their move stemmed from discontent with the state of affairs in the United States, similar to the sentiments expressed by many protesters I had encountered during my walk-through anti-Vietnam War demonstration. Given that the man appeared to be about my age probably in his early-20s, it crossed my mind that he may have been a draft dodger[33] who opted for Australia over Canada, a popular choice for many others. In retrospect, I should have asked directly, but my apprehension lingered despite the change in conversation.

After conversing for a little longer, it finally dawned on me why they had been so inquisitive. They revealed that they were part of a network that assisted American and Australian soldiers who were unwilling to return to combat or Vietnam. Their role involved providing the necessary documents to establish residency in Australia. If I decided to pursue this path, I would need to travel to the Outback and spend time with other individuals who had taken similar measures, as a precautionary measure to avoid detection. They mentioned that there was a considerable number of Americans and military personnel actively seeking individuals who had not returned to Vietnam.

While they presented this opportunity as something exciting, I responded politely, stating that I felt obligated to fulfill my duties to the soldiers in Vietnam and my country. Additionally, I emphasized that my family would never forgive me for engaging in such a cowardly and unpatriotic act. Sensing my convictions, they seemed to understand my stance and re-

---

[33] I define it as here in the US, someone who evades compulsory military service or a person who illegally avoids joining the army.

quested that I keep our conversation strictly confidential. I assured them that I would honor their request. Truthfully, I had never discussed this encounter with anyone until Cathy and I began planning our vacation to Australia, New Zealand, and Tasmania in 2020. I often wonder if that couple still resides in Australia and what they might be doing now.

After that encounter my emotions were in a tumultuous state. I found myself grappling with a mixture of worry and fear. I was concerned that my interaction with the ice cream store couple might lead to trouble. Anger also welled up inside me, directed towards those who had guided me towards that encounter. I couldn't help but question what about me had given them the impression that I would consider going AWOL. Did my appearance or behavior suggest that I was a deserter? What led the people in Sydney to believe that I would abandon my solemn oath of duty?

After indulging in a few bourbons and reflecting on the events of the day, including my encounter with the Americans at the ice cream store, a realization dawned upon me. It suddenly became clear. Their actions were not a reflection of me personally. Instead, it was an "ah-ha" moment that unveiled their genuine intention. They were trying to play their part in putting an end to the war by decreasing the number of individuals participating in the Vietnam conflict. I believed they sincerely thought they were engaging in an honorable service. They held a strong conviction that the war needed to be halted immediately.

This newfound understanding shifted my perspective. It helped me see that their motivations were driven by their passionate belief in the necessity of ending the war. It was no longer about me or any assumptions about my character. They genuinely believed they were contributing to a cause they deemed crucial.

Later that evening, as hunger set in, I sought out a restaurant and enjoyed a satisfying dinner. Taking a leisurely stroll back to my hotel, I relished the vibrant sights and sounds of downtown Sydney. Along the way, I came upon a Baskin-Robbins ice cream shop and found myself faced with the delightful dilemma of choosing a flavor. Unable to decide, I ended up purchasing a scoop of every flavor available. While waiting at a traffic light, I struck up a conversation with a young lady beside me waiting for the light to turn. We began walking together, engrossed in conversation. I discovered that she had been working late and was heading home to her apartment. During our chat, she playfully questioned whether I could consume all the ice cream I had purchased. I confidently said yes and jokingly asked if she wanted to join me in sampling all thirty-one flavors. Her smile was all the confirmation I needed, and without hesitation, we shared the lone spoon as we continued walking and talking, enjoying each scoop until the ice cream vanished. That evening, we explored various parts of the Kings Cross district and its surroundings before eventually walking together back to my hotel.

The following day, before dawn, I arrived at the R&R center. Eager to make the most of my time, I was among the first soldiers to board the bus that would take us back to the airport and, eventually, back to Vietnam. There was an undeniable energy among us as we prepared to bid farewell to Sydney. On the bus, I observed couples hugging, kissing, and saying their emotional goodbyes. Watching them, I could not help but wonder if they had fallen in love during their brief rendezvous. It was difficult for me to comprehend why one would embark on such attachments. Perhaps it was the fragility of life in Vietnam or the intensity of experiencing intimacy for the first time. Prior to joining the Army, I had no desire to have someone wait for me back home. It was only my parents who eagerly awaited my return, not a wife or girlfriend.

Throughout the journey to the airport, my mind remained occupied with thoughts about how one could fall in love over the course of six nights and seven days. I pondered the profound impact of emotions on individuals serving in combat in Vietnam. Yet, I couldn't find a definitive answer. Even as I write about my Sydney R&R experience now, that vivid mental image of the bus ride on that beautiful early morning resurfaces. The love-filled atmosphere, the bright sunshine, and the camaraderie of those bidding farewell still feel remarkably fresh, as if it were just this morning, despite the passing of more than fifty years.

Incoming

In the wake of Operation Lamar Plain, the North Vietnamese cunningly altered their strategy. It appeared they had either strategically relocated or entirely withdrawn their larger armaments from the I-Corps region. On an early morning in December 1969, just before dawn, my crew and another,

171

four each assigned to an aircraft, were getting ready for a two-aircraft mission. It was around 3 a.m., and we were inside our small mess area, having breakfast and discussing the day's mission. Suddenly, I believed I heard what sounded like a rocket heading towards us. The sound of rockets in flight was the most terrifying and dreaded sound imaginable. I immediately asked everyone to stop talking and listen. The harrowing whine of a rocket sliced through the air—a sound so dreadful, it chilled the marrow in my bones, the harbinger of death without a hint of where it would kiss the earth and explode. Then the first rocket hit, followed by several others kissing the earth and exploding. In a split second, all eight of us scrambled towards a small side door, desperate to exit and reach the safety of a nearby bunker. I ran on the right side of the other flight engineer, my friend Bob McLaughlin, elbow to elbow, as we made our way to the door. We were the last ones to reach the exit of the mess area. As we reached the door, I saw a blinding flash to my right.

An odd smell almost like gunpowder filled my nostrils, and disorientation washed over me in waves. All eight of us were incredibly fortunate that the rocket detonated beyond its intended blast zone. Had we been inside that blast zone, the explosion could have caused severe internal injuries and even cost us our lives. I genuinely believe that the door frame Bob McLaughlin and I were pushing through played a crucial role in shielding us from more serious harm. After being taken to the 91st Medevac Hospital and being thoroughly examined, I met two individuals who would come into my life again later: Dr. Ken Spence and nurse Marilyn Shertzer. As the war was drawing to a close, I was granted an early discharge, although this was not to be a permanent arrangement. Being extremely fortunate, my hearing did return within six months of leaving Vietnam.

Years later, I was having issues with my right knee, my wife, Cathy suggested I see the orthopedist she was seeing for arthritis. I made an appointment to see the orthopedist because of pain in my right knee, which I believed was from running. When I made the appointment, I didn't realize the orthopedist would be Ken Spence. As Dr. Spence walked into the examining room, I observed his white hair and that he was wearing a starched shirt and tie covered by a heavily starched lab coat. At first, I did not recognize him from my time in Vietnam. I stood up, extended my right hand, and introduced myself, saying, "Hello, I'm Bob Rodweller."

He shook my hand and said, "Hello, I'm Ken Spence." He continued shaking my hand as he looked directly into my eyes. Then he said, "I believe I know you." I smiled. "I work at the Federal Reserve Board of Governors in Washington, D.C." "No, that's not it." I said, "I participate in athletics," and he again said no, that's not it either. I mentioned, "I've been in information technology all my life. I also received my undergraduate and graduate degrees from the University of Maryland." He smiled and said he also attended the University of Maryland medical school several years before me.

"Nope, that's not it either," he said. Next, he asked, "Were you in the military?" I immediately said yes, and that's when we realized he had treated me in Vietnam at the 91st Medevac Hospital. We talked for about our lives after Vietnam and the University of Maryland during our time there and how it had changed.

Upon examining my knee, he instantly noticed a scar on the inside of my right knee. His inquiry was thorough, instantly connecting the dots to an old injury I had endured in Vietnam. I shared the tale of my mission in Laos, recounting the moment a Huey's tail section struck and sliced the inside of my right knee. He proceeded to take an X-ray, which validated the presence of an old wound. Over the next two years, I found myself returning to see him on several occasions. Each visit was not just a medical check-up but a cherished opportunity to reminisce and bond over our shared history, as two army comrades often do.

The last time I encountered Ken Spence, his fingers were wrapped in bandages. He informed me that I would be his final patient due to a muscle disease that hindered his ability to perform surgeries. There was a noticeable sadness in his eyes as he shared that his lifelong dream was to be a surgeon. Ken Spence was passionate about his career in orthopedics, which he could not continue without performing surgery. Consequently, he sold his practice and entered retirement.

While writing this autobiography, memories of Ken prompted me to reconnect with him, to simply say hello and inquire about his life post-retirement. Instead of reaching out directly, I came upon an obituary. It revealed that Dr. Ken Spence, esteemed for his work as an orthopedic surgeon in Maryland and D.C. and respected as a Vietnam veteran, had passed away from leukemia at the age of 79. This news deeply saddened me, as I had recently lost other friends from my time in the Vietnam War. The bonds I formed in the Army were profound and indispensable; they were akin to a family for me while away from home. Losing Ken was particularly hard because he had been a friend who tended to my wounds in Vietnam, someone who, at one point, knew me better than my own family.

The Helicopter Soldiers

Flying the workhorse of helicopters, the Chinook in combat during the Vietnam War was an experience that can only be described as a constant rollercoaster of emotions. Countless helicopter crews took to the skies day after day, hour after hour. Our emotions were a potent mix of exhilaration, intermittently interrupted by moments of desperation, violence, and pure panic.

I consider myself deeply grateful for the opportunity to have been a part of flying those helicopters in combat. It's hard to find anyone who served in Vietnam that doesn't still feel a sense of joy when they hear the distinct sound of helicopter blades cutting through the air above. That familiar sound, created by the top and bottom of the blades' meeting the vacuum and slapping the air due to air pressure, serves as a nostalgic reminder of the Vietnam War. It evokes memories akin to the serenades of my youth by favorite artists like the Beach Boys, Jan and Dean, or the Beatles.

To me, the sound of the helicopter blades resonated with notions of service, rescuing the wounded, delivering vital supplies of food and water, replenishing ammunition, departing from the chaos of combat, or returning casualties for essential medical care. Often, my mind drifts back to those days spent in flight, and I briefly indulge in reminiscing about those years of reckless abandonment, surrendering myself entirely to the care of a higher power.

I am incredibly fortunate to have survived when many others did not return home. The debt of gratitude that the United States owes to those who made the ultimate sacrifice cannot be overstated. They selflessly answered the call from our nation. It is by sheer grace that I am here today. I am blessed to have been able to live my days to their fullest, to receive an excellent education, and to have a successful career. Even though our departed friends are no longer with us, their spirits live on within each of us who fought in Vietnam. Instead of dwelling on their

174

deaths, they would want us to reflect on how we are living our own lives. They lived with a passion and joy that epitomized our youthful spirit, when life was brimming with energy, hope, and significance beyond words. Their music may never be sung again, but their impact on the military and on life itself was extraordinary. Through their strength, courage, attitude, and positive influence on me, I am able to share this memory and offer the following prayer.

> Almighty God has blessed us with the will and courage to do our duty. We praise you for our comrades whose death kept freedom living even for those in foreign lands. We praise you also for giving us these years we have lived since their departure. We pray that you will strengthen and sustain our devotion to truth and justice so that we may be faithful beneficiaries of their sacrifice. Continue your mercy to our comrades, keep them in your care and bring us into your presence to rejoice eternally. AMEN[34]

Reflections on My Past and Thoughts on War

Reflecting on my tour of duty in Vietnam, my service time extended far beyond the 15 months of active combat. It spanned a challenging 14-year odyssey of personal and societal upheaval. Returning from Vietnam, I often found myself feeling disconnected, like an alien, or a stranger in my own homeland.

The countries transition was arduous, as it took years for the nation's perception and appreciation of Vietnam veterans like me to evolve. In the wake of this period, I came to understand the futility of searching for clear-cut answers to the profound "whys" that life poses. Instead, I learned to accept the inherent ambiguity of some questions, recognizing that not all mysteries can be unraveled.

Describing the complexity of emotions, I felt upon learning I was going home after the rocket attack was challenging. The news came as a complete surprise, primarily because I had a deep desire to continue flying helicopters. Acknowledging that my days of flying—and the exhilarating tasks associ-

---

[34] The Chapel of the Fallen Angels prayer by the Very Reverend Robert C Martin 392nd BG Pilot Dean of the Cathedral, Retired, Erie PA

ated with it—were over was a tough reality to accept and face. Flying had always been an electrifying experience for me, akin to an addiction to the rush of adrenaline it provided. The thought of not experiencing that thrill again was difficult to accept.

Returning home from the war was a journey marked not just by the physical distance traversed but by the profound emotional shifts that accompanied my reentry into a world that felt both familiar and alien. As I previously wrote when my aircraft was shot down and crashed to earth it was a different earth that I returned to in the United States. The war, and its aftermath had changed me in ways I could not fully comprehend until I was back on home soil. My return was shadowed by the loss of close bonds forged in the crucible of conflict, a connection with the Army that had been both a source of identity and a cause of profound change and dislocation. But the most painful was the sting of rejection from those who opposed the war and saw me as a symbol of a conflict they detested.

Yet, the journey home was more than a physical return; it was a passage through a landscape of loss and memory. The friendships that had sustained me through the anxiety of combat were irreplaceably altered or severed by death, leaving a void where once there was camaraderie and shared purpose. The Army, once a source of pride and belonging, now felt like a chapter forever closed.

The reception from those who opposed the war compounded the sense of dislocation. Their hostility, born of a conflict they loathed, was directed at me, a representation of the war they protested. This negative reception was a bitter pill, adding to the alienation felt in a country I had served but no longer seemed to recognize.

Reflecting on the war and its aftermath, I am reminded of the profound sacrifices made, the friendships forged in the crucible of conflict, and the complex legacy of service. The sound of helicopter blades, once a harbinger of danger, now evokes a bittersweet nostalgia, a reminder of a youth spent in the shadow of war, of lives cut short, and of the enduring bonds of brotherhood.

As I pen this autobiography, I am compelled to honor those who served and sacrificed, to acknowledge the pain of loss, and to celebrate the resilience that has allowed me to navigate the aftermath of war. In remembering, I pay tribute to the spirit of those who did not return, ensuring that their sacrifices are not forgotten but serve as a testament to the cost of freedom and the enduring strength of the human spirit.

When I reflect upon my early missions and my time in Vietnam, I find myself questioning the nature of my involvement and the reasons for my survival. Were the missions I had participated in purposely kept hidden during and after the war? Additionally, why do my military records lack completeness, failing to capture the entirety of my training and experiences during my time in Vietnam, especially the early months of 1968?

During my time serving in Vietnam with the Army, I came to understand that the military, while formidable, was not immune to the chaos of human error; clerical mistakes were not uncommon. However, I remain perplexed at how my military records could be so devoid of the rich details concerning my training and the activities I engaged in. It's baffling how such significant experiences and accomplishments are not documented. Over the years, a retired West Point graduate who assisted me in researching this matter commented, "Bob, one day, all this information will come to light. For now, it might be stored in a warehouse or someone's basement until they pass away."

I've kept my experiences and concerns about Vietnam mostly to myself, rarely discussing those times or missions with others. Only recently have I begun sharing a fraction of those experiences with Cathy. In the past I feared I might be involved in an unfortunate or unexplained accident while running, cycling, or riding my motorcycle. Perhaps it is best to keep those times private and not release my thoughts regarding those uncertain times at this stage of my life. After all I want to continue living and those times and experiences occurred a very long time ago in a land on the other side of the earth.

A Proposed War Checklist for Presidents

I strongly believe there should be a checklist for all presidents to consider before engaging in any type of war. This checklist should cover topics such as whether war is justifiable only when all alternatives have been thoroughly explored and failed, or if the destruction of the United States and our way of life is inevitable. Another consideration would be if we are under imminent threat of invasion by a foreign nation-state. Only then should war be seriously contemplated.

Acknowledging the psychological impact of combat is essential. While there are some positive aspects to combat, as I previously noted in my observations of war, history has often emphasized and exaggerated these positives to protect combatants' self-image, rationalize their sacrifices, and garner support for war efforts. However, recognizing this manipulation doesn't negate the existence of these positive aspects. There has been a profound attraction to war and combat throughout history, but it's important not to swing from glorifying war to denying its existence.

The Complexity of War's Effects

During times of peace, nations take pride in their past and soldiers who have fought to maintain the nations' freedom and security. However, this pride tends to focus on victory and patriotism rather than the bloodshed and horror of killing. This sentiment is likely universal, regardless of nationality or ethnicity. People of all nations want to see their country as powerful and victorious, capable of defending their homeland.

The ability to recognize and confront danger while bonding for a common cause such as WWII reflect positive aspects of human nature. Yet, the cost of war, particularly for the young individuals who have experienced and been involved in combat, is tragic. Death, destruction, and the psychological toll on combat survivors are undeniable realities. This cost, often misrepresented by military and government sources, perpetuates the glorification of warfare.

Emerging from the Vietnam War, I bore only minor scars, a stark contrast to the profound wounds carried by many others. Yet, within me burned a resolute determination, fueled by a profound sense of gratitude. I was acutely aware that I had been granted an extraordinary gift by the divine—the chance to survive amidst the harrowing shadows of combat in Vietnam.

This realization filled me with a relentless drive to succeed, to honor this miraculous opportunity bestowed upon me. I perceived my survival not as mere luck, but as a sacred blessing, a testament to a higher purpose. It was a chance to transform the gruesomeness I had witnessed into a force for positive change, a guiding light to lead me through the journey of life post-war.

Combat profoundly affects all participants, regardless of background. It's been my experience that working-class individuals bear the brunt of combat due to societal dynamics. This leads to the question: "Would I make the same choice again and accept the call to duty given today's circumstances?" My experiences in the Army and Vietnam helped shape who I am, and while I still love my country, I'm disappointed and disillusioned by our government's alignment with personal gain and power. My unwavering belief remains that our country is the greatest on earth. However, I find myself disillusioned with the current state of our government, as it no longer seems to represent the interests of ordinary citizens. Instead, it appears to serve the agenda of those in positions of power, driven by a desire for personal gain and increased influence. Regrettably, I now find myself unwilling to answer the call to service for the United States. The eagerness of leaders to sacrifice young lives for dubious purposes is distressing.

Military Honors

During my time in Vietnam, I was awarded a Bronze Star and several other medals. Upon returning home, I showed those awards to my parents, observing their teary-eyed reaction. It was in that moment that I truly grasped the depth of their worry and concern for their youngest son, Bobby, during my service in Vietnam. Until then, the war had felt distant, only seen through the eyes and ears of embedded combat reporters speaking on television in living rooms across the country.

I left my awards and medals with my parents, choosing to move forward with my life rather than dwell in the past that those awards represented. When I got married in my mid-twenties, my parents returned the medals to me. I placed them in a cardboard box alongside other Army memorabilia, honoring their significance while focusing on embracing the present.

Years later in 2012, our eager for knowledge daughter Casey asked me about my time in the Army and Vietnam. This conversation occurred because her maternal grandfather, Robert Ridgway Case, a POW in WWII, had just died. After his funeral, Casey and I discussed my time in the Army and Vietnam. After those conversations, I decided to look through my Army memorabilia box and show my awards to Casey and Cathy. The three of us had spent hours reviewing the items in the box before I realized the Bronze Star was missing. I immediately scanned my DD-21438 because I believed the medal could be replaced with a copy of my DD-214 form.

I was totally surprised when I discovered that my DD-214, the official record of my military service, did not include any of the documentation for the medals I had received in Vietnam. I knew that these awards were valid because I had the signed orders for each of them. I couldn't comprehend why they were omitted from my official record. The absence of my Bronze Star in particular puzzled me. Initially, I tried to remain hopeful, considering the possibility that it may have been misplaced during the numerous relocations I had undergone over the years. I also had to face the reality that someone might have rummaged through my belongings, possibly during the period when everything was in storage during my divorce. I remembered that my first wife wore the Bronze Star medal on a bright green dress several times as she said it was beautiful addition to the dress. When I asked her about the medal, she stated she had no idea of its' location.

Then I researched and contacted every military or government location that might have copies of my military records over the next several years. To my amazement, I could only find the incomplete DD-214 records. The staff of the Army Personnel Command at Fort Knox were helpful and they assigned a person to assist me. I'm unsure if she was in the military, a civilian, or a civilian contractor, but she assured me they would find my records and call me in two weeks. She called in less than two weeks. To my astonishment, she couldn't find any of my documents either. During our discussions, I mentioned having the medals and the required orders awarding each to me. She asked if I could copy the orders and take pictures of each medal's front and back as proof. This was to ensure they weren't medals purchased from the internet, because each had my name engraved on the back of each award. Once validated, she would update my official personnel records. The problem was I didn't have the Bronze Star in its green folder with the orders authorizing it. Like the others, it wasn't documented on my DD-214.

The Fort Knox staff member coached me through the process that was required to locate the Bronze Star. She acknowledged that many records were lacking, and if the search failed to yield the award documentation, I would have to resubmit the entire package. That wasn't what I wanted to hear.

After conducting extensive research for several months, I had been unable to find any evidence of the award. I decided to approach the search process as if I were pursuing a PhD. My thesis was centered around the belief that I had received the Bronze Star and other medals. I understood that I would need to conduct thorough research and gather evidence to support my thesis, meticulously documenting every step of the process. It was a challenging and intimidating task, particularly because many of those who had approved the initial Bronze Star had since passed away.

To my astonishment, the staff contact at Fort Knox provided the contact information of Major General Lloyd B. Ramsey, the former commander of the Americal or 23rd Infantry Division in Vietnam when I received and was awarded the Bronze Star. I also succeeded in having several files declassified, which provided concrete evidence of my participation in Operation Lamar Plain in 1969 which was the original reason for me being awarded the Bronze Star. During this discovery process, I obtained six sworn statement letters signed by fellow soldiers in my company, attesting to the fact that I was awarded the Bronze Star medal.

It involved numerous steps and several years of research to locate the necessary documentation and individuals who could vouch for my receipt of the Bronze Star. Although the process was challenging, the outcome made it all worthwhile. Because there was the additional benefit of reconnecting with many of my comrades from the Vietnam War, with whom I had lost touch over time.

When I had a ready-for-review draft of the entire package, I sent it to my contact person at Fort Knox. After review, the Fort Knox contact suggested additional minor edits. Once the edits were made the Fort Knox contact said it was ready for signatures.

I immediately called General Ramsey, and to my surprise, he answered the phone. I was excited to be talking with a retired Major General of the Army. He had commanded the largest infantry division in Vietnam. I was sure he wouldn't remember me. Nevertheless, I introduced myself and explained why I was calling. I asked him if I could bring my completed materials for his review and signature. He replied he would be happy to sign the documents again for me. We spoke for a few additional minutes, then he told me during our conversation that after his wife had passed away, he had moved from their home in Alexandria to the Brandon Oaks retirement community in Roanoke, Virginia. I was somewhat joking when I stated I wished I had known he had lived that close when we lived in Maryland. I would have paid him a visit or two. He stated that he would have liked a visit from one of the young troopers from the Americal or 23rd Infantry Division. We set a tentative date for a visit. Unfortunately, as fate would have it, General Ramsey suffered a stroke before our scheduled visit. The visit was delayed. I called several times to say hello and wish him well during his recovery. Ms. Jacqueline (Jackie) Barber, who was his always helpful and cheerful caregiver, relayed my conversations to him.

Jackie was so helpful in scheduling another date for our visit. She would text me about how General Ramsey was progressing. Cathy accompanied me as we flew from Northwest Arkansas (AR) to Roanoke. I'll never forget the wonderful welcome we received when we walked into General Ramsey's apartment and introduced ourselves. Even after having a stroke, General Ramsey shook my hand firmly, looked directly into my eyes, and said, "Hello Bob, it's good to see you again after all these years." I was so moved and surprised because he spoke and acted as if he remembered me.

But the very best part was when I introduced Cathy to General Ramsey. He shook her hand and smiled, saying it was a pleasure to meet her. I was glad Cathy had the opportunity to meet him. He had represented such a critical part of my life.

Before we arrived at Brandon Oaks to see General Ramsey, Cathy and I had agreed to only visit for an hour to obtain his signature on the documents. We didn't want to tire him. He was 97 years old. To our amazement, we were there for over five hours, visiting and catching up about our lives in and after Vietnam. General Ramsey spoke highly of the 178th assault support helicopter company (ASHC), the unit I was assigned under his command. He repeatedly stated that the aviation units of the Americal division participated in intense combat that took a toll on the aircraft and flight crews. We talked about our combined history in the war. It was a magnificent opportunity to spend that much time with a great human being and share our experiences. I was so honored to share our life stories as two old veterans!

General Ramsey had invited his best friend at Brandon Oaks, Mr. Chet Lang, to join us. Mr. Lang and General Ramsey met at Brandon Oaks. They had developed a deep friendship because of their shared experiences from their military service. What an honor it was to meet another outstanding human being. Mr. Lang had been a B-24 Liberator bomber pilot during

WWII and had completed over 50 combat missions. During WWII, if a person had completed 25 missions, they were sent home. But Mr. Lang loved to fly airplanes, and because he wasn't married and had no one waiting for him at home, he stayed and continued to fly. Finally, after completing over 50 missions, the Army sent him home. Mr. Lang was in his early 90s and was extremely articulate in his descriptions of his missions and flights as a bomber pilot. It was a joy to talk with him as he described his WWII military time. We also learned that after flying all those missions he received flight training to pilot the B-29 nuclear bomber. Mr. Lang never flew again after the war. He said he would rather drive a car than fly in an airplane again.

I've thought about this over the years and how Cathy's father was shot down on his third mission while flying a B-17 over Germany in WWII. He also said he would rather drive a car than travel in an airplane. Mr. Lang and my father-in-law experienced similar actions and likely shared the same psychological effects. For me flying was my first love. I never wanted to stop flying my own airplane or flying commercially or in others' private airplanes.

Cathy and I had the privilege of visiting General Ramsey on four distinct occasions, and each of these visits filled us with immense happiness. I am inclined to believe that these visits held special significance for General Ramsey

Me with General Ramsey (seated) after his stroke and Chet Land

as well, especially considering the personal tragedies he had endured—the passing of his wife and daughter, with his son only visiting occasionally.

As I reflect on our trips, I could not help but ponder the loneliness that General Ramsey and Mr. Lang must have felt. In the gaps between our visits, I made it a point to send them handwritten letters to keep in contact. When we would visit again, they expressed their gratitude for these letters and remarked on the joy our visits brought them. Having experienced first-hand the importance of receiving letters from home during my time in the Army and Vietnam, as they always lifted my spirits, I am truly thankful that my letters had a similar uplifting effect on General Ramsey and Mr. Lang.

General Ramsey's caregiver was delightful. She was always helpful in making our visit arrangements and kept me updated on General Ramsey's health. Ms. Barber and I continue to communicate by phone or social media. The most challenging and difficult phone call I received from Ms. Barber was her call to tell me General Ramsey had died on February 25, 2016. He represented a period in my life that was exciting, exhilarating, and life changing. I felt as though I had a special connection, friendship, and bond with him. He was a wonderful human being and a great leader during that time in my life. His leadership along with many others helped me find my true north and a positive direction for my life. The memory of that time in my life is fading ever more quickly with the passing of so many good friends from that period.

When General Ramsey was still alive, we could talk about that time of our lives and how wonderful and exciting it was. With his passing, I felt my life slipping away as fast as those memories. I looked out my office window and thought of my life and how fast it was speeding toward its conclusion. I was leaving behind all those thrilling and exciting life experiences too quickly, and would never experience them again.

General Ramsey received a full military burial ceremony at Arlington National Cemetery. The ceremony included a church service, a riderless horse adorned with decorations with backward boots, a 19-cannon salute, a 21-gun salute, a bugler, a funeral caisson, and a two-wheel horse-drawn wagon accompanied by military pallbearers. To gather my comrades who had served alongside me under General Ramsey, I reached out to several of them to check if they could attend. Cathy, Casey, Eigil Rothe a dear friend and coworker from the U.S. Courts, and Bougie Criswell were present at the ceremony. It was a tremendous honor for me to be part of such a significant symbol of national service. The ceremony served as both a tribute to General Ramsey and a memorial to the sacrifices made by all those who had served in the military.

Upon our arrival at the gravesite, Bougie and I approached the casket closely to pay our final respects to General Ramsey and to listen attentively. As we stood together, our emotions intensified as the music ceased and the 21-gun salute resounded. The most challenging part of the entire funeral was witnessing one of The Arlington Ladies approach each family member, offering hugs and handshakes. At that moment, I just could not hold back my emotions any longer and instinctively looked towards Bougie. It was as if we were children, sobbing and embracing one another at a parent's funeral. Bougie has been a cherished friend throughout my life, and while we have shared numerous experiences, this particular event was unparalleled. I was grateful that both of us could participate in this exceptional occasion. Moreover, it warmed my heart to know that Cathy, Casey, and Eigil were also able to share this extraordinary, emotional, and unforgettable event with me.

Shortly after General Ramsey's death Larry Self passed away on March 2, 2016, at 73 years old. I had just talked with Larry the week before his death. That day we talked about his progress in documenting his adventurous life story. Helping him tell his story was my way of repaying him for his incredible flying lessons and our time together flying the Chinook helicopter. Near the end of our last call, Larry mentioned he hadn't felt well and had fallen the previous day. After the fall, he said he couldn't get up without help. I suggested he see a physician and continue working on his life story. When I learned he had died, I felt like another part of me had been taken away. Larry had contributed significantly to my development as a person. Larry was buried in Greenville, SC.

The passing of Larry Self, coming so soon after General Ramsey's, marked yet another profound loss in a short span of time. The final conversation with Larry, filled with reflections on his adventurous life and the sharing of concerns about his well-being, now echoes with a deeper sense of finality and loss. Losing Larry, a mentor and friend who played a pivotal role in shaping my journey, not just as a pilot but as a person, left a void that is hard to articulate. The grief of losing someone who has been a significant part of one's life is a profound experience, demanding not only recognition of the loss itself but also a navigation through the complex process of grieving.

Coping with loss and grief is an intensely personal and unique journey for everyone. It involves confronting the pain of absence, the adjustment to a life without the loved one or friend, and the gradual process of finding a way to remember and honor their impact on our lives. As I transition to discussing how to cope with loss and grief, it's important to acknowledge that while the pain of loss can be overwhelming, there are pathways through the grief that can lead to healing, acceptance, and the ability to carry forward the legacies of those we have lost. The stories of Larry and others who have touched my life are not just memories of the past but guiding lights for the future, the importance of connections, and the enduring power of love and friendship.

Coping with Loss and Grief

I must write about grief and loss because, like every other living creature on earth, I have experienced it. Whether through my experiences in Vietnam, the death of family members and our beloved friends and pets or the loss of a marriage through a painful divorce. After leaving the Army while in college I took many psychology classes. So many that one evening after class, the professor said to me, "Bob, are you aware that you are taking a lot of psychology courses that are not part of your major." He then said, "I say this because you might wind up like me with a doctorate in psychology and only be able to teach psychology!" He was an excellent coach and was most likely kidding but still making a point. During several after-class talks, he came to the realization I was trying to resolve the many confusing life issues and emotions created from the aftermath of Vietnam. Those talks helped me to understand grief and loss better.

Losing someone or something I had loved has always been painful for me. After a significant loss, I would experience complex and surprising emotions, like shock, anger, anxiousness, forgetfulness, yearning, sadness, bewilderment, depression, and sometimes guilt. At those times I believed the sadness would never go away. There have been times when years after an event, I would experience grief once again over a past loss. My feelings of grief might return when I suddenly remembered, smelled, or heard something that reminded me of the past. I would go back in time. I would experience the pain and the grief yet again. To be there again, experiencing the pain and grief, would once again remind me of the importance of those individuals or events that contributed to my life.

While these feelings were frightening and overwhelming, I realized they were normal reactions. I knew from experience that accepting them as part of the grieving process and allowing myself to experience them was necessary for my healing. I learned there is no right or wrong way to grieve. Grief is the natural reaction to loss, and it is a universal emotion. Grief is also a very personal experience. I eventually realized there are healthy ways to cope with my pain.

I also learned the grief I experienced aided me in the healing process and eventually strengthened and enriched my life. Because the person, pet, or life experience had contributed to my life in some way. Grief for me was like a building process, each hurt building on the previous one, thereby lessening the pain and suffering experienced. Those grief periods didn't hurt any less than the first. They just weren't so deep and long.

Reflecting on the loss of my mother and father, I now appreciate how others felt when they lost a parent. As I matured, I thought I would accept death as a part of life and handle all sudden losses in an appropriate adult manner. But what does an appropriate adult manner mean? That I should not be sad? Or should I be so grateful that they didn't die when I was a child and didn't have to mourn my parents' deaths in childhood?

If I considered grief from a deeper perspective, I discovered that my internal loss was the most painful. Because my internal losses represented the love to me by my parents. The deep friendship losses in war or the loss of a relationship in a divorce. The external losses like a house or a job or material things like furniture hurt but not like my internal losses. At this stage in my life, I believe the grieving process is a journey. It does not end on a particular day or date. It truly becomes an individual process for each of us. We know grief is real because loss is genuine. Each grief has its imprint on us, as distinctive and unique as our specific loss. The pain of loss is sometimes so intense and heartbreaking because when we are deeply connected with another human being in love. Grief mirrors the lost connection of a relationship that had contributed to my life. Those losses didn't diminish because I became an adult, or my mother or father lived a good life.

My experience is that society places enormous pressure on us to get over our losses quickly. Get through our grief. Be a man. Stand tall. Show no emotion. Life goes on. How long should I have grieved for the man who was my father for 27 years? Did I suffer any less for my mother of 41 years?

Those losses happened momentarily during my life, but their aftermath has remained with me. Each loss had its individual imprint on me, as distinctive and unique as the person I lost. It doesn't matter how old I was when the loss occurred; it was still excruciating. Some of us experience loss way too early in life.

For example, in a war on the other side of the world, I briefly developed a deep friendship with another flight engineer from the 1st Cavalry Division. It was the beginning of Operation Lamar Plain. His aircraft was assigned to a parking revetment next to mine. Daily we and our fellow crewmembers would assist the other helicopters in loading or unloading before or after missions. We helped each other make minor repairs on our aircraft. When the weather delayed our flights, the crews would gather in one helicopter and talk until the weather cleared and we could fly our missions.

On one occasion, the 1st Cav crew came over to my aircraft to wait out a major rainstorm. During our conversations, the other flight engineer showed me pictures of his new baby girl sent from his wife. He was a very proud father. I enjoyed listening to him talk about being a father. This was a welcomed distraction from the weather and the complexity and severity of our upcoming flights. Eventually, the rain stopped, and the weather improved enough to fly. The weather forecast anticipated continued improving conditions, which meant we could complete all our missions. When we received clearance to take off, I waved to the 1st Cav flight engineer. He still had that new Dad smile, and I felt so proud for him and his wife. That was the last time I saw him. Later that day, his aircraft approached a landing zone (LZ) and received heavy weapons fire from North Vietnamese gunners. The helicopter had taken too many rounds to continue to fly. The pilots did their best to maintain control and tried to land. The enemy fire continued until the aircraft burst into a fireball and crashed in a ball of fire. Each member of the crew died in the crash.

I heard about the crash that night when we returned with our completed missions. The flight engineer was in the helicopter's rear as it crashed, and his body was never recovered. I was shocked, stunned, distraught, and sad but I dared not show my emotions. Later after returning to my hooch, I thought about this and had to leave the hooch, not wanting others to see my emotions. I walked around trying to reconcile how the guy was a new father and was now dead. How could God let this happen?

How does one describe such an intense and rapid friendship like this and then experience its loss within a month? I was so upset I knew I wasn't going to sleep, so I went to the flight line and began helping the maintenance and repair crews. I worked twenty-four hours that day. This became a typical routine when life became too complicated, and I couldn't understand the meaning of it. I lost many hours of sleep thinking about my confusion about life and God's way in war.

When we lose an aged parent or a close friend, sometimes well-intentioned friends will try to offer condolences, by saying they had a long and excellent or productive life or some other words. Or you're so lucky they died so quickly. But those are only words and have never helped me with the pain caused by my grief.

Words of condolence did not resonate with me when I lost my father or mother. I'll never have another mother and father. We forget the depth and strength of our connection with our parents, they are often our primary connection to our developing world. Even if we have a loving spouse, children, and close friends, the death of a parent means the loss of one of our first and most important connections in living our lives. The misconception that a mature and capable adult will not need to grieve for a long time over losing a parent can cause feelings of loneliness and confusion. I felt these very emotions after my father drowned and my mother died.

My relationship with my parents changed in adulthood after returning home from Vietnam and leaving the Army. We became closer because of my several years of absence. Before a parent is gone, we intellectually understand that they will die someday. But understanding and anticipating does not prepare us for the grief we feel when we lose a parent, even if we are adults. As I reflected on the memories of my parents, I began to feel the pain of grief again. This time though, it wasn't as heart-wrenching as when they died. Now my grief lives in the wish that they could see the fruits of their labor. To know who and what I have become and know my immediate family. I pray that when it comes my turn to return home, our daughter realizes I will always be with her. I hope I will always be within her heart and memory, and all she will have to do is think of me, and I will be immediately with her. I will always be only a loving memory in her heart and mind, and I'm sure Cathy feels the same way!

After our parents die, we realize, perhaps for the first time, everything and all they did for us as children while we grew toward adulthood. When I became a parent, I learned quickly to appreciate my parents' challenges while raising me and my brothers and sisters. Being a parent gave me a new perspective on my parent's lives and the worries they experienced on my journey to adulthood. I knew they were worried when I was drafted into the Army and went off to war in Vietnam. But it wasn't until I became a parent did, I experience their type of worry.

As I turn the page from my time in Vietnam, a period marked by conflict and profound personal challenges, the transition to home and civilian life emerges as a journey of reintegration and rediscovery. Leaving behind the intensity of combat in military service, veterans like me faced the daunting task of adapting to a world that had continued to evolve in our absence. This shift not only required physical relocation but also a significant mental and emotional adjustment. The skills and experiences gained during service had to be recontextualized within the framework of civilian life. This period of adaptation was not just about finding new roles and careers but also about re-establishing connections with family and communities and seeking a sense of normalcy after living amidst conflict. As you explore the challenges and triumphs of transitioning from the battlefields of Vietnam to the day-to-day realities of home life, it becomes clear that this journey is as much about carrying forward the lessons and legacies of the past as it is about forging new paths and possibilities for the future.

IV. The Road Home

Leaving the Army
and Returning Home

Returning home from Vietnam was a transformative period in my life, filled with a sense of optimism and empowerment. It felt as though my wishes and dreams had materialized before my eyes. I could not help but wonder if it was mere luck or if something greater had been working in my favor. Perhaps it was part of God's plan for me. Regardless, it was a realization of my deepest desires, a dream come true. In that moment, I truly believed that I was capable of accomplishing anything I set my mind to. I possessed a feeling of invincibility, a belief that nothing could stand in my way.

It's difficult to ascertain whether this sense of invincibility stemmed from the fact that I had returned home intact or if it was a result of the overall promising outlook on life. Unfortunately, this optimistic perspective would prove to be short-lived, as circumstances would soon change, and the world would reveal its harsher realities.

When my aircraft was shot down and crashed, I had fallen to and collided with the same world each time, but unfortunately, I had returned home to another entirely different world altogether. The Vietnam War, while having about one-fifth of the casualties of World War II, endured for three times as long. It left an indelible mark on our nation, forever altering its essence as a beacon of hope and optimism for nearly two centuries. The Vietnam War profoundly impacted how we perceive our government and ourselves. The innocence and confidence that once defined our country were lost. While I bore no responsibility for this war, I found myself grappling with heartache and confusion in the years that followed. The weight of the war's consequences was something I struggled to comprehend.

In the late 1960s and early 1970s, during the concluding phase of the Vietnam War, American popular culture often negatively stereotyped Vietnam veterans, portraying them as unstable or criminal. This unfair depiction was met with deep resentment from many veterans returning home. To counter this narrative, I, along with many fellow veterans, actively discussed how we participated in humanitarian efforts and provided food, medicine, and financial support to the Vietnamese people.

Contrary to the widespread media narratives, research, and various articles I have come across indicate that fewer veterans struggled with readjustment after the Vietnam War than was commonly reported. Many of us successfully integrated into society to pursue fruitful careers or businesses. These challenges often stem from stressors of being exposed to combat and other war-related experiences, as well as the reception we faced upon returning home. In truth, I believe a significant number of Vietnam veterans are still grappling with personal challenges. Many veterans chose to keep their struggles private, only confronting these issues later in life. Because later in life we have more time to reflect and ponder our time in Vietnam and returning home. We may do this while writing autobiographies or getting together with other veterans at a local Veterans of Foreign Wars or American Legion organizations. Maybe, we meet fellow Vietnam Veterans at the local Veterans hospital when we are seeking treatment.

This delay in addressing their personal conflicts might be attributed to fewer life pressures in their later years, allowing more time and mental space to process and remember their experiences. This aspect reveals a more complex and nuanced reality of the long-term impacts of war on veterans, which often contrasts with the simplistic portrayals in the media and war movies.

Prior to my return home, the local Veterans of Foreign Wars (VFW) and American Legion Post combined, decorated my parents' home with heartwarming welcome home signs and flags and a large "Welcome Home Bob" sign. It was a beautiful display, and my parents were filled with immense pride for my service in Vietnam and our country. However, on the third night of my stay, a group of individuals (whom I refrain from using a

194

strong pejorative term to describe) callously vandalized my parents' home and front yard by hurling cans of trash and bottles all over the yard.

The following morning, I was devastated to see the remnants of their malicious act. They had scattered trash across my parents' once-pristine yard, damaged welcome home signs, and fallen flags. Without hesitation, I grabbed my parents' trash can and diligently picked up every piece of litter from the yard. I then took the time to straighten the signs and carefully fold the flags. The incident inflicted deep pain upon my parents, and its impact was felt by all of us. The cowardly actions of a few had a profound effect on our family.

As I walked back into the house with the now-cleaned yard and holding the folded flags, I glimpsed the anguish on my parents' faces. The hurt caused by that single act lingered, casting a shadow over what should have been a joyful homecoming.

Amidst the intense pain, I was consumed by an even stronger emotion: rage. I yearned for the opportunity to confront those responsible for this heinous and despicable act. The disbelief lingered within me, unable to comprehend how anyone could harbor such hate and carry out such a hateful deed. It struck me at a deeply personal level, and I struggled to comprehend the motive behind this repugnant act, except perhaps the perpetrators' intense disdain for the Vietnam War. In their eyes, I represented the very essence of that abhorred conflict they so vehemently despised, but why did they want to take their hatred out on me?

This incident posed a significant challenge, as it demanded great courage to maintain my composure and not succumb to the overwhelming anger that threatened to engulf me. It undoubtedly hindered my progress in finding solace and resolution regarding my own personal struggles with the war.

Soon thereafter, I found myself submerged in a flood of painful emotions, with the fear that they might drive me to engage in regrettable actions. The desire to confront those who had defiled my parents' front yard burned within me. To momentarily escape the torment of these negative thoughts, I sought solace in the embrace of bourbon, attempting to wash away the darkness that clouded my mind.

Thankfully with the dawn of a new day, a realization struck me with clarity: my rage and volatility stemmed from my failure to handle and control my emotions effectively. I had disregarded the priceless lessons imparted by the Army, that had taught me that hating someone else was a futile endeavor because I was actually inflicting harm upon myself by carrying that hate. I understood that my painful emotions would not dissipate until I chose to perceive those hurtful experiences from a different perspective.

Undoubtedly, the most challenging aspect for me was attempting to banish the haunting memories. In times of war and combat, the world resembles a harrowing horror movie. Those images would unexpectedly resurface, replaying in my mind when I least expected it. Reassimilating into a regular routine posed difficulties for anyone who had been absent for a significant period. Imagine going on a three-week vacation, flying to a destination, and leaving your car untouched. Upon returning home, you find yourself in the airport parking lot, sitting in your vehicle, and suddenly realizing the strangeness of shifting it into reverse and backing out of the parking space. That's how I would describe my homecoming from Vietnam. I believe many soldiers returning from the Vietnam War would agree with this sentiment. I imagine military personnel returning from Iraq or Afghanistan might identify with these feelings as well.

After coming back home, I realized that nobody truly understood the extent of what I had experienced, witnessed, and endured during my time in Vietnam. With the help of God, I managed to adjust relatively quickly. Outwardly, I didn't fit the stereotypical image of a Vietnam War veteran. I didn't sport jungle fatigues, an unkempt appearance, or shaggy hair. Instead, I dressed in button-down shirts, cuffed dress pants, and even wore tassel penny loafers reminiscent of my high school days.

Despite these internal struggles, there was a constant inner drive pushing me forward, urging me not to give up. This mindset was instilled in me during my time in the Army, where I learned that surrendering was never an option. This philosophy became a guiding principle throughout my life and career.

Crafting for Therapy

I stayed with my parents for about three weeks to take care of the many administrative tasks that needed completion upon returning to civilian life. These tasks included re-registering with my local draft board, updating my driver's license, registering to vote, and a multitude of duties required to re-enroll in civilian daily life. I discovered latch hooking in those first weeks. I had always loved working with my hands and had been a star potholder maker in elementary school. Latch hooking was probably a basic form of therapy for me in those early days of re-entry into civilian life.

I discovered a company in downtown Baltimore selling latch hook rugs and pillow kits. This company allowed me to design my own and pick the color of the precut wool. I created an American Eagle flag rug and two sofa pillows. After I moved to my apartment, I continued to latch-hook over the next two years whenever I had free time or began experiencing negative thoughts. My latch hooking therapy helped me immensely. Focusing on making something with my hands kept me from drifting into pity parties or back to the war mindset, and the difficulties I was beginning to experience.

I practiced good health by exchanging alcohol for fruit juice. One morning as I was eating breakfast, I poured the last bit of fruit juice from a large metal can. I remembered how resourceful the Vietnamese were and how they reused everything the Americans threw away. A voice inside my head said, "juice can lamp." I thought through what materials would be needed. "Voilà," I had a pair of matching lamps.

Making those lamps became so much fun! I cut the tops and bottoms out of the cans and placed a circular piece of pine wood on the top, middle, and bottom sections. I purchased electrical lamp kits and lampshades, used leftover wool, and wrapped the cans in rug-making material. I used fun colors to paint the wood. I even covered the top and bottom of the lampshades with fabric from a local sewing shop. I completed the lamps which adorned my bedroom nightstands. Waking daily seeing those lamps on my nightstands brought a smile to my face. If asked where the idea for the lamps came from, I couldn't answer. Maybe it was something someone said, or the Vietnamese, perhaps a message from a higher power or God.

I had the privilege of growing up next door to Mr. and Mrs. Cruickshank, a quiet and devoutly religious couple. They always treated me with kindness and warmth. It was during my high school years that their oldest daughter married a man who owned a stunning 1955 Ford Crown Victoria. I was captivated by the car's exquisite appearance and would often engage in conversations with their son-in-law whenever he visited the Cruickshanks. Over time, we developed a strong friendship.

Their son-in-law, who was on a path to becoming a minister at their church, would occasionally share snippets of his Sunday sermons with me. It seemed as though I became his practice audience for these talks. During these practice conversations, he imparted valuable knowledge and skills to me, such as the art of spray painting. He also taught me the intricacies of car maintenance. We would spend many Saturday afternoons together, tending to his beautiful vehicle. It was through these experiences and his guidance that I gained a deep appreciation for automotive care and maintenance.

Reflecting on this, I can't help but consider whether my attachment to the 1955 Ford Crown Victoria stemmed from the time I spent with their son-in-law and his car. It's plausible that those shared moments influenced my choice to have a 1955 Ford Crown Victoria during my high school years as well.

Mr. Cruickshank, a skilled carpenter by profession and a World War I veteran who fought in France, had a profound impact on my life. Despite growing up next door to him, I had no idea about his wartime experiences until I returned home from Vietnam. It was then that I discovered a deeply personal connection between us—a shared understanding of the horrors and realities of combat and war. While I had some basic knowledge of World War I, it was through conversations with Mr. Cruickshank that I gained a greater appreciation for the immense challenges faced by those who served in that conflict.

The soldiers who fought in World War I endured unimaginable physical and emotional hardships. The introduction of advanced technologies such as machine guns, tanks, and deadly gasses made the battlefields terrifying and toxic. The soldiers were subjected to appalling living conditions, and the nature of the war itself created an incredibly dreadful and harrowing experience. Millions of men and women from around the world served in the First World War, fighting in various locations spanning continents. The impact of modern warfare combined with the political circumstances of the time made it a truly terrible ordeal.

During my initial week home from the Vietnam War, Mr. Cruickshank came to visit me at my parents' house. Our conversation held a profound intimacy due to our personal times in war. Despite the differences in our combat experiences, the emotional connection between us was undeniable.

I can still vividly remember the moments spent in my parents' kitchen, where tears were shed as Mr. Cruickshank, and I discussed our war encounters. We talked about the vivid mental images engraved in our memories, the moral wounds we carried, and the toll that taking lives had exacted on us. Thankfully, we were among the fortunate ones who managed to progress without becoming fixated solely on the past.

Mr. Cruickshank revealed that religion had played a crucial role in his healing process, enabling him to bury his painful memories and nightmares deep within his subconscious. His open display of emotions and his willingness to share his coping mechanisms left a lasting impression on me. It was a testament to the resilience of the human spirit and the power of finding solace in faith. Our conversation that day helped me understand that, despite the stark differences in our wartime experiences, we were united by the shared journey of healing and finding ways to live beyond the scars of war.

I am immensely grateful for the visit from Mr. Cruickshank, my dear friend and neighbor. Our shared experience and conversation proved to be a deeply therapeutic encounter for both of us. The significance of that discussion has stayed with me throughout my life. It provided the exact support I needed at that time. Dealing with the hateful individuals who threw trash on my parent's yard and the mental imagery that continued to play in my mind. Through our dialogue, I came to realize that I wasn't the only one carrying the personal experiences and emotional burdens of war. It is possible that Mr. Cruickshank sought out this conversation as well, having recognized the immense value of connecting with fellow veterans returning home.

Regardless, Mr. Cruickshank's words and willingness to share his own experiences helped me gain a profound understanding of the emotional journey soldiers undergo when they return from the battlefield. I came to the realization that I couldn't selectively ignore or suppress certain aspects of my emotional experience, as if trying to unfreeze only half of an ice cube. There were moments when I felt fragmented, like half of that ice cube. It became clear that I had to embrace my entire emotional journey, rather than dwelling on just a portion of it.

Reconciling Past Teachings
with Post-War Transformation

Upon my return to the United States, I was shaped by the teachings of the Army, its instructors, and the impact of Vietnam. However, it was essential for me to recreate myself once I arrived home. I could not allow myself to wallow in self-pity or remain anchored in the past. I had to choose between numbness and embracing the energy of my complete emotional experience, using it to my advantage. Ultimately, I had to melt the metaphorical ice cube within me and move forward in life.

I was a mixed-up and confused young man. I believed the root of this conflict was reconciling the horrible things I had to do to survive in war, including kill or be killed. In addition to the teachings of my youth to be strong and respect the sanctity of life. As I grew up, my parents provided various animals for me to love and raise. They wanted to teach me to be responsible for these tiny living creatures. Sometimes these little creatures would lay eggs, and I would spend hours watching and helping in the emergence of those tiny living creatures inside their shell encasings. The baby rabbits were so small and soft when they were born with those amazing red eyes.

As I previously wrote, before the Army, I had never fired a weapon or hunted. I cannot remember my father ever owning a weapon, nor did I see one in our home. I often asked for a Daisy BB rifle, and each time was told no. My parents would say that I might shoot my eye out. Or they would say we didn't have to hunt and kill our food because we could buy it at the grocery store. I was always more focused on raising and nurturing animals and nature. I never thought about killing these extraordinary little creatures I loved and cared for so much.

Lessons in Courage, Strength, and Benevolence

After many years of reflection on the valuable lessons I gained from my conversations with my father and guidance from influential figures like SFC Watson, my Boy Scout leader, as well as others I respected and who had mentored me. These individuals served as exceptional role models, teachers and leaders. If I were asked today to define myself, I would choose three words: 1.

courage, 2. strength, and 3. benevolence. Each of my role models and life mentors exemplified how to cultivate these essential qualities within myself.

Courage can hold different meanings for different individuals. It encompasses a wide spectrum, ranging from simple acts of kindness to engaging in armed combat. For me, courage entails the determination to stand resolute even when faced with opposition from everything and everyone around me. This kind of courage ultimately empowers us and strengthens our resolve.

I firmly believe that courage equips us with the capacity to navigate through challenging situations, such as job loss, divorce, or life-threatening health crises. It also enables us to uphold our moral values, acting as a guiding force that keeps us aligned with our true principles. Moreover, courage bolsters our commitment to pursuing intellectual matters we believe in, with our whole heart.

Strength encompasses not only physical prowess but also mental fortitude. It signifies the possession of a significant level of determination and willpower. A robust physique grants the essential power and stamina to accomplish feats like running a marathon, cycling 100 plus miles, or swimming four miles across the Chesapeake Bay. However, strength goes beyond the physical realm, as it equips us with the mental capacity to tackle the demanding cognitive aspects inherent in overcoming physical challenges.

On the other hand, benevolence is the desire and willingness to help someone, like volunteering to fight in a war to help the oppressed. Benevolence is the feeling of goodwill toward others. I also believe benevolence refers to acts of kindness or charity, which I observed my parents' do by helping others while I was growing up. Benevolence is not altruism or simply a response to the misfortunes of others. For me, it's also the active pursuit of the value we receive from relationships with others. For example, the fathers like Howard Mager and Eigil Rothe who would take their children camping with Casey and me. Or the fathers who volunteered to be Boy Scout leaders and help with camping even when my father couldn't go. And we, as a family, helping others at a homeless shelter or a soup kitchen by serving meals. In my opinion, the act of benevolence and helping our fellow human beings is a significant virtue and key to living an extraordinary life.

I displayed benevolence in a real-life situation when I encountered a serious highway accident. Without hesitation, I rushed to help a woman who was trapped inside a severely damaged car. Her life was in danger, so I stayed by her side, offering words of encouragement and providing immediate first aid until she could be safely rescued from the vehicle.

Furthermore, I have continued to demonstrate benevolence by offering guidance and valuable direction to young individuals. I created internships specifically designed for college and university students, providing them with a constructive learning experience and helped them navigate their career paths.

To me, benevolence has always entailed embracing optimism in my interactions and relationships with others. Its essence lies in treating others with the same kindness and respect that I desire for myself. During my tenure in the Army, I adopted a mindset of treating strangers as if they were acquaintances and acquaintances as if they were close friends.

While serving in Vietnam, I frequently found myself contemplating the purpose of my life. Like many others, my search for answers often led to more questions. Despite my dedication to training and honing my Army skills, I couldn't escape the restlessness and stress caused by conflicting paths in life. On one hand, as a soldier, I was trained for combat, which presented a stark contrast. On the other hand, I was deeply influenced by religious teachings and the values instilled in me by my parents, which emphasized the sanctity of life. This internal conflict is often a source of immense pain for veterans upon their return, and it can cause some individuals to isolate themselves from society, eventually ending up homeless. The intense emotional tug-of-war can inflict significant suffering, further exacerbated by issues such as Post-Traumatic Stress Disorder (PTSD), alcoholism, drug addiction, and even suicide.

Personally, I grappled with the need for high-speed, adrenaline-inducing activities as a way to cope with these conflicting emotions. I strongly believe that Vietnam veterans became scapegoats for our country's involvement in an incredibly unpopular war. Those who survived the war often faced worse outcomes compared to those who didn't serve in the military. The most tragic consequence for returning Vietnam soldiers has been the alarmingly high rate of veteran suicides. The clash between valuing life and the actions a soldier must take to survive in combat undoubtedly plays a significant role in these heartbreaking incidents.[35]

I found that pursuing a sense of purpose in life helped me navigate those challenges. It doesn't mean I didn't go through pain. Trust me, I did. I would describe my purpose as being driven to make something meaningful out of my life because I was fortunate enough to return home by God's grace. While I experienced some disorientation, I wasn't permanently affected or broken like many other soldiers.

The Army provided me with structure and a profound sense of team unity. After leaving the Army, I deeply missed the rigor, discipline, and camaraderie it had offered. I sought to recreate that camaraderie in every position I held throughout my career, but it never quite matched up. Perhaps that's what my brother James was searching for in life.

As a result of my combat experiences, I came to realize the fragility of life and the inevitability of death. It's not a matter of if, but when. This awareness dawned on me much earlier than many of my peers who didn't serve. In Vietnam, I intimately understood my mortality, and even to this day, when I reflect on my life, I remind myself and my wife, "It's inevitability, Rodweller."

With this perspective on mortality and my other experiences in the Army, I recognized the immense potential to accomplish meaningful things each day. Perhaps the most crucial lesson I learned was that time is both limited and precious. I shouldn't squander it. This realization became my primary motivation after leaving the Army.

The transition from the Army to civilian life in the early 1970s proved to be immensely challenging. It was far from a simple process; instead, it marked the beginning of an entirely new and unfamiliar journey. Ironically, this period was anything but joyous, as it entailed overcoming numerous obstacles without faltering or failing. Dealing with the mental anguish and confusion only added to the difficulty. Despite the circumstances, I tried not to indulge in self-pity. Instead, I channeled that energy into pushing forward, seeking answers, and finding my own path.

I could not simply follow the crowd or rely on external sources to discover my true self. I had to delve deep within myself and actively create my own identity, shape my life, and build my career. Embarking on the journey

---

[35] https://bigthink.com/the-present/story-behind-mcnamaras-morons/

to discover my true self was both profound and courageous. It meant stripping away the complacency of my school days and deeply understanding that past. This quest required me to dive into the depths of my identity and fully embrace who I truly am. Contrary to the belief that such a quest might be inherently self-centered, it was, in reality, a selfless endeavor at the core of all my future actions. To become the most effective contributor to the world, whether as an employee or an athlete, I first needed to understand my values, my strengths, and what I could offer to those around me.

Every morning, I would rise before dawn, reflecting on the human being I was the day before and how I could evolve into an even better version of myself. This commitment to personal growth was not just a path I chose; it felt like a necessary expedition to unlock my full potential. It involved shedding the lethargy of my former self—those aspects that no longer served me and did not align with who I aspired to be. But this journey was not solely about discarding the old; it was equally about constructing the new. I aimed to recognize and nurture the person I wished and knew I had to become, passionately pursuing my unique destiny.

Acknowledging my personal power while remaining open and vulnerable to my past experiences was crucial, as well as necessary. This process was not to be feared or shunned but embraced with curiosity and compassion, like getting to know a fascinating new friend. Through this exploration, I learned that understanding oneself is not just an act of self-discovery; it's a way of preparing to make a meaningful impact on my life and the world, grounded in authenticity and purpose.

Navigating Post-War Life: Challenges in Building Relationships

It was a challenge for me to pursue romantic relationships or establish long-term connections. I didn't have much money, only a small amount of savings I had accumulated during my service in Vietnam, and I was uncertain about finding employment. Plus, the future was uncertain. Nevertheless, I had the opportunity to meet several attractive and interesting young women who were already forging their own paths in their careers.

It often felt awkward when a woman would ask me, "What do you do?" I could only answer truthfully, explaining that I was currently unemployed and had recently returned from Vietnam. Some of these women would express an interest in discussing Vietnam, but I didn't want to dwell on the past. I would deflect the conversation or politely say, "I'm not ready to talk about it yet." I believed they were attempting to engage in conversation, but I did not have college, work, or career aspirations to discuss.

During that time, I met a nurse at the Towson Bratwurst Haus biergarten who also lived in Towson close to her work. She had already completed her undergraduate degree and established herself in her profession. She was fun and engaging, and one Friday afternoon, she invited me to a small gathering at her house along with a few other nurses. Without much thought, I immediately accepted her invitation. Just after my return from Vietnam, I had purchased another motorcycle, which served as my primary mode of transportation. Unfortunately, when I accepted the nurse's invitation, I hadn't considered the weather conditions in January. It was bitterly cold, with temperatures dropping to the low 20s.

Nonetheless, I didn't let the freezing weather deter me. Donning my helmet, I hopped on my motorcycle, fully expecting a short ride to Towson. I was dressed in lightweight cotton chino pants and a thin, light blue jacket intended for warmer climates. I foolishly hadn't considered the sub-freezing temperatures or the fact that the journey would take about 30 minutes. My excitement stemmed from being invited to an all-girls Friday night party.

Within 10 minutes of riding, the frigid weather began to take its toll. I hadn't thought to wear gloves to shield my hands from the icy cold. After enduring 20 minutes of sub-freezing temperatures, I started shivering uncontrollably. The intense shaking caused the motorcycle's headlight to tremble violently, flickering erratically along and around the road.

Finally, I arrived at the nurse's townhouse in Towson. When I knocked on the door, I couldn't feel any sensation in my fingers, which at that point had turned a deep shade of purple. Despite my discomfort, she greeted me with a warm smile, invited me inside and offered me a drink. I requested a cup of hot coffee. While the coffee brewed, she introduced me to her friends. When they asked about my occupation, I mentioned that I had recently returned from Vietnam. Given my severe trembling, they probably assumed I was suffering from PTSD or shell shock. My entire body continued to shiver and shake from the cold as I was handed the coffee. I clumsily spilled the coffee all over the floor.

After assisting my friend in cleaning up the mess, I felt compelled to make my exit, claiming that I must be coming down with a cold or flu. I was incredibly embarrassed and still trembling. She kindly suggested that I stay, offering me a blanket and aspirin. Looking back, it would have been wise to accept her generous offer. But for some inexplicable reason, perhaps due to my wounded pride, I declined. I bid my farewells, promising to call her soon. She understood my embarrassment and attempted to put me at ease. With my ego bruised, I knew I had no choice but to leave.

To add to my misery, I now had to endure another thirty-minute ride back to my apartment in Dundalk, braving even colder temperatures. The freezing weather had intensified during my time at the nurse's house. Once again, as I rode my motorcycle, I shivered uncontrollably, causing the headlight to flicker erratically. On this return journey, I devised a desperate strategy to combat the cold. I decided to ride for a few minutes, then stop, dismount the motorcycle, and push it while running alongside it. My aim was to generate enough physical activity to get my blood flowing and warm myself by increasing my body temperature. I repeated this arduous process for what felt like an eternity. After an agonizingly cold and painful ride, I finally arrived back at my apartment. Gradually, I began to thaw, but the cold had left a lasting impression. In the warmth of my apartment, I couldn't help but chuckle at the thought of attending the Army's winter survival school in the Alaskan wilderness. I quickly dismissed the idea, realizing that my current tolerance for jungle climates and my thin blood made warmer temperatures far more suitable.

Following that chilly incident, the nurse attempted to contact me multiple times. However, my wounded pride and lingering embarrassment restricted my willingness to move beyond casual telephone conversations. Reflecting on the experience, I pondered how I could have avoided such an awkward situation. Although our conversations continued over the phone, my internal struggles impeded any progress beyond these informal chats. Deep down, I believed her calls were driven more by pity than genuine interest. Unfortunately, my assumptions were proven incorrect when she eventually ceased reaching out. I comprehended her decision all too well.

A few years later, I gained a clearer perspective on the difficulties I faced during those initial months after returning from Vietnam. I was grappling with numerous personal issues, making it nearly impossible to foster close personal relationships. In hindsight, it's easy to see how I could have handled things differently during that period of my life. I wish I could go back and rewrite those chapters. Many remarkable individuals were extending their support and assistance, yet I was either unaware of how to accept their help or unable to do so.

Finding Work
After the Vietnam War

As I previously mentioned after returning from Vietnam, I was eager to find employment to distract me from dwelling on the past. I often joked that I couldn't even find a job parking cars for a dollar and a quarter an hour, attributing this difficulty to my status as a Vietnam veteran. This joke prompted our insightful daughter to ask if I had genuinely sought such positions. I clarified that it was a metaphor to illustrate my employment challenges post-Vietnam.

While searching for work, I encountered discrimination and disdain from potential employers in the Baltimore and Washington, D.C., areas upon learning of my veteran status. Despite my desire to contribute positively to my community, I was met with widespread institutional indifference where the organization lacked interest, concern, or sympathy for the Vietnam Veteran. This was a common experience for many veterans who returned home to find their employment prospects significantly diminished.

The Vietnam War, increasingly viewed as futile by the American public, cast a long shadow over those of us who served. Our service, of 12-month tours, was largely unappreciated, as the war was considered the first lost by the United States. The lack of a celebratory homecoming starkly contrasted with the reception of World War II veterans. This difference in public perception underscored a broader misunderstanding and underappreciation of Vietnam veterans' sacrifices. Initially, I sought help from the Veterans Administration but was only offered low-skilled jobs, which was extremely frustrating.

In the Army at Fort Meade, MD

After looking for work during the first month at home and receiving only rejections, I eventually concluded that reenlisting in the Army would be my best option. The Army recruiter, realizing I had a critical Military Occupational Specialty (MOS), suggested I contact the 11th Group 1st Special Forces at Fort Meade, Maryland. He recommended contacting the administrative officer who could assist me with potential work opportunities.

My visit to Fort Meade introduced me to an unexpected connection from my past. Meeting with the administrative officer, I was surprised to learn she was a major and that she had served as a nurse with the rank of Lieutenant in Vietnam at the 91st Medevac Hospital. She was one of the nurses who cared for me after the rocket attack.

During our meeting, I shared my difficulties finding employment and educational aspirations. The administrative officer Marilyn Scherzer, the nurse from the 91st medivac hospital in Vietnam described a wonderful opportunity to me. It became clear that my Army MOS was still a highly sought-after Army skill, and she extended an incredible offer for me to join the 11th Group. Considering my previous service and experience working with and supporting the Green Berets in Vietnam, transitioning to a Green Beret would be a smoother process than expected. The major also assured me that returning to Vietnam wouldn't be required, although I could choose to do so like other Green Berets. My role there was a unique combination of soldier and civilian duties. I worked on helicopters alongside various Army aviation units stationed at Tipton Army Airfield. These units included the 195th AVN CO (ASH), 11th Group, 1st Special Forces, and the 97th ARCOM.

Throughout my five years in the Army at Fort Meade, I participated in various programs and schools that were both fun and challenging. They also gave me many rewarding and enjoyable experiences. However, I will not describe each of them in detail, as that would divert from the main story of my life in this autobiography. Instead, I will focus on those experiences that significantly enriched my life.

At Fort Meade, I had the unique opportunity to visit the White House. Robert Preston's story is significant, as he enlisted in the Army in 1972 to become a helicopter pilot. However, circumstances prevented him from completing the helicopter flight training course at Fort Rucker, Alabama, thus thwarting his path to becoming a warrant officer. Subsequently, he was assigned to Fort Meade in the role of a helicopter mechanic.

On several occasions, I worked alongside Preston and found him to be intelligent and personable, just a year or two younger than me. Rumors circulated that he disagreed with an instrument flight instructor, who allegedly used his influence to fail Preston on an instrument rating flight test. During that time, the Vietnam War was winding down, and the requirements for pilot efficiency became exceedingly challenging. Many aspiring pilots struggled to pass flight school, and the Army's demand for pilots diminished as the war ended.

While stationed at Fort Meade, Preston became involved with a local girl. However, on February 17, 1974, their relationship came to a painful end. It isn't easy to discern the exact thoughts occupying Preston's mind that day. But on that particular Sunday night, he turned to alcohol, possibly as a coping mechanism for the emotional turmoil stemming from both the breakup and his prior setback of failing flight school. Despite the obstacles he had encountered up to this point in the Army, I sympathized with Preston and firmly believed in his potential to excel as an officer and a pilot. Regrettably, the combination of alcohol consumption and his struggles likely intensified his underlying sense of unhappiness and discontent.

In his intoxicated state, Preston made an impulsive and shocking decision. He headed to the Tipton Army Airfield at Fort Meade, where, at that time, helicopters were not secured or locked. This led to an unexpected event: a helicopter theft, something no one had foreseen. Preston, who knew intimately about the Huey H model helicopters, effortlessly started one of the sixteen helicopters parked outside a hangar. He then contacted the control tower for instructions on the appropriate departure route and soon took off. Remarkably, despite his intoxication, Preston flew the helicopter skillfully within and around the Fort Meade area. His flying skills were astonishing, exceeding those of many sober pilots during daylight hours. Though I might be biased due to our acquaintance, I firmly believe that Preston was a kind-hearted and exceptionally talented pilot.

Preston could fly for an extended period and return to Tipton Army Airfield unnoticed. It would have been considered another Army aviator practicing night flying. However, the authorities learned of his actions when

210

he landed the stolen helicopter on a liquor store parking lot. Rather than shutting down the helicopter, Preston left it running with the blades turning while he went inside the store to purchase more alcohol. This frightened several customers, leading them to contact the local police, who then alerted the Maryland State Police. Within a short period, two Maryland State Police Bell Jet Ranger helicopters began pursuing Preston as he departed from the liquor store.

Preston's Huey helicopter was more significant, with a bigger rotor blade diameter and heavier weight, making it more stable in flight but using a larger quantity of fuel during flight. However, it seems that Preston hadn't accurately calculated the fuel requirements for the night. The Huey had a range of over 300 miles. Given the circumstances of trying to evade the State Police helicopters, it could have consumed that amount of fuel faster than usual, in addition to his detour to the liquor store.

As Preston became aware of the low fuel warnings, he had already flown inside the Washington, D.C., district lines. Eventually, he landed the Huey on the south lawn of the White House because of all the bright lights, mark-

Robert Preston's Huey with bullet holes from landing on the White House lawn

ing a significant security breach. Secret Service agents assigned to the White House responded to this unauthorized landing by firing handguns, automatic weapons, and shotguns at the helicopter, striking it with over 300 bullets. Miraculously, Preston survived the hail of gunfire with only a minor injury to his right foot, which had been momentarily pushed off the control pedal by one of those bullets during the landing. It was a remarkable feat, considering he was heavily intoxicated, showcasing his remarkable helicopter-flying abilities under such circumstances.

I was part of the team that was called to inspect the helicopter at the White House. It was astonishing to see that Preston had escaped grave injuries despite being targeted by so many bullets. Furthermore, the aircraft's flight control systems remained undamaged. The entire situation was a testament to his extraordinary luck. Preston was undeniably a fortunate individual.

Marriage

Marriage is the number one cause of divorce.
Most women believe men should be like Kleenex:
soft, strong, and disposable.

While at Fort Meade in the Green Beret unit, I continued my education and pursuing technology positions, eventually securing an entry-level IT position at the Social Security Administration (SSA) in Baltimore. This was one of three job offers I received simultaneously, a testament to the adage that "good things come in threes." The other offers included a position with the FBI and an opportunity with Air America in Southeast Asia, both of which I declined in favor of furthering my education and career in technology.

I started as a programmer trainee at SSA, working with much younger peers who had only high school diplomas. However, my diverse background in the Army and Vietnam quickly opened opportunities for me to work on non-technology assignments. This marked a positive shift and a starting point in my career trajectory. My involvement in non-IT related tasks gave me a unique insight into SSA's operations, which distinguished me from my colleagues.

Those non technology positions allowed for promotions to senior programmer roles to follow. Along with those professional and personal milestones, which included meeting my future wife, Rose. My experiences at

SSA, while demanding, paled in comparison to the rigors of service in Vietnam, allowing me to excel and embrace new opportunities with gratitude and resilience.

Also, upon my return from Vietnam, I committed to a strict vegetarian diet and chose to abstain from alcohol. This choice was rooted in a desire to achieve optimal mental and physical health. It also demonstrated a profound dedication to a disciplined and mindful lifestyle. Through vegetarianism, I discovered comfort in the clean, simple benefits of plant-based foods, reflecting my deep respect for all life on Earth. Similarly, eliminating alcohol from my life proved to be a pivotal change, enhancing my mental clarity and focus. This decision enabled me to interact with the world with greater awareness and intention, significantly enriching my sense of purpose.

One day, I saw a fellow classmate from one of my classes at Dundalk Community College. She was eating lunch and reading a book by herself. I approached her and introduced myself and discovered her name was Rose. We soon started having lunch together at work. Then I asked her out on a date.

I continued dating Rose and even had the opportunity to meet her family. While her family was friendly, I sensed a certain reservation in our interactions. Connecting with them proved to be a challenge. I couldn't help but feel that they found me peculiar due to my decision to become a strict vegetarian and refrain from alcohol after Vietnam. It seemed as though they were uncomfortable with someone who didn't consume meat or engage in drinking. They might have bought into the stereotype perpetuated by the media, portraying Vietnam veterans as "crazy."

Despite the perceived differences, Rose and I continued to date, and I remained committed to working through my personal issues. There was still a persistent void in my life that needed addressing—the feeling of being adrift in the storm of life. While I poured my passion into my work and dedicated myself to full-time schooling, the bigger picture of what I would do with my entire life remained hazy. I held onto the belief that my education and career commitments, both during my time in the Army and afterward, were of utmost importance and should never be forsaken. Nevertheless, there was something gnawing at me, something I couldn't quite put my finger on.

214

Then, one day, it struck me that what I lacked was marriage. I believed that marriage could serve as my guiding light, keeping me on a steady course towards my true north. In all honesty, I thought that Rose could contribute positively to my life. She was providing support as I continued to grow and develop. She also helped in fortifying my determination and character. Little did I know that this fortified resolve and character would prove crucial in navigating the devastating storm of our eventual divorce.

I knew that I shouldn't compare myself to others, but I couldn't help but compare myself to my high school friends who were already married with children. Meanwhile, many of my Army comrades had settled down and started families of their own. It dawned on me that marriage seemed to provide a sense of stability and purpose that I yearned for. All I had to show for myself at that time was my education and a demanding job that required long hours. I must admit I loved my work, but I didn't have a purpose or a sense of stability.

After dating Rose for over two years, we made the decision to tie the knot. Approximately a year later, we took the plunge and bought a home on the west side of Baltimore, conveniently located near our work. Despite the commitments of married life, I remained dedicated to pursuing my graduate education alongside my professional endeavors.

Then we decided to buy an airplane. This would allow me to continue pursuing my passion for flying while also reducing its associated costs. We were having fun flying to cities and states up and down the East Coast as well as several central states. During our travels, we met and became friends with other plane owners. Several of these owners were retired military pilots from the Maryland area. Some of those retired pilots were also instructor pilots. I would schedule time on Saturdays to learn the advanced training techniques these pilot friends had acquired in the military. I trained with retired Navy, Air Force, and even commercial pilots.

One long weekend Rose and I flew to Ada, Oklahoma. We wanted to meet and talk with an individual who started a regional air carrier and cargo service. I had heard about this entrepreneur and read about him in a flying magazine. He owned eight Cessna 206 aircraft and leased four others when his business needed additional aircraft. His company provided cargo or air hearse services for the central part of the United States. His company transported the deceased between funeral homes or back to an individual's home state for burial.

During our brief trip, we met with the owner, his wife, and most of the pilots who flew for him. He had an extraordinarily successful business providing air hearse services throughout the central United States. During our conversation he suggested that we should start a similar business on the East Coast. I thought, why not try it along with the air hearse business, we could deliver checks for the Federal Reserve up and down the East Coast. At that time, the Federal Reserve had an entire fleet of contract airplanes for check pickup and delivery. We could become part of that contract fleet.

In addition, Atlantic City had recently opened many new casinos. It had become an East Coast destination for gambling and an alternative to Las Vegas. The casino owners would charter planes to fly high rollers to Atlantic City. These casinos were looking to expand their air taxi flying services. At first blush, all these options sounded like a great business opportunity. This was the type of experience I had gained in the military, and my career working with technology could provide the planning experience.

I began preparing a detailed business plan with projected financials. As part of this plan, I knew we would have to complete the Federal Aviation Regulations (FAR) paperwork requirements. Due to my prior experience in writing government papers, I began working on this necessary documentation. These regulations mandated that all aspects of commuter and on-demand flight services be thoroughly documented. This involved providing a written description of how an organization planned to transport passengers, human remains or cargo for compensation, as well as outlining the processes for hiring pilots and ensuring their safety training. It also required that I detailed the specifics of how the entire organization would operate.

During this period, I became friends with the head of the aviation loan department at the First National Bank of Maryland. A former Air Force B-52 pilot and instructor, he often flew with me and helped enhance my flying skills. His department specialized in airplane leasing, financing, and occasional sales. I shared our business plan and financials for launching a commercial air charter service with him. After a thorough review, he submitted the plan and supporting financial documents to the bank's management for consideration.

216

The bank was interested in our concept but requested additional up-front funding to comfortably finance the expensive airplanes. Unfortunately, I was unable to raise the extra capital needed for the down payment.

As it turned out, this setback was a blessing in disguise. Atlantic City soon experienced a significant downturn in its gambling industry, severely impacting local aviation taxi services. Around the same time, the Federal Reserve launched the Check 21 project to reduce daily check writing by consumers. Concurrently, airlines expanded their cargo operations to include the profitable transport of human remains. Given these developments, it became evident that our business plan was no longer viable. Fortunately, we did not incur any financial losses.

My career was going very well, and I continued to receive promotions. Meanwhile, Rose completed her undergraduate degree and joined me in graduate school. She had also made a career change from being a secretary to becoming a management analyst, and she was making progress in her new field.

Rose's parents purchased a campsite at Indian Acres, a permanent camping resort located on the Chesapeake Bay in Cecil County, MD. This campsite was open year-round, allowing us to go camping whenever the opportunity presented itself. They had acquired a 34-foot Prowler pull-behind camper that provided all the necessary amenities: a bathroom, shower, and a kitchen with a full-size refrigerator. It felt like staying in a cozy studio apartment.

Our flying trips also took us to see our friends on the eastern shore and visit our dear friend from Vietnam, Bougie Criswell, and his wife Chris. We would lend a hand in building their home near Ocean City, MD. Another close friend from Vietnam, John LeCates, and his wife Beverly would often join us on these trips. Bougie was constructing a house without nails, only wood pegs, it was fascinating to witness and be part of the process.

We would also travel to the mountains of western MD, particularly the Deep Creek ski area. We cherished the time spent skiing down the trails, thanks to the breathtaking views of the lake. Life was truly treating us well.

Rose was doing well in her new career track as a management analyst, and many evenings she would call to say she had to work late on a project for the SSA administrator. I never thought to ask her what she was working on during those after-hours tasks because I was constantly returning to work to assist in resolving the latest technology crisis in my work world.

We had a friend who lived in an apartment near the SSA headquarters. On several occasions, Rose said our friend had asked her to go to her apartment and meet the telephone repair person. I was so involved with my work that I never thought this sounded odd or thought to question her.

For me, working in the field of technology never felt like work; it was fun, more like doing something I genuinely enjoyed. As I progressed further in my career, I noticed that promotions were less frequent. A friend had faced a similar situation to that, and he decided to seek promotional opportunities in other organizational components within SSA. It didn't take long for him to become a senior executive. I congratulated him on his career success, and during our conversation, he suggested that I consider moving out of technology to further my advancement.

I took some time to reflect on his suggestion, weighing the possibilities. After serious thought, I soon realized that the field of technology was my passion, and I didn't want to pursue other career paths. I had a genuine love for the work I was doing, and that was what truly mattered to me.

Shortly after our conversations, I received a phone call from a recruiter in New Jersey who asked me if I would be interested in a career change. The telephone call surprised me, as I questioned how she obtained my direct telephone number? At first, I wasn't interested, but the recruiter continued to call and talk about this opportunity. Rose and I discussed the position for several weeks and we agreed I should follow up. I went on four interviews for a position with a private, family-owned, multibillion-dollar New Jersey corporation. I even traveled to the company's headquarters in Edison, New Jersey, to meet with the corporate officers.

The company extended an offer with a salary that was over double what I was currently earning. In addition to the impressive salary, they included a comprehensive benefits package and an enticing bonus rewards program. It all sounded almost too good to believe. In hindsight, I should have heeded my internal cautionary advice that warns when something appears too good to be true.

I discussed the offer extensively with Rose, and ultimately, I decided to accept the new position. However, before finalizing my decision, I made sure to request an offer letter detailing specific provisions regarding salary payments and the continuation of benefits in case of termination. Once I had that letter as my official contract, I submitted my resignation from the SSA and commenced my new role.

With my new job, I found myself commuting more than a hundred miles every day. After a month of this tiring routine, Rose and I discussed selling our home and constructing a new one closer to my workplace while staying reasonably close to SSA for Rose's position. We also considered the possibility of her transitioning to the private industry. Surprisingly, she strongly opposed the idea of switching organizations. I was really surprised by her quick and adamant response. Given her long working hours, I believed she could potentially earn more money and have a better work-life balance elsewhere. However, every time I broached the topic, she instantly became angry, stating that she had no desire to change her career path. I assumed she interpreted my intentions as an attempt to push her out of her current profession.

There continued to be instances when she would call me at work, informing me that she had to work late on a project and would not be able to make it home in time for dinner. Whenever I inquired about the specifics of her work, she would mention a project name or a particular department within SSA where she was assigned to work with. I thought about this during my lengthy commutes to and from my new workplace. I interpreted her actions as a sign of her ambition to progress in her career. I chose to disregard any negative thoughts that may have arisen.

Meanwhile, our discussions about the possibility of relocating closer to my new workplace became more serious about possibilities. To my relief, she did not object to the idea. I tried to identify areas that were conveniently situated between our respective workplaces. During weekends, we embarked on a quest to find a suitable home that met our requirements. Despite our two-month long search, we struggled to find a house that both of us liked. While I had discovered several options that perfectly matched our criteria, Rose consistently found reasons to dismiss those houses as unsuitable. As a result, my frustration grew. The extensive time and money I spent on commuting felt increasingly wasteful. Instead of sitting in a car, I could have utilized those precious hours and resources for more fulfilling activities like flying, biking, running, swimming, or almost anything else.

We eventually found a building lot and a builder in northeastern Baltimore County. We engaged an architect to create a set of building plans for our new home. I thought Rose was excited about this new phase in our marriage. She seemed interested in selling our existing home quickly. Because of my lengthy commute, Rose managed the entire process of selling our house herself, much to my surprise.

Upon my return from a business trip, she was excited that the real estate agent had suggested a selling price for our consideration. We heatedly discussed this price. I thought it was too low and was very hesitant. We had completed many improvements to the house, and I didn't believe the suggested selling price would allow us to recover our improvement expenses or to break even. Nevertheless, she was adamant about setting the selling price at the recommended amount for a quick sale. I was stubbornly opposed to it, but reluctantly agreed because the commuting was definitely wearing on me.

Rose said if our home sold quickly, we could put all our belongings in storage and move in with her parents. Her parents had finished their attic and created two small bedrooms. I did not want to do this and was vehemently opposed. I continued to argue that we should at least look at apartments or other options before moving into her parents' house. We looked, and again, nothing worked for her, just like looking for a house. She continued to press the point that we could save money by living with her parents and use the savings for building the new house.

I wondered why she didn't want to agree on other temporary living options. When I angrily brought up the rental options, she would reply it was my idea to save and invest money for our retirement. That was true. Therefore, I couldn't and didn't object, but I was still resentful of her inflexible attitude about moving and living arrangements.

As soon as there was a contract on our house, she immediately engaged Wheaton Moving and Storage to pack, move, and store our furniture and belongings. Nearly everything we owned went into storage. We only had the bare minimum essentials when we moved into her parents' home. I believed this would be a short stay. Still, I was impressed by her efficiency in making all the arrangements. I was glad she took this on because I needed to focus on my new job. It never occurred to me that there was a master plan she had established beforehand, and every step had been planned perfectly. Her plan was like a giant funnel directing us to an endpoint, but I didn't realize this or even understand that the endpoint was not moving into a new house.

Less than a month after we moved into her parents' home, Rose began receiving calls in the evening from coworkers. She said the calls were about a project at work. At first, I didn't think anything of this because I had received after hours calls while working at SSA, and even from the new employer. But it wasn't long before those after-hours work calls occurred almost every evening. Her parents' telephone volumes were loud. It was easy to hear what was being said over those phones because they were like little speakers.

On a Tuesday evening during the second month of living with her parents, I returned home later than usual, and I missed dinner. As we were getting ready for bed, the telephone rang once again. Her parents answered it promptly. They called upstairs to Rose, notifying her that it was a work call. Due to the loud volume of the phone, I overheard a male voice asking her if she had informed him yet. It became evident that both of us could hear the question. She ended the call abruptly. I continued preparing for bed. I'm sure I had a puzzled expression on my face.

Just as I was about to pull back the covers on the bed, she stood there for a moment, looking directly into my eyes. Then she uttered the shocking words, "I want you to let me go so I can live my life the way I want to live it." Followed by, "You need to go. Leave now. Go."

I was completely shocked and speechless. Rose wanted me to leave immediately. I could only muster the usual questions, asking her what this was all about and why she was doing this. She simply stood there, either unable or unwilling to respond. Her silent pause allowed me a few moments to regain my composure. I asked her if she was certain about her decision, to which she replied with a resolute "yes." That single "yes" marked the definitive end of our marriage.

My mind raced, evoking memories of the intense moments I endured during my time in Vietnam when life itself hung in the balance. Amid this overwhelming realization, it became clear to me that this entire situation had been orchestrated with the help of someone else. In due course, I would uncover the identity of that individual. Gathering my essentials, which included a week's worth of clothes, suits, two homemade juice can lamps, and my trusty clock radio, I swiftly packed my bag and departed.

There was no possibility of ever going back; nothing anyone could say or do would alter my decision. I could not fathom reconciling with a person who exhibited such deceit, dishonesty, unfaithfulness, and selfishness. How could someone who made promises break them to commit such a profoundly hurtful act? The devastation I felt was immense. Nevertheless, I recognized the importance of moving forward and not allowing myself to sink into an emotional abyss. I had to tap into the strength I had cultivated during my time in the Army to navigate through this challenging period.

As I loaded my car with my few possessions, I realized that I had to maintain a positive attitude. I was in a challenging situation, but I wouldn't lose the power to get through this successfully. With my mind still racing as I drove around looking for a nice hotel, I concluded that all our possessions in storage, the so-called comforts of life, were not essential. Clinging to them would hinder my personal growth in the attainment of a better life from this experience. In Vietnam, I had only the basics to live and here I was again. But this time I was more experienced and mature.

I felt a deep anger towards Rose and her family. I was convinced that her parents were aware of the situation even before we moved into their house. As this anger intensified, I decided to channel it into productive energy to propel myself forward. In due course, I discovered a hotel along Route 40 where I planned to stay for the upcoming nights.

Following my work hours, I actively searched for apartments to rent. Fortunately, I came across one that perfectly matched my desired location and commuting requirements. I took the necessary steps, writing a check for the deposit and another for the first month's rent.

I will never forget my first night in that unfurnished apartment. All I had with me were my clothes, juice can lamps, clock radio, shaving gear, toothbrush, and toothpaste. As I was lying on the floor and about to turn off the lights, I looked through the empty apartment, at my juice can lamps and clock radio, thinking this isn't so bad. I'm inside, it's not raining, and no one is shooting at me or trying to kill me. What more could I want, and I then turned off my lamps and went to sleep.

At work the following day, the apartment rental office called to say my checks were returned due to insufficient funds. How deeply embarrassing! I said I could stop by after work to resolve this situation. I checked our joint bank and investment accounts and found that only five dollars remained in each account. Rose's divorce plan was well-prepared and expertly executed.

If Rose had taken all the money from each account, I would have been notified of the account closings. I explained my entire situation to the apartment rental office manager that afternoon. The agent said she could rent the apartment to me until Friday, and I assured her I would pay her on Friday once I received my weekly paycheck.

I began thinking through everything required to realign my life. Over the next several nights of lying on my apartment floor, I remembered from my Army days, that attitude equals altitude. I knew I had to envision my world NOT from the past or the painful present, but the future. This vision had to include how I viewed myself, my accomplishments, and my abilities. The Army taught me that no one could create my attitude. I began envisioning what and where I wanted to be in my future, asking myself what was important to me and what really mattered.

I continued to think that my attitude should focus solely on what I could control. I believed being in control of my thoughts and actions, was essential. Lying on that carpeted floor I thought of my mother's quote from the poem "Invictus": "I am the master of my fate, and I'm the captain of my destiny." My destiny was working toward my purpose in life. Feeling in control and intrinsically motivated I would not let this one event deter me from achieving my purpose in life that God or my higher power had in store for me.

I was astonished by the extent of Rose's deception, which left me feeling blindsided and embarrassed. To make matters worse, she continued to use my last name, Rodweller. Throughout my life, I had prioritized upholding the integrity associated with that name. I understood that respect is earned through consistent actions, reliability, and trustworthiness. I always followed through on my commitments and treated others the way I wished to be treated. Unfortunately, Rose seemed to have disregarded these principles, making me feel as if she was tarnishing the reputation of my family name.

Being a victim was a new and unwelcome feeling for me. Initially, I was deeply hurt and wondered if she had betrayed me intentionally for some inexplicable reason. However, as the days passed, I came to realize that her actions were not about me at all; she had always been focused solely on herself.

Not long after the separation, I found myself deep in thought during a long bicycle training ride. I realized I had a choice: to be angry with Rose, to hate her, or to pity her. This was a breakthrough moment for me. To move on successfully, I needed to let go of negative emotions and focus on the future. Life's only constants are uncertainty and change, so embracing a positive attitude was crucial for navigating its ups and downs. Changing my attitude was not easy, but over time, my negative feelings about Rose began to fade, allowing me to concentrate more positively on my life and what lay ahead.

During this reflective period, I also pondered the nature of autonomy and destiny, influenced by my interest in physics that had started in college. Physics often suggests that the universe operates like a mechanical system, but what role does free will play? This led me to question whether life's challenges were the result of my past choices or simply the workings of natural laws. Could my current hardships be traced back to earlier lapses in judgment or decisions I had made? Regardless of the answer, I resolved to maintain a positive and proactive approach to life.

However, these philosophical musings did not negate the practical struggles I faced. With no savings and only a weekly paycheck, I had to manage a car payment, apartment rent, utilities, and other living expenses. To make matters worse, the attorney I initially hired proved ineffective and expensive. After accumulating substantial legal bills for seemingly pointless work, I decided to terminate his services. I then reached out to Rose to request a face-to-face meeting. We agreed to meet on the steps of the Towson Library.

When we met, I brought up the matter of retrieving our belongings from storage. Rose didn't answer, so I suggested that she should take everything. I knew she only wanted the newer items. Her response made it clear that this was what she had wanted all along. She seemed invigorated by my offer and immediately said she would contact Wheaton Moving and Storage.

When the items arrived, I noticed she kept all the newer and more valuable things, sending only the older items to my apartment. She had already taken our savings, proceeds from selling our house, investments, and certificates of deposit, showing no remorse for the end of our marriage or the turmoil she had caused.

Despite these challenges, I felt liberated from the emotional burden of resentment and anger toward Rose and her partner. While I regretted not asserting my claim over what was rightfully mine, I realized that letting go of material possessions set the stage for a brighter future. Those were just things that would eventually wear out or break, whereas she would also eventually deplete all the money. This perspective made me see that she had inadvertently given me the opportunity to become the person I was meant to be.

During this time, I continued working at a diverse manufacturing corporation specializing in various technologies like heating and cooling systems, thermometers, and thermostats. A thought struck me one day: Did I want to be a thermometer that merely reflects its environment, or a thermostat that actively influences it? I chose the latter, opting for a proactive approach to reshape my attitude and life.

After our meeting, I immediately instructed my attorney to prepare and serve the divorce papers. It was a state law that I couldn't file for divorce before one year had passed since separating. Exactly one year after Rose had asked me to leave her parents' house, she was served the papers, surprised by the timing. I often wonder why she was astonished. Given her actions over the prior year, it's difficult to believe she might have thought reconciliation was on the table. Her actions had definitively closed a chapter in my life.

Once the divorce was finalized, my aim was to swiftly relegate that period to the past. I had a plethora of goals to achieve, and I was determined not to be hindered by the aftermath of a divorce. My experiences in the Army and Vietnam had taught me the importance of focusing on adaptation and refining strategies and ideas as circumstances demanded. I had learned to take hold of the reins of change and steer towards the future.

Rose never offered an explanation for the divorce, prompting me to question my potential contribution to it. Had I invested too much time in work, flying, or athletic pursuits? Did I create an environment that left her discontented? I realized once more that the issue was not centered around me; if something in our marriage had been troubling her, she would have communicated it. Instead, I circled back to the understanding that this was about her desires and her path in life—a new life that excluded me. Regardless of her reasons, my shift in attitude enabled me to see that she had done me a great service. She provided me the opportunity to continue evolving and becoming the person I was meant to be!

V. Work Life

Education and Career

Upon returning from Vietnam, I recognized the significance of acquiring a college education. Despite having the option to attend various colleges or universities via the GI Bill, I opted to pursue my education independently. This choice was driven by my belief that I could have more influence over my studies and the institution I would attend.

While I was in Vietnam, my mother sent me a letter that included a small announcement from our local weekly newspaper, the Dundalk Eagle. This announcement detailed plans for the establishment of a community college in Dundalk. Reading those lines, I knew that achieving an associate of arts degree from Dundalk Community College was my first goal in my overall educational plan. Earning that first degree at Dundalk Community College would be an exceptional accomplishment for "One Cool Cat" from Dundalk.

I have never let my schooling interfere
with my education.
— Mark Twain

Choosing to attend Dundalk Community College (DCC) was one of the wisest educational decisions I ever made. Initially, I opted for refresher courses that helped me build upon the habits and skills I had developed during my time in the Army. To my surprise, it didn't take long for me to realize just how much I had missed during my high school years.

There are two notable experiences from my time at DCC that significantly impacted my personal growth and transformation into a more confident student. The first experience took place in a speech class where I had an opportunity for self-reflection and development. During one class session, I found myself seated at the back with a fellow student who had recently left the Marine Corps. We engaged in quiet conversation, sharing our experiences and enjoying each other's company. Unexpectedly, the instructor called upon me to be the first to approach the podium, introduce myself to the class, and describe my life in less than 10 minutes. The sudden spotlight startled me, and my nerves kicked in. It wasn't the time constraint that bothered me; rather, it was my anxiety about speaking openly about myself.

As I walked toward the podium, I pondered, "Why am I feeling anxious when I have faced combat situations?" Taking a deep breath, I looked at each person in the class and introduced myself, saying, "Hi, I'm Bob Rodweller, and I have just returned from Vietnam." What followed was a nearly 10-minute talk that proved to be a pivotal moment for me. This experience had a profound impact on my career trajectory. I realized that people were genuinely interested in what I had to say, even in that class setting. It also dawned on me that we listen to others because everyone's life story holds significance. Each person has a compelling narrative to share, and I had not fully grasped the value of my own story until that moment in class.

This experience in the speech class not only helped me overcome my initial anxiety but also instilled in me the belief that our lives matter and that our stories deserve to be heard. It was a transformative realization that stayed with me throughout my career and beyond.

Another notable experience occurred when I enrolled in an advanced math and physics class. The course description had caught my attention, but after attending the initial session, I thought to myself, "Oops, this is beyond my grasp. I am likely to fail." Unwilling to accept failure, I took the initiative the next evening. I arrived early, seeking advice from an academic counselor about potential solutions. The counselor recommended seeking a tutor to aid with the class. Determined to conquer this intriguing course, I asked for tutor suggestions.

One of the recommendations happened to be the college's Chief Financial Officer (CFO). The counselor mentioned that the CFO might be available for tutoring if time permitted. Acting on this, I contacted the CFO the following day and arranged a meeting. In our discussion, he agreed to provide tutoring and I discovered that he also taught math and physics classes. We established terms and objectives that ultimately led me to succeed in the course.

My tutor maintained periodic check-ins to offer encouragement across my other classes as well. Dundalk Community College proved to be the ideal educational institution for me due to the exceptional and supportive professionals who were part of it. Their guidance and dedication played a crucial role in my academic journey.

In 1976, after completing my Associate of Arts degree, I decided to transfer to the University of Maryland. I earned my undergraduate degree in 1978 and, upon being accepted into graduate school, approached one of my undergraduate professors to serve as my academic advisor. We had developed a good rapport during my undergraduate studies. Given our positive past interactions, I believed he would be an excellent mentor. I requested his review of my application package, during which he discovered I was a Vietnam War veteran. Unfortunately, he harbored a strong disdain for the war, and everything associated with it. He viewed the war as inherently evil, and this perspective extended to veterans, whom he considered both evil and foolish. This revelation led me to believe that his treatment towards me was influenced by my veteran status, a realization that served as a harsh lesson.

Despite this initial setback, I remained determined and consistently sent him drafts of my thesis. I even took time off from work to personally deliver these drafts to his office in College Park. However, he consistently failed to provide feedback. After numerous unsuccessful attempts, I approached the Dean of the University of Maryland Graduate School and requested a change in academic advisor.

I was fortunate to be assigned another advisor, a 29-year-old psychologist who had recently earned his Ph.D. His guidance was invaluable from the start, significantly influencing my academic direction. Our discussions about his academic achievements provided insights and examples of how I could pursue advanced education, potentially to the Ph.D. level.

However, life's unforeseen circumstances such as a divorce shifted my aspirations and plans. Echoing the Rolling Stones, "You can't always get what you want, but if you try sometimes, you'll find you get what you need." I adapted to these changes and moved forward.

The importance of a master's degree cannot be understated. When I graduated in 1984, I felt immense gratitude for achieving such a significant milestone. This accomplishment opened numerous doors in the field of information technology, offering me abundant opportunities.

Reflecting on my career, I occasionally wonder if pursuing a Ph.D. would have provided the same range and depth of challenging and rewarding projects I have been privileged to work on. Although there are moments when I ponder continuing my academic journey, these thoughts are infrequent and fleeting.

Data Centers and New Family Members

Over time the term data center has seemed to have evolved into what is now called the "cloud." Nevertheless, cloud computing is slightly different from data centers. A data center is a facility used to house computer systems and associated components, such as telecommunications and storage systems. Cloud computing[36] on the other hand is the on-demand availability of computer system resources, especially data storage and computing power, without direct active management by the user.

Most of my extracurricular work assignments were in or somehow associated with SSA's data center. I was becoming very knowledgeable in all aspects of their complex operations. Like humans, data centers have a lifespan, with different events marking each stage of their existence. They have an extended and sometimes painful beginning because building a data center is complex. A data center may have had a difficult birth but then had a long and productive life. Like people, data centers pass through multiple relationships in their lifetimes. They form lasting partnerships with owners and other clients operating within their space. They may become part of a more prominent family or spinoff because of mergers and acquisitions or because owners want to increase market share.

---

[36] Cloud computing is on-demand access, via the internet, to computing resources—applications, servers (physical servers and virtual servers), data storage, development tools, networking capabilities, and more—hosted at a remote data center managed by a cloud services provider (or CSP). The CSP makes these resources available for a monthly subscription fee or bills them according to usage.

After successfully completing a major data center programming project, my next assignment at the SSA would be a significant turning point in my life. Little did I know then, it would open doors to a new and exciting chapter that I had never anticipated. The task at hand was to collaborate with the General Services Administration (GSA) on a major data center upgrade, involving renovations to the SSA computer rooms and programming work areas. This endeavor, known as the data center facilities project, carried immense importance.

Given the challenging and intricate nature of the project, my supervisor's decision to assign it to me was both flattering and daunting. She entrusted me with the responsibility to liaise with the regional GSA administrator, Jack Booz, a retired Marine known for his assertive demeanor. Stories of his forceful presence and tendency to hire former Marines circulated, and many found themselves intimidated by his reputation, as his booming voice could reportedly be heard for miles when he became angry.

Jack Booz held a position comparable to that of a corporate president and was among the highest-ranking employees at GSA. Prior to my meeting with him, my supervisor provided me with a brief overview of his background and emphasized that she believed no one else was better suited for this task than me. Honestly, I believe it was my Army experience that gave her that confidence. Nonetheless, I was grateful for her confidence in my abilities, I thanked her and eagerly reviewed the project documentation at my desk in preparation for my meeting with Booz the following morning.

The significance of the assignment weighed heavily on my mind throughout the day and persisted into the evening. I was determined to leave a positive and lasting impression, I carefully selected a three-piece suit and ensured my shoes were impeccably polished. The following morning, I drove to the GSA office, where I was warmly greeted by Bernie Segal upon my arrival. Bernie and I had collaborated on previous SSA/GSA projects, fostering an excellent working relationship.

I explained to Bernie that my supervisor at SSA had assigned me to the data center upgrade and had suggested arranging a kickoff meeting with Mr. Booz to discuss the project. Bernie informed me that Mr. Booz was tied up in a conference call and running behind schedule. In the meantime, Bernie introduced me to the entire staff, a group consisting of retired military personnel or individuals who had served in the Marine Corps. We engaged in lively conversations about our military experiences helping pass the time until Mr. Booz became available.

At last, the much-anticipated moment arrived as Mr. Booz, an imposing figure towering above me, approached. Despite my nervousness, I endeavored to hide my unease as he drew near. I extended my hand to introduce myself, resolute in creating a favorable and lasting impression.

When I greeted Mr. Booz with a friendly "Hello, Mr. Booz, I'm Bob Rodweller," he held onto my hand instead of releasing it. He maintained his handshake and, while looking directly into my eyes, said, "Bob, it's good to see you again. Come into my office." He gestured for me to sit and offered me a cup of coffee. Then, he surprised me by asking, "Bob, do you remember that your father and I were in the Marine Corps together? I haven't seen you since you were a little boy."

I was surprised by his statement. It seemed impossible. My father had four children, and I was fairly certain the Marine Corps wouldn't have accepted him during WWII. As I reflect on this encounter, I can't help but burst into laughter because I was so caught off guard. It was such an unexpected revelation that I felt like I had been transported to a different reality. The whole situation made me quite uncomfortable, and I distinctly remember thinking I had entered some alternate universe.

Fueled by determination, I mustered all my courage and responded, "No, Mr. Booz, I wasn't aware of that." I remembered my supervisor had advised me against disagreeing or saying no to Mr. Jack Booz. Recognizing the importance of being a team player and avoiding conflicts with Mr. Booz, I decided to navigate the situation without causing any disruptions.

Although I wanted to support my supervisor, the initial meeting with Jack Booz seemed to be veering off course rapidly. I wasn't certain about the conversation's direction, but I decided to go along and see where it led.

Believing I didn't remember my father's Marine history, he continued telling me how he and my father were in the Pacific together and fought on almost every island campaign in the Pacific theater during World War II. Their combat ended when they were wounded and sent back to the United States for medical care and recovery. He said they were both assigned to teach Reserve Officers' Training Corps (ROTC) program classes at Princeton University.

He asked me how my father and mother were doing these days. I sat there for what seemed like an eternity while pondering my response to this question. I took a deep breath and said, "Mr. Booz, I believe you're mistaken." He looked at me like I was from another planet, then shaking his head, he said, "Oh no, I think you're mistaken. Let me show you our association directory. You'll see your father's name and rank right here with many of us who fought together in the Pacific. Also, he was from Princeton, New Jersey." I tried to interject and explain my family's move to Baltimore from Princeton at the beginning of World War II. We both went on for the better part of a half-hour before we realized that Jack Booz was talking about my father's stepbrother unknown to me at that time, Leo Rodweller. It was a long and convoluted conversation, and I feared he would be angry.

To my surprise, he wasn't angry and asked me about my service in the Army. I'm sure Bernie Segal had told him about me before arriving. I explained I was a trained and experienced flight engineer on a CH-47 and a private pilot. I then explained I was in the 23rd Infantry division, the largest in Vietnam, flying daily combat for 15 months and how another battle buddy and I had mixed it up with a Vietnamese 122-millimeter rocket and that the rocket won that fight. He asked many questions about my training and education in and out of the Army.

Before that pivotal meeting, I had no knowledge of the existence of my step-uncle, Leo, and my aunt, Florence, who resided in Warwick, Rhode Island. My parents had never mentioned them during my upbringing, leaving me entirely unaware of their presence in my extended family. It was only when Jack Booz provided me with their contact information that I learned about their connection to me. According to Jack, Leo had enlisted in the Marine Corps in 1939 and had enjoyed a successful career spanning two decades. It was during his service in the Marines that he met his wife, Florence.

Jack emphasized, in a commanding tone, that I should call Leo and Florence that very night, introduce myself and convey his regards. Furthermore, he expected a detailed status report on my call with them first thing the next morning. Responding with a respectful "Yes sir," I agreed to carry out his directive. It felt like I had been given a mission order and was determined to execute it successfully. Finally, after a two-hour interview, we shifted our focus to the data center facilities project.

Later in the evening, after dinner, I dialed the number Jack had provided. The phone rang several times before eventually diverting to voicemail. Leaving a message that identified myself and the purpose of my call. I hoped Leo and Florence would return my call. The following morning, I arrived at work early, filled with a sense of duty akin to that of a young Marine under strict command. Aware of Jack's expectations for a status report, I felt a mixture of apprehension and determination. I feared he might perceive my failure to reach Leo and Florence as a shortcoming. Drawing a deep breath, reminiscent of my experiences in Vietnam when embarking on daunting missions, I dialed Mr. Booz's number, ready to provide my report.

I called so early that he and many of his staff hadn't yet arrived at work. I felt so relieved because I called before the boss arrived at work. I immediately thought, Rodweller, that's one gold star for initiative in your plus column. Jack Booz will like that. I then walked to my supervisor's desk, provided her with a status update, and told her the entire story. At first, I believed she was worried. Because she sat in her chair for a minute, not responding to what I told her, finally she smiled, saying, "Jack will love you. I'm sure you and he will get along just fine. Don't worry. This will turn out great." I thought about her confidence in me and hoped she was correct.

After finishing our conversation, I returned to my desk feeling a mix of relief and satisfaction. I dialed Jack Booz's number once again, and to my surprise, he answered on the second ring. It impressed me that someone of his stature would pick up his phone. Throughout our conversation, he displayed a remarkably friendly demeanor, as if we had been long-time friends.

I proceeded to provide him with my status report, anxiously awaiting his response. However, instead of criticism or yelling, he calmly asked me to keep him informed and requested that I convey his greetings to Leo and Florence when I spoke with them. I assured him that I would fulfill his request. Before concluding the call, he expressed his anticipation for working together on the data center facilities project. I expressed my gratitude for everything, especially the unexpected discovery of my previously unknown aunt and uncle and conveyed my excitement about collaborating with him as well.

Engaging in the data center facilities project proved to be an invaluable opportunity for me to expand my knowledge and expertise in upgrading not just the data center, but also various other facilities and building skills. When the project was successfully implemented, I was pleased that management recognized my ability to handle such a complex endeavor. This undertaking was just one of many successful projects involving the creation or upgrade of computer centers throughout my career. I was grateful to have had the guidance and mentorship of professionals like Jack Booz and his staff.

A week later, Leo and Florence returned my call, informing me that they had been golfing in Hilton Head, South Carolina. That evening, we engaged in a delightful hour-long conversation, catching up on family information and backgrounds. They mentioned their plans for another trip to South Carolina in a month and a half and expressed their willingness to stop by my house in Baltimore if their schedule permitted. The following morning, I promptly contacted Jack Booz again, providing him with an update on my conversation with Leo and Florence. Judging by his tone, I could sense his satisfaction, and he even requested that Leo and Florence call him if they had the time.

I discovered an uncle and aunt from this facility project assignment with Jack Booz. I also established a close relationship with a senior executive GSA regional administrator. Jack Booz was one of the kindest and most professional people I enjoyed working with over my career. I believe he used his rough and gruff Marine persona to keep individuals in line. But once he got to know me, he was like a best friend, great neighbor, and mentor. Several times, I considered applying for promotional positions within his GSA organization but didn't because of my love for technology.

Leo and Florence's visit to my house on their way to South Carolina was a memorable occasion. When I opened the front door and saw Leo for the first time, it felt as if my father stood before me. The resemblance between them was striking, with the only notable difference being Leo's robust, barrel-chested physique I suppose developed from his years of service in the Marine Corps. It was a truly wonderful visit, and it became evident that Leo and Florence were exceptional individuals. They shared many captivating stories from their time in the Marines and their life together. They had a son named Robert Allan Rodweller, who was born in 1953 and happened to be five years younger than me. Unfortunately, Robert Allan and I never had the opportunity to form a close bond over the years. Tragically, Robert Allan Rodweller passed away in 2015 at the age of 62.

After discovering my newfound uncle and aunt, we would have numerous visits over the following years. Whenever Leo and Florence visited me in Baltimore, I would take them to explore the historical sites in Maryland and Washington, D.C. I would occasionally call them to say hello and check in on their well-being between our visits. Sadly, Leo developed bone cancer and passed away on November 12, 1998. Florence asked me if I would speak at Leo's funeral in Palm Bay, Florida. I was deeply honored by her request and readily agreed. I vividly remember observing the anguish on the face of my cousin Robert Alan who seemed to struggle with his emotions throughout the service. Perhaps Florence entrusted me with speaking because she knew Robert Alan would have been very emotional. During my speech, I recounted how I discovered Leo and Florence's existence, our journey of reconnecting, and emphasized what an extraordinary individual Leo was. I also highlighted his remarkable career in the Marine Corps and the incredible life he and Florence had built together. After the funeral, as I drove away from Palm Bay a profound sense of loss enveloped me. A newfound part of myself had been taken away, and I was filled with sorrow and grief throughout the journey to the airport.

Florence stayed in Palm Bay, and Cathy, Casey, and I would visit her from time to time. In 2012, Cathy and I moved to Fayetteville, Arkansas, and that first Christmas, we decided to go on a Caribbean cruise with Casey, who still lived in Baltimore. We arranged for Casey to meet us in Miami several days before our cruise departure. We rented a car, drove to Melbourne, and visited Florence during our stay. She had moved into a lovely assisted-living facility in Palm Bay, not far from the ocean. We spent the night in Melbourne, picked Florence up the following morning, and spent the day visiting with her and taking in the sights of Melbourne. It was a wonderful experience for all of us. We continue to call and visit with Florence. In September 2023, she celebrated her 99th birthday and continues going strong.

Another GSA Project

Thanks to the success of the GSA/SSA facilities data center project, I was consistently assigned to other GSA projects involving minor aspects of technology. One of these projects, which was truly unconventional, involved repainting the parking spaces at one of the SSA outlying buildings.

As a technical person, I couldn't comprehend why I was involved in such a task. However, I soon realized that the building housed a small data center, making it relevant to my expertise. While it may have been a stretch to consider it a technology project, I saw it as an opportunity to expand my knowledge, gain experience, and meet new people.

The project entailed reducing the size of each parking space, because the SSA needed to accommodate more cars with its limited 21,000 parking spaces for 37,000 employees. The SSA administration contracted with GSA for a contractor to handle the work. This was the first of several parking lots to be restriped. Unfortunately, the precise project requirements were either changed or inadequately documented during the contracting process. This led to complications once the project began. The lack of clarity in the contract documents would pose significant challenges throughout the entire endeavor.

I arrived early with the project documentation, taking the time to acquaint myself with the requirements and tasks. However, on Saturday, the GSA contractor arrived with just three individuals to undertake the job, even though its scale necessitated a team of at least six people. The task involved restriping the parking lots and having them ready for employee use by 5 a.m. on Monday morning. Given the limited manpower, this seemed like an almost insurmountable challenge.

I approached the contractor supervisor and suggested I could assist if he showed me how to mark the asphalt for the new striping. Most of the time was spent on taping, painting, and cleanup, while the preparation work of marking the new parking spaces could be done by me. Although it was an unconventional project, I found enjoyment in the work. Mark Twain once wrote, "Find a job you enjoy doing, and you will never have to work a day in your life." I considered myself fortunate to have fun and get paid for it. I saw this weekend project as an opportunity to learn a new skill, marking and striping parking lots. While I may not have another opportunity to do asphalt striping, it added to my repertoire of skills, abilities, and experiences. Even today, when I come across parking lot striping, I'm reminded of that enjoyable weekend project.

Project Planning

In the 1970s, project planning wasn't widely practiced at the Social Security Administration (SSA). Supervisors often delegated tasks based on trust and relationships. When I began developing training classes, I introduced project planning, its history, and benefits to introductory technology courses. Many SSA managers and technical staff found this new concept challenging, preferring traditional planning methods. However, as the technology industry evolved, SSA needed to adopt more structured planning and development processes.

Previously, SSA employed project planning sporadically, mainly for significant projects, using the waterfall development methodology. This linear approach required completing each project phase—analysis, design, development, testing—before moving to the next. While effective for issue identification, the waterfall method didn't always catch all potential project problems, leading to work duplication or delays when necessary, staff were unavailable for programming tasks.

Trained at the University of Maryland in the latest project planning and scheduling methods, I advocated for their use at SSA, despite resistance from many supervisors who found the structured planning process too complex. To gain practical experience and demonstrate the value of project planning, I created project plans and GANTT charts for myself and the project teams. Eventually, I developed ways to consolidate multiple projects into a single master project plan, facilitating simultaneous review and status checks of several projects and identifying potential inter-project impacts.

Over time, recognizing the advantages of project planning, SSA's technology management acquired the Artemis mainframe project planning software. Artemis, a pioneering package combining project planning, scheduling, cost control, and resource management, required substantial investment in large tabletop color printers. It was also the world's first commercially successful relational database system. As a programmer working with Artemis, I deepened my expertise in relational databases and project planning. Tasked with evaluating the software's cost-effectiveness annually, I confirmed its break-even point after three years, validating the investment.

Throughout my time at SSA, I consistently requested access to this planning software in new positions, appreciating its benefits across the project lifecycle. I helped others unfamiliar with the application or planning principles learn how to use the software, supporting the team's goals and objectives.

As project planning processes matured, companies like Microsoft developed similar software for personal computers. Initially basic and challenging to use, this software evolved into a suite aiding developers and professionals in various fields. Utilizing this PC-based software even in management roles, I was asked to develop a training class on planning and scheduling. This experience allowed me to address programmers' planning challenges, offering solutions that were integrated into future training.

Advancing into management, I led programming teams and modernization efforts at SSA, transitioning from technical duties to a strategic managerial role. As a technology program manager, I balanced various responsibilities, including design, development, finance, cost control, scheduling, coordination, and subcontractor management.

This promotion didn't mean abandoning my technical roots; instead, it offered a chance to blend management and technical work. Initially, I risked stepping out of my managerial role to help develop classes in new programming languages, learning them first. I enjoyed leading user requirements meetings and creating documents, a blend of technical and management tasks that satisfied my passion for technology. Working on projects with over a million lines of code was tedious but fulfilling, allowing me to indulge in what I viewed as a hobby rather than just a job.

Social Security Solvency

In the 1980s, concerns about the solvency of the Social Security system were prevalent among many individuals. As someone working with actuaries, I had firsthand involvement in creating tables that would be incorporated in the programming changes made to various SSA programs. I also began questioning the long-term financial viability of the Social Security program. It became evident that the program was on the verge of bankruptcy during that period.

Witnessing wasteful practices within the system, I found it hard to imagine Social Security surviving as a national program. I would engage in discussions with others daily, as we were programming the applications and were intimately familiar with the issues at hand. Elected officials in Washington, D.C., must have also recognized the severity of the situation, as they received our weekly reports on issues and statistical analysis from the actuaries.

Prior to this time, President Jimmy Carter was in office, and the Social Security program was facing the depletion of its asset reserves. I remember reading a trustee's report that contained alarming recommendations aimed at restoring fiscal stability to the program. This report caught President Carter's attention, leading his administration to work with Congress to amend the Social Security legislation. These amendments included raising the payroll tax, increasing the maximum amount of earned income subject to Social Security taxes, reducing benefits, and removing the annual cost-of-living adjustment (COLA). As a result, technology had to be modified to implement these program changes. Despite these efforts, it was widely believed that additional changes would be necessary within five years, given the rapid depletion of the trust fund.

In the early 1970s, Alan Greenspan assumed the role of Chairman of the Council of Economic Advisers under President Gerald Ford. Through this position, Greenspan established a significant network of political connections, which would prove valuable in the future. In 1981, President Reagan appointed Greenspan as the Chairman of the National Commission on Social Security Reform. Prior to these appointments, Greenspan had served as Chairman and President of Townsend-Greenspan & Co., Inc., an economics consulting firm based in New York City.

Two years after its formation, the National Commission on Social Security Reform issued a report outlining recommendations for Social Security reform. Following the report's release, President Reagan appointed Greenspan as Chairman of the National Commission on Social Security Reform to oversee the implementation of the Social Security Amendments of 1983.

The amendments made to the Social Security system in 1983 did indeed involve a significant increase in the payroll tax. The intention was to generate surpluses that would support the program for the next three decades. These surpluses were to be saved and invested in marketable Treasury bonds, which could be sold in the future to provide the necessary funds for benefit payments. It was believed that this approach would ensure the financial stability of Social Security.

However, as an employee at the SSA, witnessing the inner workings of the program, I grew skeptical of relying solely on Social Security for retirement income. This skepticism led me to seek out an investment advisor to establish a retirement-saving plan. I questioned the feasibility of the government's promise to provide Social Security benefits as the primary source of income for millions of Americans during their retirement years. I felt that many individuals would not receive a full refund of the money deducted from their paychecks over their lifetimes.

Alan Greenspan, in his role as an influential figure, played a significant part in another issue that impacted Social Security. He advocated for raising Social Security taxes and using the revenue for non-Social Security purposes. The over $3 trillion generated from the 1983 payroll tax increase was diverted from Social Security and combined with general revenue funds, which were then spent on other government programs. In return, the Social Security trust fund received non-marketable government IOUs known as special issues of the Treasury. These IOUs could not be sold or redeemed for their full value.

President Ronald Reagan and his advisers were aware of the impending cash shortage faced by the government. The substantial cuts in income tax rates, a key aspect of the new supply-side economics, were not sustainable in the long run. To bridge this gap, Reagan implemented Greenspan's proposal to increase the Social Security payroll tax. The additional revenue from the tax increase would be transferred to the general treasury funds and used to finance government operations while avoiding massive deficits. Raising Social Security taxes was seen as a politically viable alternative to increasing national income tax rates at the time. The preservation of Reagan's income tax cuts was seen as a positive outcome, and both Reagan and Greenspan received praise for their efforts to ensure the long-term solvency of the Social Security program.

I was working on enhancements to the Social Security payments systems to ensure the Social Security program would not go into bankruptcy. I learned a lot about politics in Washington and how most politicians were more focused on their pet projects than on supporting the taxpayer. I along with my branch of programmers and analysts reported directly to Greenspan. This organizational change meant I would provide Greenspan with in-person updates on our progress with program enhancements. I learned so much. It was an exciting time for all of us. We worked so many hours that occasionally, I would take everyone out for dinner on a Friday night.

One Friday evening, we had dinner at Tio Pepe's in downtown Baltimore. It was the only restaurant in Baltimore that offered excellent authentic, Spanish and Mediterranean food at a very reasonable price. Price was an essential consideration of restaurants because I was paying for everyone's dinner and drinks. Restaurant Tio Pepe was a real treat because it was a one-of-a-kind experience.

Tio Pepe was known for its Sangria wine served in handmade pitchers. It was the perfect combination of blended fresh fruits, liqueurs, and chilled wine. I was trying to be the life of the party and ensured plenty of Sangria was on our table. It wasn't long before most of us had consumed too much Sangria. Our group was feeling the effects of the Sangria when one of the programmers spotted Greenspan in the restaurant.

My team members encouraged me to go over and say hello to the boss. This challenge continued for about 20 minutes. I finished two additional glasses of sangria, got up, and walked over to the table where Greenspan and his date were eating dinner. Because of my consumption of Sangria that evening, I'm unsure if it was Barbara Walters or his wife-to-be, Andrea Mitchell. I said hello and introduced myself to the lady at the table. She said, "Hello, Bob. Alan has told me about you." I sat down and began talking about how exciting it was to work with Mr. Greenspan. While I was talking, Greenspan continued eating his meal.

I finally got the hint to leave them alone, got up, said my goodbyes, and walked back to my table. I didn't think I embarrassed myself too much and believed I was polite. After returning to SSA the following Monday, I was worried that Greenspan might say something when I briefed him on Monday morning, like, don't ever bother me again when I'm outside of work having dinner. To my surprise, over the following weeks and months, Greenspan never commented on our brief restaurant encounter. For some reason, he did appear to be friendlier toward me, however.

After the resignation of Chairman Paul Volcker in 1987, President Reagan appointed Greenspan Chairman of the Board of Governors of the Federal Reserve (the Fed). This appointment didn't come as a surprise to those who knew or worked for Greenspan. He was the consummate politician. He knew exactly what he wanted and pursued it with a passion. He certainly had the President's attention due to the improvement in the Social Security program as a revenue generator for the rest of the United States government.

In 1991, President George H.W. Bush nominated Greenspan for a second term as Federal Reserve Chairman of the Federal Reserve's Board of Governors, and the Senate confirmed his nomination. President Bill Clinton appointed him Federal Reserve chairman for his third and fourth terms. President George W. Bush appointed him for his fifth and final term, which concluded in 2006.

Health Care Financing Administration Data Center

During one of many reorganizations at the Social Security Administration (SSA), a new healthcare component was formed that needed a separate data center. I was reassigned to this division to oversee the design, development, and equipment acquisition for this new data center. Since no data center buildings were available at the SSA, we leased a warehouse to set up a temporary data center. While I enjoyed the work, it was demanding and required me to work seven days a week for over a year.

On a particularly stressful day, I found myself frustrated with certain individuals causing project delays. These individuals weren't directly under my supervision due to our matrix management system. In this system, employees report to multiple supervisors across different organizational units. I wasn't a fan of this approach because it made it challenging to evaluate an employee's overall performance when they weren't solely under my purview.

At that time, SSA had not provided adequate training for this new management structure, leading to widespread confusion and inefficiency. Even though senior management was enamored with the cost-saving potential of matrix management, the reality was far messier in day-to-day operations.

Feeling exasperated, I was approached by a co-worker who noticed my distress. He encouraged me to "Be Bob"—to step back and objectively assess the situation. Taking his advice to heart, I spoke directly to the supervisor of the individuals causing the delays.

When I returned to the data center, these individuals were waiting for me. We had an open discussion and discovered that the root of the issue wasn't with me or them. Rather, their home unit's supervisor had not fully embraced the matrix management concept, inadvertently causing bottlenecks in multiple departments. After addressing this with their supervisor, the individuals became much more productive and contributed meaningfully to the project.

This experience taught me several important lessons. Firstly, my exhaustion had clouded my judgment and prevented me from identifying the underlying issues. Secondly, taking a moment to reassess the situation allowed me to find a constructive solution. Overall, it reminded me that even when working under intense pressure, taking a step back to assess the situation can make all the difference.

In our temporary warehouse data center operations, everything was going well. We were providing additional online user capabilities daily. Because the data center was operating within a warehouse there wasn't adequate air conditioning for all the computer equipment. We had installed large free-standing air-conditioners to cool the main processor rooms in place of large rooftop units that had been used for traditional data centers. We had to inspect these air conditioning units several times daily and manually replenish the water supply for cooling. It was humorous to see a person in a suit carrying two buckets of water to replenish the air conditioning units. This continued for approximately three months until permanent traditional rooftop air conditioning units were purchased and installed.

Our daily operations had finally settled into a normal data center routine. We were able to complete our day-to-day operations without disruptions. But then, one Thursday afternoon, I finished filling the water supplies and was headed home. Everyone had already left for the day. Extremely heavy rainstorms were in the forecast. Walking out of the building, I saw Marv Ferguson working at his desk. Marv was the senior programmer in charge of transferring and operating the existing programs from SSA to the new data center. Walking toward the door to leave, I said, "Don't stay too long because heavy rain is forecast in the area." He replied he had to remain at work until the storm was over because he had ridden his motorcycle that day.

246

On my drive home, the sky opened, and it began to thunder and lightning. It rained so heavily it was hard to see the road surface or markings. It was almost impossible to see the road ahead of me, making for very dangerous driving. My usual commute would only take about 12 minutes, but this day it took me almost 30 minutes before I arrived home. As I parked the car, my pager went off, and I saw Marv's work phone number. Once inside my house, I dried myself off and immediately returned Marv's telephone call. He informed me that he believed a tornado had hit the data center and that most of the building was destroyed. It took less than 10 minutes for me to return to work because of my speed, and there was hardly any traffic on the roads.

When I returned to our temporary data center, a scene of devastation unfolded before my eyes. The destructive force of the tornado had mercilessly rampaged through the building, leaving behind a trail of utter destruction. The sheer brutality of its impact was evident in the twisted remnants of the once-sturdy structure. The roof had been mercilessly torn away, leaving exposed sections throughout the structure. The recently installed air conditioning units were still in place because they were bolted to heavy steel anchor beams. Broken glass from the shattered windows littered both the interior and exterior, a testament to the ferocity of the event. Marv, visibly shaken, awaited me outside. His tense demeanor gradually eased as we engaged in conversation. It was then that a realization struck me like lightning—the equipment inside was still operational and in dire need of an immediate shutdown.

Without a moment's hesitation, I sprinted through the waterlogged premises, wading through nearly two-and-a-half inches of water, determined to reach the circuit breaker panel. Each step was an exercise in urgency. Flipping breaker switches one by one, I cut off the electricity supply to every piece of equipment, ensuring their safety. It was in that moment, as I turned to survey the main circuit breaker, that I fully comprehended the peril I had just escaped. The enormity of my luck sank in. My heart raced at the realization that I had risked electrocution by sprinting through that treacherous water. Because of a loose connection or a frayed power cord exposing electrical current to the water. Talk about a narrow escape. It sent shivers down my spine.

After the power went out, I proceeded with caution, navigating around glass and debris, until I reached Marv's desk. This desk was positioned at the center of the data center's programming area. Right in the middle of his desk, there lay his motorcycle helmet, pierced by a large shard of thick window glass that had broken. The glass was sticking through both sides of the helmet. Had Marv been sitting in his chair at that moment, the glass would have passed through the center of his back and emerged from the front of his chest.

Fortunately, Marv managed to escape harm on that particular day by finding shelter in one of the inner offices, which happened to have sturdy brick walls. Interestingly, despite the close call, Marv chose not to wear his helmet as he rode his motorcycle home later that evening. It crossed my mind that he might have kept the damaged helmet as a memento, proudly displaying it to his family and friends, akin to a trophy.

Almost immediately, we were back to work rebuilding the data center. The rebuilding took several months, but this time, it went much faster because of the initial experience in setting it up. Thankfully, almost all the equipment was still salvageable and operational. Vendors were extremely helpful in obtaining the needed replacement equipment and materiel in noticeably short timeframes.

Dedication of Vietnam Veterans Memorial, November 13, 1982

In 1979, the Vietnam Veterans Memorial Fund (VVMF) was established by Vietnam veterans to honor those who lost their lives or went missing during the Vietnam War. They successfully raised $8.4 million for the construction of the memorial. The chosen location for the memorial was a three-acre site adjacent to the National Mall, northeast of the Lincoln Memorial. To make space for the memorial, an old-World War I munitions building was demolished with the approval of Congress.

To determine the design of the Vietnam War memorial, a national competition was organized. A total of 1,421 design submissions were received and meticulously reviewed by the selection committee. The winning design, chosen from these submissions, was created by Maya Lin, an American designer and sculptor. Maya Lin grew up as a second-generation Chinese born in the United States after her parents immigrated from China in the 1940s. Her East Asian heritage shaped her world through her parents' upbringing. When she won the competition, she was an undergraduate student at Yale. Her design featured a unique V-shaped reflective black granite wall that stretched for 493 feet. Initially, the design faced opposition due to its unconventional nature due to the black color, and lack of ornamentation. Within the VVMF, it was even referred to as a "black gash of shame." James Watt, the Secretary of the Interior under President Ronald Reagan, initially denied a permit for the memorial. However, a compromise was eventually reached, with the agreement to include a bronze statue of American soldiers near the left side of the wall.

Construction on the memorial commenced on March 26, 1982. The stone for the monument, sourced from India, was specifically chosen for its highly reflective surface. The stone cutting process took place in Vermont, while the sandblasting and etching of the 57,939 names into the stone was completed in Tennessee. As of May 4, 2021, the wall bears the names of 58,281[37] men and women who were either missing or killed in the Vietnam War. As someone residing in Washington, D.C., at the time, I had the privilege of witnessing the progress of the wall's construction. I would visit the site nearly every week to observe the ongoing work. During one of these visits, I had the fortunate opportunity to meet Maya Lin in person. We engaged in a lengthy conversation about her design and submission.

Maya Lin was an engaging young lady who took a keen interest in my background as a Vietnam veteran. She inquired about my experiences in Vietnam and my subsequent career in technology. Our discussion delved into how I became passionate about computers. As we walked together, I shared how the aviation industry began using the term "computer" in the 1960s and how captivated I was by this new technology. I then described my insatiable desire to learn everything I could about it, which eventually led to a lifelong appreciation for and involvement with technology.

While strolling along the reflecting pool in front of the Lincoln Memorial, Maya Lin explained her entire design process. She mentioned

---

[37] 2021 Name Additions and Status Changes on the Vietnam Veterans Memorial: https://www.vvmf.org/News/2021-Name-Additions-and-Status-Changes-on-the-Vietnam-Veterans-Memorial/

that one of her classmates had come across a competition poster calling for designs for a Vietnam Veterans memorial in Washington, D.C. Since Maya and her classmates had recently completed a project involving the creation of a memorial for World War II, they decided to conclude the course with this undertaking.

In researching their previous assignment on war memorials, Maya noticed how war memorials were not consistent in how the fallen were recognized. Some listed only the victors or high-ranking officers rather than the individual soldiers who had lost their lives in combat. The use of basic identification tags, akin to today's "dog tags," emerged during World War I. Soldiers in the trenches of France were issued two coin-like metal discs, each marked with their name. They would wear these tags into combat, with one staying on their remains if they were killed. However, even with these rudimentary dog tags,[38] not all fallen soldiers could be identified.

She explained that the sight of dog tags had a profound emotional impact on her and inspired her to focus on honoring each individual soldier who had lost their life. She described her vision of cutting open the earth and inserting a memorial while engraving the names of the fallen soldiers and polishing the exposed sides like a geode. She was inspired by the geode rock formations and the idea of a wound that is closed and healing.

When her class received the competition details and guidelines, it was specified that all the names of the fallen soldiers needed to be included, and the memorial should be apolitical and contemplative. Her design evolved from the geode concept into two black granite walls below ground level. The names of the men and women who died in the Vietnam War were engraved chronologically. At the meeting point of the two walls, or the apex, an inscription read:

> In honor of the men and women of the Armed Forces of the United States who served in the Vietnam War. The names of those who gave their lives and of those who remain missing are inscribed in the order they were taken from us.

---

[38] Dog Tag History: How the Tradition & Nickname Started https://www.de-fense.gov/News/Inside-DOD/Blog/Article/2340760/dog-tag-history-how-the-tra-dition-nickname-started/

The dates 1959 and 1975 marked the beginning and end of the war, symbolically closing the circle of the war period. Maya Lin intended for veterans to find their time of service on the wall and for visitors to see their reflections in the names they viewed, aiming to establish a personal and intimate connection between each viewer, the soldier's name and the memorial.

The placement of the memorial was intentionally related to the nearby Lincoln Memorial and Washington Monument, both physically and historically, creating a connection between the three landmarks. As her semester was ending, she decided to enter her design in the spring competition, not with the expectation of winning, but to convey a message about making the memorial personal, human, and centered on individual experiences. I distinctly recall Maya Lin expressing her intention to present that time of conflict truthfully, encouraging reflection on our relationship with war and loss. I expressed my gratitude to her, acknowledging how her design made me reflect on my own time in the war and the friends I had lost. The extraordinary meeting and experience on that Saturday have stayed with me over the years.

Construction of the wall concluded in late October 1982, and preparations for the dedication ceremony began promptly. A week-long tribute to Vietnam veterans preceded the dedication, with thousands of veterans marching through Washington on November 13, 1982, to attend the ceremony. During the parade, I had the opportunity to greet General Westmoreland and exchange waves with several fellow veterans. It was a brisk, chilly day in Washington, D.C., and I was accompanied by Rose, John and Beverly LeCates.

The poignant theme from the movie "Chariots of Fire" played near the memorial, setting a dramatic tone for the ceremony. The event drew a crowd of 150,000 people and was broadcast live on local Washington, D.C., radio and television stations. One veteran expressed, "Being known as a Vietnam veteran used to be a dubious distinction, but on that day the situation changed." Another speaker proclaimed, "This memorial symbolizes the sacrifice of over 58,000 young Americans and renews our awareness of our collective capacity." Even with that speaker's comments I found it challenging to contain my anger and emotions due to the difficulties I had faced upon returning to the United States. I am certain I was not the only one who felt that way on that momentous day!

I believe the most significant additions to the Vietnam Veterans Memorial were made two years after the initial ceremony. These additions include The Three Soldiers sculptures, depicting a Marine and two Army soldiers of different races. In 1993, the Vietnam Women's Memorial was added, featuring uniformed women nurses providing aid to a wounded soldier. Finally, in 2004, a memorial plaque was installed, honoring the men and women who served in the Vietnam War and later died due to their service.

Trip to New Zealand

Because of the data center project, I found myself with a considerable amount of unused vacation and compensatory time. When my management suggested taking some time off, I didn't hesitate. I really needed this type of break, and I excitedly planned a 34-day adventure in New Zealand during 1984. To kick off my trip, I spent the first week at the stunning hillside home of my friends, Joan and Brian Smith, in Auckland. They managed the hotel I stayed at during my R&R visit to Sydney in 1969. It was a great reunion!

While in Auckland, I embarked on several day trips. One memorable excursion took me north to the Ninety Mile Beach, a stretch of coastline boasting magnificent sand dunes at the tip of New Zealand's North Island. Along the way, I encountered numerous delays due to sheep leisurely crossing the roads. Those wooly creatures seemed more interested in engaging me in their own language of "Baa, Baa" than in letting me pass.

Sitting in my rental car, engine off, I found myself captivated by their antics. In that moment, I realized there was no need to rush. After all, I might never have the chance to experience this again, and the sheep appeared to enjoy our peculiar form of communication. Finally arriving at the beach, I was awestruck by its sheer beauty. The area, both on and off the beach, felt like an endless paradise. I also discovered an interesting fact, despite being called Ninety Mile Beach, it measured only 56 miles in length. Nonetheless, it remained a true paradise in my eyes.

Ninety Mile Beach, officially designated as a highway, is a captivating destination. However, it's important to note that only 4WD vehicles can navigate its sandy terrain safely, and driving is only feasible during specific tide conditions. Rental companies, prioritizing safety and vehicle maintenance, prohibited their cars from venturing onto the beach. Despite this, I decided to drive my trusty little blue Toyota Corolla as close to the beach as possible before parking it. Determined to experience the wonders of the coastline, I continued on foot. I couldn't help but recall the cautionary words of the rental car employee in Auckland, advising against driving onto Ninety Mile Beach due to the risk of getting stuck or damaging the vehicle.

Returning to my car, I moved it further north and found another public parking lot, where colossal sand dunes obstructed my view of the Tasmanian Sea. The sound of crashing waves and the rhythmic pounding of the sandy beach echoed in my ears. Thankfully, a gap in the dunes beckoned me toward the beach, and as I stepped onto the other side, I was greeted by yet another breathtaking vista. To my delight, I found myself alone in this paradise, with unspoiled beauty stretching as far as the eye could see. It was a moment of pure bliss, a personal connection with nature's magnificence. I was tempted to spend the rest of my trip in this idyllic spot, but practicality prevailed. Nonetheless, I savored every second as I strolled along the most captivating beach I had ever encountered.

On another day, my adventurous spirit led me to Whangarei, a traditional native Maori village adorned with homes and shops built by the Maori people. Known as Whangarei Terenga Paräoa, meaning "the swimming place of the whales," this village witnessed the gathering of whales during the summer months. The term "Paräoa" referred to the revered sperm whale, a symbol of high status among the Maori people. As I wandered through this Maori wonderland, set against a backdrop of erupting geothermal activity, I couldn't help but immerse myself in the rich Maori culture. Engaging with the local shop owners, I delved into conversations about New Zealand's history and traditions. Thanks to the knowledge shared by Joan and Brian before my visit, I felt a deeper appreciation for the island's heritage and enhanced my interactions in the village.

The following day, my journey led me to Rotorua, a town and lake nestled within the embrace of an active volcano. Here, I had the extraordinary opportunity to enjoy a dinner prepared entirely using volcanic geothermal steam. Clad in traditional attire, the Maori residents skillfully prepared the meal, captivating us with descriptions and demonstrations of their ancestral language. Exploring Rotorua further, I discovered an abundance of handcrafted New Zealand Maori arts and crafts. The allure was irresistible, and I was prompted to bring home several cherished mementos that continue to remind me of that enchanting trip.

To begin the second part of my journey to the South Island I departed from Wellington, the capital of New Zealand. From Wellington I flew, to the enchanting city of Christchurch on the South Island. The flight to Christchurch was relatively short, but it presented a unique opportunity to interact with a high school rugby team who were on the same flight. The young men were eager to engage with someone from the United States, and I thoroughly enjoyed our conversations, answering their curious questions and sharing laughs along the way.

Once I checked into my hotel, I set out to explore Christchurch. In the evening, I embarked on a leisurely stroll, immersing myself in the city's English heritage. One captivating aspect of Christchurch was the Avon River, which flows through the heart of the city. The river not only showcased a diverse array of plants and animals but also served as a hub for recreational activities. Serene flat-bottomed boats gracefully glided along the water, transporting visitors to various shops dotted along the city center. As I walked, I couldn't help but notice the multitude of cyclists whizzing past me, reminding me of the joy it would be to explore this beautiful city on my own bicycle.

Alongside the banks of the Avon River, I discovered a stunning botanical garden. As I made my way through the garden, I found myself captivated by the breathtaking display of flowers adorning the river's edge. The historical buildings that graced the streets of Christchurch further added to the city's charm, evoking images reminiscent of England. Given more time, I would have gladly extended my stay, but unfortunately, a hotel reservation forced me onward to the next city. Christchurch was undoubtedly a place where one could spend several delightful days exploring, perhaps on my next trip.

The following morning, I embarked on a scenic drive along State Highway 1, tracing the southern scenic route along the eastern coast. It was an awe-inspiring journey that led me to Dunedin, yet another picturesque city nestled on New Zealand's eastern shores. The presence of Scottish influence in Dunedin was clearly evident and easily recognizable.

During one of my stops, I stumbled upon New Zealand's only castle which was constructed in 1871. I was astounded to learn that it took over 200 workers three years to build the castle's magnificent exterior. Intrigued by its grandeur, I indulged in a tour of the castle, where I discovered that master European artisans had dedicated an astonishing 12 years to completing the intricate interior. The woodworking craftsmanship and meticulously handcrafted wood paneling and trim throughout the castle were simply breathtaking.

As I wandered through Dunedin, I had the chance to speak with another store owner who shared fascinating insights about the city. He associated Dunedin's past to that of many American towns, explaining how a gold rush in the 1860s had brought prosperity to the city. The influx of gold sparked investments in education, religious buildings, and public infrastructure projects. Streets, roads, bridges, water systems, sewage systems, and waste facilities all saw significant improvements. What caught my attention was the abundance of bicycle paths throughout Dunedin. I briefly contemplated renting a bike to explore the city, but ultimately decided against it. I wanted the freedom to visit and carry items from the numerous shops and stores I planned to explore. Witnessing the bustling presence of cyclists everywhere sparked thoughts about the potential benefits of having more bike paths in cities back home in the United States. It could alleviate traffic congestion and promote a healthier lifestyle for citizens. Fortunately, there is hope, as many cities are now developing greenways and bike friendly infrastructure, just like here in Northwest AR.

Leaving Dunedin proved to be challenging, as I realized I could have easily spent more time in this enchanting city. Nevertheless, my road trip beckoned me forward, and I embarked on State Highway 1 again enjoying its stunning scenery as I journeyed to Invercargill, the southernmost city of New Zealand and the capital of the South Island. Invercargill had a distinct obsession with all things wheeled, particularly bicycles. Being a long-time follower of bicycle racing, I discovered that the city had constructed an indoor velodrome,[39] catering to those passionate about cycling around a

---

[39] In the cycling world, there are several categories of racing styles. One of the lesser-known styles is track racing, a team or individual event in which competitors ride fixed-gear—or non-coasting—bicycles with no brakes on an oval track

banked oval track. Moreover, there were dedicated truck and motorcycle museums. The motorcycle museum was particularly special, as it showcased the achievements of New Zealand's own Herbert James "Burt" Munro, who held the world speed record for Indian motorcycles for many years. The film "The World's Fastest Indian" recounted his remarkable journey to set that record by racing an Indian motorcycle on the Nevada salt flats. It was an odd experience to realize that I had actually seen the very Indian motorcycle portrayed in the movie during my visit to New Zealand. The film prompted me to delve deeper into Burt Munro's story, uncovering the remarkable details of his record-setting feat. At the age of 68, he rode a stripped-down, 47-year-old Indian motorcycle with an engine under 1,000 cc's, essentially a standard street motorcycle without any special enhancements or tires. It was a true testament to Munro's unwavering spirit and determination.

Continuing my journey northward, I arrived in Queenstown, a town that immediately felt welcoming and became my favorite destination throughout my trip in New Zealand. Its charm reminded me of the picturesque ski towns found in the beautiful western United States. I couldn't resist taking a tram ride to the top of one of the mountains, and the views from there were absolutely breathtaking. Queenstown was a haven for adrenaline enthusiasts, offering an overabundance of thrilling activities such as skiing, jet boating, whitewater rafting, bungee jumping, mountain biking, skateboarding, hiking, paragliding, and skydiving. The river buzzed with jet boats zooming over it. I couldn't help myself from inquiring about taking a ride on one of these high-speed adrenaline machines. However, upon learning the cost, my practical side kicked in, reminding me to save money for more meaningful purchases I could take back home to family and friends. It was undeniably tempting to participate in one or more of these exhilarating activities, but sometimes budget considerations prevailed.

With my adventurous spirit awakened, I eagerly delved into the multitude of outdoor activities available during my two-day stay in Queenstown. Although I didn't personally participate in every exhilarating endeavor, I couldn't help but be captivated by those who did. To say that leaving

---

called a velodrome. A velodrome is typically made of wood and has ramped corners to accommodate a racer's high speed in sharp turns; they may be built as outdoor or indoor tracks.

Queenstown was a challenge would be an understatement. As I checked out of the hotel the following morning, a pang of reluctance tugged at my heart. Every fiber of my being urged me to stay, to soak in more of the enchanting atmosphere. Reluctantly, I summoned the willpower to start the car and embark on the next leg of my northbound journey.

Leaving the allure of Queenstown behind, I made my way towards the Fox and Franz Josef Glaciers. Upon arrival at the Fox Glacier Lodge, I discovered that there had been a mix-up with my reservation. Hotel rooms were unavailable, but to my delight, they offered me an A-frame cottage instead. This charming abode had the capacity to accommodate twelve people, yet I had it all to myself for the price of a single room. The A-frame cottage, nestled away from the bustling central hotel, provided a cozy retreat with its spacious rooms and fully equipped kitchen. It felt like a home away from home, albeit one without the distractions of a television and phone.

The following day, I embarked on a hiking adventure on the magnificent Fox Glacier. The cloudy skies and cool temperatures set a tranquil ambiance for the hike. I didn't have to rush so I allowed myself time to pause, savor the scenery, and refuel with granola bars and water during a thirty-minute break. Recharged, I resumed my journey, reaching the pinnacle of the glacier to be greeted by awe-inspiring views. The return trek was effortless, marked by frequent stops for taking photographs or just enjoying the stunning landscapes. The next day, I reached the Franz Josef Glacier. I followed a popular trail that led to the glacier's highest point. The ice was more brilliant than that of the Fox Glacier, reflecting a golden radiance from the sun's glow. The captivating blue shades were even more enchanting. This picturesque scene remains imprinted in my memory as a display of unparalleled beauty.

After bidding farewell to the Fox and Franz Josef Glaciers Lodge, I made my way back to Christchurch in time for a late morning flight to Auckland. The evening was spent in the warm company of Joan and Brian, savoring the last moments of my New Zealand adventure. The following day marked the beginning of my 23-hour return flight to the United States. I was grateful for the foresight to plan a two-day return trip, as even for someone young and fit like me, the journey took its toll, leaving me thoroughly exhausted. Once I had enjoyed a restful good night's sleep, it was time to return to the routine of everyday life, armed with cherished memories and a renewed spirit.

After the memorable vacation, my connection with Joan and Brian Smith remained strong over the years. We made it a tradition to call each other every New Year's, catching up on life and exchanging well wishes for the upcoming year. However, our conversations took a somber turn about two years after Cathy and I got married in 1989. Joan and Brian reached out to inform us of Joan's devastating diagnosis of incurable cancer. They also shared the challenging news that Brian had been battling issues with skin cancer. The shock intensified when we later received word from Joan's brother that both of them had succumbed to cancer within the same year.

Returning to work at SSA after that much-needed 34-day vacation brought a renewed sense of enthusiasm. I was entrusted with managing a skilled development staff responsible for creating applications for end-users. Additionally, I oversaw the development of test environments to ensure seamless testing of new and enhanced applications. Maintenance, upgrades, and the management of production databases were also part of my responsibilities. Adhering to the standard practice at the time, we employed a method of copying production data into a test environment. This allowed programmers and testers to identify any issues in a production-like setting without compromising the integrity of the live data and file structures. I was determined to ensure the readiness and smooth functioning of my production software.

Yet, unforeseen challenges could arise even after the systems and applications were in use by clients. Early on in my career at SSA, I grasped the importance of continuous testing throughout the development process to avoid software flaws. This invaluable experience taught me that testing not only served as a means to practice using the application but also involved installation, configuration, and familiarization with its functionalities before its release to the client organization.

Thoroughly testing an application before deployment granted our team the opportunity to swiftly identify and resolve problems that might arise. These issues could range from hardware or network failures to data corruption or communication breakdowns. Testing also shed light on how the system or application would perform in diverse user environments, potentially unveiling logical design flaws such as overly complex screen layouts. Armed with this knowledge and experience, I was well-prepared for future career opportunities that would require implementing comprehensive testing capabilities to ensure the optimal performance of multifaceted systems.

The White House

While working at SSA on a crisp December day in 1987, I found myself stepping onto the grounds of the White House for the second time. My first visit, etched in memory by the audacious flight of Robert Preston, paled in comparison to the unforgettable moments that awaited me during the Washington Summit. From December 8 to December 10, amidst a backdrop of diplomatic fervor, I had the distinct honor of witnessing history unfold as President Ronald Reagan and General Secretary Mikhail S. Gorbachev began their series of historic meetings.

The arrival of General Secretary Gorbachev, flanked by a convoy of big and imposing black Soviet cars, captured my imagination. These massive, seemingly indestructible vehicles were escorted by a formidable entourage of security. Joking about their fuel efficiency, I found common ground with a towering Russian security guard, when I stated, "these cars aren't exactly fuel-efficient and probably don't get very good gas mileage." His puzzled smile broke into understanding as he agreed, "No, not very good gas mileage. They burn lots of fuel."

As leaders mingled on the South Lawn, our conversation ventured into realms of military service. Discovering he was a Spetsnaz soldier sparked a spontaneous gesture of camaraderie—I offered him my 11th Group 1st Special Forces challenge coin. His initial hesitation gave way to a shared moment of respect as he accepted, then he offered me his Spetsnaz lapel pin, a token of gratitude that underscored an unspoken bond. "Thank you," he said, marking an exchange that transcended mere words. Though we parted ways as he returned to his duties, that encounter epitomized the essence of human connection amidst the grandeur of diplomatic ceremonies.

Reflecting on the day's events from my home that evening, I felt a deep sense of pride in having subtly fostered the U.S.-Russian relations through a simple, yet profound, exchange. The privilege of shaking hands with President and Mrs. Reagan, and the honor of meeting General Secretary Gorbachev and his wife, provide me with memories of unparalleled significance. That day, rich with historic encounters and personal connections, will forever remain a memorable highlight in my life's journey, a testament to the enduring power of diplomacy and the unexpected bridges we can build with gestures of goodwill.

My participation in the arrival ceremony on that pivotal Tuesday, followed by a poignant ceremony on the White House's South Lawn and the deeply moving farewell to the Gorbachev's, marked chapters in an extraordinary narrative of peace and diplomacy.

Department of Justice

Throughout my career, I had the incredible opportunity to work in many interesting organizations and one of them was the Department of Justice (DOJ). My role there involved leading a team in the design and development of a national Litigation Case Management System (LCMS). As a Senior Computer Specialist, I played a crucial part in creating this centrally managed application that aimed to streamline case management for attorneys nationwide within the DOJ.

The purpose of the LCMS project was to develop a solution for sharing case information among seven of the Department's litigating components— the Executive Office for United States Attorneys (EOUSA) and United States Attorney's Offices (USAO); Criminal Division (CRM); Civil Division (CIV); Tax Division (TAX); Civil Rights Division (CRT); Environment and Natural Resources Division (ENRD); and Antitrust Division (ATR).

Being one of the initial technologists on the development team, my duties were to perform LCMS program management activities. These activities included tracking and managing the program schedule, development activities such as requirements gathering, programming, testing, documentation, and monitoring and managing the program risks while providing performance monitoring in meeting budget and schedules. I also had to collaborate closely with seven of the Department's litigating components to gather and document the application design requirements to begin the design phase of this important technology project.

I also had the opportunity to manage two major technology procurement projects for the DOJ. This role required that I had to lead the development of detailed requirement documents with actual use cases describing the processes supporting the requirements. In addition, working with the procurement staff to develop the necessary administrative and procedural information. This included such items as the cover letter that briefly introduced the project and invited vendor participation. The programmatic information and its development were my responsibility. This included developing the statement of needs that clearly defined the project the DOJ was trying to address by such large procurements. Then the detailed project description that provided detailed specifications of the products and services, required, including technical requirements/specifications, timelines, and deliverables. The selection process had to be developed and provided to all vendors for their information and use in developing their specific proposals.

These two procurement projects were in the completion phase when I was recruited by the Administrative Office of the U.S. Courts as a Development Manager.

Information Technology Test Laboratory

In the early 1990s, my testing expertise came to the forefront when I found myself involved in a remarkable project: planning and designing a comprehensive information technology test laboratory. This exciting endeavor unfolded during my tenure at the Federal Judiciary, the third branch of government. Prior to my arrival, the Administrative Office of the United States Courts had enlisted the services of a prominent international technology consulting firm. Their mission was to conceptualize, construct, and implement a national data network for the organization. This network aimed to facilitate the smooth transmission of large files and provide user access to applications across three data centers.

When I joined the Administrative Office of the United States Courts as a development manager, the original network implementation had been completed several years prior. Approximately six months into my role, we encountered significant performance issues plaguing most of our computer applications. Determined to address these challenges, we reached out to the international technology firm responsible for the network's original design and construction. Swiftly responding to our concerns, they dispatched a team of experts to investigate the matter. Within a week, they presented their findings to the CIO and executive management, revealing a startling truth: our network was ill equipped to handle user access to applications, large file transfers, or even sizable email attachments. Essentially, the original network design fell short of meeting the technological demands of our organization, serving primarily as only an email conduit.

Regrettably, due to the contractual terms, our organization lacked the power to compel the contracted company to redesign or rectify the network issues. We were left with two alternatives. The first option involved the contracted firm re-engineering the national communications network, a costly endeavor. The second option entailed upgrading the entire network in-house, a solution estimated to be more economical than the contract modification. However, this approach came with its own set of challenges, including the need for replacement hardware and software, resulting in substantial costs. Additionally, our in-house staff would need to redesign all the applications to align with the upgraded network.

The subsequent decision would have a significant impact on the organization, ultimately shaping our technological landscape for years to come. The CIO summoned me to his office to delve into option two and its associated challenges. As our conversation unfolded, he inquired about the feasibility of my team handling the network upgrade and application rewrites. I assured him of our capabilities, but stressed the need for additional qualified personnel to tackle such an immense undertaking. Responding to my concerns, he entrusted me with the responsibility of formulating a comprehensive plan and determining the exact number of staff members required. With the plan in hand, meticulously crafted and refined, the CIO assigned this monumental project to me and my team.

To kick start the process, my team embarked on preliminary testing to ascertain the network's precise requirements. Recognizing my expertise in establishing testing environments, the CIO entrusted me with an additional task: designing, developing, and implementing an innovative information technology testing laboratory. This cutting-edge facility would serve as the testing ground for all applications, ensuring their smooth transition into production and subsequent availability for end users. Additionally, I arranged for the training of user support staff, enabling them to provide valuable assistance to end users once the applications were deployed. Unexpectedly, the project took an intriguing turn when it became evident that existing mainframe-based applications required modification and transition. Swiftly adapting, I reallocated resources from other project areas to fund this unforeseen phase.

Over the course of the next two years, our dedicated staff labored tirelessly, operating in three shifts per day, seven days a week. To meet the demanding workload, we bolstered our ranks with developers, system administrators, and testers. This assignment proved immensely rewarding by allowing me to leverage my extensive testing experience and knowledge acquired throughout my career. It presented an opportunity to acquaint myself with the latest testing tools and equipment, staying at the forefront of technological advancements. However, the true highlight was collaborating with a diverse group of talented individuals, both existing team members and new recruits. Together, we fostered a dynamic team environment reminiscent of my days in the Army, learning and growing from one another's expertise.

At the outset of this assignment, I found camaraderie with six talented Vietnamese programmers in my organization. Our bond was strengthened by the shared knowledge that I had served in Vietnam. These programmers possessed exceptional skills, always offering innovative ideas and approaches to our work. Working alongside them was an absolute pleasure due to their meticulousness and expertise. At a certain point during the project, we decided to create a sign bearing a profound quote by Lao Tzu, which we proudly displayed on the wall:

Deal with the difficult while it is still easy.
Solve large problems when they are still small.
Prevent large problems by taking small steps.
It's easier than solving them by small actions.

The national network had been upgraded to transport all types of large and small files. My development team transitioned to modifying numerous applications to operate efficiently without consuming large amounts of network bandwidth. We were approximately six months from completion when my career took an unexpected turn; I received a compelling offer from the Federal Reserve Board of Governors to manage and oversee the consolidation and management of a national technology organization. Before diving into the intricacies of that role, it's essential to grasp the significance of the Federal Reserve, often referred to as the Third United States Central Bank.

Origins of the Federal Reserve

The origins of the Federal Reserve remain forgotten from history classes or relatively unknown to many American citizens. Nevertheless, its origins can be traced back to the establishment of our first national bank by George Washington and Alexander Hamilton in 1791. This bank served as a central repository for federal funds. The initial bank's charter expired, leading to the founding of the Second Bank of the United States in 1816.

Traditionally, the management of the bank was entrusted to a board of directors with ties to the industrial and manufacturing sectors. As a result, the bank was perceived to be biased towards the urban and industrial northern states. This created tensions, particularly with President Andrew Jackson, who embodied the spirit of the frontiersman. Jackson was dissatisfied with the bank's reluctance to provide funding for the expansion into unsettled Western territories.

Furthermore, Jackson objected to the bank's significant political and economic influence, as well as the lack of congressional oversight over its operations. In a decisive move known as the "Bank War," President Jackson publicly declared on September 10, 1833, that the Federal government would cease utilizing the services of the Second Bank of the United States, effectively ending its status as the country's national bank. He then exercised his executive authority to remove all federal funds from the bank, concluding the conflict surrounding the Second Bank of the United States' existence.

Following a series of financial panics, culminating in the Panic of 1907, the Aldrich-Vreeland Act was passed by Congress in 1908. This act established the National Monetary Commission, a committee of eighteen members led by Senator Nelson Aldrich of Rhode Island. The commission was entrusted with the task of reforming the nation's monetary system.

In November 1910, a group of six individuals gathered for a duck hunting trip at the Jekyll Island Club in Georgia. The participants included Nelson Aldrich, A. Piatt Andrew, Henry Davison, Arthur Shelton, Frank Vanderlip, and Paul Warburg. The public did not have a clue that the true purpose of their meeting was to devise a plan for reforming the country's banking system. Nor were the citizens aware that these six individuals intended to draft the legislation that would create the extensive powers of the Federal Reserve System. This clandestine meeting played a pivotal role in reshaping the entire financial structure and operations of the United States, with long-lasting effects.

The meeting and its intentions were kept highly confidential, and it was not until the 1930s that the participants publicly acknowledged its occurrence. The notion of influential individuals gathering behind closed doors without public awareness of their agenda continues to evoke legitimate concerns even today. In the aftermath of the 2007/2008 financial crisis, we have gained more insight into this kind of behind-the-scenes negotiations. The men who convened on Jekyll Island would likely find familiarity in the covert meetings depicted in the film "Too Big to Fail," which aired on HBO in May 2011. This television film was based on Andrew Ross Sorkin's non-fiction book, "Too Big to Fail: The Inside Story of How Wall Street and Washington Fought to Save the Financial System and Themselves" (2009). The participants of the Jekyll Island gathering would likely take pride in their ability to keep their top-secret meeting concealed from the media and cinema. In 1910, leaks were simply nonexistent.

Originally, the Federal Reserve System was conceived as a privately operated banking system. A group of private banks would contribute to funding federal government bailouts, when necessary, like what J.P. Morgan accomplished during the financial and banking panic/crisis of 1907. At that time, the United States lacked a central bank, and a federal government bailout was impossible.

In the original design there was never any intent to create the Federal Reserve as it exists today. The original design was altered dramatically by lawyers over the years who never understood banking and would later become elected officials to pursue power as politicians. In my opinion, it's not much different today in Washington, D.C., either.

It can be discouraging to realize that one of the most respected institutions in the United States, the Federal Reserve System, began during secret meetings. Sometimes such clandestine conferences are necessary to protect national security. Sometimes, they are held to avoid public backlash and enable some of society's most affluent and powerful to steer economic policy without governmental oversight or public debate. Yet, one only has to look back over the past 20 years and read about the many secret meetings that ultimately changed our nation in one way or another forever and never for the best interests of the people.

The Federal Reserve

Upon taking on a new role at the Federal Reserve Board of Governors in Washington, D.C., my career path took an unexpected turn. Transitioning from managing a national technology organization, I was unprepared for the surprise that greeted me during my first week. In a chance encounter in the elevator, I was stunned to meet Alan Greenspan face to face again. Recognizing me, he warmly greeted me by name and recalled our previous meeting at Tio Pepe's, where I had inadvertently disturbed his dinner while working at the Social Security Administration. We shared a friendly conversation about the restaurant, carefully steering clear of mentioning my less-than-graceful intrusion that evening.

In my role overseeing the information technology program across all 12 Federal Reserve banks, I was required to present quarterly financial status reports for my national IT program. This meant I was immediately thrust into board meetings that were as insightful as they were daunting. Seated at a table beneath large brass chandeliers, surrounded by walls adorned with framed $1,000 certificates and flanked by grand fireplaces, the setting was nothing short of imposing. Describing these meetings as merely intimidating doesn't quite capture their full impact; they were a profound learning experience. Maintaining a neutral expression, a skill I had honed throughout my career, became particularly challenging in this environment. A moment that stands out vividly involved the term "too big to fail." It was during one of these meetings that I fully grasped the extent to which massive financial institutions could dominate the Federal Reserve System, leaving me utterly astonished. My visible surprise and confusion were not, I realized, conducive to professional advancement.

My interest in business history dates back to my college days, particularly the story of Standard Oil's breakup in 1911. Back then, the consensus was that Standard Oil had become too large and needed to be dismantled. Interestingly, the breakup revealed that the parts of the conglomerate were

266

more valuable than the whole. This historical example led me to ponder whether today's financial, banking, and technology organizations, often labeled as "too big to fail," are indeed too large for our good. Could it be time to consider breaking them up, akin to Standard Oil? In my opinion, these entities have grown alarmingly large, exerting undue influence and power over our society.

The meeting took an unexpected turn, surprising not just myself but also Vice Chairman Roger W. Ferguson, as evidenced by our exchanged glances of disbelief. It was clear we weren't alone in our astonishment; similar reactions were visible among other boardroom attendees, though many maintained a composed exterior.

During my first financial presentation to the Board of Governors, a Federal Reserve Bank president interrupted me, claiming I was overstepping boundaries and challenging their authority over technical staff. Despite their rudeness, I stayed calm, striving for a diplomatic resolution.

Tension rose when this president criticized my questioning of his preference for an in-house document management system without fully considering its total cost of ownership. He wrongly assumed that assigning additional tasks to salaried staff would incur no extra costs. I countered his flawed logic by explaining that diverting staff to a new project would detract from their primary responsibilities.

In a robust discussion, the president made bold cost estimates for the system. I challenged his vague figures, emphasizing the need for precise financial planning. I proposed creating a detailed business case, including documented costs, savings over five years, and the benefits of a large-scale enterprise application, despite his disregard for already established project guidance procedures.

Anticipating resistance, I was mentally prepared for the president's objections. However, Vice Chairman Ferguson intervened with a pertinent question about the necessity of executive sponsorship for national projects, which helped ease the tension and allowed me to clarify the roles involved in project management. His support was crucial, marking the start of a strong partnership.

My tenure at the Federal Reserve involved setting standards and challenging the status quo, often facing resistance from bank presidents reluctant to adopt national standards and procedures. They preferred relying on in-house staff despite a clear lack of expertise in developing national applications. Yet, in another meeting, a president's suggestion to consider commercial software led to a mutual recognition of the need for a comprehensive business case, highlighting the importance of cost, savings, and total ownership considerations—key metrics I was tasked with reporting. This experience underscored the Federal Reserve's tendency towards independence among its banks and the challenge of aligning them under unified standards and practices.

Following our discussion, we arrived at a cooperative decision: my team would work with the Reserve Banks to evaluate the possibility of adopting a system-wide applications solution. This led to the innovative idea of creating an oversight board. Made up of executive representatives from each Reserve Bank, this board would oversee the development of a comprehensive business case and supporting documentation to secure system-wide approval. Additionally, it would act as a dedicated technology oversight entity within the Federal Reserve.

With the establishment of the oversight board, a significant shift occurred in the management of the Federal Reserve's extensive system-wide information technology program. Comprised of senior vice presidents from different Reserve Banks, the board took on the responsibility of overseeing information technology initiatives. It carefully examined and discussed proposed projects to ensure they met established standards and policies. Before any new or updated policies and procedures were implemented across the system, they were submitted to the board for review and feedback. Importantly, these board members also worked closely with the senior staff of Reserve Bank presidents, involving them in the system-wide IT efforts to ensure their support and endorsement. This cooperative strategy eliminated the practice of making decisions without broader consultation, which in turn eased the political tensions I had previously encountered with the bank presidents.

September 11, 2001

In the wake of the September 11, 2001 attacks, chaos emerged. A remarkable chain of events unfolded at the Federal Reserve. Chairman Greenspan and William J. McDonough, President of the Federal Reserve Bank of New York, were departing from a central bankers' meeting in Switzerland when the terrorist-piloted airplanes struck the World Trade Center. Because of the unfolding tragedy, Greenspan's U.S. bound aircraft was fortunate enough to be able to return to Zurich, unlike many other flights that were forced to land in remote locations. Vice Chairman Roger Ferguson, at his office at the Federal Reserve Board of Governors, found himself at the forefront of an unprecedented situation. His presence became vital as he took on the responsibility of safeguarding the global financial markets.

Meanwhile, I was in my office, engaged in a meeting focused on enhancing the Federal Reserve's video conferencing capabilities to curb soaring travel costs. Little did I know that the world outside was spiraling into chaos. Just as the discussion began, an unexpected interruption shattered the room. A colleague burst into my office to deliver the shocking news of an airplane crashing into the World Trade Center. Sensing the gravity of the situation, I suggested a break, but before we could proceed, my phone rang. Little did I know that it would be my last call for the next three days. The Department of Defense had declared the nation under attack, prompting the immediate suspension of all communications within Washington, D.C.

The events of that morning reshaped our nation's priorities and brought into sharp focus the resilience and adaptability required in the face of unforeseen challenges. The Federal Reserve, with Vice Chairman Ferguson at the helm, would navigate uncharted territory to ensure stability during the crisis.

As Vice Chairman Ferguson entered his office that day, he instinctively switched on the television to monitor the financial markets. The moment the second plane struck the World Trade Center, he didn't need anyone to tell him that the nation was under attack. The deliberate targeting of Lower Manhattan World Trade Center buildings made it painfully clear that the assault aimed to disrupt the very foundation of the global financial system. In response, Ferguson wasted no time in declaring a state of emergency, setting into motion the meticulously crafted Year 2000 (Y2K) emergency procedures.

The Joint Y2K Committee, which Ferguson had chaired, proved to be a priceless resource during the crisis. The Federal Reserve system swiftly implemented the committee's plans and training, relying on them as the events of Wednesday, September 11, 2001, unfolded. A dedicated group of individuals at the Board convened in a conference room, making crucial decisions under Ferguson's guidance. Their actions averted a potential catastrophe, preventing a disastrous collapse of the world's financial markets.

Amid the evacuation of Washington, D.C., roughly 100 determined Federal Reserve staff members remained at their posts, standing alongside Vice Chairman Ferguson to coordinate emergency operations. Some of us took on the responsibility of facilitating the evacuation of personnel from the Martin and Eccles buildings. Once completed, a small group, including myself and Chairman Greenspan's executive assistant, gazed out onto the burning Pentagon before seeking refuge in the building's basement graphics department. There, we anxiously watched various news channels, absorbing the latest updates on the unfolding crisis.

At 9:25 a.m. the Federal Aviation Administration grounded all planes, effectively halting air travel nationwide. Within a mere 40 minutes of the second plane's impact, Ferguson issued a concise and reassuring statement to member banks and institutions. His message emphasized that the federal fund transfer system remained fully operational, and the Federal Reserve Banks would remain open, providing stability in uncertain times.

The Federal Reserve Bank of New York, located just blocks away from the World Trade Center, found itself in a critical position. Swiftly responding to the crisis, the bank's police secured vaults and entrances, creating a safe zone while clearing the streets for emergency vehicles. Federal Reserve personnel, equipped with two-way radios, coordinated efforts to transfer operations to the Continuity of Operation (COOP) backup facility in New Jersey. This resilient location served as the hub for managing the bank's operations and maintaining authority during and after emergencies of this magnitude.

One of the primary concerns that consumed us at the Board of Governors was the sudden loss of communication with the New York Federal Reserve Bank in the aftermath of the attack. All channels of communication to and from the bank had been abruptly severed. It was a worrisome situation considering the crucial role the New York Federal Reserve

Bank played as being the largest repository of gold worldwide. No other place on the planet possessed such an extensive collection of this precious metal. This vulnerability made it a prime target for potential theft, and the chaos of the attack presented a golden opportunity for would-be thieves to make off with billions of dollars' worth of gold. To ensure some level of communication, we repurposed the lone active data communications line to facilitate voice communication, particularly with the New York Police Department (NYPD). This arrangement allowed us to receive additional police protection during those critical initial hours. Despite the severity of the attack, the Federal Reserve managed to restore normal operations within a year, implementing significantly enhanced security measures to safeguard against future threats.

I could delve further into the details, but I must emphasize the composed and resolute demeanor displayed by Vice Chairman Ferguson as he took decisive actions to avert a global financial catastrophe. In my personal opinion, his remarkable leadership during the crisis should have positioned him as the natural successor to the Chairman of the Federal Reserve System.

Attack or Robbery at the Chicago Federal Reserve Bank

Six months later, on an early Tuesday morning around 3 a.m., my world was jolted again when the board's switchboard operator relayed news of an attack or robbery at the Chicago Federal Reserve Bank. Management promptly contacted me, instructing me to catch the earliest flight to Chicago. My mission was clear: assess the technological implications of the incident and provide an immediate report to the board that would shed light on the unfolding situation.

As I arrived at the scene, a striking sight greeted my eyes. The Chicago Federal Reserve police force, armed with assault rifles and clad in body armor, patrolled the streets and sidewalks. The atmosphere was tense, with an underlying uncertainty hanging in the air, as everyone pondered the possibility of a major robbery unfolding before them. However, the truth turned out to be far less nefarious. What had caused the commotion was an enormous hole in the road, stretching approximately 200 feet long and 150 feet wide. This cavernous gap unleashed a torrent of mud and water, transform-

271

ing the area into a chaotic battlefield-like landscape. Local television stations swiftly dispatched reporters to the scene, capturing the unfolding events live on television. Speculation ran rampant, with some of the reporters initially theorizing that the Federal Reserve Bank had fallen victim to a daring heist. Eventually, their stories shifted as city officials clarified that it was, in fact, a water main break.

As the City of Chicago swiftly deployed its employees to shut off the water and commence repairs, a sense of calm gradually settled over the area. Drawing upon my experiences in Vietnam, I swiftly assessed the situation and contacted my management in Washington, D.C., and provided them with a comprehensive briefing. Throughout the day, I remained at the Chicago Fed, diligently relaying updates back to Washington. Once the situation had stabilized, and the bank staff had assumed responsibility for monitoring the repairs, I made my way to the airport to board a late evening flight back to BWI airport.

The Adventurers Club of Towson

After my divorce from Rose, I found comfort by continuing my active lifestyle through running, biking, and swimming. A friend introduced me to a unique athletic club located in Towson, MD. It was no ordinary athletic club. The club was founded by a husband-and-wife duo of clinical psychologists. It catered to individuals who avoided sports due to their deep-seated fear of failure and competition. Known as the Adventurers Club, it served as a safe haven where the psychologists' patients could participate in sporting events without the overwhelming burden of their anxieties. What intrigued me even more was discovering that the psychologists themselves were active participants in the club's athletic pursuits.

I embarked on a transformative journey, in my mid-30s when I joined the Adventurers Club. Despite not being a young man anymore, I was fueled by personal growth, numerous life transitions, and a perpetual stream of challenges. My mind and spirit were in a constant state of evolution. Surprisingly, when I pushed myself to my physical limits, something magical happened. I discovered my faithful companions, endorphins. I affectionately called them my endofriends[40] because they brought me joy and happiness. These endofriends had the incredible power to minimize discomfort and pain, while simultaneously amplifying feelings of happiness.

[40] Endorphins. Endorphins are your body's natural pain relievers. These neurotransmitters, or chemical messengers in the brain, are also responsible for feelings of pleasure we can get after certain activities like hiking or running, eating chocolate, and laughing with friends. https://www.verywellhealth.com/endorphins-definition-5189854

With these elevated emotions, my confidence soared, and optimism filled my being, while bolstering my self-esteem.

When I joined the club, it boasted a membership of around 200 individuals. Prospective members, including myself, were required to undergo a one-on-one meeting with the psychologists. Additionally, we had to attend a meeting and take part in several activities to ensure compatibility with the existing group. As the only non-patient and veteran, I embarked on this unique journey.

The club provided exceptional weekly training sessions that became an avenue for open conversations among members. During these sessions, fellow Adventurers would share their personal struggles, discuss their fears of failure, and address other issues. As they confided in me, I listened attentively, offering support and encouragement. Remarkably, their narratives inadvertently aided my own healing process, allowing me to confront residual challenges stemming from my divorce and experiences in the Vietnam War. Witnessing their methods of overcoming obstacles and seeing their progress was an invaluable source of inspiration.

Upon completion of each training event, I would make it a point to look each member in the eyes, warmly shake their hands, and express my heartfelt gratitude for being part of their journey that day. I wanted them to know that their willingness to include me in their training meant the world to me, and I genuinely appreciated their camaraderie.

In the realm of the Adventurers Club, the pursuit of physical activities went far beyond mere exercise. It became a sanctuary where shared experiences and the power of empathetic connections allowed us all to grow stronger, conquer our fears, and embark on transformative personal journeys.

During the monthly gatherings of the club, we were treated to enlightening presentations by guest speakers covering a wide range of topics, including training techniques, sports medicine, and healthy eating habits. Among these speakers were the respected physicians who founded the Union Memorial Sports Medicine Clinic in Baltimore. Their membership and involvement in the club provided us with invaluable insights into the realm of sports medicine and enhanced both our training routines and our performance in competitions.

One particular area that captured my attention was their in-depth discussions on knee injuries and surgical interventions. Through captivating videos, images, and firsthand accounts of knee and leg surgeries, the physicians educated us on how to prevent such injuries. Another topic that really resonated with me personally was their talk on adjusting bicycle seat height and angle. Previously, during bicycle time trials and fast-paced races, I would often experience numbness in my delicate personal regions as well as my extremities such as my feet and toes. This numbness would take several days to subside.

The discomfort and concern of experiencing numbness in these intimate areas haunted me and fueled worries of potential embarrassment. During a Q&A session following one of the physicians' presentations, I mustered the courage to inquire about this issue. The physicians explained that this condition could affect both men and women due to the presence of soft tissue in those areas. Incorrect alignment of the bicycle seat could lead to inflammation in the soft tissue, and other critical body parts causing numbness in our private parts, legs, feet, and toes. Fortunately, they provided valuable guidance and techniques to properly adjust saddle height and angle, preventing such discomfort.

Furthermore, the physicians delved into the significance of heart rates in training and competition. I was intrigued with this topic, because after leaving the Army I had always taken my pulse manually while running, swimming, and cycling. Their insights prompted me to adopt a more meticulous approach. I began diligently tracking and charting my heart rate during training sessions. Each day, I methodically documented my resting heart rate upon waking, tracked my sleep duration, and charted my dietary intake from the previous day. I even added a "notes" column to capture my mental and physical state during each session to form a comprehensive record of my progress.

These presentations by experts not only expanded my knowledge but also instilled a sense of purpose and scientific precision in my training regimen. The dedication to monitoring and understanding the intricacies of my body allowed me to fine-tune my routines and make informed adjustments to optimize my performance.

I understand that my charting practices may be perceived as excessive, but these charts offered valuable structure and insights into my training and physical well-being. Each month, I eagerly reviewed my precisely kept notes, assessing my progress and determining if any adjustments were necessary. This systematic approach served as a tangible measure of my advancement toward both psychological and physical goals.

In my younger years, during high school, I participated in cross-country running. However, my approach to running back then was more recreational than competitive. It was all about the sheer joy of the sport, not about racing against others. Everything changed when I underwent Army training. The military instilled in us a mindset of constant competition, not only with others but, more importantly, with ourselves. Every minute of the day, we strived to better ourselves and overcome the limitations of our old habits and ways of living.

The Army introduced us to a fierce culture of competition rooted in the principles of war, dominance, and conquest. It was a necessary preparation, knowing that many of us would soon be thrust into the realities of combat. In the face of life-or-death challenges, the ultimate contest awaited us. What I failed to realize at the time was how profoundly this competitive ethos of the military would shape my future, even after my departure from active service.

Throughout my life, I have realized that engaging in sports serves as a tremendous stress reliever. During my time in the Army, I unearthed another extraordinary facet of physical activity: adrenaline. Adrenaline became a natural, healthy drug that enabled me to surpass both my physical and mental limitations. It also acted as a delay mechanism, postponing the onset of pain following an injury. As human beings, we naturally seek pleasure and avoid pain. Consequently, if an activity made me feel good, I was more inclined to participate. Although training can be arduous and challenging, the rewards of physical fitness and good health far outweigh any temporary discomfort.

Understanding that we are inherently social creatures, I recognized the importance of community. As my mother always said, no man is an island. I understood that endorphins played a pivotal role in strengthening social bonds. At this stage of my life, I craved social interaction and knew I could not retreat into a world of isolation. Throughout human history, people formed social groups to survive, reproduce, and defend themselves and their communities. I passionately believe that the psychologists who founded the Adventurers Club shared this understanding and recognized the significance of social connections as a fundamental reason for establishing the club.

Another reason individuals joined the Adventurers Club was to cultivate positive attitudes. Until then, I had learned that possessing a positive attitude was the key to making a difference in myself. This became especially crucial when competing or engaging in team sports. In such environments, negative attitudes had no place. It was abundantly clear that developing a positive mindset was paramount to achieving success and fostering a harmonious team dynamic.

My last Triathlon

During my time in the Army, I discovered a crucial ingredient for success in any endeavor: a positive and confident attitude. It was this mindset that propelled me forward, enabling me to conquer tasks and overcome the myriad of negative mental challenges that often arose. Seeking to refine this essential skill, I turned to the Adventurers Club. My training regimen not only bolstered my confidence but also fostered self-reliance and honed my social skills through increased team interactions. Additionally, I developed new and improved methods of self-motivation and discipline through my meticulous charting processes.

Joining the Adventurers Club opened a world of opportunities to connect with like-minded individuals, each navigating their own life challenges. Together, we embarked on a series of exhilarating competitions, ranging from triathlons, foot races to half and full marathons, and bicycle races. The allure of triathlons captivated me after reading a fascinating story about this emerging sport in a running magazine. Intrigued, I decided to incorporate swimming and cycling into my regular routine, seamlessly transitioning into the world of triathlons.

Eager to delve deeper into the sport, I eagerly subscribed to *Triathlon* magazine, devouring each issue for valuable insights. As I immersed myself in its pages, I uncovered the origins of triathlons. In 1978, a group of Navy Seals pioneered the first Ironman Triathlon in Hawaii. The more I delved into the Ironman Triathlon, the more I grasped why it was regarded as one of the most grueling events in the world of sports, second only to the Tour de France bicycle race. Picture this: a grueling 2.4-mile open water ocean swim, followed by an arduous 112-mile bike ride, culminating in a full marathon spanning 26.2 miles, all completed consecutively. Participants were given a strict 17-hour window for completion. The event would typically commence at 7 a.m. and end at midnight on the same day.

Soon after, in 1980, I eagerly paid my entrance fee and embarked on my first triathlon in Groton, Connecticut. This race encompassed a mile swim, a 10K run, and a 26-mile bicycle race. It was a transformative experience that left an indelible mark on me. What struck me the most was the realization that my true competition was not against others, but rather against myself. This understanding brought a profound shift in perspective.

Beyond the obvious cardiovascular benefits, training for triathlons enhanced my overall strength and fitness. Each discipline, swimming, running, and cycling contributed to building both my upper and lower body strength, as well as core stability. Triathlons became more than just races; they became catalysts for personal growth in physical fitness.

Every triathlon presented a unique challenge, and the opportunities to participate in races across the United States seemed boundless. The mental benefits were just as significant as the physical ones. The rush of positive stimulation and the sense of accomplishment after each race was unparalleled. As a member of the Adventurers Club, I found companionship and camaraderie among fellow triathlon enthusiasts. We would encourage and motivate each other to sign up for multiple races throughout the year to accumulate points that would rank us nationally.

Even after Cathy and I married, I remained an active member of the Adventurers Club, along with her understanding and support. She recognized the joy I found in the club and the positive impact it had on my well-being. Among the club's numerous events, one of my most enjoyable experiences was the exhilarating bicycle races held in various shopping center parking lots. Every Sunday morning at 6:30 a.m., Adventurers Club members would gather at different Baltimore-area shopping centers. The perimeter roads and parking lots would be transformed into a criterium course,[41] where we would race against the clock, recording our times. It was from these races that the club leaders compiled a list of racers to participate in the annual September Baltimore to Ocean City bicycle road race, a cherished tradition eagerly anticipated by all.

I vividly recall the early days of the Baltimore to Ocean City bicycle race, when only a dozen brave souls took on the challenge. It was a casual affair, with most racers donning gym shorts and tennis shoes instead of proper cycling gear. The race kicked off at 5:30 a.m., shrouded in darkness. To navigate the dimly lit roads, we strapped flashlights to our handlebars, casting beams of light as we zipped through the western side of Baltimore County. Our first milestone was reaching the service road near the Chesapeake Bay Bridge toll booths in Annapolis, marking the halfway point of the race to Ocean City. Arrival times were accurately recorded, and our bikes were transported across the Bay Bridge to the eastern shore. The following leg of the race would commence from the eastern shore, with racers departing in the same order they arrived in Annapolis. That initial stretch from the Towson/Lutherville area of Baltimore to the bay bridge encompassed approximately 75 miles.

I must admit, the first stage of the race was a thrilling adventure. Racing through the darkness at speeds exceeding 20 miles per hour, with a trusty flashlight affixed to my handlebars, was both exhilarating and fun. However, the condition of the roads in Baltimore County presented a challenge. Countless potholes caused several flashlights to detach from handlebars and meet an unfortunate demise. To mitigate this, I had ingeniously secured a heavy-duty plastic flashlight to my handlebars using electrical tape, ensuring it stayed firmly in place and illuminated the road ahead.

Given that the Ocean City race was an annual tradition, I had not invested in an expensive bicycle light, as my makeshift solution served me well

---

[41] A bicycle race of a specified number of laps on a closed course over public roads closed to normal traffic.

enough. Yet, after two years of participants voicing concerns about safety on those roads, race organizers decided to make changes. The start time was shifted to a later hour, and a new starting location was chosen in the charming town of Northeast, MD. From the town center, we would embark on our journey, racing out to Route 40, then heading north for 10 miles. Upon reaching Route 213, we would turn south, passing through countless historic and scenic small towns until finally arriving at Route 50. This revised race-course boasted better roads that facilitated higher speeds. This route was approximately 185 miles long, ten miles longer than the previous route.

By the time September rolled around each year, I would be in peak physical condition for the Ocean City race. While there were younger, more formidable athletes in the club, it was a fantastic opportunity to compete alongside them. They pushed me to my limits, encouraging me to achieve faster speeds and better times. With my daily commute to Washington, D.C., spanning two to four hours, balancing a career and family, training wasn't easy. As a result, the top spot on the podium often eluded me. Nevertheless, I consistently finished in the top third to fifth place. I was satisfied with the progress I made.

In one particular year, I tasted victory, albeit with a twist. The second-place finisher's front tire was mere inches behind from being level with mine, an incredibly close call. Unfortunately, the judges didn't catch this detail. Since we didn't employ photo finishing, they declared the race a tie for first place. While some might have protested, I saw no need to do so. I knew in my heart that I had won, and that was enough for me. I always competed to better myself, and I let the decision stand, content with the personal achievement I had attained.

While I've shared my experiences with triathlons before, I haven't delved into the world of marathons. Let's talk about my first marathon, the Baltimore Marathon. Those grueling 26.2 miles proved to be quite a challenge, mostly because I had not trained as diligently as I should have. My work as a computer programmer often fascinated me, whether it was coding, troubleshooting hardware, or simply enjoying the intricacies of my computer tasks. Unfortunately, that enjoyment sometimes led to neglecting my training runs.

Despite my less-than-ideal preparation, the marathon course offered breaks at various mile markers, where I could slow down and replenish myself with water and refreshing Gatorade type drinks. Curiously, it always felt like those oases appeared after the 17th-mile mark. Because those last miles were the true test of my resolve in completing the marathon. I had to dig deep, mentally encouraging myself with the thought that it was merely another block, just a few more steps, or only half a mile left to conquer. The marathon route took me through charming sights, including a scenic loop around Lake Montebello, the attractive Inner Harbor waterfront, Fells Point, Federal Hill, and ultimately, a triumphant finish near the USS Constellation. Additionally, I took part in several 10-mile races in Annapolis and the annual Vietnam Veterans 10-miler.

One memorable morning, while training for the legendary Ironman Triathlon[42] in Hawaii and its 26.2-mile marathon, I found myself running on South Rolling Road near the vibrant campus of the University of Maryland Baltimore County (UMBC). It was early morning, and the Baltimore area was still shrouded in darkness, as I completed a 10-mile run. As I was on my way home running down South Rolling Road, a fascinating sight unfolded to my left, the radiant lights of Baltimore City. The view from there gave me an indescribable sensation of being on top of the world, a moment of sheer exhilaration. I guess that is what is called "runner's high."

As a devoted member of the Adventurers Club of Towson, I dedicated myself to a rigorous training routine. Swimming became a regular activity, and I aimed to run daily while squeezing in bicycle rides whenever possible. I would rise before dawn, mount my bicycle, and traverse the perimeter road and parking lots of the University of Maryland Baltimore Campus (UMBC). The empty early morning paved streets ensured a safe and enjoyable ride, as the towering parking lot lights cast a vibrant glow upon my path. It was an opportunity to simulate the intensity of a Sunday club criterium race, honing my skills and embracing the thrill of the sport.

Throughout my journey, I remained one among many passionate athletes in the club, crisscrossing the United States to participate in exhilarating races. Detroit, Miami, Chicago, Baltimore, Richmond, and Boston became significant landmarks on our race map. These triathlons held great importance as we fervently competed, striving to amass points and secure

---

[42] This race consisted of a two-mile ocean swim, a hundred and twelve bicycle race, and a twenty-six mile-marathon run to the finish.

our qualification for the highly anticipated 1986 National Triathlon Championships in Hilton Head, South Carolina, an event I previously mentioned and eagerly anticipated.

Most of our journeys to triathlons were by car, ensuring we could reach each race and return home in time for work on Monday. I vividly recall arriving home in the early morning hours, with just enough time to hastily shower, dress, and hit the road for work. While the competitions were thrilling, they also left me fatigued on that first day back or during the commute. On many occasions, I found myself dozing off on the train ride to and from Washington, D.C. Thankfully, I never missed my stop going home although I could not help but worry, having heard stories of others unknowingly riding all the way to Elkton, MD, near Wilmington, Delaware. They would then have to call someone to pick them up or find other ways of returning home. I'm sure their days were a lot longer than normal because of sleeping and missing their stop.

There were moments when fatigue overwhelmed me even before a race began, often due to lack of sleep leading up to the event. A particularly vivid example happened during a triathlon in Detroit. My exhaustion was so severe that I could not rest in the car beforehand, which led to a momentary lapse in focus during the race. This lapse caused me to miss a critical turn on the bicycle course, adding extra miles to my route—one mile off course and another mile to return to the proper path. While this detour may seem minor, closing the distance was a daunting task as other competitors were moving at impressive speeds. I managed to make up for the lost time, but it required a significant effort and greatly drained my energy reserves.

Yet, I had the swim portion in the Detroit River still awaiting me. Typically, I would swim in a wetsuit for speed and insulation, but that weekend, in my exhausted state, I left it behind in my laundry room. Thus, I dove into the water wearing only my trusty Speedo swimsuit. As I emerged from the swim and stepped out of the river, I found my entire body coated in a repugnant, brown film. This unwelcome coating made the ensuing run even more grueling, as the film acted like sandpaper against the areas of my body that rubbed as I moved. With the exhaustion from the demanding bicycle leg and swim, I had not even noticed the odor until after completing the race. Walking around post-race, I couldn't stand the stench emanating from my body. Unfortunately, no showers were available. I settled for a quick rinse with a cold-water hose before embarking on the drive home. The thought of subjecting my fellow race companions to my pungent aroma during the car ride was unfathomable.

Upon completing the race, the officials delivered fantastic news, I had accumulated enough points to qualify for the prestigious national championship race in Hilton Head. What made it even more exhilarating was that all my race companions from the Adventurers Club had also secured their spots through their impressive performances. The sense of club pride was massive, and we could not help but feel thrilled for one another. Amidst the celebration, one of the younger racers, despite his remarkable achievements, fell victim to an upset stomach. His discomfort led to frequent toilet stops, elongating our journey back home.

The National Triathlon Championship race at Hilton Head, South Carolina was not for the faint of heart, as it attracted international champions and was renowned. Because it was one of the toughest events for tri-athletes worldwide. While I knew my career commitments meant I wouldn't finish in the top 25 rankings, I was proud to participate. Cathy accompanied me as I raced the Hilton Head event, viewing it as her own vacation and supporting me every step of the way.

I received a gold key ring and a collection of commemorative tee shirts, hats, and other nifty giftees that proudly displayed my completion in the 1986 National Triathlon Championship. To my surprise, the race officials also thoughtfully provided a goodie bag filled with nutritious health bars and drinks, perhaps offsetting the cost of my $250 entrance fee.

A few memories from this event stand out vividly. The most notable one occurred during a last-minute training swim in the ocean. As I swam in the open ocean, I immersed myself entirely in perfecting my form and focusing on my breathing, mainly due to the presence of higher waves in the open ocean. The Atlantic Ocean presented a formidable challenge, with potential storms brewing off the coast. The anticipation of above-average storm waves added an extra layer of difficulty to the swim portion of the race the following day. I had never experienced such massive waves before, and at one point, I paused to assess my location, only to realize I had drifted over half a mile away from the shore, and the current was relentlessly pushing me farther out.

Realizing the urgency, I had to swim back swiftly as the sun had begun its descent. It would not be long before dark. Frantically propelling myself through the water, I suddenly heard peculiar sounds emerging from the depths. Instantly, the thought of "SHARKS" echoed in my mind., I must have appeared like a delectable feast to any passing shark, clad in my wetsuit resembling a thrashing seal. The thought of becoming a shark's dinner along the Atlantic coast sent adrenaline coursing through my veins, propelling me to swim like never before. Finally, I reached my original starting point, gasping for breath as I emerged from the water. As I walked further up the beach, I turned back to identify the source of those mysterious sounds. To my relief, they emanated from porpoises. However, a fleeting concern crossed my mind, don't sharks' prey on porpoises too?

One of my most cherished memories stems from a training run I embarked on with a group of the world's fastest milers. Together, we covered approximately six miles, and it turned out to be a truly extraordinary experience. Over the years, I had been fortunate to receive guidance from running coaches who imparted valuable insights to enhance my skills and technique. However, this training run provided an unparalleled opportunity for professional-level coaching from these world-class athletes themselves.

To my surprise and delight, the pros didn't simply leave me in their dust; instead, they engaged in conversation throughout the entire run, generously sharing their wisdom and experiences. They attentively observed my form and offered invaluable hints to optimize my running technique. It was a remarkable instance of camaraderie and mentorship, as they selflessly took the time to connect with me on a personal level. This incredible encounter propelled me to achieve one of my personal best running paces and times both during that training run and subsequently in the race itself.

Running alongside these world-class athletes, receiving their guidance, and witnessing their dedication, was an unforgettable experience that left an indelible mark on my journey as a runner. It served as a testament to the power of support and the incredible strides we can make when we have the privilege of learning from those who have reached the pinnacle of their sport.

VI. Perfect Match

Meeting the Best
Human Being Ever

Over the years, the tale of how I met my wife, Cathy, has been a recurring query among friends and family, each time reminding me of the serendipitous moment that would forever alter the course of my life. Before Cathy, I often joked that the first 37 years of my life were merely a rehearsal, a series of trials and errors in preparation for something grand. Indeed, that grand moment arrived unexpectedly, high above the clouds on a routine flight to St. Louis, MO. It was there, amidst the hum of the aircraft and the expanse of the sky, that fate introduced me to a petite, beautiful blonde named Cathy A. Case.

This chance encounter, seemingly mundane in the grand tapestry of life's events, was anything but ordinary for me. Cathy's presence, marked by a feeling of warmth and a captivating smile, drew me in from the moment I laid eyes on her. Our initial exchange of pleasantries soon blossomed into a profound conversation that made the miles disappear beneath us. With each word, it became increasingly clear that this was not just another chance meeting, but the beginning of a journey I had been unconsciously preparing for all my life. Cathy, with her infectious laughter and insightful views on life, illuminated a path I hadn't realized I was seeking, guiding me towards a future filled with love, companionship, and endless adventure.

Whenever I spent time with her, I could not help but notice her qualities as a loving, caring human being. Those moments solidified my decision to take a chance and see where this could lead. And so, my relationship with this amazing woman I had unexpectedly met on a plane continued to flourish. I questioned myself repeatedly if I was willing to expose my vulnerability once more. However, I can confidently say that choosing to move forward was the right decision. My love for Cathy Case, that petite beautiful blonde, grows stronger each day we spend together!

It was a Monday morning, and I was on my way to a trade show where I would oversee the company's presence, showcasing their products with brand new marketing material. Typically, when I traveled for business, I preferred an aisle seat. However, for some reason, I was assigned a window seat on this particular trip. As everyone settled in, the flight attendants prepared the aircraft for takeoff and closed the overhead compartments. Just as the main cabin door was about to be shut, a petite blonde woman burst through the entrance, catching everyone's attention. She hastily boarded the plane, juggling a giant carry-on duffle bag, a large purse, and a briefcase slung over her shoulder. Oh, and let's not forget the sizable cup of coffee she managed to hold in her other hand. I was genuinely impressed by her ability to handle all her belongings without bumping into anyone, dropping anything, or spilling a drop of coffee.

In my row, the aisle seat was occupied, but the middle seat remained vacant. Secretly, I hoped no one would claim that middle seat since I intended to review my new investment information after going through the marketing materials for the upcoming trade show. As I observed, the blonde woman valiantly attempted to stow her hefty duffle bag in the overhead compartment. Eventually, a flight attendant came to her aid and closed the compartment for her. But, as luck would have it, she ended up taking the middle seat next to mine.

After exchanging a cordial "good morning" greeting with the passenger next to me, I resumed reviewing the materials related to my new investments. Following my divorce, I had prioritized rebuilding my financial future, leading me to work together with a financial planner in Hunt Valley, MD. As I was looking over the details of my investments, I became conscious of the privacy of the information. To prevent any inadvertent disclosure to nearby passengers, I decided to discreetly put the folder back into my briefcase. Then, I shifted my attention to a Money magazine, which coincidentally featured articles about the very assets I had recently invested

288

in. This allowed me to continue my financial education without risking the exposure of personal investment details.

As I sat beside the blonde lady, I couldn't help but notice the delightful fragrance she wore. It reminded me that my female training friend, from the Adventurers Club, had an upcoming birthday in two weeks. I thought of giving her perfume for her birthday. Leaning over, I complimented my new seatmate, saying, "Your perfume smells absolutely delightful. May I ask what it's called?" In my enthusiasm, I did not fully consider the potential implications of my comment. *It suddenly dawned on me that she might interpret my inquiry as a feeble attempt as a pickup line, on a Monday morning, no less.*

She hesitated for a moment, gazing directly into my eyes, before answering, "It's called 'Galore.'" I quickly jotted down the name on a piece of paper and placed it in my shirt pocket. Thankfully, my question broke the ice, and we began discussing investments. She shared her experience attending a company-sponsored investment seminar at The Rouse Company in Columbia, MD. Furthermore, she revealed that she was a marketing executive traveling to Union Station in St. Louis to work on an inner-city train center renovation project. It was fascinating to hear about her involvement with the renovation of such a significant train station. I thoroughly enjoyed our conversation. Before I knew it, the pilot announced that we were about to land.

Once the plane landed, I mentioned I had rented a car and offered her a ride to either her hotel or Union Station. Upon seeing the lengthy queue at the car rental counter, she explained that her boss had scheduled a meeting she couldn't afford to miss. Realizing she could not wait for a rental car, she had to hail a cab. Just as she was about to leave, she handed me her business card, and we shook hands. Our eyes met as she reiterated her name, saying, "I'm Cathy Case. If you'd like a tour of Union Station, feel free to give me a call." I watched her depart with all her belongings, and a thought crossed my mind, I should follow up and give her a call.

After finally securing a rental car, I drove to my hotel, checked in, and proceeded to the St. Louis Convention Center to set up the trade show display area. Throughout the process of arranging the display panels and engaging with other individuals, I couldn't shake the memory of the blonde lady's face and name. Even though I recognized that our meeting on the airplane was merely a chance encounter, thoughts of her persisted until Wednesday afternoon. That's when I gathered the courage to call her and invite her to lunch on Thursday. Surprisingly, she accepted and suggested meeting at a specific spot in Union Station. Following our meal, she would fulfill her previous promise of giving me a tour.

As the trade show progressed smoothly, my mind remained fixated on this lady and the serendipitous encounter we had shared aboard the plane. I marveled at the fortuitousness of meeting someone in such a way and pondered how a single chance encounter could have such profound effects on our lives.

On Thursday, as I arrived at Union Station, she apologized, explaining that her boss had called yet another urgent meeting, leaving her only a few minutes to grab a quick sandwich. Eager to spend time with her, I purchased our sandwiches and beverages while she found us a spot to sit. During our conversation over a hurried lunch, I sensed an undeniable charm emanating from Cathy. It was difficult to pinpoint whether it was her beauty, warmth, generosity, or intellect that captivated me, but one thing was certain, I wanted to see her again.

Once we finished our meal, she handed me another business card, maintaining eye contact once again as we shook hands. She said, "If you're interested in a tour of Harborplace in Baltimore, don't hesitate to reach out." The fact that she had extended another invitation made me contemplate if I was pushing too hard, receiving two offers in a row. Reflecting on my behavior after receiving consecutive invitations from Cathy, I pondered whether I had been too eager or assertive in my responses, prompting her repeated offers. My introspection centered on the dynamics of my eagerness in re-engaging socially with Cathy following a divorce. I questioned whether my enthusiasm was overly keen, driven by a desire for connection yet wary of misinterpreting social cues in our interactions. My concerns were rooted in self-reflection, aiming to navigate the delicate balance between showing interest and not rushing into a situation I wasn't ready for—I didn't want to jump from the frying pan into the fire. Then on Friday, I packed up the trade show supplies, made arrangements for their return shipment, drove to the airport, and boarded my flight back to Baltimore.

I was still grappling with the aftermath of my divorce, and to make matters worse, I found myself working in a job I accepted while working at

SSA in a manufacturing corporation that did not fulfill my career needs. From the very beginning, warning signs emerged in this company because it was hindering my creativity and left me yearning for new challenges to expand my knowledge and expertise. The leadership resisted embracing technological advancements and modern management practices. It was my daily task to introduce and educate employees on new ways of utilizing technology in their work. It was a family-owned business where long-standing employees clung to outdated methods, reluctant to embrace change. Stepping into each corporate division felt like a time warp, transporting me back to what I thought would be like working in the 1940s and 1950s. Their resistance to technology was astonishing. They were content with pencil and paper, citing the tired phrase, "we've always done it this way." Dealing with such attitudes created an immensely challenging environment for me.

At this point in my career, I had come to realize that success alone, without acquiring new skills or gaining valuable experience, did not bring me happiness. While I received a handsome salary and a multitude of benefits, the stifling work environment hampered my creativity and professional growth. It was only a matter of time before I would once again confront the decision to chart a new career path.

Amid these struggles, there was a glimmer of hope. Even after the trade show in St. Louis, thoughts of Cathy Case lingered in my mind. I couldn't forget her face and the captivating feeling I experienced when we were together. Although my emotions from the divorce still haunted me, here I was, intrigued by a woman I had recently met. Yet, cautionary whispers within my mind reminded me of the perils of exploring such thoughts and feelings at this particular stage of my life, following a devastating divorce.

Consequently, it took three months before I mustered the courage to call Cathy and invite her for that long-awaited tour of Harborplace. We agreed to meet on the following Saturday at 5 p.m. outside Phillips's Seafood Restaurant in Harborplace. Eager to make a good impression, I arrived early but struggled to find a parking spot. I eventually settled for a spot several blocks away. Determined not to be late, I briskly walked the distance to ensure I arrived on time.

I sat at a table in the outdoor dining area of Phillips, ordering a soda and eagerly awaiting Cathy's arrival. As the minutes ticked by and it reached 5:30 p.m., doubts started creeping in. Would she stand me up? By 5:45 p.m., those doubts were almost a certainty. I couldn't help but feel perplexed because Cathy didn't strike me as the type to stand someone up. It was a new experience for me, and perhaps my instincts and emotions had been mistaken about her.

In those days, there were no cell phones for us to communicate with each other. Disappointed and somewhat hurt, I reluctantly put on my coat and made up my mind to leave. I contemplated how I could have misjudged Cathy as I tidied up the table, pushed in the chair, and turned towards the exit. Just then, to my surprise, Cathy burst through the atrium doors across from me, near where I was standing with my coat on. She asked if I had been waiting long. I couldn't help but think, seriously? Nearly an hour! Waiting long would be an understatement.

Her tardiness and dramatic entrance reminded me of our initial encounter, making me wonder if she was always disorganized and late for everything. Red flags waved in my mind about her, but I maintained a polite smile and didn't show my upset as we walked back to the table, I had just vacated to order dinner. It took a few minutes for my disappointment to fade, and I began to feel at ease again. We engaged in conversation about our careers and life, just like two individuals on a first date. After dinner, we strolled around Harborplace while she explained the workings of the shopping center business and how revenue was generated. When it was time to part ways, I took a leap of faith and decided to ask her out for dinner the following Saturday. Little did I know that this would mark the beginning of several subsequent Saturday meetings, as I delved further into my initial impressions of her beauty, warmth, generosity, and intellect over time. It was clear that being late for our first date was a fluke. She was never late for any future dates.

Prior to meeting Cathy, there was another woman I had trained with on weekends and occasionally had dinner with. She was the intended recipient of the perfume I wanted to give as a birthday gift. We both were going through difficult divorces, and I wanted to keep our relationship purely friendly without any romantic involvement. While she was pleasant, I made sure to maintain emotional distance. I believe she understood this, especially when I began dating Cathy regularly. Eventually, she started dating a divorced man and moved in with him. Soon after, she stopped attending training sessions and Adventurers Club meetings. I didn't make an effort to keep in touch, and before long, we lost contact.

Cathy and I shared countless memorable moments together. One date, in particular, still brings a smile to my face. It was our third date when we decided to drive to Loch Raven Dam. As we strolled along the shoreline, savoring the breathtaking scenery, time seemed to slip away. Eventually, the afternoon sun reminded us that it was time to leave Loch Raven and head back to Cathy's house in Columbia, MD. Before making our way home, we stopped at a small store to purchase sodas. We sat in the parking lot, sipping our drinks, while Cathy entertained me with stories of her upbringing in Flora, Illinois, a town with a population of 5,800.

As we resumed our drive to Cathy's house, she suddenly expressed the need to use the bathroom. The closest option happened to be a Shell gas station near the Towson Town Center Mall, roughly a 10-minute drive away. Once I parked the car, Cathy swiftly grabbed the restroom key and flashed a smile to me before disappearing around the corner towards the ladies' room. I stayed in the car, lost in the music and reflecting on what a beautiful and enjoyable day it had been with her. I continued listening to the radio for another five minutes, then 10. However, as the minutes stretched into 20, concern started to creep into my mind. In a playful mood, I couldn't help but wonder, did she call a cab and leave?

Unable to figure out why it was taking so long to return to the car, I decided to investigate and check the bathroom. Smiling to myself I thought if Cathy had indeed left, I could at least return the key. As I approached, a loud banging noise emanated from the direction of the ladies' room. With each step, it became increasingly clear that Cathy was inside, banging on the door from within. Somehow, the door had become jammed, trapping her inside. She couldn't exit until someone pushed hard from the outside to release it. The question that lingered was whether she had intentionally jammed the door, hoping to be rescued by her Prince Charming, or if she had simply found herself stuck in a gas station bathroom for an unexpected 20 minutes. Regardless, it became yet another delightful, funny and amusing memory we shared together.

Cathy played a pivotal role in helping me overcome my bitterness and view my divorce in a different light, as something that was in the past. She made me realize that I should not let this single event define who I had the opportunity to become. Cathy reinforced the idea that forgiveness is a trait of confident and courageous individuals who are better off in the long run. She constantly reminded me that this painful situation could be an extraordinary opportunity if I were willing to accept that simple fact. And deep down, I knew she was absolutely right.

I often found myself wondering why we hadn't crossed paths years earlier. However, maturity has a way of revealing the truth. We both acknowledged that our separate paths would have likely continued if we had met earlier, because we were different people back then. There were moments when I contemplated putting an end to this budding relationship.

However, I can confidently say that choosing to move forward was the right decision. My love for Cathy Case, that petite beautiful blonde, grows stronger each day we spend together!

Cathy Moving to Lutherville

When I first met Cathy, she owned a charming and compact home in Columbia, MD. Her daily commute to work was a breeze, taking less than 10 minutes even during peak traffic times. The size of her property was perfect for a single woman who frequently traveled for her job. There wasn't much yard to maintain. It was an ideal setup for her lifestyle.

However, living in a planned community like Columbia presented certain limitations for Cathy. Around six months into dating, Cathy began actively searching for homes in the Towson and Lutherville areas. One of the major reasons she wanted to move was the lack of close single friends in the area. The community was predominantly inhabited by married couples, many of whom were fellow employees of the Rouse company. In contrast, Cathy had friends residing in Baltimore, specifically in Towson and Lutherville. I couldn't help but think that one of the motivations behind her desire to relocate was to be closer to me, although it could have been wishful thinking on my part.

She found a house on Morris Avenue in historic Lutherville. She was considering making an offer on the house. She called me, excited and eager for my opinion. We met at the house. I initially assessed the home and wondered why she was interested. It seemed to require extensive repairs and updates compared to my lovely two-year-old home, which had no maintenance issues. The house she had her eye on was nearly three decades old and needed significant attention. The owner, a cardiothoracic surgeon and was more focused on his stock investments and neglected the necessary repairs and modernization of his home. We visited the house multiple times, and with each visit, the list of repairs and upgrades seemed to grow longer.

Cathy was particularly drawn to the house in Lutherville because of its location in the historic neighborhood. The streets exuded charm, adorned with majestic, mature trees and numerous well-preserved historic homes. Unlike the planned community of Columbia, this area had organically evolved over time, retaining its timeless allure.

After receiving and accepting an offer on her Columbia house, Cathy made the purchase and officially became a resident of historic Lutherville. Around the same time, I found a new position in Washington, D.C., which meant spending extra hours commuting between Baltimore and the capital. Despite the demands of my job, I made sure to carve out time to assist Cathy with the necessary repairs, aiming to minimize her move-in costs. Before long, I sold my townhouse to a couple who happened to live just two doors away from my former home. They had previously rented a unit nearby before deciding to purchase my townhouse.

To my pleasant surprise, Cathy's new Lutherville neighbors turned out to be warm and welcoming. Just two houses away, I discovered the residence of Mimi and Dave DeGrafft, who happened to be my fifth-grade teacher. Reconnecting with Dave after so many years was a delightful encounter. He showed genuine interest in my life and career. We reminisced about my time in the Army, combat experiences in Vietnam, and my journey through education, obtaining both undergraduate and graduate degrees at the University of Maryland. Mimi, his lovely wife, shared stories about their wonderful family and grandchildren, painting a vibrant picture of their lives.

On Cathy's right side lived Charles and Martha Robinson. Charles held the respected position of director of the Baltimore County library system. He was the longest-serving library system director in the entire United States at the time. He had achieved legendary status within the library community across America. Martha was a skilled handworker proficient in needlepoint and cross-stitch. She quickly became a close friend to Cathy. When our daughter Casey was born, Martha proved to be an invaluable source of guidance and support for Cathy. There were occasions when Martha and Charles graciously offered to babysit Casey if either of us had to work late.

On the left side of Cathy's home resided Bill and Ruth Halum. Bill had dedicated many years to the Marine Corps Reserves, while Ruth served as a nurse at St. Joseph Hospital. They had a large family, with several children and numerous grandchildren. It was always a joy to witness the lively family gatherings, especially during the festive Christmas season.

Visiting Cathy's Parents

As our second Christmas together approached, Cathy extended an invitation for me to spend the holidays with her parents in Hot Springs Village, AR. After dating for over two years, I could tell Cathy really wanted me to meet her parents. We flew from Baltimore to Little Rock, where Cathy's mom and dad eagerly awaited us at the airport's baggage claim area. Cathy had told them a lot about me, and they were excited to finally meet me in person. The warmth of their greeting was overwhelming, instantly making me feel at ease and as if we had known each other for years. Throughout the drive to their home in Hot Springs Village, Cathy's parents demonstrated a genuine desire to get to know me better, asking numerous questions that allowed me to share my life story, where I had been, and my aspirations for the future.

At one point during our ride to their home, Cathy's father initiated a conversation about my military service. He said, "Cathy tells me you were in the Army and served in Vietnam." I respectfully replied, "Yes, sir, I was in Vietnam." Curious to know more, he asked, "Did you see combat?" Once again, I responded, "Yes, sir, I did." To shift the focus away from myself and Vietnam, I quickly added, "Cathy mentioned that you flew B-17s in World War II. She also told me that you had been shot down, captured, and spent the rest of the war as a prisoner." This revelation sparked a lively and engaging discussion, making our hour-long ride to their home feel much shorter. Upon our arrival, Cathy's parents graciously showed us to our respective separate rooms.

After settling in, we reconvened downstairs, where Cathy's father, Bob, kindly offered me a drink. With pride, he announced the presence of Old Grand-Dad and Wild Turkey bourbon. I was so impressed that they had paid attention when Cathy shared details about me, like my favorite bourbon, it really made me feel like they cared already. As we sipped our drinks, our conversation continued to flow. I expressed my admiration for their beautiful home, and they eagerly shared the story of how they acquired two adjoining lots and built their residence. Situated overlooking the picturesque 18th fairway of the Cortez golf course, their home was nestled within the captivating Hot Springs Village, a community of mostly retirees and boasted seven enchanting golf courses.

The abundance and variety of food prepared by Cathy's mother, Betty, indicated that she had been cooking and baking for weeks in anticipation of our arrival. Each dish was a delight, leaving me in awe of her culinary skills. After dinner, she presented an array of incredibly delicious desserts, including mouthwatering shortbread cookies, zesty lemon bars, delectable chocolate chip cookies, assorted cakes, and, of course, Cathy's father's favorite treat, vanilla ice cream. While all the desserts were exceptional, those shortbread cookies were my favorites and Betty noticed. Over the years, she would bake multiple batches and send them to me on birthdays, holidays, or just any time of the year simply out of her kindness and generosity. Her pure heartedness was one of her most precious qualities and made me feel cherished, like a son.

Cathy's mother, Betty, was not only lovely but also a kind and nurturing soul. On numerous occasions, as I observed Cathy and her mother together, I could not help but see the striking resemblance between them, both in terms of their physical features and their genuinely warm personalities.

Seeking Blessing for Marriage

Before summoning the courage to ask Cathy's parents for their blessing to marry their daughter, I found myself wrestling with a whirlwind of emotions. Doubts and fears gnawed at me. Was I simply rebounding from my previous relationship, or was I leaping from one uncertain situation to another? However, deep within my heart, I sensed that this was different. Once again, I felt the desire to embark on a journey into the unknown. Despite my reservations, I passionately believed that Cathy had become my closest companion, and I wholeheartedly believed she was the one. Our relationship had reached a significant level of seriousness, and I was ready to take the leap into marriage. I had an almost spiritual certainty about Cathy's love for me as it had grown and her unwavering commitment to our future together. Ultimately, I knew in my heart that Cathy was on an entirely different level from any of my previous female friends. I realized it was time to embrace the future without allowing the past to potentially overshadow the beauty that lay ahead.

Seeking her parents' approval felt like the right course of action. It was important to me that Cathy knew how deeply I cared for her and that I respected her relationship with her parents. Moreover, I believed that her parents would appreciate the gesture of a formal request. Her parents held a significant place in Cathy's life, and their blessing carried immense weight. I was genuinely curious about Cathy's parents' impression of me, considering that she had shared a great deal about my background with them. She had covered various aspects such as my career, age, and Catholic heritage. I wondered if any of these factors might raise concerns regarding our future together. To prepare for any potential questions, I took the time to reflect on each aspect and formulate my responses. However, as I geared up for this conversation, a small voice in the back of my mind pondered what would happen if they objected due to my Catholic faith, prior divorce, or Vietnam veteran status.

Nevertheless, I reassured myself with thoughts of how could they possibly say anything other than yes? After all, I loved their daughter, and not to mention my dashing good looks, impeccably pressed clothes, and highly shined shoes. But before seeking Cathy's parents' approval, I needed to ensure that she wanted to marry me. It would have been awkward to obtain their blessing only to have her decline. Just kidding, I had already proposed to her on Thursday before we departed from Baltimore. Yes, I got down on one knee in her kitchen and asked, "Cathy Ann Case, will you marry me?"

One evening, while Cathy's parents were busy preparing dinner and she was in her bedroom, I approached them and requested a moment of their time to sit down and talk. We gathered around the kitchen table, and as I looked into their eyes, I poured out my heart. I passionately explained why I believed I was a good match for her and how committed I was to our relationship of two years. With sincerity, I expressed the immense joy she brought into my life and my desire to spend the rest of my days by her side.

Taking a deep breath, I finally mustered the courage to ask, "May I have your permission and blessings to marry Cathy?"

At that moment, Cathy's mother stood up, approached me with open arms, and hugged me. She planted a loving kiss on my cheek and then while hugging me she wholeheartedly said yes. Meanwhile, her father, wearing a warm smile, shook my hand and uttered his approval. To my surprise, he then went a step further by enveloping me in a warm hug and planting kisses on both of my cheeks. WOW, I was not accustomed to such affectionate gestures from other men. That beautiful encounter marked the beginning of countless memorable and loving visits to Cathy's parents' home.

Cathy and Bob's Wedding July 12, 1987

Cathy and I, both in our late 30s, eagerly took on the task of planning our wedding, embracing the chance to work together on this significant milestone. The first step in our journey was finalizing the invitation list. With the guest count in hand, we could accurately determine the quantities of food and drinks needed for our celebration.

Recognizing the importance of finding the perfect setting for our nuptials, we simultaneously began the search for our dream wedding venue. We both envisioned an outdoor ceremony that would incorporate our religious beliefs, a vision that added complexity to our search beyond the simplicity of choosing a church and reception hall.

As we explored various locations, our weekends were dedicated to preparing for the post-ceremony festivities. For an entire month, we made regular trips to Edgeway Discount Liquors just outside Bel Air, MD. These excursions allowed us to gradually stock up on bottled water, soda and alcohol, and by the end of our shopping endeavors, Cathy's basement on Morris Ave had transformed into what resembled a charming boutique liquor store. This methodical approach not only ensured we were well-prepared for our celebration but also allowed us to enjoy the planning process together.

After approximately two months of exploration, we came upon the Hampton Mansion in Towson. The staff graciously provided us with information about hours, costs, and regulations. As we embarked on a tour, we were impressed by the sight of the impeccably preserved 18th-century estate, complete with grand Georgian structures and exquisite formal gardens.

It was a visual masterpiece. Ultimately, we concluded that the Hampton Mansion was the perfect setting for our wedding and reception.

The rear lawn of the mansion emerged as the ideal outdoor spot for our ceremony. Beneath the shade of two colossal trees that had stood since the Revolutionary War, we would exchange our vows. Moreover, the ground was even, ensuring a safe walk for the ladies in their high-heeled shoes. Adjacent to the lawn, the Orangery served as the staging area for our food and beverages, and most importantly our wedding cake. The cake, a work of culinary art, was lovingly crafted by an associate of Cathy's at The Rouse Company. On the big day, several of Cathy's co-workers lent their assistance, contributing to the success and beauty of our wedding.

My beautiful bride

In the days leading up to our wedding, I found temporary residence with one of Cathy's associates after selling my house. They found my routine peculiar on the morning of the wedding, when I woke at the crack of dawn. Without delay, I showered and dressed in my cycling gear and embarked on a 25-mile bicycle ride. This unconventional activity had a purpose. During my ride, I focused on memorizing and rehearsing my vows. I was determined to recite each commitment flawlessly.

After completing my cycling session, I refreshed myself with another shower and got dressed in my wedding attire. As I readied myself to depart, the weather took a sudden turn. Dark clouds loomed ominously, threatening to unleash heavy thunder and lightning at any moment. Yet, amidst the gloom of a large thunderstorm, a glimmer of hope emerged, a patch of blue sky resided directly above the Hampton Mansion, where our ceremony was to take place. Guests who had driven to the wedding recounted their travels through the thunderstorms and torrential rain on their way. That day, it seemed as though divine intervention smiled upon us, for the rain spared the Hampton Mansion from its downpour and blue sky was exposed above!

Father Joe Webb, the Episcopal Priest from Holy Comforter church in the historic town of Lutherville, officiated our wedding ceremony. Interestingly, not many people know about the surprising twist in our pre-marriage counseling

Husband and wife

with Joe. He had administered various tests that highlighted our divergent tastes and personalities. We were both shocked and very surprised when Joe advised against marriage. Yet here we are, more than 35 years later, still going strong. In the end, his intentions were good, and he conducted a truly memorable wedding service for us at the enchanting Hampton Mansion.

Following the festivities, we thoroughly cleaned up the venue, packed away the remaining food and drinks, and returned to Morris Avenue. After a quick change of clothes, we embarked on a drive to the Embassy Suites Hotel at Baltimore Washington International (BWI) airport, where we spent the night. The next morning, at the crack of dawn, we set off on our airplane journey to New York, marking the start of our much-anticipated honeymoon in England. The transatlantic flight was relatively smooth. We managed to catch up on much-needed sleep during most of the journey. I glanced over at Cathy several times and noticed she was exhausted and desperately needed sleep. The cumulative effect of the wedding preparations and the actual wedding had finally taken its toll. Despite being overly fatigued, she eventually drifted off to sleep. Nevertheless, even with her tiredness and slight puffiness under her eyes, she remained a vision of beauty as the radiant bride she was to me.

Upon reaching England, we picked up our rental car and embarked on a scenic drive through the breathtaking southeastern English countryside. The quaint houses that lined the roads added to the charm of the journey. However, a bewildering change came over Cathy, leaving me puzzled and concerned. Her demeanor shifted, and she began making snarky remarks and providing curt responses during our conversations. At times, my mind wandered back in time, questioning whether I had once again made the wrong choice. As we checked into our hilltop hotel and entered our room, I summoned the courage to ask her directly, "What's wrong Cathy, don't you want to be married to me?"

Her response was laced with anger as she expressed her desperate desire for a cig-

The happy couple

arette. I was shocked and stunned, feeling as if someone had knocked the wind out of me. Months prior, Cathy had assured me that she had quit smoking, but evidently, she had not. Here I was, married to a woman who indulged in smoking cigarettes, despite promising myself I would never marry someone who smoked cigarettes. Confusion clouded my thoughts as they went into overdrive. Should I call it quits, pack my bags, and return home?

To clear my mind and dispel the negative thoughts, I got up and retrieved a room key, then walked outside for what felt like an eternity. Eventually, I came upon a small store that sold cigarettes. Yes, I caved and purchased a pack along with matches before making my way back to the room. Handing them to Cathy, I implored her to genuinely commit to quitting smoking this time. The following week, she discarded the remaining cigarettes, and I firmly believe she has never smoked since.

I am sure there were aspects of my personality that gave Cathy pause because we were in a period of adjusting to another person's ways and mannerisms. However, her cigarette smoking truly bothered me, especially considering she had assured me that she had quit. I couldn't help but wonder if she was like my previous wife, who hadn't been entirely truthful. Nevertheless, I chose not to give up easily and decided that time would reveal the truth. The next two weeks would be a perfect opportunity to assess this situation.

After time on the Isle of Wight, we made our way back to the mainland and spent two delightful days in Bath. During our drive, I casually mentioned to Cathy that since we were so close to Ireland, it would be a shame not to visit. In a half-joking manner, I added that if we didn't go there while in England, my mother would never let me hear the end of it. To my surprise, my wonderful new bride took charge and arranged a short trip to Ireland. This was an exciting prospect for me, as I had never been to the land where my mother's family originated. In contrast, Cathy had fond memories of vacationing in Ireland with her parents after college, so she was equally eager to explore the country once again with me.

Cathy took care of booking our flights and accommodations for our brief excursion to Ireland. We departed from Bristol Airport and landed in Cork, a short flight away. I had no idea where we were headed or where we would stay, but it turned out to be a delightful surprise. Stepping foot on Irish soil meant that my mother would continue to speak to me after we returned home.

Just before our wedding, I purchased a new Timex Triathlon watch with a waterproof design and a bright night light. My previous Triathlon watch had stopped working during one of my workouts, so I wanted to ensure this one served me as well as the other had. Like its predecessor, I would place it on the bedside table each night of our journey. However, our first night in a Cork hotel would bring an unexpected twist. In the middle of the night, while I was still asleep, I shook Cathy awake and presented her with the watch, showcasing its illuminating night light. Oblivious to my actions, I returned the watch to the side table, peacefully laid my head back on the pillow, and continued sleeping. The next morning, I had no recollection of this incident. It was Cathy who informed me that I had awakened her to show off the watch's glowing feature. She kindly requested that I refrain from waking her in the future for such demonstrations. Little did she know that this would be just the beginning of technological surprises she would encounter from me over our married life. As a lover of all things tech and gadgets, I consistently introduced new technologies into our home over the years. I also assisted Cathy in embracing and mastering new technologies throughout her career and into retirement.

During our travels in Ireland, we discovered the Ballymaloe House Hotel, a charming family-owned country house hotel, cooking school and restaurant nestled amidst the picturesque countryside of southeastern Ireland, not far from the Cork coast. This place was a hidden gem, exuding a unique and magical atmosphere thanks to its stunning natural surroundings. We felt incredibly lucky to have stumbled upon this tranquil and idyllic retreat. It was also known as a top-tier cooking school, offering exceptional culinary education to students from around the world since 1983. As we arrived, we were greeted with tantalizing aromas and the sight of freshly prepared dishes and delectable desserts meticulously arranged on long tables adorned with crisp white linen tablecloths. As we stepped inside to check in for the night, the attentive staff even offered us plates filled with warm, mouthwatering food.

That evening, our dinner seemed to go on indefinitely. Course after course arrived at our table, accompanied by delightful local wines. What amazed us the most was the affordability of our stay, considering the abundance of food, wine, and desserts, as well as the excellent room and service we received. What a wonderful and successful find.

The following day, we made a visit to Blarney Castle & Gardens to fulfill the tradition of kissing the Blarney Stone. My mother had always told me that those who kissed the stone would be blessed with eloquence and lifelong good luck. It was a must-do for me before leaving Ireland. To accomplish this, I had to lie down on my back, tilt my head under a stone wall, and plant an upside-down kiss on the ancient rock. Cathy, however, had no interest in contorting herself into such an uncomfortable position and kissing a stone that countless others had done before. I couldn't argue with her on that, as I wasn't entirely sure about the hygienic aspects myself. I never mentioned to her how discolored the bottom of the stone was. Nevertheless, I went ahead and did it. Now I can proudly claim that I've kissed the Blarney Stone, thankfully my teeth haven't fallen out as the old joke goes.

The castle's gardens were absolutely beautiful, and we leisurely strolled around the entire estate, taking in the breathtaking scenery. Once again, we set off to explore more of the Irish countryside, but this time we encountered intermittent heavy rain throughout the day. Luckily, we again found an inn with a cozy bar to seek refuge until the rain subsided. Nestled in comfortable leather chairs, we gazed out through large windows at a stunning deep green valley, warmed by the crackling fire in the fireplace. We savored the view until the rain finally ceased. I recall the sight of majestic trees adorning the rolling hills in the distance. Even with the rain, I found myself imagining how perfect this place could be as a place to call home.

After visiting Cork and Blarney, we made our way to Tipperary, the ancestral land of my mother's family, a fact she had often reminded me of while I was growing up. Our accommodation was a small castle undergoing conversion to a bed-and-breakfast, still it was a work in progress. Our room was only halfway painted, and the shower was so small and cramped that Cathy and I kept accidentally knocking our arms against the round doors while showering. Nevertheless, staying there provided us with opportunities to engage in conversations about Tipperary's history with the innkeepers and locals.

The next morning, we took a leisurely stroll through the charming town of Tipperary, exploring its many small shops and stores. We even stopped by a bookstore to peruse the reading preferences of the locals. Surprisingly, the book selections were not much different from those found in bookstores back in the States. As I viewed the magazine shelves, I came across a Ph.D. dissertation on the history of Tipperary and its people, encompassing the surrounding countryside of Ireland. It was a well-written account of the area, and I decided to purchase it to read during the remainder of our trip and the flight back home. Once I finished reading it, I passed it on to my mother and brother Bill. When I asked my mom if she enjoyed it, she expressed her thanks for learning more about the history of Tipperary and its people, particularly their connections to Scotland. As for my brother Bill, I'm not entirely sure if he ever read it, because when I asked for it back, he casually mentioned that he had thrown it out with the garbage after reading it. So much for preserving our ancestral history, right?

This leg of our Irish honeymoon was filled with new and captivating experiences, truly embodying the magic, mystery, and marvel of Ireland.

The enchanting accents, the legendary Blarney Stone, and the vibrant ambiance of the pubs offered just a glimpse into the country's enchantment. I vividly recall driving down a narrow Irish road, uncertain if we were on the right path to our next overnight stay. It was then that I decided to stop a man I spotted walking along the secluded road and asked him for directions to Clonmel. However, his speech was unintelligible to both Cathy and me, he was either speaking Gaelic or he was inebriated, or maybe he simply didn't wish to engage in conversation at that moment with anyone. We graciously thanked him and proceeded on our way, sharing a laugh at our mutual inability to comprehend a word he said.

The most unnerving experience occurred during our flight from Ireland back to England. Given the security concerns between England and Ireland in the late 1980s, due to the ongoing conflict involving the Irish Republican Army (IRA), we felt a heightened sense of caution. Our flight was scheduled to depart from Dublin aboard a small regional aircraft that could accommodate approximately 20 passengers. After the ground crew had loaded the baggage and we had boarded the plane, we settled in for our short flight back to England. We noticed the considerable amount of time it took for the flight crew to close the cabin door. There was no communication regarding the cause of the delay. It was then that we observed the pilot and co-pilot leaving the aircraft. Looking around, I realized that the two front row seats were unoccupied. Finally, a crew member entered the plane and informed us that two bags had been checked for those seats, but the passengers had not yet been located. A wave of tension and concern washed over the cabin. At that moment, I couldn't help but contemplate the possibility of a catastrophic event, especially after having survived combat in Vietnam and enduring multiple instances of being shot down. Trying to alleviate some of my uneasiness, I turned to Cathy and jokingly suggested that the passengers were likely stuck in traffic.

Although I wasn't certain if my comment provided any comfort, Cathy appeared less worried, and it provided some relief for me as well. As time passed, I found myself hoping that the aircraft would be evacuated. Eventually, accompanied by local police, the ground crew emerged from the terminal building. They were escorting two older women who had been completely unaware of the time while they browsed the duty-free shop and had lunch. The immense relief that swept over me was intense. I'm sure others felt the same, but we couldn't help but feel a mixture of relief and frustration towards those women.

Once back in England, we had the pleasure of staying at several wonderfully unique accommodations. On one occasion, we slept in a room situated above a pub. The room was illuminated solely by a pull-chain light with a meager 45-watt bulb hanging from a ceiling over 15 feet high. It was the only source of illumination in the entire room. The distant sound of music, people chatting, and laughter from the bar downstairs added to the ambiance. We chuckled at the dimness of the room, as even reading a few pages in our books proved challenging. Nevertheless, the experience was worth it, for just across the street awaited the magnificent Cambridge University, where we would spend several hours exploring.

The following day, as we drove towards Stonehenge, it began to rain heavily. Seeking refuge from the downpour, we stopped in a quaint little town where we purchased a bottle of wine, a selection of cheese, and freshly baked bread. Our original plan was to enjoy this delightful feast once we reached Stonehenge, but the aroma of the bread proved irresistible. Unable

Me with bread and cheese

to resist its allure, we found ourselves nibbling on the bread almost immediately. Upon our arrival at Stonehenge, we sat in the car, eagerly awaiting a break in the rain, and finished eating the remaining delicious cheese and bread, accompanied by sips of wine. Even after all these years, the memory of that moment remains vivid, and it evokes a mouthwatering sensation. It was a truly magical time for me, being in the company of the most wonderful person on Earth. Together, we sat in the rental car, gazing out at the rain, savoring those unplanned and special moments while waiting for the rain to cease at Stonehenge, England.

Following our visit to Stonehenge, we embarked on a drive to Brighton Beach. The subsequent day, we had the pleasure of exploring the illustrious 200-year-old Royal Pavilion. Situated in the heart of Brighton, this exotic palace has a rich and colorful history. Originally constructed as a seaside pleasure palace for King George IV, it was a beautiful blend of the grandeur of Britain and the enchanting visual elements from India and China. The palace boasted an array of beautifully painted rooms and ceilings that captivated our senses. It was intriguing to learn that the Royal Pavilion also served as a local government building and even a hospital during World War I.

After our delightful time at Brighton Beach, we made our way back to London where we spent the night. The following morning marked our departure, as we caught our flight back to the United States. During our journey home, Cathy wore an outfit I had bought for her prior to our marriage. She looked stunningly beautiful, and exhaustion eventually lured her into a peaceful sleep once again on the plane ride back to the United States and home. I couldn't help but smile, realizing that this would be just one of many exhilarating yet tiring vacations we would embark on throughout our lives together.

Reflecting on the years we've weathered side by side, it's undeniable that life has thrown its share of trials our way. From the heart-wrenching illness and eventual loss of her mother to the painful farewells we've had to say to my siblings, grief was an uninvited guest that lingered too long in our lives. Before Cathy entered my world, I was no stranger to sorrow. Yet, it's within the crucible of these hardships that our bond was forged stronger, her love acting as a balm to the wounds of loss. The shared weight of our grief became, paradoxically, a source of comfort and made the burden just a bit lighter to bear. Amidst this backdrop of challenges, we've also carved out spaces for joy, laughter, and shared dreams. Our life together has been a tapestry of profound love and harmony, punctuated by countless smiles, infectious laughter, moments of pure bliss, and numerous journeys taken hand in hand. I am deeply thankful for every lesson learned, every moment of support, and the abundance of blessings that have enriched our shared path in life.

The Beginning of the Best Chapter of My Life

Our honeymoon, a beautiful prologue to the symphony of our lives together, was not merely a journey across England and Ireland but a voyage into the heart of our love, setting the stage for a deeply connected, loving marriage that has flourished over 37 years and still does today. Reflecting on those initial days, I see them in a light so different from my first journey down the aisle. With Cathy, each moment was infused with profound learning and an unspoken promise of togetherness, teaching us the essence of navigating life's waters as partners in love.

Adaptability and patience became our early lessons as we transitioned from the high of our wedding into the reality of intertwining our lives. Cathy's mood shift due to tiredness upon reaching England was a stark reminder of the need to flow with the tides of each other's emotions, embracing each moment with understanding and grace. Our adventures, from the tranquil drives through the English countryside to the spontaneous decision to explore Ireland, became a canvas for our shared dreams, teaching us the beauty of seizing life's spontaneities together.

Our journey was also about peeling back the layers of our hearts, where I discovered the importance of honesty and open communication. Cathy's struggle with smoking was a hurdle we faced early on, but addressing it candidly laid the foundation for a relationship built on transparency and trust. It was a pivotal moment, showing me the depth of Cathy's commitment and her willingness to overcome personal battles for the sake of our love. Her victory over this challenge was a testament to the strength and support that would define our journey together.

In the quirks of our daily lives, from the whimsical moments waking Cathy to admire my Timex Triathlon watch light in the still of the night, to our shared laughter in a dimly lit pub, I found the magic that binds us. These instances, seemingly small, have been the building blocks of our enduring bond, celebrating the joy in each other's unique selves.

But beyond the laughter, we've navigated through storms together, our bond a beacon of support and empathy. Our ability to share in each other's grief and joy has not only tested but strengthened our love, proving it a steadfast anchor through the years.

Looking back, I realize how our honeymoon was much more than a beginning. It was a promise fulfilled each day, a lesson in love, adaptability, and mutual support that has blossomed into a life rich with understanding and affection. Cathy's inherent qualities, the same ones that I admired as we embarked on our married life together, have made her not only my beloved partner but the best human being ever to touch my life.

Friends, Neighbors, Speedos, and Plumber's Helper

Prior to marrying Cathy and before Casey's arrival, I invested a significant portion of my free time in triathlon training. Enhancing my swimming speed and refining my technique became paramount. I was determined to excel in the water by increasing my velocity and minimizing water resistance. Over time, I gradually opted for a smaller swimsuit, eventually selecting the tiniest Speedo swim trunks available. Admittedly, referring to Speedos as proper swim attire is challenging due to their minimalistic design. The less external material translated to reduced water drag, allowing me to swim faster.

The entire time of dating Cathy, we hadn't gone to a beach or pool together, so she remained unaware of my affinity for Speedos. Prior to our wedding, Cathy's Lutherville coworkers hosted a pre-wedding pool party in our honor. Cathy consistently reminded me to pack my swim gear and towels for the event.

In preparation, I readied my swim bag, ensuring I had all the essential equipment. After dinner, I changed into one of my customary Speedo swimsuits. As I stepped out of the house onto the pool deck, Cathy greeted me with a startled expression, as if she had encountered a ghost. Could it be that she wasn't accustomed to men wearing Speedos? When I walked around the pool, her friends also cast curious glances, making me feel somewhat exposed and ill at ease. Their unexpected reactions puzzled me, as in my experience swimming training at local pools, both men and women who regularly swam sported Speedos or TYR swimsuits. Needless to say, I certainly made a memorable impression at that gathering.

Another weekend not long after our marriage, Cathy and I received an invitation to a dinner party at the home of an executive from The Rouse Company. I pondered the purpose behind the dinner, was it a celebratory occasion or more of an executive social gathering? Given my limited understanding of The Rouse Company, I assumed it to be the latter, a gathering of corporate leaders. Following dinner, the male executives gathered in the family room for after-dinner drinks, engaging in discussions about investments, weather and sports. Our host, a Rouse executive, turned his attention to me, launching into a line of questioning that immediately clued me in on his intent. He sought information about my workplace, my position, and my connections, all with an eye toward potential future access. This type of introductory conversation was standard practice in the Washington, D.C., area.

As someone who grew up in Dundalk and had experienced combat, I found myself in a room filled with individuals who had not served in the military but nevertheless had achieved successful careers. While chatting, memories resurfaced of my previous attempts to secure technology positions at The Rouse Company after my time in the Army and Vietnam. Unfortunately, these attempts had been met with consistent responses that the positions were already filled. I could not help but sense the pervasive unfair judgment that often greeted returning Vietnam veterans and institutional indifference.[43]

Engaging with The Rouse Company executives was a pleasant experience, and I could have easily been mistaken for one of them. I was dressed in the appropriate corporate attire, wearing a Brooks Brothers suit and Allan Edmonds shoes. The corporate executive host directed a question at me, asking about my line of work and place of employment. I had anticipated this type of inquiry due to my past experiences in D.C. and was fairly certain it would come up during the evening. Feeling a playful, teasing mood coming

---

[43] I use my definition of institutional indifference toward Vietnam Veterans seeking work after the war that was a complex issue marked by a disconnect between the sacrifices made by veterans and the lack of support by institutions during their reintegration into society.

over me, I deliberately paused before answering. Gazing at each executive in turn, I playfully responded, "I'm a plumber's helper by trade, working towards becoming a licensed plumber, and I come from Dundalk." Their immediate change in demeanor was quite telling. Dundalk was and is a working-class community, not the upscale neighborhood of the party's location. It was amusing to see their expressions shift abruptly. I might as well have shown up in the nude, the surprise was so evident. With a slight raise of my glass, I remarked that I needed to freshen my drink and asked if anyone else wanted or needed anything. Then I walked away from the startled group.

Thirty years later, Cathy and I found ourselves on vacation with the same Rouse Company executive who had hosted the party. During the course of that vacation, he confided in us. He admitted that after the party, he had looked up my name and discovered my position as a senior executive at the Federal Reserve Board of Governors. He also confessed that when he had posed those questions at the party, he believed he had put me in an awkward position and embarrassed me when I responded about being a plumber's helper from Dundalk. This revelation came while Cathy and I were sailing on a catamaran with him and his neighbor friends around the British Virgin Islands. Nevertheless, even with this new perspective, I harbored no regrets about my responses during that party many years prior. When someone asks such questions, they should be prepared to accept the answers they receive.

Dinners for Eight

Living in Lutherville, we discovered that our most enjoyable dinner gatherings began at Holy Comforter Episcopal Church. These delightful events, known as Dinners for Eight, allowed us to savor both delicious food and warm fellowship, surrounded by a mix of familiar faces and new acquaintances. The dinners took place in welcoming homes located not far from our own house and the church and created a sense of closeness within our community.

When we first joined the Dinners for Eight program, there was already an established list of gracious hosts. So, as eager participants, we simply signed up and initially attended as guests. Eventually, we became active church members and continued to relish these gatherings. These homes were thoughtfully arranged to accommodate eight adults, randomly selected to share a memorable dinner.

The host would generously provide the main dish, while the guests contributed their culinary creations in the form of a side dish or dessert. Once the groups were assigned to a specific home, the host would reach out to the guests, sharing the exciting details of the main course. This allowed everyone to plan accordingly and bring a complimentary dish. What made Dinners for Eight even more delightful was the fact that culinary expertise was not a requirement. A simple bagged salad or a store-bought cake was just as appreciated as a gourmet masterpiece. These dinners were never about the intricacies of the food itself, but rather, the time spent together in heartfelt fellowship. Eventually we felt the need to move closer to Washington, D.C. This wonderful dining experience would be greatly missed after our move.

VII. Family Man

Creating Our Family

Journey to Parenthood: Adventures, Missteps, and Serendipity

One of the greatest blessings in my life has undoubtedly been my loving family. After Cathy and I married, the idea of having children became a topic of discussion for us. In July 1989, after I completed the Baltimore Triathlon, we took a vacation to the beautiful Pacific Northwest and ventured into Vancouver, British Columbia, Canada. We only made hotel reservations for the early part of our trip. I anticipated that we might deviate from our planned route much to Cathy's dismay, I was hoping to discover unique accommodations along the scenic backroads. She wanted to plan the route, hotels, activities, and sights to see along the entire trip.

Our journey began in Baltimore and brought us to Portland, where we spent the first two days exploring the city and its surroundings. On our first evening, we decided to dine at a lovely Chinese restaurant. As we looked over the menu, we noticed several spicy options. I have never been a fan of hot or spicy food, so I opted for a salad, while Cathy expressed her desire for something hot, tangy, and salty. When the server warned Cathy about the intense spiciness of her choices and suggested a milder alternative, she reconsidered her initial selection and opted for the recommended dish. However, even the second option was described as hot and spicy by the server. Despite the warning, Cathy remained undeterred and went ahead with her choice.

As our meals arrived, I happily ate my salad, unaware of the ordeal that awaited Cathy. The moment I glanced at her face, I knew she was in for a fiery experience. Her complexion turned beet red, and beads of sweat began to trickle down her temples and forehead. I discreetly scanned the restaurant and noticed curious onlookers observing Cathy's crimson face. Suppressing the urge to burst into laughter, I offered her my glass of water. She had already consumed her entire glass of water in an effort to soothe the intense sensation of heat. Thankfully, she accepted the water I offered, even though it provided only temporary relief. Unfortunately, the intensity of the spicy dish left her unable to take more than a few small bites. After a minute or two, she gradually began to cool down. With a smile, she jokingly remarked that it was just a tad warm, prompting us both to burst into laughter over our memorable meal. From that day on in Portland, I can't recall a single instance when Cathy willingly ordered anything that hot or spicy again.

It was during that unforgettable dinner that we made a life-changing decision to have children. We had discussions about our future and the joys of parenthood. The following morning, as we left for our journey to Vancouver, British Columbia, the topic of starting a family continued to occupy our conversations, prompting us to ponder the possibilities and consider what steps we could take at our almost too late stage in life to conceive a child.

Due to my boneheaded decision of only reserving a hotel room in Portland, we were unable to secure accommodations as we continued our journey along the scenic coast towards Vancouver. Naively, I failed to consider that we would be traveling during Canada Day on July 1st and the Independence Day celebration in the United States on July 4th. It turned out to be a rookie mistake on my part, as Canada Day is a festive national holiday celebrating the Canadian country's pride and identity. In hindsight we should have secured lodging arrangements during these heavily traveled holidays well in advance to avoid the possibility of struggling to find accommodations. Nonetheless, my amazing wife graciously accepted my ill-conceived and foolish notions.

One night, as we drove through the west side of Olympic National Park, known for its abundant rainfall of about 12 feet per year, we encoun-

318

tered a beautiful park-like jungle rainforest with a grand and majestic lodge. I was optimistic that they would have a room available for us. To my disappointment, they were fully booked.

The closest available room was in Seattle, which was a considerable distance away. Frustration and anger overwhelmed me as I realized we might have to spend the night in the car. I didn't want Cathy to go through such an uncomfortable experience. Standing at the hotel entrance, I deliberated for what felt like hours, grappling with my anger towards myself and the guilt of putting us in this predicament. Returning to the car, I explained the situation to Cathy, and in that moment, she looked at me with a mix of disbelief and amusement. For a split second, I feared she might seriously consider divorce, but it turned out to be a playful response. Nonetheless, I desperately hoped for a miracle as we drove out of that enchanting rainforest and national park.

Cathy and I found ourselves spending hours in a phone booth along the highway, making calls to potential accommodations for the evening. Eventually, we decided to try our luck finding lodging along the road as we continued our drive along the coastal highway. Our new plan involved making hotel reservations several days in advance, if possible. It was during this vacation that I learned a valuable lesson: God watches over and cares for babies and foolish people like me. God must have seen my stupidity and boneheadedness and came to our rescue. Within an hour, we located a small hotel along the coastal highway, but it didn't solve the problem I had created regarding the rest of our trip's accommodations.

The following night, we found ourselves staying in a lady's home. She had converted her two-car garage into a comfortable bed and breakfast in Port Angeles, Washington. Over breakfast the next day, she shared the story of her husband's passing and how opening the bed and breakfast helped her make ends meet and maintain her home. She was a delightful woman who kindly provided us with contact information for other bed and breakfasts along our journey.

Out of adversity often springs opportunity, and thanks to the lady's recommendations, Cathy and I had the pleasure of meeting several captivating couples who ran bed and breakfasts out of their homes. On our final night in the United States, we stayed with a couple who owned a stunning home on a hillside overlooking Puget Sound and Whidbey Island. The husband had enjoyed a successful career as a dentist, and his wife had worked alongside him in his practice. However, after a severe heart attack that nearly claimed his life, they decided he should retire and sell the practice. Uncertain about how to spend their retirement, they realized the most fulfilling aspect of their dental practice had been meeting and engaging with people. After considering various options, they chose to transform their home into a bed and breakfast, allowing them to continue connecting with others. The couple's hospitality was exceptional, and that evening, they invited their guests to join them for a glass of wine. As we sipped our wine, they shared fascinating tales about the history of Puget Sound and the Whidbey Island area.

The next morning, we reconvened for breakfast in the B&B's dining room, which offered breathtaking views of Puget Sound and Whidbey Island. As we enjoyed our meal, the couple shared more insights about the area. The retired dentist then asked if I had served in the military, to which I replied yes. The conversation shifted from geography to the Vietnam War, with discussions about young men who evaded the draft by seeking refuge in the San Juan Islands of Canada.

Curious, the dentist's wife inquired whether I had ever considered leaving the country after being drafted. I responded with a firm "no," explaining my family's strong military background and how I felt compelled to follow in their footsteps. The dentist then mentioned the presence of "Dodgers" in the San Juan Islands and along the coast. My mind raced, trying to make sense of the term. I thought to myself, "Dodgers? What does that have to do with the military?" Suddenly, a sports-related realization struck me. Without thinking twice, I blurted out an incredibly naive question, accompanied by a smile, "Which sports teams train here, the Brooklyn Dodgers or the Los Angeles Dodgers?" The room erupted in laughter, with even Cathy playfully kicking my leg under the table, saying, "Oh Bob, you're hilarious, talking about draft dodgers like that." The dentist and his wife joined in the laughter, assuming I had made a humorous remark about the sports teams. Though slightly embarrassed, we all shared a hearty laugh, and to this day, Cathy and I fondly recall that amusing breakfast conversation in Everett, Washington.

From Everett, we continued our journey to Anacortes, WA, where we boarded the Washington State ferry that connected Anacortes and Vancouver. The ferry route treated us to stunning views of the San Juan Islands, including Lopez and Orcas Islands, amidst breathtaking scenery and a refreshing breeze from the Pacific Ocean. That evening, we finally settled into an excellent hotel with picturesque harbor views, conveniently located near the renowned Butchart Gardens. This enchanting 55-acre park boasted a variety of incredible gardens that delighted visitors throughout the year. Being there in July added an extra layer of magnificence to the vibrant colors. Cathy, being more knowledgeable about the gardens, graciously led me on a private tour. As we strolled among the countless roses, hydrangeas, lobelias, begonias, fuchsias, and blooming trees and shrubs, a delightful medley of scents enveloped us.

The hotel's prime location allowed us to explore various shopping areas and the art district, including the picturesque Fairmont Empress Hotel. We discovered fliers inside the visitor center of Butchart Gardens that detailed the afternoon high tea service at the Fairmont Empress Hotel, and we thought, "Why not give it a try?"

It promised to be a delightful and enjoyable experience, and indeed it was. While we weren't dressed in elaborate turn-of-the-century attire like characters out of a period drama, we did make an effort to don elegant attire suitable for a fine dining experience. Stepping into the elegant lobby of the hotel, we were greeted by a spacious and grand atmosphere that seamlessly blended turn-of-the-century charm with contemporary refinement.

The sight of pristine white tablecloths, exquisite dinnerware, and elegant utensils transported us to an era that displayed how royalty lived in the early 1900s. The delectable spread included scones with strawberry jam, delightful pastries, honey sourced from the hotel's own beehives, scrumptious finger sandwiches, and an array of premium teas. It was yet another wonderful moment shared between Cathy and me, adding to the collection of cherished memories.

The following day while exploring the city of Vancouver, we embarked on a leisurely stroll through the charming gardens of Stanley Park. This sprawling 1,000-acre public park was on the outskirts of downtown Vancouver. We leisurely walked along the six-mile multi-use path encircling the park, pausing at various points to enjoy the picturesque vistas along the waterfront. As we made our way back to the hotel, I noticed a sign advertising bicycle rentals.

Excitedly, I suggested to Cathy that we rent bicycles and embark on a leisurely ride around Stanley Park together. Initially hesitant, she eventually agreed to my proposal, and we made plans to rent bicycles the following day. Returning to the rental shop the next day, we paid for a half-day rental, assuming we would return the bikes before noon. The staff provided us with a map that emphasized a crucial turn we had to make near the shop. Understanding the significance and IMPORTANCE of that turn, we listened attentively, even reviewing the map with the staff and marking the exact crucial point.

The rental bicycles surprised me with their high-quality components and prestigious brand names. The ride itself was a joy with smooth paths. I was confident that we would complete our ride in time for lunch, even if we took occasional breaks to revisit places we had explored during our previous walk. However, as we approached the critical turn, I noticed several city buses unloading passengers. Attempting to navigate around them and continue towards our very IMPORTANT turn, I made a fateful error.

As you can probably guess, things didn't go as planned. We missed our turn, and unknowingly, we pedaled our way deeper into Vancouver. I attempted to demonstrate my prowess in map reading, and initially, Cathy trusted my guidance. I don't want to shift blame, but truth be told, the maps provided by the rental shop seemed to be poorly drawn, resembling the work of an eight-year-old. Nevertheless, drawing from my experience as a seasoned Army veteran, I felt confident in my ability to interpret this basic map. Concern started to creep in as we found ourselves lost amidst the intricate streets of Vancouver. It was around 1:30 p.m. when Cathy finally asked, "Shouldn't we have found the bike shop by now?" Trying to reassure her, I replied that the shop was probably just a block away, and we should keep pedaling forward.

Another hour passed, and we were still peddling. It would be evident to the casual observer that Cathy truly loved me because she was willing to put up with my wrong directions. She was so cute with her comments about maybe calling the bike shop. My response was still just another block or two. After two additional hours, we were near the city docks. Cathy's face was bright red from the heat and the exertion of riding such a long distance. I was experienced riding and racing bicycles over a hundred miles, but Cathy wasn't. For a casual bicycle rider, this was an overly long distance. Suddenly, it hit me like a two-by-four on the head. Was Cathy's redness on her face anger or from the heat and effort of riding? I tried to soothe the situation by saying we were close to the bicycle shop. As I previously wrote, God cares for babies and stupid boneheaded people like me. To my amazement, luck, and God's intervention, we were only a block away from the bicycle shop. If we had ridden further, I'm sure divorce court would have been in my future again.

When we returned home from that trip, we immediately began trying to conceive a child to no avail. After many doctor visits and tests, we still were not successful. After considering all our options, we decided that adopting a child was the safest and best choice. What was interesting about this entire process was years before, while at a doctor's office for a bad case of poison ivy, the physician asked me if I was planning on having children. When he asked me the question, I immediately responded that I'd like to adopt a child to provide them with opportunities for success they might not have had otherwise. After leaving the doctor's office, I thought about that conversation and my statement for years. What amazed me was I just blurted out that I wanted to adopt a child. What made me make such a statement like that? Was it something inside of me that knew I would not be able to produce a child? Or could it have been destiny or divine intervention? I didn't have an answer.

I continued to think about my adoption statement for years because I had not consciously thought or talked about it with anyone. As I wrote in the introduction, over my life, I have learned that we are guided by laws that operate without concern for our destination. This is about physics and the laws of the universe in which we are bound. We emerge from those laws that, as far as we can tell, are timeless, and yet we exist for the briefest moment of time. We are guided by laws that operate without concern for destination, and yet we constantly ask ourselves where we are headed. We are shaped by laws of physics that seem not to require an underlying rationale, and yet we persistently seek meaning and purpose in our lives and our destiny. Yet, we constantly ask ourselves where we are headed. We are shaped by laws that do not require an underlying rationale, yet we persistently seek meaning and purpose in our lives. I can safely say that my meaningful life direction was to marry Cathy and adopt a child.

In the late 1980s, the process of adoption appeared intimidating and mysterious at first. We began our adoption journey by conducting thorough research and consulting with other adoptive parents. We considered all our options: Catholic Charities, domestic private adoption, foster care adoption, and international adoption. Each one had its positive and negative attributes. Most depressing was that Catholic Charities and other adoption agencies said we were too old to adopt a child. At the time I was 39 and Cathy was 37. Still, we didn't let that hurtful and depressive rejection deter us. Instead, it just provided us with more energy and will to succeed.

After carefully considering our options, we determined that private adoption was the best path for us. This type of adoption involved hiring a lawyer who would act as an intermediary between us and the birth parents and guide us through the complex legal procedures. Once we settled on this approach, we reached out to a highly recommended attorney who specialized in private adoptions. With her assistance, we connected with another attorney who would represent the birth parents. We were confident that this attorney's experience and track record would benefit everyone involved. With our legal team in place, it was time to start the process of finding a birth mother.

At this time, I was serving as the deputy director of an information technology organization overseeing 13 hospitals. During my evenings, I taught technology classes at the graduate school of Johns Hopkins University on a part time basis. I utilized this opportunity to post adoption business cards on bulletin boards across the campus and outside bookstores. Additionally, we placed adoption advertisements in local and regional newspapers and set up a separate telephone line to receive adoption inquiries.

Cathy's work at The Rouse Company allowed her to network with business associates across a national community of shopping centers, expanding our search for a potential birth mother. Her business trips also connected her with contacts throughout the United States who had adopted children in the past. Between my demanding full-time job and teaching graduate classes in the evenings at Johns Hopkins University, I also found time to devote to our adoption pursuit.

At that point, my role as deputy director involved leading a complete overhaul of the hospital information technology system. At the start of each shift, I conducted rounds throughout the hospital, ensuring that the technology was operational and could effectively support the medical staff. On the Thursday morning of November 16, 1989, four months into our birth mother search, during my routine check of the operating rooms and emergency department, I unexpectedly came upon the birth of a baby in the emergency room. Pausing briefly, I marveled at the sight of this tiny life actually being born in front of me and watched as it took its first breaths. Careful not to interfere, I continued on with my duties, while the baby was entrusted to an emergency room nurse. However, the experience lingered in my thoughts. I contemplated the existence of the baby's soul or spirit before its arrival in the emergency room. Considering the immortality of our souls, I pondered many thoughts and whether the baby had a pre-birth "life." These thoughts, which seemed to come from nowhere, would later become integral to one of the most cherished blessings in my life.

Upon returning to my office, I shifted my focus back to the complex task of rewriting the hospital's computer system. Just as I began delving into this major project, my concentration was interrupted by my ringing phone. Expecting a technical matter requiring immediate attention, I was surprised to find the head of pediatrics on the other end. He called to inform me about the mother of the child born in the emergency room and her desire to have her baby adopted, and if I might be interested. According to him, the baby girl was born prematurely, weighing only five pounds and two ounces, but both the mother and baby were in excellent health. We discussed the delicate nature of the process should I choose to proceed further, and our conversation lasted several minutes.

I thanked the doctor and ended the call. I immediately headed to the birth mother's hospital room. Introducing myself, I briefly explained to her that my wife, Cathy, and I were eager to adopt a child and had established an adoption process. I wanted to assure her that we would provide a loving home and be great parents if she chose to entrust us with her baby. It was essential to gauge the birth mother's seriousness about adoption and ensure her comfort with us. I mentioned that my wife was currently on a business trip in Texas and that I would call her to return home promptly. Expressing gratitude for her time, I assured her that we would visit her at the hospital as soon as my wife arrived.

Hurriedly returning to my office, I informed my secretary that I would be taking two hours of vacation time off and swiftly left the facility. I went to a coffee shop in Towson, to call Cathy. I chose not to use my work phone for a very personal matter. Our conversation was brief but significant. I recall saying, "Come home NOW. I believe we have a baby." The next crucial call was to Dr. Hall, the pediatrician we had chosen for our prospective baby. Our attorney had recommended him, and given our similar ages, we found it easy to connect. Dr. Hall wasted no time in meeting me outside the nursery, where we stood together, gazing at the babies and discussing the health checkup procedures he would perform for the delicate, beautiful baby girl. As we observed the babies through the nursery window, I couldn't help but blurt out, "I have no idea how to be a father. I'm a middle-aged techie and sports jock. Parenting is uncharted territory for me."

In a reassuring manner, Dr. Hall responded, "You and Cathy will naturally know what to do. Your maturity and life experience will make you good parents." During the baby's health checkup, Dr. Hall diagnosed her with a slight case of jaundice, prompting him to recommend that she remain in the hospital over the weekend due to her small size. She had actually lost weight and now weighed less than five pounds at that point.

Cathy's return home that afternoon marked yet another remarkable chapter in the day's unfolding narrative. I explained my deep feelings of divine intervention as I shared with her the day's extraordinary event: the chance witnessing of a birth in the emergency room, a moment that marked my first encounter with the genesis of life. The awe and amazement I felt as I observed the emergence of a new heartbeat from the tranquil abyss was and is still overwhelming. It was a profound spectacle of life beginning the extreme opposite of the weighty experience of life ending in death. Nevertheless, this awesome new experience stirred deep within me questions about the mystical forces that guided me to be a witness to the arrival of this new soul. I pondered, perhaps, was it the divine breath of God that infused life into that tiny, pulsating heart? From what celestial origin did this baby's journey commence, leading it to cross our paths on this very moment of this very day?

I found myself immersed in wonder and astonishment, humbly admitting my lack of answers, yet captivated by the profound mysteries of the universe and the divine intervention in the orchestration of life. This experience of witnessing the miracle of birth—a sacred dance of life coming into being, continues to resonate deeply within my soul. The intricate and profound path that life takes to reach its moment of birth, guided by unseen forces and perhaps a divine hand, remains a source of endless fascination and reverence for me. The beauty and miracle of life, with its ability to weave such an intricate tapestry leading to that pivotal moment of birth, is a testament to the awe-inspiring complexity and majesty of creation.

After our conversation we promptly returned to the hospital to meet the birth mother and see our beautiful, tiny baby girl. After our initial greetings, Cathy delved deeper into the detailed questions our attorney had discussed with us, which served as red flags to consider. We inquired about the birth mother's motivations, mental and physical health, and her relationship with the birth father. We also wanted to know if her parents supported her decision to place the baby for adoption. During this conversation, the birth mother revealed that she herself had been adopted.

Since the hospital was a Catholic institution, the birth mother was required to have a meeting with Catholic Charities adoption services the following morning before proceeding with a private adoption placement. Mid-day, the birth mother called us to inform us that she had attended the necessary meeting with Catholic Charities and still wished for us to adopt her baby. This was wonderful news, but we still needed the birth father's name and his approval, as well as the approval of both sets of grandparents.

The remainder of the day and the weekend seemed to pass by in a blur. It felt as though I was operating on autopilot, effortlessly completing each necessary task without prior thought. It was as if a higher power had guided me through the entire adoption process, preprogramming my actions and decisions.

After visiting the birth mother, we headed straight to the nursery where the enthusiastic nursing staff provided invaluable guidance. They taught us how to hold and feed our precious new baby girl. I was filled with worry about handling her delicately, afraid of inadvertently causing harm or dropping her. However, the moment I embraced her, an overwhelming sense of gratitude and blessing washed over me like never before. It surpassed any achievement I had ever experienced before. Nothing could compare to the sheer wonder and joy I experienced at that very instant. I realized that she was a divine blessing from God. Holding her in my arms, I was flooded with an immense wave of love, happiness, and appreciation, as I looked at Cathy and knew that my adoration for both of them would last forever.

Throughout the weekend, we made several trips to the hospital for feedings and met with Dr. Hall during his numerous visits. I couldn't help but notice how he went above and beyond to assist us in our adoption journey. His kindness and generosity during that weekend left a profound impression on us, and we were incredibly grateful for his support.

During that period, our attorney had a meeting with the birth mother to ensure her decision remained unchanged and to discuss the adoption process. The attorney explained the preliminary forms that needed to be signed as part of our discussion. Once the birth mother signed the initial forms, she met with another attorney who would represent her throughout the adoption process. At that point we needed the birth father's name, his signature on the adoption agreement, and approval from both sets of grandparents. It was important to note at that time in the late 1980s that even with all the necessary approvals, the birth parents could still change their minds up to six-months after the adoption. To navigate this uncertain time, our families, friends, and church community joined us in continuous prayer. Thankfully, our prayers were answered, and the birth parents did not have a change of heart.

With only three days to prepare, our home had to be swiftly transformed to welcome our beautiful baby. The urgency to choose a name, secure clothes, diapers, and everything else essential enveloped us. Originally, our hearts were set on connecting with a birth mother at the outset of her pregnancy, granting us ample time to craft the nursery, deliberate on a name, and orchestrate all necessary arrangements. Yet, fate had a different timeline in store for us, hastening our need.

Amidst the whirlwind, I was enveloped by a profound sense of divine guidance, as if each step was being directed by a force greater than myself. It was as though God's hand was gently guiding me through each decision, each purchase, and every preparation with grace and ease. This serene journey, I believe, was also illuminated by the blessing of sharing my life with the most extraordinary partner one could ever dream of encountering. This confluence of divine intervention and human partnership made the impossible seem effortlessly achievable.

Meanwhile, our friends were also scrambling to provide us with baby essentials such as clothing, blankets, cribs, and car seats. Their generosity was overwhelming. They organized baby showers for us and even brought daily supplies to our home. It was astounding how our lives had changed in less than a day.

Cathy and I transformed the smallest bedroom in our Morris Avenue home into a cozy nursery for our baby girl. I painted the ceiling trim a bright white, and we covered the walls with a lovely ivy print wallpaper. We purchased a new crib along with other furniture for our little girl's room. Cathy had an heirloom bassinet with rollers that had been passed down through her family for generations. After cleaning it and buying a new mattress, we placed the historic bassinet at the foot of our bed. We were excited to have our baby girl close by, ready to tend to her every need if she cried.

One important matter that required immediate attention was choosing a name. Cathy and I discussed various options and consulted a baby name book for additional ideas. In a seemingly unexplained act of divine intervention, an idea emerged. Since Cathy had not changed her name after we got married, and everyone knew her as Cathy A. Case, she suggested, "People call me Casey. Let's name her Casey Rodweller." I found it to be a beautiful name, and then I proposed the idea of giving her my father's first name as her middle name, but in its female form. We instantly agreed and said it out loud, Casey Alexandra Rodweller. It was the perfect name for our little girl, and her initials, CAR, were easy to remember.

Dr. Hall wanted to schedule weekly visits with Casey for the next three months. During the first week, both Cathy and I took Casey to see Dr. Hall, as we wanted to hear his advice and guidance on parenting. From the second week onwards, Cathy took her to the appointments. She had the benefit of a month-long maternity leave. Whenever possible, I would join them when I could take time off from work. I was still involved in leading and managing the rewriting of the hospital information system.

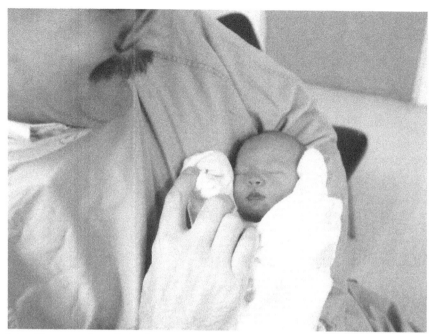

Me with our newborn Baby Casey

During one consultation, Dr. Hall explored Casey's sleep patterns, and we shared that she found peaceful slumber in her bassinet within our bedroom. He scrutinized our decision to keep her so close during the night, probing into our emergency plan should she encounter breathing difficulties. Our immediate thought was to either dial 911 or rush her to the nearest hospital. Yet, Dr. Hall illuminated the grim reality of the possible lag in receiving medical assistance and the dire risk of mortality prior to obtaining aid. He advised us, with a tone of urgency, to transition her to her personal bedroom at once, underscoring it as a crucial step for her wellbeing and to alleviate our anxieties.

Luckily, I worked just three miles away from home, allowing me to visit during lunch breaks and check in on Cathy and Casey. One day, when I arrived home, I noticed that Cathy was still in her bathrobe and looked exhausted. It became apparent to me that she needed a break. Despite the challenges of being new parents, particularly at our age (I was 41 and Cathy was 39), I convinced Cathy to take some time for herself. I promptly called work and took the rest of the day off as vacation time.

Casey proved to be a wonderful baby with minimal difficulties. However, the real challenge for Cathy and me was taking care of ourselves while learning to be good parents. It required hard work, but the rewards were immeasurable, especially when Casey would flash us her beautiful smile, and in those precious moments, the world became more beautiful, and time seemed to stand still.

Shortly after Casey's birth, we held her christening at Holy Comforter Episcopal Church in Historic Lutherville, MD, the same church that married Cathy and me. Reverend Janice Gordon, the church's new rector, had spent considerable time discussing adoption with us prior to Casey's arrival. We also discussed the importance of raising a child within a church community. Janice's excitement for us was evident when she visited Casey in the hospital every day until she came home. Afterward, she continued to call and visit us regularly each day. It felt as if Janice was just as eager to hold and play with baby Casey as we were. She provided unwavering support throughout the entire adoption process and the following years.

As a member of the vestry at Holy Comforter, I had regular discussions with Janice about various church matters and operations. One of my primary responsibilities for the church was developing and maintaining the church's strategic plan, as well as overseeing the annual operating plan. This connection with Janice extended beyond church matters and played a significant role in our adoption journey with Casey. Janice became a loving family member, offering unwavering support and nurturing care for baby Casey.

Janice suggested a full church service for Casey's christening, emphasizing the significance of a religious ceremony to formally welcome Casey into the Christian faith. Christening held deep religious and symbolic meaning, marking a significant milestone in life. We invited our family and friends to witness this beautiful ceremony and hosted a luncheon at our home afterward to celebrate the occasion.

Every Sunday, we attended church with Casey. We would always be seated on the right side, or groom's side, of the church at the end of the second pew. We took great pride in being parents and never missed a Sunday service while we lived in Lutherville. It was important for us to set a good example for Casey and establish a routine, even from a young age. I wanted her to have a solid foundation and understanding of religion, so that she could engage in meaningful conversations about it when the time came.

Invitation to Casey's Christening

The experience of holding our beautiful baby girl was simply incredible. For the first three months of her life, Casey wore preemie diapers. They were so adorable that we decided to keep a few as mementos to share with her as she grew older. Even after thirty-four years, we still have those tiny diapers along with other memorabilia and keepsakes that remind us of our little girl. Eventually, there will come a time when Cathy, our daughter, and I will have to part with these items. It will be a bittersweet moment for me, as each item holds a cherished loving memory.

Casey Learning to Go to Sleep by Herself

I should also share our experience of the most challenging three nights of our lives when we transitioned Casey to sleeping alone without being rocked to sleep. Dr. Hall advised us to help her learn to go to sleep independently as early as possible. He recommended establishing a consistent bedtime routine and allowing her to fall asleep on her own.

However, he acknowledged that around 20 percent of babies may not respond well to sleep training due to various factors such as gas, acid reflux, or separation anxiety. Dr. Hall's guidance was invaluable as he sought to assist us and Casey in growing together as a family unit. He emphasized the importance of parental consistency in sleep training since babies thrive on routines, and we wouldn't be effective if we were constantly exhausted during our workdays.

The first night of separation was incredibly difficult and challenging for Cathy, me, and Casey. We decided to time how long we would let her cry before comforting her. We had read that it could take up to 30 minutes for most children to cry themselves to sleep. While it felt like a prolonged period for a child to cry, we needed to start somewhere. Setting my watch timer, we placed her in her bed, kissed her goodnight, and walked across the hall to the TV room. Cathy and I sat together holding each other's hand or hugging and being overwhelmed with anguish, as we listened to our beautiful baby girl cry. Each minute of her crying seemed like an eternity, testing our instincts as parents. We questioned how we could allow our baby girl to cry like this, despite consulting our parenting books written by Dr. Spock and following Dr. Hall's instructions. The discomfort was profound, striking at the core of our hearts. Finally, after what felt like an endless 24 minutes, Casey stopped crying. Although we wanted to check on her immediately, we decided to wait a couple of additional minutes. When we eventually went into her room she was peacefully asleep, looking utterly beautiful. What struck me as profound about that night was how I will forever remember the overwhelming sense of gratitude for having such a remarkable child in our lives.

During the second night, after giving Casey a warm bath and reading to her, we embarked on the same mission. We went into the TV room and once again embraced each other or held hands. This time our anguish lasted only approximately 18 minutes which once again was excruciating. We had to remain strong, seeking solace in each other's arms throughout the evening. On the third night, following her bath and reading time, it only took approximately 10 minutes before Casey fell asleep. By the fourth night, her crying lasted merely a minute, and by the fifth night, she drifted off to sleep almost immediately. Dr. Hall had instructed us to consistently establish a set bedtime and wake-up time for Casey. Following his advice, we started putting her to bed at 8 p.m. each night and waking her at 6 a.m. She rarely woke up during the night and slept through the entire night on most occasions. I remember Cathy remarking that this was God's way of caring for older parents, and I believe she was right. It felt like a blessing from God to have such a beautiful and easily manageable baby in our lives.

Casey Falling and Cutting Her Lip

Cathy and I always ensured Casey was enveloped in love and attention as she blossomed. I took particular delight in selecting charming outfits for her, including dresses and swimsuits, from a beloved children's boutique on Connecticut Avenue in Washington, D.C. Dressing her up for various outings and showcasing her in her pretty dresses at church filled us with unparalleled love and happiness. In our eyes she truly was a sight to behold.

On one memorable Sunday following church services, we found ourselves reveling in the beauty of our backyard, engaging in a playful game of catch with our petite Maltese, Biff. The yard, a picturesque setting featuring terraced landscaping adorned with ivy, daffodils, and wildflowers, all under the canopy of a grand oak tree, was simply breathtaking. It boasted a cozy seating area crafted from red bricks and featured several steps leading up to it. Casey was in her element, her laughter and smiles filling the air with joy. It was a moment that beautifully captured the essence of our cherished family times.

As lunchtime approached, we decided to head inside to change. Cathy ascended the brick steps first, beckoning Biff to follow. Casey, at a year and a half and still mastering her balance, clutched my hand for support. Tragically, she stumbled on the second step, her grip slipping from mine, leading to a fall that resulted in her lower lip striking the bricks. With only two lower front teeth at the time, the impact caused them to pierce her lip.

I scooped her up as her cries pierced the air, her blood, a stark and vivid reminder of my days in Vietnam, flowing freely. During those times, I had witnessed grave injuries and losses, learning to stifle my emotions to assist the wounded effectively. However, confronted with our daughter's agony and the sight of her blood, I found myself overwhelmed, my attempts to communicate reduced to frantic pleas to stem the bleeding. In that instant, I was transported back to the battlefield, my mind engulfed by the death and trauma of the past.

Cathy, sensing the urgency, implored us to rush inside to prevent excessive blood loss. Once indoors, the gravity of my reaction became painfully clear. Not only did Cathy have to address Casey's injury, but she also found herself needing to soothe her husband, who was visibly shaken and unable to act rationally. Casey's lip finally stopped bleeding, but I was calmer and was able to go on with our Sunday activities.

Reflecting on that day has always been a source of inner turmoil for me. I've pondered deeply on my reaction, attributing it to the distress of seeing our daughter in pain and the triggering of harrowing memories from Vietnam. The sight and smell of Casey's blood unwittingly dredged up those past experiences, linking them subconsciously to fear and loss. Although my response might not have had a rational foundation, it revealed the unpredictable workings of our subconscious minds.

At that moment, I was immobilized, caught in a state of shock, my usual capability for swift, problem-solving action abandoned. This has remained a point of deep personal reflection, as I struggled to understand my inability to transition into the effective problem-solver action-oriented individual I had always been.

New Father Bob or Dead Last Rodweller

After Casey was born on November 16th, I devoted all my free time to being with Cathy and our daughter, forming a strong bond and learning the ropes of fatherhood. Despite my affection for my work in Washington, D.C., I eagerly looked forward to returning home to my beautiful wife and baby girl. I believed that building a solid foundation and nurturing a close-knit family was vital for overcoming any challenges that life might throw our way.

Although many friends from the Adventurers Club extended invitations to join them in training runs, swims, or bike rides, I consistently declined in favor of spending time with Cathy and Casey. Often, my friends would visit us after their training sessions, and Casey's infectious smile brought warmth and joy to our home.

In early December I realized that I had previously signed up for a 10-mile winter cross-country foot race over the summer. The race was scheduled for the second Sunday in December at Druid Hill Park, a sprawling 745-acre park in northwest Baltimore. Consumed by the joy of fatherhood, I had not gone for a run since Casey was born. Life was wonderful, and I naively believed I could forgo training and still breeze through a 10-mile race without any problems.

The race weekend arrived accompanied by snowfall, starting on Friday evening and continuing through Sunday. Despite the snow, the 10-mile race was still scheduled for early Sunday morning. I woke promptly, had my coffee, showered, and dressed warmly in my running clothing, complete with a hat and gloves. After kissing and saying goodbye to Cathy and Casey, I departed our home, cleaned the snow off our car and drove to my 10-mile run, feeling confident and unfazed by the upcoming race. I was convinced that my good physical condition would carry me through the snowy race, even if I hadn't trained adequately. While victory wasn't my focus, I was certain I wouldn't come in last. But as life would have it, challenges lay ahead.

Arriving at Druid Hill Park, the snowfall had intensified, creating a picturesque winter scene reminiscent of a Norman Rockwell painting. The race organizers consulted the runners about proceeding with the race despite over six inches of accumulated snow. The resounding response was a unanimous "Yes, let's continue." The notion of running a cross-country 10-mile race in a snowstorm seemed like a fun and adventurous undertaking.

As the runners gathered and awaited the starting signal there was much talk about being unsure of the footing in the snow. Once the starting gun went off we cautiously began running in the snow. I managed to keep pace with the leading group of five runners for the initial couple of miles. However, after those initial miles a new sensation set in at this point in the race, rapid fatigue. How was it possible that the snow was sapping my energy more than my regular runs? It reminded me of running in sand with combat boots during my time at Fort Bragg. My ego reassured me, "No worries, you've done this many times. Just breathe deeply from your belly."

Before the race, each runner received a trail map to navigate the course, which I occasionally consulted. Slowing my pace and falling behind the faster group, I suddenly noticed I was becoming excessively overheated and sweating profusely. This was unexpected, as I had never perspired so heavily in cold weather before. Additionally, the snow's wetness smeared the ink on my running map, obscuring the route. After a quick glance down, I looked up to find I had lost sight of the front group. Poor visibility due to falling snow made it challenging to see ahead or behind.

Undeterred, I pressed on, yet my breathing grew heavier and labored. Approaching a right-hand turn, I believed it would lead me around the lake's east side. Contentedly making the turn, I continued to run amid the enchanting snowfall, embracing the moment's joy and feeling thankful for my remarkable wife, beautiful daughter, and my blessed life. With these positive thoughts, the sweat and intense breathing bothered me less. I opted to slow down and savor the run, basking in life's beauty. My misguided belief that I could rely on my inner committee of three composed of me, myself, and I to guide me through the remainder of the race, as it had in the final stretch of past marathons, was a major error. However, my inner committee reminded me that they had also advised me to train for this race and were less than pleased about trudging through heavy snowfall.

It felt strange not to hear or see any other runners around me. Glancing at my triathlon watch, I realized nearly 50 minutes had elapsed, meaning I had covered over six miles. This seemed promising, as I only needed to complete four more miles to finish the 10-mile race. Nonetheless, my running form continued to grow even sloppier, and I was relieved that no other runners were observing my less-than-impressive stride. Suddenly, realization struck me like a two-by-four to the head, I had made a MAJOR mistake! Instead of turning left as I should have at the last turn, I turned right. This now meant I'd have to circle the entire Druid Hill Lake. As I continued running, it dawned on me that I'd need to add an extra three miles to my already 10-mile run to reach the finish line. I tried to pick up my pace, but overwhelming exhaustion washed over me. I felt drained, utterly spent. The temptation to quit was strong. Drawing upon my past marathon experiences, especially after passing the 17-mile mark, I struggled to muster the strength and determination to push through. Digging deep was a challenge that day, but I ultimately summoned the willpower to complete the race.

The most gratifying moment of the run arrived when I finally crossed the finish line. Other runners cheered and applauded as I secured the dead last position. The announcement of the top finishers and their times was followed by a new addition to the tradition—introducing the last-place finisher, me, "Dead Last Bob Rodweller." That moniker remains, and even as I write about this run in the snow a smile emerges on my face, recalling that memory. It took a few years for Baltimore's running community and the Adventurers Club to let go of my memorable "Dead Last Rodweller" finish. Nevertheless, I finished, adding another unique chapter to my athletic journey, dead last place!

Move to Allanwood Place

Before our move to Allanwood Place, Cathy had already endured yet another Rouse Company reorganization, which required her to travel more frequently. In addition, I was recruited by an organization in Washington, D.C., and my daily commute often stretched well over two hours. To make matters more challenging, we hired a caregiver in Lutherville to look after Casey during the day. It weighed heavily on me when I would arrive home well past dinnertime due to work or commuting delays. To address these new travel and transportation issues, we made the decision to relocate closer to Washington, D.C., in Montgomery County.

Armed with a map of Maryland and Washington, D.C., we drew two 30-mile half circles using a compass. One originated from the center of The Rouse Company building in Columbia, MD, while the other radiated from the Board of Governors of the Federal Reserve office buildings in Washington, D.C. We also considered the proximity of the three major airports, taking into account Cathy's travel requirements. It was remarkable to discover an area such as Olney that lay precisely halfway for Cathy and me, where the two 15-mile half circles intersected.

One Sunday, we found ourselves in the Olney area of Silver Spring, MD, exploring various neighborhoods. Serendipitously, we stumbled upon an older community and were on the verge of leaving when a large sign caught our eye at the end of a street. To our delight, we learned that a new cul-de-sac neighborhood Allanwood Place, featuring six custom-built homes by John du Fief was in the works. Eager to gather more information, we took note of the contact details from the sign and made the call. We left our contact information. The listing agent returned our call and provided us with extensive details about the builder and the planned homes. After the call, we arranged a meeting with the builder himself, John du Fief, and his real estate agent. It was during that meeting that we made the decision to purchase his very first home, it was simply perfect!

Our new home was beautiful, and we were thrilled to learn that the builder would commence construction on another house just a month after we had settled into ours. Unfortunately, due to a slowdown in the real estate market, the potential buyer for the second home backed out of their contract. Momentary worries crept in because we didn't want to be the only house on a cul-de-sac making us question the timing of our move and the potential loss of value. But those negative thoughts dissipated when I realized that we could potentially sell our new home for a higher price than what we had paid. After all, the Olney and Silver Spring areas were highly sought-after in the real estate market. Many professionals chose to reside in and around Allanwood Place due to the highly rated schools. When we first arrived in Allanwood, we knew it was an ideal location to raise Casey.

Approximately two months later, we received exciting news from John du Fief, lot two had been purchased, and construction would commence within a week. The proud new homeowners turned out to be Lou and Sandy Walter, accompanied by their 17-year-old twins, Joe, and Jennifer. I will never forget meeting the entire family.

This information brought us great joy, as it meant that Casey might have babysitters next door. With our workplaces now closer to home, we found ourselves with more quality time to spend with Casey. Living in Allanwood offered us the perfect blend of urban and suburban living. The area boasted a plethora of restaurants, shops, and parks. Moreover, Washington, D.C., and its surrounding areas were renowned for their historical attractions, abundant outdoor activities, and vibrant atmosphere.

As much as we loved our new home, it didn't take long for us to start missing our Lutherville neighbors and friends from our Church Dinners for Eight groups from Holy Comforter. Yearning for new friendships and connections, we extended an invitation to our new neighbors, the Walters for dinner. That dinner marked the beginning of a close and wonderful friendship. As more families moved into Allanwood, we eagerly invited them to join our gatherings. The Allanwood Place family grew to include six families with nine children. Eventually, these get-togethers evolved into neighborhood dinners held for every holiday, snowstorms, or simply any reason to celebrate and bring our families together.

Living in Allanwood was a truly idyllic way of life, much like our experience in Lutherville. We were part of a community of six families, raising our children in an environment that felt like an extended family. The memories we created during our time at Allanwood are so special that I could easily fill another book with those life events. However, for now, let's save that for another book. This extraordinary chapter in our lives lasted for over 20 years.

Driveway Coating and Snow Throwing or Snow Blowing

In the early days at Allanwood, there were always home maintenance projects to tackle. The asphalt driveways required annual sealing as recommended by the builder, John de Fief. Initially, we hired someone to seal the driveways collectively, thinking it would save us time and money. Unfortunately, after a heavy rain, the sealant washed away, leaving discolored and cracked asphalt behind. It seemed the contractor had planned for repeat business. Determined not to face the same issue at an exorbitant price, I took it upon myself to research how to seal our driveways.

I discovered that all the necessary materials were readily available and could be purchased from Home Depot. The total cost of the materials matched what we had paid previously for professional services. However, I didn't factor in the amount of labor and effort required to complete the task. Regardless, I enjoyed the process and didn't mind taking on the work myself, even though it took an entire Saturday to finish.

As I neared completion of my own driveway, my neighbor and friend, Lou Walter approached me to discuss the sealing process. He mentioned that his driveway also needed sealing, and I offered my assistance. This collaborative effort over the years strengthened our friendship. Lou and I became great friends.

The following week, Lou purchased all the necessary materials, and early Saturday morning, we embarked on cleaning and sealing his driveway. Through our joint efforts, we grew even closer. Lou was around the same age as my brother Jimmy, who was nine years older than me, yet I found more common ground with Lou than with my own brother. With Lou's Ph.D. and his research background, our educational and scientific interests aligned well. We defined our roles on the first day of seal coating Lou's driveway. I cleaned the driveway and applied the material, while Lou ensured the mixture in each bucket was thoroughly stirred and ready for spreading. I still remember the image of Lou sitting on one of those large plastic buckets, diligently stirring the material as I coated the driveway. With our collaboration, time flew by, and we completed the driveway sealing in half the time it would have taken individually.

Working with Lou was truly rewarding, especially because we had the opportunity to share and discuss various personal aspects of our lives. We delved into our childhoods, military experiences, first marriages, their reasons for ending, as well as our careers. Our conversations covered a wide range of topics, solidifying the depth of our relationship. Lou was not just a friend; he was a dear and extraordinary friend. I believe he felt the same way about me.

After completing the driveway sealing for Lou and Sandy, we started gathering on Friday evenings for drinks and intellectual discussions. On one memorable Friday, Lou shared his experience attending a colloquium at NASA headquarters that focused on life in space. The conversation that evening was so captivating that we continued long past our usual end time. The previous week's sermon at church had sparked additional thoughts about life, death, and eternity which provided ample material for questions and discussions that night. Meanwhile, on Saturday mornings, Cathy and Lou's wife Sandy attended yoga classes together. During their yoga sessions, Lou would come over and we would either fly a flight simulator on my computer or take the opportunity to mow our lawns while our wives exercised.

During one of our seal coating Saturdays together, I learned of Lou's desire to fly an airplane. This revelation inspired me to rent an aircraft at Montgomery Airpark and take him flying as a birthday surprise. Our neighbor John Meyer, a retired Air Force pilot, joined us. Since neither John nor I had the necessary hours to fly the plane ourselves, I rented the aircraft along with an instructor pilot (IP). It turned out to be an incredible full day spent with two of my closest friends, indulging in our shared love for flying.

Snowstorms were often the highlight of our time in Allanwood. The camaraderie among the men was especially evident during these snowy occasions. As soon as the snow began to fall, we would gather to clear our driveways. It became a friendly competition, with the first to finish lending a helping hand to neighbors until every driveway was snow-free. The women affectionately dubbed us the "Men of Allanwood."

In the beginning, we relied on snow shovels to tackle the snowy burden. However, after a week of sore muscles and exhausted arms, we collectively decided to invest in a small snow thrower[44] for the neighborhood. This handy machine became our trusted companion for several years, making the task a little less physically demanding.

One winter, a heavy snowstorm struck overnight, leaving us with a thick layer of wet snow. Eager to start clearing, I fired up our faithful snow thrower, only to encounter an unexpected issue, it quickly became clogged with the wet snow. Pausing to clear the chute and spraying it with WD-40 in hopes of preventing further clogs, I soon realized that the clogging persisted. Determined to find a solution, I resorted to using a small wooden paint stirrer to unclog the chute. While not the safest method, it was a better alternative than risking injury by using my hands or a metal object.

Once I finished clearing our own driveway, I took the snow thrower to the Walters house for their use. Unfortunately, the same issue arose as the chute clogged again. Alarmed, I rushed outside, clutching my trusty paint stirring stick before I could yell to our neighbor Pete Wasilewski to stop. To my dismay, I witnessed Pete attempting to clear the clog by pushing the snow toward the turning blades with his bare hand. Running over to Pete, I urged him to stop the machine and use the wooden stick instead. Troubled by what I had witnessed, I went from house to house, cautioning each neighbor about the dangers of using their hands to unclog the snow and stayed with them until they finished clearing their walkways and driveways.

It was a long and eventful day for me, but I found solace in the fact that there were no injuries. The experience served as a stark reminder of the importance of safety and vigilance, even in the face of a seemingly mundane task like snow clearing.

---

[44] A snow blower is more powerful than a snow thrower. A snow thrower is a single-stage machine, meaning it gathers snow and tosses it out a chute in a single motion. The power generated by a horizontal spinning auger picks up the snow while also creating the force that expels snow out of a discharge chute, usually to a distance of 15 to 25 feet away. A snow blower works in two stages; like a snow thrower, it has a rotating auger to scoop up snow, but the snow is then fed into an impeller, which is akin to a powerful fan that launches the snow up to 35 feet away or farther. At the even more powerful end of the snow blower spectrum are three-stage blowers that feature accelerators that chew through hard-packed snow and even ice, crushing it and feeding it into a mighty impeller that can launch snow up to 50 feet away.

During one of our dinner gatherings, I proposed an idea that would revolutionize our snow-clearing efforts in Allanwood. It was time to upgrade to a larger, safer snow blower. The suggestion sparked a lively discussion that lasted well over two hours. One of the neighborhood wives voiced concerns about the cost and the infrequency of snowfall in our area. Despite the reservations, we ultimately reached a consensus. Each family agreed to contribute, and we pooled our resources to purchase a brand-new snow blower.

Just three days later, on a snowy Friday, the arrival of our new snow blower couldn't have been timelier. The snowfall started and seemed relentless for the next three days. It was during this snowy period that the true value of our investment became evident. The men of Allanwood, myself included, were immensely grateful for the larger and more robust snow blower that effortlessly tackled the heavy snowfall.

With the new snow blower in our possession, a new chapter unfolded in Allanwood's snow removal saga. I took on the responsibility of caring for the machine, diligently changing the oil twice a year and giving it a thorough cleaning and waxing after each use. When the snow came, all the men and boys of the neighborhood would gather for our snow-clearing missions. We worked together, taking occasional breaks in each other's garages to seek respite from the biting cold. Those breaks offered a chance to warm our bodies and spirits with a fine selection of bourbon. We had a theory, you see, that the bourbon provided a quicker warmth, allowing us to take shorter breaks and get back to the task at hand.

As we shared stories and laughter over glasses of bourbon, our snow blowing team of Lou, Pete W, Mark, John, Pete L and me grew stronger. The snowy days became an opportunity not only to clear our driveways and the streets, but it also strengthened the bonds within our tight-knit community. The combination of teamwork, the powerful snowblower, and the shared enjoyment of good bourbon made our snow-clearing endeavors both efficient and enjoyable.

Another memorable snow story came from a quick snowstorm that dumped a lot of snow quickly. One of those snow dumps came as I was leaving work in D.C. The subway was TOTALLY jam packed with people trying to get home in hopes they would not get stranded in D.C. I finally got on one of the last red line subway trains to the Glenmont Metro station that was six miles from our home in Allanwood. Once I arrived at the metro station, I had difficulty driving home. I had to take several diversions because of cars stuck in the snow.

Ultimately, I had to park my car on the side of the road because I could not drive in the snow any further. This meant I would have to walk home in 10 to 12 inches of snow wearing my tassel penny loafers carrying a full briefcase and my laptop computer. When I began to walk, I immediately knew it would be one of the most arduous walks of my life. My feet immediately became extremely cold and wet. But as luck would have it, one of my Allanwood neighbors, Mark Townsend, had parked his car not far from mine. It took us three hours to walk the four miles home that night. I'm glad he was with me because we could commiserate together about our cold, wet feet, and our miserable walk home in the snow. We also talked about how we were looking forward to having a bourbon or two when we arrived home. We spoke of that walk for years and laughed about it every time.

When it wasn't snowing, the men would plan a cul-de-sac yard maintenance effort in the spring and summer months. We would order pallets of different fertilizers and grass seeds to be delivered to our cul-de-sac. That area of our cul de sac was our staging area for dispensing the materials. We would usually complete our work in one long, full day. When we would do aeration with grass seed and fertilizers, it would take a Saturday and Sunday. After each of these activities in the evening, everyone would gather at a neighbor's home for a group dinner. During another one of our cul-de-sac dinners, we all agreed that each family would contribute to planting trees along the road approaching the cul-de-sac into Allanwood place. Over the years, it was beautiful to see the trees lining the street, touching and forming a canopy. As I write about those times, my heart is warmed by many fond and enjoyable memories of fellowship with my neighbors of Allanwood.

As our neighbors affectionately dubbed me the "Mayor of Allanwood," they bestowed upon us a parting gift for our eventual move from Allanwood that encapsulated our shared memories: the snow blower. It was a kind and thoughtful gesture, a token of the joyous times we had spent together battling the snow. Living in Northwest AR snowfall has been a rare occurrence. Consequently, the snow blower remains in my possession, awaiting its purpose.

I have made attempts to sell the snow blower, recognizing that it may find better use in the hands of someone in a snowier region. Yet, despite my efforts, it remains unsold. Perhaps in the future, I'll have to part ways with my special gift and give it to someone in need. Nevertheless, whenever I step into our garage and catch sight of that pristine snow blower, it serves as a vivid reminder of the cherished moments of fellowship we shared. Memories of laughter, camaraderie, and bourbon-fueled snow-clearing adventures flood my mind and bring a smile to my face.

Though the snowblower may no longer serve its original purpose, it has become a cherished memento, symbolizing the bonds forged in Allanwood and the joyous times we experienced as a community. Its presence in our garage preserves a tangible connection to those wonderful days and forever memories.

Celebrations

On July 4th, our Allanwood neighborhood would come alive with bicycle and tractor parades, where American flags and ribbons adorned the bikes and lawn tractors. It was a joyous sight to see parents and children riding their decorated bicycles and driving the tractors around the cul-de-sac and along the driveways. One 4th of July, I sat on a front porch step with John and Jeanne Meyer, retired Air Force members, watching the parade of bicycles and tractors pass by. We reminisced about our experiences living on military bases and celebrating Independence Day. After the parade, we continued our celebration with a cookout.

At Allanwood, Christmas and New Year's held a special place in our hearts. Every home was beautifully decorated, but the highlight for me was spending time with my beloved partner, Cathy and baby Casey. We both adore Christmas and took delight in decorating our home and tree. Cathy took charge of how our Christmas tree would look and where each decoration would be placed throughout our home. She also arranged the table settings with holiday china, linens, and centerpieces. The Allanwood families hosted progressive Christmas and New Year dinners, sometimes even dressing up in gowns and tuxedos for our formal New Year's dinners and parties. In our previous neighborhood of Lutherville, when we participated in Dinners for Eight, one of our neighbors would always say a prayer before the meal. I cherished hearing those prayers, so at Allanwood, I continued the tradition by composing a formal written prayer for every meal we shared as a community. Soon, my prayers were requested before all our meals, and I eagerly awaited the opportunity to write them. Casey has asked me to create a pamphlet with all my prayers, but I am uncertain if I have saved all of them. Perhaps one day, I will search to see how many prayers I still possess.

During the early years at Allanwood, when our children were young, Cathy managed to borrow a life-size Easter Bunny costume for me to wear at Easter. I would start at church as the Easter Bunny, and walk among the children, distributing Easter treats during the egg hunt. After church, we would return home, where I would once again put on the Easter Bunny costume for an Easter egg hunt in Allanwood. As

Cathy and me during one of our Christmases at Allanwood

time went on, I expanded the egg hunt to include a nearby street, walking up and down, offering candy eggs to the children. Following the Easter egg hunt, we would gather for a neighborhood dinner at one of the homes, with everyone still dressed in their Sunday clothes. It became another formal and eagerly anticipated event for our community each year. The children were all so lovely and handsome, always adding to the charm of the occasion.

Allanwood was a truly enchanting place, providing a wonderful and delightful environment for our children to grow up. With children of similar ages, they would spend their days playing and even having afternoon tea at small tables on the grass. On other occasions, they would transform an unfinished basement into a makeshift fitness center and sell tickets to adults for entry. It was incredible to witness their creativity as they turned a partially unfinished basement into a fully functional fitness center.

346

Living in Allanwood felt like being part of one big family. We were constantly finding ways to come together and celebrate. One Mother's Day, I decided to create a special Allanwood Mother's Day card for all the mothers in our neighborhood. It was a joy to write heartfelt sentiments and design the card's graphics. The best part was having each husband personally sign the cards to honor their wives and the Mothers of Allanwood. Then, the Men of Allanwood joined forces to deliver each card to its intended recipient and treated all the mothers to a delightful brunch prepared by the guys.

The Tenth Anniversary of the Vietnam Veterans Memorial

The Tenth Anniversary Commemoration of the Vietnam Veterans Memorial on November 11, 1992, was a deeply meaningful day for me in many ways. It marked the anniversary of the end of America's most agonizing war. Most Vietnam veterans were draftees, making it a unique experience. Moreover, having Casey with me on this special day held great significance. Bringing her along was my way of staying focused on the present and what mattered most to me, my family.

The highlight of the day was spending it with nearly three-year-old Casey. Cathy had to work, so we had agreed that Casey would accompany me to the ceremony in Washington, D.C. We had a fun subway ride to the Foggy Bottom-GWU stop and then walked for about ten minutes to the mall. Casey, always talkative, held my hand and engaged in a conversation, asking numerous questions. Her inquiries ranged from the challenging why wars happen, to the playful why were there so many birds in the trees along 23rd street and near the State Department building.

During the ceremony, several individuals spoke to honor the Vietnam veterans, both living and deceased, for their service to the nation. I vividly remember an odd statement by Al Gore, pledging to investigate if there were still POWs and MIAs from Vietnam. It struck me as peculiar that such investigations were not already being conducted by the U.S. government. But the most ironic part of the speech was his promise to improve veterans' healthcare. Under the Clinton/Gore administration, many previous healthcare benefits for veterans were eliminated and replaced with fee-for-service arrangements, shifting the financial burden to the veterans themselves.

Some of the speakers discussed the new enhancements and future plans for the memorial. As Casey grew tired from listening to all the long speeches, we found an unoccupied chair and sat until the ceremony concluded. When we resumed walking, she expressed her fatigue, saying, "Daddy, I'm tired of walking." I lifted her onto my shoulders, and as we approached the wall, viewing the names, Casey blurted out, "Daddy, do you have any more chewing gum?" Her innocent remark brought me back to the present moment, away from my war memories and emotions. I smiled and reached into my pocket, pulling out a large packet of gum. Casey made me realize that she and Cathy represented the here and now, the most important aspects of my life.

As Casey slept on my lap during the subway ride home, I began putting things into perspective. Being with our beautiful little girl on that subway car allowed me to identify the essential aspects of my life: health, purpose, love of family relationships, time, experiences, memories, and friendships. I had already decided not to dwell in the past, but these moments solidified my determination. Without getting weighed down by memories, I realized that there were countless life and career opportunities yet to seize and master.

Throughout our lives, we go through different stages and phases. We start as infants, become teenagers, transition into adults, grow old, and eventually pass away. While children and teenagers may not fully grasp these life changes, as adults, we must acknowledge and adapt to the significant facets of our changing lives. Understanding these phases empowers us to make the most of each period. It means living life to the fullest in its simplest terms.

Taking Casey to Daycare on the Washington, D.C., Subway

During the period between the ages of 3 and 5 and a half, Casey accompanied me on the Metro subway to and from Washington, D.C., for daycare. Those two and a half years were absolutely wonderful and cherished moments in my life. I adored being her father and spending time reading books, magazines, and articles to her. We would engage in activities like finding hidden pictures in Highlights magazines and books, filled with numerous captivating photographs and objects. As we traveled in D.C., and rode the subway, we would discuss and marvel at the various sights and sounds we encountered. Every second spent with this lively and beautiful little girl was an absolute joy.

After approximately six months of riding the subway together, I taught Casey the etiquette of standing to the right on the escalator, allowing others to pass on the left. The following week, to my surprise and amusement, Casey confidently walked onto the escalator, urging me to join her and move to the right to allow others to ascend the stairs. She exclaimed, "Come on, Daddy, get on and move to the right so others can walk up the stairs." It was incredibly endearing and demonstrated her understanding and application of the lesson.

Another memory that stands out is that of the flower man. In the early 1990s, charitable organizations in D.C. provided opportunities for the homeless to earn money by selling flowers. On our walks to and from day-care, we would pass by a man selling flowers. One day, we stopped and purchased flowers for Mom/Cathy. Casey's face lit up with a smile as she carried the flowers home, excited to present Mom with a beautiful gift. Buying flowers from the flower man soon became a daily routine for us. Casey always wanted to personally carry the lovely flowers home for Mom, and once we arrived, she eagerly assisted in arranging them in a vase. She would rush to the cabinet where we kept the vases and carefully select one. Placing each flower inside with precision, she would remind me to adjust its position if it didn't meet her expectations. When she said, "Daddy, put this one in next," I would gladly comply with her directive.

Several months later, Cathy's sister and her two sons came to visit us at Allanwood. We decided to take them into D.C. so they could experience the sights and sounds of the city by riding the subway. Casey was thrilled about their visit and became the perfect ambassador for the D.C. Metro subway and escalators. During our subway ride, Casey confidently took charge, instructing everyone on what to do and how to do it, whether it was purchasing tickets, navigating the turnstiles, or entering the subway car. Despite being only five years old, she guided others on how to ride the subway like a seasoned pro.

On one particular subway ride home, Casey was dressed neatly and wore a pair of adorable new shoes. As our scheduled train arrived, I noticed that the gap between the platform and the subway car floor was larger than usual. I cautioned Casey to watch her step to avoid falling into the gap and hurting her foot or ankle. Additionally, I positioned her behind me on my right side to ensure she wouldn't get bumped or pushed by anxious passengers exiting the train in a hurry to get home. She listened attentively, observed others disembarking, and began walking alongside me. For only a second, she lost focus and accidentally stepped into the gap, getting her shoe stuck between the subway car and the platform. Reacting quickly, I grabbed her ankle and pulled her foot out of her shoe just as the train bells rang and the doors began to close.

Casey began to cry because of the sudden pull on her ankle. Her shoe had fallen into the subway pit below. I reassured her that everything would be alright, and that Daddy would retrieve her shoe. Peering down into the pit, I estimated its depth to be about five feet. I removed my suit coat and laid it across my briefcase. Instructing Casey to stay where she was, I made a daring decision to jump into the pit. To my surprise, it turned out to be over six feet deep. However, I managed to retrieve Casey's shoe. Now faced with the challenge of getting out, I attempted to jump up onto the platform but failed to do so. It was rush hour, with numerous trains running. Hearing the approaching sound of the next train from the previous station, I felt a surge of emergency energy. Tossing Casey's shoe onto the platform, I took a short running jump and successfully pulled myself up, scraping my elbows and knees against the concrete and steel. My pants, shirt, and tie were covered in dirt and grease, but I had managed to retrieve Casey's shoe. She smiled and commented, "Daddy, you're dirty," before handing me my suit coat. I felt a sense of accomplishment and appreciated that she returned my jacket and briefcase. To this day, I am amazed that no one on the platform offered to help me. I assume they must have thought I was some kind of eccentric trying to impress my child. It was yet another exhilarating experience that Casey and I shared while riding the subway together.

During our subway rides, the most unforgettable experience was when I offered Casey's seat to a woman due to the crowded subway car. I had been reading a Disney storybook to Casey and then shifted her onto my lap so the woman could sit down. Unlike other subway riders who interacted with Casey and me, this woman simply gazed out the window. I couldn't help but notice a hole in her left nostril, likely from a nose piercing. It was winter, and many riders had colds and the flu. The woman frequently wiped her runny nose. With Casey on my lap, I instinctively leaned away from her. At one point, the woman sneezed, causing a large mucus bubble to emerge from the hole in her nose. Casey, in her innocent excitement, exclaimed, "Daddy, look! The lady is blowing bubbles!" I couldn't help but burst into laughter, finding the situation both funny and embarrassing for the woman. That incident remains one of the most vivid and memorable experiences from our two and a half years of riding the subway with Casey.

Camping as a Family

Camping has always held a special place in my heart, serving as the ultimate bonding experience between fathers and their children. My own cherished memories with my father, where he was both a mentor and a friend, taught me the profound respect for nature through our adventures. These experiences were not just about the joy of the outdoors but also about learning life lessons, such as the importance of leaving no trace and caring for our gear to ensure countless future adventures.

One of my most memorable camping trips was Casey's first. She was just a baby when we joined several families, their children, and dogs for an adventure that would mark the beginning of a lifelong love for camping. This trip wasn't just about introducing Casey to camping; it was about sharing the joys and bonds it could foster within a family. To prepare Casey for the outdoors, Cathy and I simulated camping experiences right in our living room, setting up a tent and a make-believe campfire. Despite Cathy's reservations about sleeping on the floor, her support was unwavering, helping Casey quickly embrace the camping lifestyle.

Camping, for many, is a retreat from technology and a chance to reconnect with nature and family. It's an opportunity for children to learn practical skills and develop an appreciation for the natural world around them. My desire was for Casey to experience the same deep connections and lessons I did, fostering a love for the outdoors and an understanding of its importance.

As Casey grew, so did our camping circle. Our initial trips with other families soon evolved into a tradition with fellow dads Howard Mager and Eigil Rothe, sharing our love for camping and creating over 15 years of memories.

Precocious Casey and Cathy camping in the living room at Allanwood

These weren't just outings; they were elaborate, planned events in Maryland, Pennsylvania, and Delaware, where meal preparation became a friendly competition, and evenings were spent under the stars, sharing stories and laughs.

Our favorite spot, Trap Pond in Delaware, offered more than just a camping experience. It was a place for adventure, learning, and laughter, from navigating with maps and compasses (despite the temptation of GPS technology) to exploring the natural beauty of bald cypress trees and local wildlife. Our culinary adventures, too, became a highlight, with my infamous introduction of Boca Burgers turning me into the group's breakfast chef—a role I embraced as fun and with dedication.

The essence of these camping trips was captured in Howard's photographs, a tangible reminder of the bonds formed and the adventures shared. From special activities like hayrides to the simple pleasure of meals shared under a makeshift roof, these experiences enriched our lives, creating a legacy of memories and lessons for Casey and all the children involved.

In reflecting on these camping adventures, it's evident that the true joy of camping lies in the connections made and the experiences shared. It's a testament to the lasting impact of nature on fostering relationships and creating cherished memories that endure for a lifetime.

My 50th Birthday

In 1998, as I reached my 50-year milestone, I initially thought it would be just another birthday just a half century old. However, upon reflecting on my life, I realized that reaching the age of 50 was a cause for celebration and acceptance. I had been fortunate to lead a full and enjoyable blessed or fortunate life thus far, surrounded by a loving family. Instead of dwelling on any negative aspects, I chose to embrace this new phase, make plans, and set goals for the next 50 years. Little did I know that this birthday would turn out to be truly exceptional.

A week prior to my birthday, Gay Williams, a former colleague of Cathy, contacted me with an exciting invitation. She was a commercial pilot managing the Bay Bridge Airport in Maryland. Gay asked if I wanted to go flying with her on my birthday in her V-tail Bonanza airplane. Without hesitation, I enthusiastically accepted. I was thrilled at the prospect of piloting her aircraft and looked forward to our flying adventure. I had no idea Cathy had put her up to it. Gay's V-tail Bonanza was a stunning aircraft that looked new. Painted in midnight and light blue with white stripes, it boasted a luxurious leather interior and had seating for six people. This 1987 Bonanza was equipped with a powerful 300-horsepower engine and a three-bladed propeller, allowing it to cruise at speeds exceeding 200 miles per hour. As I settled into the left front seat of this remarkable airplane, I found myself enjoying the experience of flying it. While communicating with air traffic control and meticulously following our assigned route and altitude, memories of my first flight in the Army came flooding back to me. That inaugural journey aboard the Boeing CH-47 Chinook helicopter ignited my passion for aviation and set me on the path to obtaining my pilot's license. Learning to fly a fixed-wing aircraft had been an exhilarating journey, filled with a sense of freedom and the satisfaction of conquering a complex challenge. The skills and problem-solving abilities I acquired through my flight training in the Army had proven valuable in various aspects of my life, emphasizing the need for meticulous and methodical thinking in the world of aviation. I had wanted to reflect on my first 50 years, this was a great way to do it.

And here I was once again, engaged in an activity that I had truly loved since the very beginning of my first flight. It was a remarkable experience to reconnect again with my first true love as a celebration of my 50th birthday. Memories and emotions flooded my mind, leaving me with an ear-to-ear smile. However, my attention was quickly brought back to the present when the New York Center alerted me to be mindful of commercial aircraft landing at JFK International Airport, referring to my aircraft by its identification number.

Gay and I discussed our flight plan that took us out over and along the Atlantic Ocean route and reviewed emergency procedures. It was a perfect day for flying, and the speed of the airplane made the flight seem remarkably quick. It felt as though we were landing at Block Island in Rhode Island shortly after departing from the Maryland airport. During the approach, I circled the island with a standard rate of turn, but Gay playfully encouraged me to bank the plane at a steeper turn. With a smile, I increased power, executed an extreme bank angle, and notified the airport of our landing intentions before circling the island again. This turn felt like we were tethered to the ground by a short rope, creating a small, tight circle. To my surprise, Gay's Bonanza made the landing so easy and smooth on the Block Island State Airport. After parking the airplane, we walked to a restaurant for coffee and lunch, surrounded by buildings that reminded me of historic revolutionary structures I had previously seen in pictures and movies.

Following lunch and completing the pre-flight checks and once again initiating our flight plan with flight services, we were ready for departure. After taking off, I circled the island one last time, again executing a very steep banked turn and then set our course back home. Once we reached our cruising altitude, Gay enjoyed becoming familiar with her newly purchased handheld GPS device. We retraced our previous route over the ocean, but this time heading southward and maintained a 1,000-foot altitude difference. As I began communicating with the New York Center for flight services and monitoring, the controller told me to be alert for the "Heavies," large aircraft landing at JFK International Airport. Instantly, I understood the significance of the controller's warning. These massive aircraft, such as 747s, 777s, or giant military planes, generate enormous vortices in their wake for many miles, causing unstable flying conditions for smaller aircraft.

This understanding stemmed from a profound lesson I learned during my time in the Army on a night flight from Mattituck, Long Island, to Fort

Meade, MD. We had flown to Mattituck to have the engines of a twin-engine Cessna 310 rebuilt as part of an Army contract. After leaving the Cessna to have its engines rebuilt, we flew home in a repaired Huey helicopter, with Colonel George Gorsuch.as the pilot in command. After we had stopped for fuel at Dover Air Force Base, the co-pilot, another full-time Army/civilian, asked me to switch seats with him because he was becoming very sleepy and fatigued.

Gay and I were now flying the same route and altitude as that night back in the early 1970s with Colonel Gorsuch. However, on that particular night, as we left Dover Air Force Base in the Huey helicopter, there were multiple colossal C-5A Galaxy cargo planes performing practice takeoffs and landings. Just after takeoff, the Huey started gyrating dangerously up, down, and sideways. The sounds emanating from every corner of the helicopter were alarming. It felt as though the helicopter could be torn apart at any second. After we settled down, Colonel Gorsuch explained the vortices. Thankfully, everyone onboard had their seat belts tightly fastened, preventing injuries from the extreme turbulence. This experience taught me a valuable lesson to maintain a safe distance from larger, heavier aircraft when flying smaller planes.

During Gay's and my flight back from Block Island, I engaged in conversation with the flight center controller and expressed gratitude for their precise location updates on those massive aircraft. Aware of the potential turbulence, I reminded Gay to ensure that her seat belt was tightly fastened. She reassured me with a smile, indicating that the other planes wouldn't pose a problem and then reminded me of the importance of maintaining our assigned altitude and speed. I tried to convey my concerns and sought her confirmation once more. Unfortunately, before she could reply to my concerns, we ended up flying through the vortex of one or possibly multiple large passenger planes. Almost immediately, the Bonanza began gyrating and severely bounced around in the air causing us to lose and gain altitude. It brought back memories of my earlier experience in the Huey helicopter. In the chaos, Gay's hand-held GPS device flew from her hands, hitting the ceiling before bouncing around the cabin with each violent jolt.

This incident caught Gay's attention, prompting her to switch into instructor pilot training mode and assume control of the aircraft. Fortunately, the worst of the turbulence had passed by then. We shared a laugh about the experience, and I recounted my previous encounter with vortices in the Huey helicopter. Based on the stories I had shared and our firsthand experience, I believed Gay would be more cautious about avoiding vortices caused by larger planes in the future. She relinquished control of the airplane back to me, and we continued our flight to the Annapolis airport and safely landed. After making the necessary logbook entries, we returned the airplane to the hangar and then set off separately for Allanwood.

During my drive home, I called Cathy as she had requested, checking if she needed any items from the grocery store. Cathy's sister, Jane, was visiting, and we had discussed the possibility of going out for dinner that night. I eagerly anticipated the evening meal, unaware that it wouldn't take place at a restaurant. As I approached home, I noticed around 20 of my friends gathered on our hill, each holding up a sign letter spelling out "HAPPY BIRTHDAY BOB." What a delightful surprise! Remarkably, Gay had been aware of the surprise birthday party but managed to keep it a secret throughout our hours spent flying. She truly excelled as a secret keeper. Even my colleagues from work had managed to keep the party a surprise as well. With over 50 attendees, it turned out to be an immense and enjoyable surprise celebration! Cathy had done a remarkable job organizing the party with patriotic themes, making it a truly unforgettable occasion. I could easily fill many pages describing the event because it remains a birthday party that has stayed with me throughout the years.

Loss of Dear Friend/Neighbor

Soon after celebrating my 50th birthday in 1998, my close friend and dear neighbor, Lou Walter, began discussing his retirement plans. Having worked as a scientist at NASA, he wanted to remain active and had accepted a position with FEMA before eventually retiring. We would often commute together on the subway into D.C., using our travel time to engage in conversations about our work and to stay updated on government affairs.

Unfortunately, not long after Lou's tenure with FEMA, he received a distressing diagnosis: a cancerous spot was discovered on his lung. This news deeply affected him and his family as well as Cathy and me. Lou and Sandy were our closest friends in Allanwood, and they felt like an extension of our own family. The rapid progression of Lou's illness and the subsequent treatments were overwhelming.

In search of expert medical care, Lou and Sandy sought a consultation at Brigham and Women's Hospital, a renowned teaching hospital affiliated with Harvard Medical School in Boston. The hospital's skilled surgeons specialize in various types of cancer surgery and treatments. Before long, Lou and Sandy returned to Boston, this time for Lou's admission and potential surgery. I prayed fervently for Lou every day, as he was like a brother to me. Sadly, our prayers proved insufficient, as Lou eventually succumbed to his illness. His passing had a profound impact on Cathy, Casey, and me, leaving a void that was difficult to bear.

A week after Lou's funeral, I found myself sitting on our front porch steps, reflecting on the memories we shared especially, how many Saturdays we spent sealing the driveways and Fridays having deep philosophical discussions. Before long, the rest of the neighborhood gathered at our house for an impromptu gathering to honor Lou's memory. It was yet another instance of our close-knit community coming together to commemorate the life of our dear friend. We shared our thoughts, reminisced about our time spent with Lou, and supported one another through the grieving process. It was an incredibly moving experience, as we all mourned the loss of our beloved neighbor, Lou.

Family Bicycle Rides

Cathy and I made it a tradition of taking Casey on bicycle rides with us during weekends. As Casey grew, we accumulated a collection of bicycle seats tailored to her height and weight. These seats were always attached to my bike. When she was just a baby, our rides were short, usually covering only a mile or two. However, as time progressed, we gradually increased the distance to 20 miles. One of our favorite routes took us from our Lutherville home to the Hunt Valley Shopping Center, passing through a warehouse district. This particular route was enjoyable due to the minimal automobile traffic, especially on Sundays after church. It provided Casey with fresh air and allowed her to experience the joy of riding on a bicycle. In the colder months, these rides presented an opportunity for us to dress baby Casey in her adorable snowsuits, complete with hats and mittens. She had three particularly cute snowsuits, and she looked absolutely precious in them, along with her tiny skull cap, mittens, and boots.

During our summer vacations at the Outer Banks of North Carolina, we always brought our bicycles along. Sometimes, we embarked on family rides, while other times I would go on day-long training rides. On several occasions, I took Casey with me in her child seat. It was delightful to have her accompany me. She would engage in endless conversations, sharing her thoughts on any and every topic. Eventually, she would tire and fall asleep, slumping over in the seat. I recall taking her on maybe five longer rides spanning 40 miles. Throughout these long rides she would chatter away until drifting off to sleep. I jokingly suspect that those 40-mile rides may have deterred her from wanting to ride bicycles today, but, I believe she truly enjoyed those rides with me.

Antietam Battlefield and the Bicycle Ride from Hell

Every December, the Antietam National Battlefield in Sharpsburg, MD, holds a Memorial Illumination[45] to pay tribute to the soldiers who lost their lives at the Battle of Antietam during the Civil War. This annual event takes place at the start of the Christmas season and serves as a reminder of the sacrifices made by military members and their families.

During the event at twilight, 23,000 luminaries are lit, symbolizing each soldier who was killed, wounded, or went missing in the bloodiest one-day battle in American history. The five-mile driving tour constitutes the most extensive memorial illumination in the United States. Cathy and I considered visiting the Antietam Battlefield at night to drive through the park and witness the luminaries along the roads. Since we couldn't make it for the scheduled nightly tour, we decided to go on Saturday morning and ride our bicycles instead. Casey received a new Schwinn children's bicycle with Shimano DuraAce components and brakes as a Christmas gift from Santa the previous year. It was an extraordinary bicycle, beautifully painted in green and blue.

After loading our bicycles and gear into the car, we set off for the Antietam Battlefield for a family bicycle ride. We even took Binker our little

---

[45] Candles are lit and placed in a brown paper sandwich bag with sand in the bottom to hold the candle. Each bag is called a luminary.

Maltese dog, who rode in a plastic milk carton crate attached to the rear wheel of my bicycle. Binker seemed to enjoy riding in the crate, which was equipped with double-folded faux sheepskin to provide comfort. Upon reaching the visitors' center, we explored the surroundings, obtained maps, and gathered information about the park and recommended cycling routes.

Once our bikes were unloaded and prepared, we began our family adventure on bicycles, armed with maps. As we stopped at various spots within the park, everything seemed to be going well. Casey, Cathy, Binker, and I appeared to be enjoying the experience, and I felt delighted to have my family actively participating in an activity that I loved. I continued to wear a smile as we pedaled on our tour.

I had initially planned for our joyful family outing to last no more than four hours. After less than an hour, I was surprised when Casey started to feel exhausted. She expressed her fatigue and desire to stop. Despite Cathy's best efforts to offer words of encouragement, Casey remained unmotivated. To add to the situation, Binker seemed to sense Casey's uneasiness and grew restless and anxious. He started barking and showing signs of wanting to escape from the crate. Thinking he needed to relieve himself, I made a brief stop and let him down on the grass for a short potty break. Afterward, I lifted him back into his crate, assuming he would now be comfortable. During this potty break for Binker, Casey continued to voice her complaints about being tired and wanting to stop.

During the ride, I failed to anticipate the difficulty of the hills. I was accustomed to tackling the challenging incline of hills on my bicycle. It did not take long before I overheard Cathy sternly urging Casey to pedal up the hills. Meanwhile, Binker had reached his limit with the yelling and decided to free himself by leaping out of the milk container. His leash became entangled and prevented him from landing on the grass. He was hanging by his leash next to my rear tire. I immediately halted and untangled Binker, so he could breathe freely once again.

Cathy's stern coaching persisted for another half an hour. The more she pushed Casey, the more frustrated Cathy became. Eventually, Cathy lost her temper and yelled, "Just pedal up the hills and stop complaining!" Casey voiced one final complaint, prompting Cathy to exclaim, "Shut the hell up and ride your bicycle!" It was at this moment that I realized our bike ride had come to an end. I suggested let's call it a day and I will ride back to the car and return to pick you up. I silently rode my bicycle back to the car, with a sense of disappointment the ride had not gone well.

That day turned out to be quite stressful for all of us. However, we now laugh about it whenever Casey brings up the memory of her mother passionately urging her to cease complaining and pedal up those challenging hills. It has become a humorous anecdote that we fondly recall.

Kiawah Island via Fort Bragg

During another one of our family outings, we embarked on a trip to Kiawah Island for spring break. Our journey took us south along Interstate 95 from Maryland to Kiawah Island, South Carolina. As we were driving through North Carolina on Interstate 95, I noticed signs indicating Fort Bragg. These signs reminded me of the memories I had developed during my time there. I thought it might be worth visiting the place where I received my Army training. I asked Cathy and Casey if they wanted to stop and see Fort Bragg, but they seemed uninterested and responded with a "nah." I continued driving, contemplating whether or not to make a stop. Something inside me urged me to seize the opportunity. I believed this could be my only opportunity to visit Fort Bragg again. I was also curious to see how the base had changed since my time of service and training.

Surprising Cathy and Casey, I took the offramp and drove onto the base and located the public affairs office. I had a conversation with a helpful staff sergeant who provided me with a map and plenty of information about Fort Bragg. I mentioned my being stationed there in the late 1960s and various times from 1970 to 1975.

With the map in hand, I expressed my gratitude and began exploring the base, reminiscing about my Army days. We drove around the main base facilities, passing by the areas where I completed my basic training, the jump school, the special forces training area, and the 1960s Delta training area. It was remarkable to witness how much had changed. The Delta training area had been relocated to a more remote location, hidden from view or their activities heard. Even the airborne jump zone and landing area had shifted.

As we drove through areas that were once dedicated to intense military training and operations, we encountered breathtaking pine forests. Suddenly,

Cathy spotted some beautiful and massive pine cones scattered on the ground. She eagerly requested that I stop the car. Initially, I assumed she only wanted to capture some photographs of these pine cones. To my surprise, she swiftly jumped out of the car and began darting through the forest, collecting pine cones. Concerned about potential dangers such as unexploded ordnances or other hazardous munitions, I worried about her safety.

I imagined a horrific scenario in which a sudden explosion would envelop us in a cloud of blood and body parts. Thankfully, she returned to the car, out of breath but grinning from ear to ear, clutching armfuls of magnificent pine cones. Rendered speechless, I chose not to voice any negative remarks. Instead, I commented on the beauty of the pine cones she had retrieved from the forest floor. To this day, we still have several of those pine cones, serving as a constant reminder of the daring adventure my remarkable wife had embarked upon searching for the perfect pine cone at Fort Bragg.

As we continued our drive toward Kiawah Island, after our detour to visit Fort Bragg, Cathy and Casey began dozing. It was then I realized that this side trip unexpectedly shifted my journey, not only geographically but also emotionally, immersing me in a flood of memories from my military service. Fort Bragg, renowned for its pivotal military role in the United States, occupies a special place in my heart. It stirs feelings of patriotism, respect, and profound reflection. That time of revisiting allowed me to realize how deeply my experiences at Fort Bragg have impacted and influenced me, intertwining with my identity and shaping my perspective and direction in life.

As I navigated through Fort Bragg with my wife and young daughter, years removed from the soldier I once was, my thoughts became the silken threads through the loom of my existence, allowing me to traverse the corridors of my deepest introspection. Amidst the labyrinthine of the whispers of time, I pondered the delicate balance between choice and inevitability over my life. Each step, a brushstroke upon the canvas of my soul, painting narratives of purpose, yearning, and achieving.

This experience, shared with my family, underscored the profound transformation I've undergone. Reflecting on my journey from a high school graduate, drafted and sent into the unknown, I realized how the innocence and exuberance of my youth had been both a shield and a vulnerability.

Military life led me into a world fraught with challenges and dangers but also ripe with opportunities for growth and self-discovery. The dichotomy of serving when others did not, far from breeding resentment, illuminated the unique path of personal fulfillment that became my compass.

This juxtaposition of my former military identity and my current role as a husband, father and professional technologist invited a rich, introspective examination of the person I have become. It was a poignant reminder of the passage of time and the evolution of my character, shaped by both my service and my experiences since leaving the uniform behind.

It was at Fort Bragg, the Center of the Universe for many a paratrooper, amidst the rigorous discipline and the camaraderie of fellow soldiers, that I underwent a metamorphosis. The term 'indoctrination' echoed through my mind, not with the coldness of manipulation but as the warm embrace of enlightenment. At Fort Bragg I was taught the power of positive attitudes, cognitive strategies, and professional methodologies—lessons that were not merely about survival in combat but about thriving in the complexities of life itself.

As we drove past the familiar landmarks—the training fields, the barracks, and the ranges—each location stirred within me a cascade of emotions. The faces of those I trained with flashed before me, their names just beyond reach, yet their spirits and the lessons they imparted indelibly etched in my heart. The exhilaration of those times, the pride of wearing my Army uniform, and the sense of purpose that military life instilled in me, filled me with a profound sense of gratitude. Fort Bragg was not just a place where I had trained; it was the crucible that forged my identity.

The camaraderie, the shared purpose, and the stark confrontations with the potential training mortality at Fort Bragg and in the jungles of Vietnam enriched my understanding of life's true value. These experiences, though fraught with peril and hardship, instilled in me a resilience and a perspective that transcended the ordinary pursuits of youth. They taught me the importance of living with purpose, of cherishing the bonds formed in the face of adversity, and of the enduring strength of the human spirit. Yet this journey back through Fort Bragg with my family, reminded me of the importance of memories and the lessons they hold.

In that reflective return to Fort Bragg, I realized that the journey of transformation, from youth to soldier and beyond, was not merely about the places I've been or the battles I've fought. It's about the internal battles won, the personal growth achieved, and the realization that the experiences which shaped me are the most significant legacies I carry forward. My time at Fort Bragg, and in the service of my country, reshaped not just my identity but my understanding of life's profound depths, teaching me lessons of resilience, purpose, and fulfillment that I will cherish and hopefully pass on to future generations through my life's actions and this autobiography. Finally, we finished the drive and arrived at Kiawah Island, bringing our journey full circle.

Skiing Family Outings

Over the years, I developed a love for snow skiing and enjoyed it with friends and later with my family. I realize that I didn't have enough time to further develop my skiing skills before or after my time in the Army. Growing up, skiing was not a common activity for my family. Despite my early years of limited practice, I managed to become a proficient skier.

After marrying Rose and working at the Social Security Administration (SSA), I joined the SSA ski club and had the opportunity to ski at various resorts across the United States. Additionally, Rose, and I would drive to Roundtop Ski Resort in Lewisberry, Pennsylvania, to go skiing. We even had the fortune of winning ski trips through Jack Diamond, a DJ from Baltimore's AM radio station WCAO. He generously gave away enough free tickets to fill a bus, for a trip to ski at Roundtop. After the divorce, I sold my ski gear and ceased skiing altogether. It was not until I married Cathy and we had Casey that my desire to return to skiing resurfaced.

This renewed desire to ski came about during a long weekend visit with friends in New Hampshire who lived near the Dartmouth Ski Way, a delightful community ski area. Casey and I had discussions about various aspects of skiing, and those conversations sparked my interest in the activity once more. Despite the proximity, I could not bring myself to put on a pair of skis again. It had been years since my last ski experience, and I worried that I would not perform as well as before.

After leaving our friends' home in New Hampshire, Cathy and I had a conversation about future skiing as a family. This was precisely the motivation I needed to rekindle my passion for skiing. Not long after that discussion, we arranged a Christmas ski trip to Big Mountain, just outside Whitefish, Montana. It was during this family trip that Casey learned to ski. We stayed in a lodge on the mountain and celebrated Christmas in the charming town of Whitefish.

On Christmas morning, we attended a beautiful Episcopal church service in Whitefish. We were warmly welcomed by the congregation who made us feel like part of their family. After the service, we stayed and socialized with fellow parishioners during coffee hour. It was one of our most memorable Christmases away from home.

Since the time I first learned to ski, I made it a habit to refresh my skills and learn new techniques by taking lessons before hitting the slopes. On this inaugural family ski trip, I arranged for private ski lessons with John Gray, an expert skier and instructor at Big Mountain. John provided excellent instruction to Cathy, Casey, and me, to the extent that after just one day, Casey was ready to ride the lift to the highest peak of the mountain and ski all the way down. I vividly remember that morning because, as we reached the top of the mountain to begin our descent, we could see airliners below us approaching Kalispell airport, located 30 miles south of our position.

Casey, full of enthusiasm, jumped off the ski lift before I did and challenged me, saying, "Come on, Dad, I'll race you

The three of us on a ski trip to Big Mountain in Montana

down the mountain." With a glance over her shoulder, she took off, leaving me shocked and concerned. I quickly followed her, crossing over the mountain's peak and looking down with a sense of impending trouble. But to my surprise, she skillfully navigated the slopes and reached the bottom of the mountain without any mishaps. Her excitement was contagious, and she convinced me to do it again. I was genuinely impressed by her natural ability and fearlessness, feeling immensely proud and determined to support her in her skiing endeavors.

On another occasion at Big Mountain, Casey and I decided to ski at night. The trails were illuminated, creating an almost daylight like atmosphere. We continued skiing for three more hours before calling it a night. Casey pulled out her trail map and suggested, "Hey, Dad, let's take this shortcut back to the lodge." She headed towards a small unlit trail and paused at the top, acknowledging its challenges but expressing confidence in our abilities. "Come on, Dad, let's go." In an instant, she was off, skiing down that double black diamond run like a professional, even in the darkness. I'll never forget the pride she exuded and how proud I felt of her. It was at that moment that I knew our family would continue skiing together for many years to come.

Over the years, we explored numerous ski areas across the country, with Alta Ski Resort near Salt Lake City, Utah, becoming our favorite. During our first year at Alta, we joined Susan Haight and stayed in a house on the mountain, generously provided by Susan. The house offered a perfect location, nestled on the mountainside, granting us breathtaking views and convenient ski-in and ski-out access. We could be at the chairlifts as soon as they started operating at 8 a.m. and at the end of the day, we were able to ski or walk back to the house. We returned to Alta for several years to enjoy skiing there.

During one particular ski trip, I noticed something different after two days. Casey had honed her skills to the point where, whether consciously or subconsciously, she was competing with me. Initially, it was enjoyable because she was genuinely talented, and I couldn't help but feel proud of her abilities. What father wouldn't? On the third day, nearing 5 p.m. we embarked on our final ski run of the day. We had to navigate through several technical areas to meet up with Cathy and Susan, who were waiting for us at the lodge. As we descended, our speed increased, adding to the excitement of the skiing experience. As we reached the crest of the last hill, still gaining momentum,

Our first trip to Alta in Utah with Susan Haight (left)

I stuck to the groomed portions of the trail, which allowed me to travel further down the slope due to my larger size and weight. Seeing me ahead triggered Casey's competitive spirit. Ignoring the signs warning against skiing in the ungroomed powder, she took a shortcut across that area, perhaps missing the warnings while intently focused on catching up to me.

Just as I turned to assess the distance between us, I witnessed a dramatic and devastating fall. A colossal cloud of snow erupted as her skis and poles went flying in different directions. Without hesitation, I veered off the groomed trail and skied towards her. We carried small walkie-talkies, so I immediately called Cathy over the radio, urging her to contact the ski patrol and request assistance for Casey with a ski stretcher. Initially, she believed I was joking, but as I described the situation in earnest, she realized the seriousness of the situation.

The ski patrol arrived promptly and carefully placed Casey in a covered litter, skiing her to the local hospital on the mountain. After undergoing X-rays and examinations, she was cleared and advised against skiing for the remaining two days of our trip. In a way, I felt a sense of relief. Being in my early 50s, I had to acknowledge that I was physically exhausted from skiing eight full hours every day without breaks.

Unfortunately, despite recognizing the warning signs from my body, my competitive nature kicked in, mirroring Casey's determination to continue skiing. On our final day, Susan proposed the idea of riding the lifts to the highest jumping-off point, hiking to the summit of a nearly 15,000-foot mountain, and skiing down. Seizing the opportunity, I agreed, thinking it was our last day of skiing.

Reflecting on that decision now, I can't help but laugh at my foolishness. In my 50s, I deluded myself into believing I was still 29 and pushed my limits. Moreover, I had skied relentlessly for four days, trying to keep up with Casey, and by the fifth day, I was utterly exhausted. Nevertheless, I bid my family farewell, expressing my love, and embarked on the journey with Susan to the lifts. It was a stunning, sunny day with only a few clouds scattered in the sky. The ascent on the ski lifts seemed endless. Once we reached the end of the lifts, we had to walk up a steep incline, carrying our skis to the mountain's peak. It felt like trekking through the sand at Fort Bragg with an 80-pound rucksack on my back. As I climbed, my breath grew labored, and I keenly felt the fatigue, particularly in my legs. Finally reaching the summit, I was breathless and exhausted. Susan and I took a few moments to catch our breaths and put on our skis. I expressed my fatigue to Susan, to which she responded, "Take your time. I'll go first." And off she went.

My pride could not resist the challenge of keeping up with this compact bundle of energy racing ahead. I immediately began skiing behind her, initially feeling confident. I thought it would be a fantastic way to conclude a week of intense skiing, admiring the breathtaking mountains and scenery around me. That was my critical mistake. Right after that thought, I realized I had lost my focus on skiing and had fallen behind where I should have been focusing. It was too late to execute the next crucial sharp left turn. I could not complete the maneuver, and my right ski caught an edge, digging into the snow. The sudden halt caused my right ski to stop while my body continued hurtling down the hill at a perilous speed.

If I hadn't been so exhausted, my focus might not have wavered, and I could have lifted my ski earlier, recovering as I had done countless times before. Unfortunately, this time was different. I tumbled down the mountain with my left ski still attached to my boot, while my right ski remained stranded further up the slope like a stalled car. Through the swirling snow powder cloud enveloping me, it was difficult to spot my right ski. Eventually, when I came to a stop, my right ski made its way down the mountain towards me, as if instinctively returning. Both my pride and body were bruised. I experienced pain in my leg and knee, but unwilling to display any vulnerability, I cautiously put on my ski and descended the mountain.

For the rest of the trip, I made an effort not to limp, though it proved challenging. Over the weekend at home, the pain in my leg and knee intensified. Monday morning, I promptly called an orthopedist to schedule an appointment. Within two weeks, I was in an outpatient clinic, undergoing a left knee arthroscopy. The orthopedist discovered torn knee tissue, along with a bruised kneecap and shin bone that had been struck by my ski. The bone bruises were quite painful. That fall served as a lesson that I wasn't 29 years old anymore, and I should refrain from attempting to be that age, regardless of how youthful I may feel!

Skiing in Innsbruck, Austria

In the early 80s, I had the opportunity to visit Innsbruck, Austria with the Social Security Administration's ski club and I absolutely fell in love with Innsbruck. The combination of Innsbruck's charm, the majestic mountains, and the overall beauty of Austria left a lasting impression on me. When Casey entered high school, Cathy and I thought it would be a fantastic idea to plan a family trip to Innsbruck for Christmas, including some skiing. I wanted them to experience the same awe-inspiring country that had captivated me years ago.

Upon our arrival in Austria, the drive from the airport to our hotel took us through picturesque little towns and stunning countryside, just as I had remembered. Innsbruck itself offered a delightful mix of urban comforts, snow-capped peaks, and a historic old town adorned with Christmas markets. Our hotel was located in the old-world historic district, faced the mountains and provided a perfect setting for leisurely walks, window shopping, and the enjoyment of delicious meals.

To enhance the festive atmosphere of the Christmas season, grand Old World Christmas figurines were scattered throughout the historic district. One notable attraction was a large Rapunzel figure with blonde hair cascading down from a third-story window to the pathway below, adding to the charm of a historic building. These charming fairytale figures could also be spotted in various storefronts, as Innsbruck was renowned for its enchanting holiday decorations.

Given Innsbruck's pedestrian-friendly nature, we chose to explore the city on foot and managed to cover almost every corner. Skiing was next on our holiday agenda. To my surprise, the ski areas had significantly improved since the early 1980s. We rented our gear from a local ski shop and then ascended the mountain by gondola. At the top of the Alps, we paused to capture breathtaking photos and soak in the panoramic views of the Alpine peaks and Innsbruck. The scenery was nothing short of magnificent, and I could tell that both Cathy and Casey were equally impressed as they pointed out various landmarks in the mountains and the surrounding areas.

Cathy felt quite apprehensive about skiing down such slopes, due to the sheer height of the mountains. Compounding her unease was the fact that the ski trails were not clearly marked to indicate their difficulty level, unlike the U.S. ski areas that provide clear safety indicators (green for easy, blue for more difficult, black for expert). Casey and I tried to alleviate her concerns and reassure her, but ultimately, she decided to ski down the mountain only once, accompanied by Casey. We started our descent together, but Cathy's apprehension caused her to lag behind, and soon I found myself skiing ahead of them. I continued down the mountain until I reached the bottom, feeling as though I had been skiing for well over an hour by the time I arrived.

I had already completed three exhilarating runs down the mountain, but on the fourth one, I encountered a sizable patch of ice that nearly caused me to lose my balance. Proceeding with caution, I made my way down the remaining part of the slope and, upon reaching the end, assessed the state of my muscles. Deciding it was wise to call it a day, I prudently decided to end my skiing early.

During our stay in Innsbruck, we embarked on a bus trip to St. Moritz, one of the world's oldest and most renowned winter sports resorts. St. Moritz had the honor of hosting the Winter Olympics in 1928 and 1948. Our gondola rides to the mountaintop were memorable experiences, particularly because we shared the gondola with a charming British gentleman in his twenties (as described by Cathy, not me). Cathy, sensing my surprise, leaned over, and whispered that she was attempting to set Casey up with him. She engaged in conversation with the young man throughout the gondola ride claiming he must be connected to the British royal family due to his striking looks and refined speech.

Pondering on that moment still brings a smile to my face. It was amusing to witness Cathy transform into an infatuated sixteen-year-old girl, convinced she had encountered a male movie star. Even Casey felt a bit embarrassed by her mother's behavior. The British guy remained friendly and polite, but it was evident he couldn't wait to get out of the gondola and distance himself from our eccentric family.

At the mountaintop, we encountered Switzerland's beautiful people. They lounged on oversized leather recliners adorned with sheepskin covers and blankets, while they indulged in champagne, wine, and cigarettes—yes, cigarettes. I was shocked by the number of people smoking, creating a thick plume of smoke that resembled a wood-burning stove. This really surprised me, as I had expected St. Moritz to be a haven for health-conscious individuals seeking outdoor activities like skiing.

After savoring a cup of coffee and realizing that Cathy had lost track of the British twenty-something, we made our way down the mountain and strolled through the town. St. Moritz is renowned for its elegant and exclusive dining establishments and vibrant social scene. We settled for a modest cheese fondue lunch in a restaurant, accompanied by coffee and soda. The bill totaled $110. Amused by the price, I jokingly asked Cathy and Casey, "Can you imagine the cost of a nice dinner with a glass or two of wine?"

In the afternoon, we leisurely explored the town, as we window shopped. One shop displayed Rolex watches, and there was a stunning Submariner Rolex listed for $15,000. As someone who appreciates Rolex Submariner watches, I owned a knock-off version that I purchased from a street vendor in New York. However, in my opinion, this genuine watch, while undeniably beautiful, didn't justify its hefty price tag. Moving on, we continued our window-shopping spree, and as the day drew to a close, we returned to Innsbruck, where we ate a delicious dinner at our hotel's excellent restaurant.

That evening, during dinner, Casey discovered that the Neuschwanstein Castle, which served as the inspiration for Disney's castle, was only a two-hour drive south of Innsbruck. Growing up, we would read Casey all the en-

The beautiful people at St. Moritz, sitting on sheepskins and drinking champagne

chanting Disney fairy tale stories, and she developed a deep fascination with castles, princesses, unicorns, and glass slippers. The magical tales of Cinderella, Snow White, and wicked stepmothers captivated her imagination. I remembered how excited she would get as I read those Cinderella-type stories. Both Cathy and I had a desire to see the real castle.

The Neuschwanstein Castle not only emitted fairytale splendor but also had a historical significance as the former residence of an actual king. Our knowledgeable tour guides provided information about King Ludwig II's reasons for commissioning the construction of this elaborate castle. It was meant to be a retreat for the reclusive king, and he financed its construction using his own fortune rather than Bavarian public funds. Construction began in 1869 but remained incomplete when Ludwig passed away in 1886.

Walt Disney found his inspiration for Sleeping Beauty's castle during a European vacation with his wife, before the construction of Disneyland in California. The enchanting design elements of Neuschwanstein Castle influenced the iconic castle design at Disneyland and Disney World.

To tour the castle, we had to ride a tram and walk what seemed like a mile uphill. It was a bitterly cold day, and we were wearing our heavy jackets and gloves. Not only was the outside temperature freezing, but the interior of the castle felt equally frigid. The tour guide mentioned that each floor had functioning toilets and heating and cooling systems, which made me wonder why they weren't turned on. Despite the chilly conditions, Casey and Cathy were thoroughly enjoying the experience of walking through a real-life fairytale castle.

After the tour, we made the mile-long walk back down the mountain to catch the tram that would take us to the parking lot below. Cathy held my right hand, and Casey held my left as we chatted about our incredible tour of this fairyland castle. Lost in conversation and admiring the scenery, we failed to notice the walkway ahead of us. Unrecognized to us, we walked onto a large patch of slippery black ice. Cathy began to lose her footing, causing her to yank my hand and arm upward and backward. I, too, lost my balance, and as Cathy fell onto her backside and thigh, I found myself falling backward, landing with a jolt squarely on my back. Fortunately, I managed to avoid hitting my head.

Many other castle tourists witnessed our fall and rushed to assist Cathy in getting back on her feet. Meanwhile, I lay there laughing, gazing up at Casey, who stood over me, and I asked her how she managed to avoid falling. "Just luck, Dad. I wasn't on the ice," she replied. To add to the humor, there was a large dirt stain on the back of my black jacket, clearly marking the spot where I had landed on the dirty road and ice. We shared lots of laughter over our mishap at dinner and continued to find it amusing over the following days.

Skydiving with Casey

There are so many memories of our time living in Allanwood, but let me share one of the most exciting, shared times. The sun bathed the sky in a radiant glow, accentuated by white, fluffy clouds, as our plane prepared for takeoff at the jump zone in Orange, VA. This was no ordinary skydiving day; I was introducing Casey to the captivating rush of freefall. Fresh from her undergraduate studies and on the cusp of grad school, she had asked me to take her on this unique adventure to celebrate her graduation. Memories from my Army days flooded back, a time when jumping wasn't just for thrill but had a purpose and I could do it often.

Before the aircraft engine roared to life, I made a request to the pilot, "Could we ascend to 14,200 feet for our jump today? I'd love my daughter

Casey and I prepare to jump out of the plane on our tandem sky dive

Casey to be able to claim she's jumped higher than the Green Berets from my era." The pilot chuckled and then said, "Consider it done.

Casey was securely harnessed, a medley of excitement and anxiety painted on her face. Over the hum of the engines, she locked eyes with me, "Are you scared, Dad?" Gazing deeply into her earnest eyes, I replied, "Yes." Then after a moment's pause I replied, "I'm scared of becoming addicted again to this adrenaline-charged sport."

Her laughter eased some tension, and I saw her anticipation growing. The plane's climb was steeped in nostalgia for me, the jitters, the expectations, and the electrifying atmosphere. It's akin to being intoxicated by adrenaline, a potent hormone that primes our bodies to react quickly, pumping our heart faster, and driving blood to vital organs.

For many, including myself, an adrenaline rush that I learned in the Army isn't merely a bodily reaction; it's a captivating, overwhelming sensation and testament to the human body's prowess.

Upon reaching our target altitude, the cabin door was opened revealing a breathtaking panorama below. Casey and I harnessed to our tandem jumpers, looked down, and the world beneath seemed vast and infinite. As soon as Casey was ready the four of us leaped, embracing the freefall.

373

Casey and I on our way earthward

Then I felt that immediate adrenaline rush from many years ago in my youth, time seemed to warp, as memories past enveloped my senses, with gusty winds in our ears, and the ground zooming closer. I could see and sense the adrenaline rush in each of us and just when the rush was peaking, our parachutes deployed, guiding us gently back.

As we touched down, an exhilarated Casey remarked, "That was exciting and surreal, Dad, even though my stomach is in knots!"

With a grin, I reassured her, sensing this might be our only jump together. Yet, a part of me hoped the sky's allure would one day draw her back, inviting another shared leap into the adrenaline void.

A Saturday Evening Outing to Montgomery County General Hospital

One eventful and memorable family outing took us to the Montgomery County General Hospital emergency room on an early Saturday evening. After finishing mowing the lawn, cleaning the lawn tractor and showering, I returned to check the gasoline levels in the gas cans I kept in the garage for next week's grass cutting. Meanwhile, Cathy was busy planting bulbs and flowers near the back of our garage, and Casey was inside watching TV. Suddenly, I heard a piercing scream, and Cathy rushed into the garage, shouting that she had been stung by an enormous wasp she had disturbed while working in the soil. This was a critical situation since Cathy had previously been diagnosed with allergies to bee and wasp stings. I quickly accompanied her to the kitchen to retrieve her EpiPen from her purse, and we settled her in a chair next to the counter, where she self-administered the EpiPen shot.

As I watched, Cathy's eyes began to swell to the point where her vision was affected and her face turned bright red, resembling someone who had been severely beaten. I grew increasingly concerned. It was evident that Cathy was on the verge of passing out, so I picked her up and informed Casey that we needed to take Mom to the emergency room at Montgomery Hospital. We managed to get Cathy into the car, secured her seatbelt, and set off for the hospital's emergency room on that Saturday evening.

Upon arrival, Casey swiftly ran inside the emergency room and returned with a wheelchair. After transferring Cathy from the car to the wheelchair, I pushed her into the emergency room, where we were greeted by one of the triage nurses. Sensing the urgency of Cathy's condition, the nurse directed us to a registration station. Given the influx of patients requiring medical attention, the emergency room was crowded, and only standing room was available.

The registration station was small, accommodating just one chair, so Casey stood beside Cathy on her left, while I stood a few feet behind them on the right. The triage registrar nurse worked as quickly as possible, momentarily pausing to create a new folder for Cathy's paperwork.

Despite the packed emergency room, a hushed atmosphere prevailed as everyone spoke in whispers. Suddenly, Cathy turned her head to the right and shouted at the top of her lungs, "Rodweller, if you ever do this to me again, I will call the police on you!" I was utterly stunned and rendered speechless, aware of the murmurs spreading among the room's occupants. Just like that, Cathy composed herself and resumed the admission process. I felt incredibly embarrassed by her outburst. In response, another nurse swiftly seized her wheelchair and wheeled her away from the registration desk, heading toward the treatment area. All eyes followed as Casey and I trailed behind.

As I followed Cathy and Casey into the treatment area, the staff regarded me with judgmental looks, as if I were some kind of monster. Cathy was wheeled to an unoccupied gurney enclosed by curtains on all sides. There she was asked to change into a hospital gown and lie down on the gurney. On the other side of the curtain, a husband and wife were able to witness and overhear everything Cathy was saying and doing. The wife, who had Alzheimer's disease, was receiving treatment for allergies. Shortly after the nurses closed our curtains, I heard the neighboring lady speak in a normal voice, "Bill, that lady's husband beats her. Isn't that awful?" Now, I felt even worse and more embarrassed. I asked Cathy why she had shouted about me beating her, but she simply looked at me, smiled, shrugged her shoulders, and offered no response. She continued to wear a satisfied smile, much like the cat that had just eaten the canary.

I was in the midst of renewing my top-secret security clearance at work and was relieved that the police had not been involved, or so I thought. My relief was short-lived when two Montgomery County police officers in uniform approached me and asked if I was Robert Rodweller. Confirming my identity, they instructed me to accompany them. They took me to a room and proceeded to interrogate me. Despite repeatedly asserting that I hadn't hit or punched Cathy, they kept me confined until a physician arrived and confirmed that she had been stung by a mud dauber or a type of Vespidae or wasps. The physician mentioned that they were awaiting further test results to determine the exact species of the insect. The police politely explained that they were obligated to ask those questions due to the prevalence of spousal abuse cases they encountered. Rather than becoming angry, I thanked them for ensuring I hadn't hurt Cathy in any way.

It didn't take long for the medical staff to identify the creature that had stung Cathy and administer the necessary medication to counteract her allergic reaction. While she received treatment, the woman in the adjacent area, for the second time, informed her husband that the lady next door had been beaten by her husband. Within a few additional hours, we returned home. The following day, I took precautions by spraying the area behind the garage to ward off bugs and flying insects, ensuring that Cathy wouldn't suffer another sting.

From that incident, I realized that Cathy was an exceptional role model and teacher for our daughter, Casey. Casey truly took after her mother in many ways, with one trait standing out above all others. One evening, while preparing a family dinner, I playfully patted Casey's cheek as if I had lightly slapped her. In response, she immediately turned, burst into tears, and hurried upstairs. Cathy noticing Casey's distress, questioned me about what I had done to make her cry and flee the room. I explained that we were just playing, and Casey had abruptly left. We were both flabbergasted by her reaction. Feeling terrible about the situation, I continued with dinner preparations, believing it was best to wait and see what happened when Casey returned. After approximately 20 minutes, she reentered the kitchen, tears streaming down her face, and that's when I truly felt awful. She exclaimed, "Look what you did to my cheek!" Her cheek appeared all red. I thought to myself that patting her couldn't have caused such a mark. Cathy and I approached our sobbing daughter to examine her cheek. As she turned towards us, we noticed she had playfully applied Cathy's red lipstick, creating a light coat on her right cheek. Then she said to me, "Gotcha Dad!" Oh goodness, it was a clever move on her part. From that moment on, I knew that our beautiful and wonderful daughter possessed a sense of humor just like her mother, and we all shared a hearty laugh.

Thoughts of Casey Growing into Adulthood

As I sit here and reflect on the journey of my life, I find myself dwelling on one of the most profound transformations I've had the privilege to witness—the growth of our daughter, Casey, from a precious little girl into a remarkable adult. It's a transformation that, despite the inevitability of time, has caught me and I believe Cathy off-guard, leaving us with a complex blend of pride, nostalgia, and a subtle sense of loss.

From the moment I saw Casey being born and enter this world, her very existence redefined my purpose and aspirations. Her early years were a tapestry of simple joys and discoveries, moments that seemed inconsequential at the time but have since crystallized into the most precious memories. The sound of her laughter, her curious eyes exploring the world, her tiny hands clutching mine—each memory is a treasure, a reminder of a time when I was her hero, her guide, and her safest place.

As Casey grew, so did her dreams, ambitions, and her very essence. Watching her navigate the challenges of life, from the trials of adolescence to college and then university transitioning onto the daunting threshold of adulthood, has been a journey filled with awe. Her resilience, her boundless spirit, and her relentless pursuit of her dreams has been an evolving tapestry of beauty. Yet, with each step she took toward her independence, a part of me yearned for the days when her world was smaller, and I was a bigger part of it.

Now, standing on the other side of this journey, as Casey embraces her role as an adult, a professional, a wife, and a partner, I am confronted with the bittersweet reality that my little girl is no more. In her place stands a woman of strength, determination, and grace, qualities that Cathy bestowed upon her, ready to forge her path in the world. It's a transition that fills me with immense pride yet also a quiet mourning for the end of an era. The realization that the chapters of her childhood are forever behind us is a poignant reminder of the fleeting nature of time and my life.

In this reflection, my daughter, my once little girl, has grown into an adult, and in this transformation, I have discovered the depth of my love, the strength of my pride, and the eternal joy of being Casey's father. Casey's journey from a little girl to an adult is a testament to the beauty of life and inevitability of growth. It serves as a reminder that our roles as parents evolve, but the essence of our love remains unchanged. I find solace in the knowledge that my role in Casey's life, while transformed, is no less significant. I pray I remain her steadfast anchor, her unwavering supporter, and hopefully her silent confidante as she navigates the complexities of adulthood. I believe in my heart my love for her, unaltered by time or distance, continues to be a source of strength for us both into and for eternity.

VIII. New Horizons

A Bicycle Ride
Across the United States

Embarking on a bicycle journey across the continental United States is a dream for many cyclists. It often finds a place on their bucket list. There's something remarkably pure and awe-inspiring about traveling coast to coast on a bike. It allows you to witness the splendor of our beautiful country up close, especially as you pedal through the heartland. What I cherished most about this adventure was encountering people from diverse backgrounds in small rural towns. I experienced their incredible kindness and generosity. I often used my bicycle ride as a conversation starter and found that it brought out the best in the individuals I met and spoke with each day.

I could easily fill another book with stories from my incredible journey through 13 states as I pedaled across the United States. For instance, in my opinion, if you could flatten out the hills in Missouri, it would surpass California in size. And let us not forget the jokes shared along the way, like the one about the difference between beer nuts and deer nuts. Beer nuts cost $1.89, while deer nuts are under a buck! Join me as I pedal across the country, navigating challenges, embracing the support of the community, and discovering the resilience of the human spirit. This is more than a journey; it's a narrative of adventure, preparation, and the kindness that connects us all.

I'm sure most people have fond memories of their first bicycle ride. My parents must have given me a bike at a very young age, as I don't recall using training wheels. It seemed like riding a bicycle was something I always knew how to do. I can still feel the sense of independence that it brought, allowing me to explore new places in and around Dundalk and gaining invaluable experiences. My bike taught me how to gauge distances and understand travel time, fostering responsibility as I grew older. Those positive experiences prevented me from becoming a couch potato as well. During the summer months, when school was out, my mother would let me ride my bike to Bear Creek, a tributary to the Chesapeake Bay, for swimming. Those delightful days were filled with exercise and fun adventures. The bicycle remained my primary mode of transportation until I obtained my learner's permit and started driving a car. I rediscovered my love for biking and even participated in races after leaving the military.

One day, a co-worker shared a touching story about his parents, both battling terminal cancer. His mother had passed away, and his father's oncologists had suggested cycling as a way to cope with grief and alleviate the emotional burden of his illness. Taking this advice to heart, my friend's father purchased a bike and started riding. Initially, he wasn't expected to live beyond six months.

He found solace in cycling as he rode further each day, and he continued well past his projected life expectancy. He pedaled across his home state of Ohio and embarked on rides through various other states. He continued to push himself beyond his limits and extended his journeys for several more years. He eventually upgraded to a high-quality, state-of-the-art bicycle. Remarkably, he survived cancer for a decade, culminating in a ride across the entire United States. Not content with that accomplishment, he traveled to Europe and conquered several countries on his bike before returning home. He continued riding and lived another ten years before cancer ultimately took its toll. His determination and passion for cycling were truly inspiring.

That story left a lasting impact on me. Whenever I raced or trained on my bicycle, I would think about my co-worker's father and realize how fortunate I was to have the life I had. It made me reflect on the importance of aligning my present life with my future aspirations. This realization, like many profound moments I had while cycling, spurred me into action. Shortly after retirement, I started discussing the idea of riding across the United States with Cathy. She was always supportive and asked insightful logistical questions. Our conversations evolved, and we began formulating concrete plans.

In 2004, during a skiing trip with Casey and her school ski club at Whitetail Ski area in southern Pennsylvania, I had an encounter that further inspired me and my ride across America. I met a man on the ski lift who told me about the Fisher House Foundation. In addition to teaching amputees how to ski, he also taught them kayaking and canoeing on the Potomac River. He described how the Fisher House Foundation builds group homes where military families can stay for free while their loved ones are recovering in the hospital. I discovered that living with family members helps military personnel heal and recover faster. The Fisher House Foundation not only supports military families but also encourages families to support one another.

Visiting the Fisher House Foundation in Rockville, MD, I learned about their initiatives. They construct homes at military and VA medical centers, providing up to 21 suites with private bedrooms and baths. The Hero Miles program uses donated frequent flier miles to bring family members to be with their injured service members. Additionally, the Hotel for Heroes program arranges hotel stays near medical centers when homes are not available, using donated hotel points to cover the costs. The foundation also offers grants to support other military charities and provides scholarships for children of fallen and disabled veterans, as well as spouses.

After discovering the crucial work of the Fisher House Foundation, I decided to fundraise for this worthy cause. I knew that preparing myself mentally and physically would be essential for such a demanding bike ride. However, if someone like my co-worker's father, who was older and battling terminal cancer, could complete a ride like this, then surely, I could. It would be a meaningful way to give back to a charity that supports wounded veterans and their families.

In 2005, when I retired from the Federal Reserve, my retirement lasted only six months. I was offered a position with Computer Sciences Corporation (CSC) and only had one condition to be approved before I accepted the position. I requested the flexibility to take up to three months off in 2007 for my cross-country bicycle ride in support of the Fisher House Foundation. My request was approved, and I began working at CSC while simultaneously preparing myself for the challenging journey ahead.

Early in my training, I realized that success required both determination and thorough preparation. To adequately prepare myself for the physical and mental challenges of such an ambitious and physically demanding endeavor, I knew I needed to invest a significant effort. I recalled a motto from my past: "The less you do, the less you want to do." I desired more, which meant I had to commit to extensive preparation and training.

I continued engaging in races, group rides, and century, 100-mile rides while constantly reminding myself of my goal to ride across the United States. Throughout this journey, Cathy, my biggest supporter, encouraged me to train diligently and complete the required training miles each week. It was challenging to leave work in the evenings or mornings to go on a ride. Consequently, I fell short of my target of riding 400 to 450 miles per week. Achieving those weekly mileage goals would have minimized potential discomfort or injuries, ensuring that I could successfully complete the multiple 100-plus mile riding days and mountain climbs.

Cathy and I were members of a fitness club that had a dedicated spinning room for indoor cycling. When I couldn't ride outdoors during the day, I attended early morning spin classes at 5:30 a.m. and after work on Mondays, Wednesdays, and Fridays. These classes played a crucial role in strengthening my legs, ultimately enabling me to ride over challenging terrain such as the Sierra Nevada and Rocky Mountains. Despite the internal conflict between my love for work and my passion for cycling, I only rode 375 training miles per week.

Cathy and I discussed how she could support me during the ride. We considered purchasing a van to serve as our mobile home. We quickly dismissed this option due to the associated costs and logistical challenges. Another consideration was driving our car and staying in hotels, but we ultimately ruled it out due to the expense and the wear and tear on the vehicle. We determined that our best course of action was to find a company that specialized in supporting rides like this. I reached out to local bicycle shops and conducted research on several companies offering such services.

While many companies provided recommended routes, the rides were primarily self-supported, requiring participants to camp out each night and arrange their own meals. I enjoy camping but I didn't want to rely on it every night while cycling across the United States. There were various concerns associated with that approach, the foremost being personal hygiene. I knew that maintaining cleanliness and wearing clean clothes during the ride were crucial. A friend of mine had cycled part of the Lewis and Clark trail, endured five consecutive days of rain while camping each night. Sleeping in damp or wet clothes and lacking regular bathing opportunities led to significant saddle sores that required medical attention in an emergency room. Despite the discomfort, he had to continue and complete his ride. Hearing about his challenges solidified my decision not to camp while cycling across the United States.

Cathy and I compiled a list of questions for each company regarding their approach to supporting bicycle rides across America. After thorough research and inquiries, only two companies possessed the necessary expertise. I selected the one we deemed to offer the most value, America by Bicycle. They were highly accommodating and promptly addressed all my additional questions that arose. Moreover, they proved invaluable in helping me prepare materials and plan for fundraising on behalf of the Fisher House Foundation. Plus, I would be one of 24 riders who would be fully supported by America by Bicycle riding across the United States.

Cathy played a crucial role in creating my marketing strategy and business cards for the fundraising bicycle ride across the United States. On the front side of the business cards, she included a picture that closely resembled me on a bicycle. These cards proved to be highly beneficial as I could easily share my contact information with people I met during the ride and potential donors. The business cards also featured essential details about my fundraising campaign, including information about Fisher House, my website, and a brief explanation of my cause.

Additionally, a friend of Marcy Holtermann, who is the daughter of my friend Bob McLaughlin, skillfully designed an outstanding website for me. This website became the key platform for all information pertaining to my fundraising endeavors. The website provided in-depth details about why I was embarking on this cross-country ride and the significance of supporting the Fisher House Foundation. It included a map of the route and served as a platform for sharing regular updates on my progress.

The website played a crucial role in facilitating online donations, making it convenient for donors to contribute using various payment methods. One of the most significant advantages of the website was its ability to visually narrate the story of my ride. I could share captivating photos, engaging videos, and written posts about my journey, allowing people to connect with my experience on a deeper level. The website also showcased my fundraising milestones and goals, enabling me to celebrate and express gratitude to those who contributed. It also encouraged both existing and new donors to continue supporting me.

Overall, Cathy's business cards and the website designed by Bob McLaughlin's daughter Marcy's friend greatly amplified my fundraising efforts, ensuring that my cause reached a wider audience and making it easier for people to support me throughout the journey.

Embarking on a cross-country bicycle ride for charity required meticulous planning and preparation, starting with ensuring my bicycle was perfectly tailored to my body. A retired professional racer and bicycle shop owner in Damascus, MD, helped me with a comprehensive refit, making my bike feel like an extension of myself.

With a packing list from America by Bicycle and a 30-pound weight limit, I began evaluating my gear two weeks before departure, daily reassessing what was essential. This period of scrutiny led to a conversation with my neighbor, John Meyer, about the number of tires and tubes I planned to carry. Despite my confidence in the durable Continental Grand Prix Four Season tires I'd been using for years, I decided to take four sets to be prepared for any situation. Choosing the right chamois (pronounced shammy is a padded section in the crotch area) cream was also crucial, especially given my sensitivity to friction from riding long hours on the bicycle saddle. The brand varied with the climate and ride length.

My final packing list included the four sets of tires and tubes, five changes of clothing, rain gear, toiletries, sunscreen, a laptop, basic repair tools, and spare spokes. For leisure, I brought along a book on fundamental physics for evening reading. I also packed two cell phones with chargers from different carriers for constant coverage and emergency preparedness.

The day before my journey began, filled with anticipation, Cathy drove me to the airport. There, a chance encounter in a gift shop led to a conversation with the manager about my ride for The Fisher House Foundation. Moved by the cause, he made a generous donation, marking the start of the incredible support and kindness I would experience throughout my journey across the United States.

Cathy says goodbye to me before I fly from BWI to the West Coast to begin my trip.

On the eve of our departure from San Francisco, our group of 24 America by Bicycle riders gathered for a meeting to introduce ourselves and set our expectations for the journey ahead. This diverse assembly included individuals from around the globe, such as two from England and one from Israel. At 59 years old, I had thought I would be the oldest participant, but that distinction went to a 74-year-old retiree from Arizona. Our group also boasted a 73-year-old retired math teacher from Colorado, a 67-year-old grandmother with a lifelong dream of cycling across the U.S., and the youngest among us, a 24-year-old woman whose husband was stationed in the South Pacific. Additionally, a 14-year-old joined us for two weeks, accompanied by his father and uncle, and a physician from Gettysburg, Pennsylvania, whose medical skills proved invaluable.

During our introductions, I shared my excitement and the transformative potential of our journey, drawing on my personal evolution from my time in the Army and Vietnam. I looked forward to experiencing a simpler, carefree way of life, reminiscent of my childhood days spent biking.

The dawn broke on our journey as we ceremonially dipped our front wheels into the Pacific Ocean's embrace, marking a promise we aimed to fulfill at the Atlantic's edge. This ritual, brimming with anticipation, heralded the commencement of our cross-country odyssey. As we set forth, I dwelled on the inevitable transformations and obstacles awaiting us, acknowledging the complex tapestry of emotions woven through our group.

Drawing on my training and the advice from America by Bicycle, I braced myself for the daily goal of riding at least 80 miles, despite potential headwinds and the mental challenges. This determination and expectation of fluctuating mental states would accompany me across the country, as I anticipated moments of both struggle and triumph in the pursuit of our collective goal.

The therapeutic value of my cross-country bicycle ride was immeasurable, particularly in providing support to the young men and women of our military through the Fisher House Foundation. As a Vietnam veteran, I understood the challenges faced when returning from war, reinforcing my commitment to support those who serve in the Armed Services. Their sacrifices, along with their families', deserve unwavering support, regardless of personal opinions on military engagements.

Me after dipping my front wheel in the Pacific Ocean at San Fransisco before heading off on my cross-country bicycle trip

Before embarking on my cross-country quest from Maryland to California, an unexpected phone call from Chief Master Sergeant Christine Thomas Flores presented a unique opportunity. She was the highest enlisted airman at Travis Air Force Base and invited me to visit the Travis Fisher House complex. An offer I accepted with enthusiasm as I was keen on visiting the Fisher House complex and meeting the service members stationed at Travis Air Force Base. I asked maybe six of my fellow America by Bicycle riders to join me on my visit. Upon our arrival, we were warmly welcomed by Chief Master Sergeant Flores and close to 30 members of the Travis Hawks bicycle club (Travis Air Force Base had a thriving bicycle racing club), a moment that felt both humbling and exhilarating. Riding alongside the Travis Hawks members to Sacramento, California I was so impressed by these young, dedicated service members (both male and female), it was an experience filled with honor and camaraderie. Our journey took an inspiring turn at the University of California at Davis to view the campus's thriving cycling culture, and then on to lunch where we discussed our service, sacrifice, and dedication, adding layers of depth and connection to our day's cycling adventure.

The following day, after leaving Sacramento, I faced a new challenge: riding in the snow. The freezing temperatures in the Sierra Nevada Mountains tested our resilience, but the stunning transformation from drizzle to snow as we climbed higher was a first in my cycling experiences. Alongside my friend Andrew from England, we navigated a snowstorm on Interstate Highway 80, an experience made surreal by the fast-moving traffic and our need to continuously clear snow from our sunglasses.

In the midst of the snowstorm, a couple's act of kindness provided a profound sense of warmth and humanity. They offered us makeshift ponchos from black plastic bags to protect us from the cold and wet conditions ahead. This gesture was deeply touching, and I made sure to express my gratitude and later sent a hand written note again thanking them along with a Gold Fisher House Challenge Coin as a token of appreciation.

This moment of generosity was but the first in a series of kind acts encountered throughout my journey. It served as a powerful reminder of the goodness in people and the impact of compassionate actions. My gratitude for such kindness remains boundless, a testament to the spirit of generosity that spans across the country.

I often find myself thinking of those who helped/supported me, and I hope that they continue to be blessed in life. May their good deeds always be returned to them in kind. Kindness is a contagious force that, once received, inspires us to touch others with our own acts of compassion and generosity. In these times, the world is in profound need of more grace and kindness.

With that heartwarming encounter behind us, we resumed our daily routine of cycling through the magnificent and breathtaking landscapes of the United States. As planned, I would continue reading my book, "Decoding the Universe," before going to bed. This physics book explored the universe and the underlying design of our existence, presented in layperson's terms, making it easily comprehensible. One chapter that stood out to me was about communication. It delved into humanity's fascination with finding extraterrestrial life and our continuous efforts to communicate with them. The author also pondered why we don't prioritize communication with other life forms on Earth, instead of investing billions in attempts to communicate with extraterrestrial beings. After reading this chapter, it struck me that if we could effectively communicate with other life forms on Earth, we might all become vegetarians and wouldn't eat our distant animal cousins.

Me in my plastic-bag rain/snow gear

The next morning at 6am, as I rode alongside my friend and fellow rider Andrew from England, I began greeting the cows, saying "good morning" and wishing them a great day. Andrew gave me a puzzled look and in his deep English accent, he exclaimed, "Bloody hell Bob, do you expect them to respond with 'Good morning Bob'?" I jokingly replied that if I kept trying, maybe one of them would surprise us with a response. We continued our ride, and Andrew muttered something under his breath that I couldn't quite catch. Each morning, I greeted the animals, and Andrew would play along with his "bloody hell Bob," statement in the same tone and manner. It was funny in a thoughtful way, bloody hell Bob.

Before the ride began, I had concerns about traversing the Sierra Nevada Mountains, expecting them to be the most challenging part of the journey. To my surprise, they weren't as tough as I had anticipated. Don't get me wrong, they were still formidable mountains to climb on a bicycle, but thanks to my spinning classes and strength training, I was able to conquer them with minimal discomfort. This was just the beginning, as I still had the Rocky Mountains and the ascent up Monarch Pass awaiting me.

Our cycling in the Rockies began around Salt Lake City, Utah. The colors and terrain were simply breathtaking. On the day we departed Salt Lake City on the way to Green River, we set off before sunrise. As daylight emerged, the mountains unveiled a magnificent array of hues that shifted throughout the day, treating me to ever-changing vistas of colorful rock formations. I was grateful to be traveling on less-traveled back roads that allowed me to dedicate a significant portion of my pedaling time to marvel at the beauty and grandeur of the surrounding landscape.

Green River, the Arches, and Green River Missile Launch Complex

Arriving at our hotel in Green River, UT, and taking some time to refresh and shower. It wasn't long before the adventurous spirit among us proposed a journey to Arches National Park to catch the sunset. The moment we laid eyes on the park's iconic red rock landscapes, we were utterly spellbound. Arches National Park, renowned for its unparalleled concentration of natural stone arches, showcases over 2,000 of these awe-inspiring formations, ranging from delicate fissures to majestic spans stretching over

391

300 feet across. Witnessing the grandeur of these natural sculptures, sculpted by millennia of erosion and geological activity, was a moment of profound appreciation and wonder for me. Amidst this natural splendor, my thoughts inevitably turned to Cathy, wishing she could stand beside me to take in the breathtaking views as the sun dipped below the horizon, painting the sky in vibrant hues.

That longing, however, would not linger indefinitely. In October of 2016, Cathy and I finally seized the opportunity to visit Arches National Park together. Standing amidst the same majestic formations I had marveled at alone, now with Cathy by my side, the experience took on a new, deeply personal dimension. Sharing the awe-inspiring beauty of the sunset casting its golden light across the arches, we were reminded of the enduring power of nature to connect, inspire, and kindle the flames of adventure in our hearts. This shared experience, set against the backdrop of Arches' dramatic landscape, not only deepened our bond but also etched an indelible memory in our journey together.

My bicycle adventure across the United States continued. After our overnight stay, we were in for an exciting discovery. We departed the town and headed east on the south side of Interstate 70. We caught glimpses of the abandoned structures and remnants of old roads leading to the obscure military installation called Green River Missile Base. This hidden gem is one of the Western United States' most forgotten and overlooked military sites. Over the years, its story has faded away, neglected by the passage of time and forgotten generations. During its prime in the 1960s and 1970s, the Green River Missile Base and its auxiliary structures nearly doubled the town's population.

Situated just a few miles southeast of the town, the U.S. Air Force established the Green River Missile Launch Complex. Notably, the base served as an annex of the U.S. Army's White Sands Missile Range and was officially decommissioned in 1983.

What makes this discovery even more fascinating is the fact that countless individuals have driven past this site, unaware of its existence. The majority of passersby would barely spare a second glance at the deserted buildings south of Interstate 70, missing out on the intriguing history hidden within the sand and backdrop of beautiful mountains.

From Green River, we biked toward the Rocky Mountains, reaching Grand Junction, CO. After spending the night, we set out the next morning for Gunnison, CO. The mountain terrain made me realize the Rockies' challenges due to the length and gradient of the climbs. As we approached Monarch Pass, my fellow riders frequently discussed the difficulty of the upcoming climb. Although I anticipated the challenge, I believed the Sierra Nevada Mountains posed a tougher test. Nonetheless, I remained focused on enjoying the current ride and the stunning scenery. Upon arriving in Gunnison, we spent the night at a hotel situated near the local airport, which offered a unique view of planes landing and taking off.

In need of a haircut, I rode my bicycle around town until arriving at a barber shop that was open, with the door and cash register unlocked, but no one working. It was late afternoon, and the barber had stepped out for a meal. When he returned, he greeted me like a long-lost friend and apologized for his absence. During my haircut, we engaged in lively conversation, and he shared insights about the town and the excellent skiing at Monarch Pass. Riding back to the hotel, I contemplated the appeal of relocating to Gunnison. However, my focus soon shifted back to the next day's challenge: climbing over Monarch Pass and the Continental Divide.

The following morning, I ate a much larger breakfast than normal because of the anticipated energy output required to pedal over the 12,000-foot mountain. One of my fellow riders had been calculating the energy we were expending each day and the calories we were taking in through meals and our SAG stop foods. The word **SAG** stands for *support and gear*. His calculations were that on an average day of 80 plus miles we were burning about 12,000 calories and on mountain days up to 15,000 calories a day. I guess all those giant peanut butter and jelly sandwiches at the SAG stops helped me.

Alongside my friend Andrew, I ascended the mountain, our journey fueled by mutual encouragement and shared determination. My support extended beyond Andrew; I also motivated other riders on a tandem bicycle (two person) struggling with the climb, aiming to lift their spirits. It was a collective success, with every member of our group reaching the summit. There, welcomed by a federal park ranger station and the option of a gondola ride to the peak, we reveled in our accomplishment.

The emotional release at the summit was joyful as emotions of joy were shed, and hugs exchanged, as we were united by a deep sense of achievement and the marvel of life. This journey transcended the physical challenge, touching the core of human resilience and joy. Climbing this mountain became more than an athletic feat; it was a profound emotional journey that allowed us to experience the essence of joy and human spirit.

Conquering the mountain marked a significant milestone in my life, showcasing my physical fitness and the enveloping beauty during the ascent. The breathtaking scenery and crisp air induced a state of grace, with each pedal stroke feeling effortless. Every small victory of reaching a somewhat flat portion of the road felt monumental, infusing me with a sensation of standing atop the world, possibly amplified by the high altitude and thin air. Reflecting on that day, the feelings of euphoria and awe at my own capabilities are still vivid.

This experience at the mountain's peak was a powerful testament to our capacity to achieve greatness. It highlighted the beauty of shared victories and the realization that our limits often extend far beyond our perceptions. The joy and fulfillment from this communal achievement underscored the value of camaraderie and human connection, binding us in a collective experience of triumph and wonder. It was not merely a physical journey but an emotional and spiritual voyage that emphasized the importance of support, encouragement, and unified objectives throughout our paths.

The distance from Gunnison, CO to Monarch Pass was about 50 miles of climbing and then 30 miles downhill to Salida, CO. I had enjoyed many of my downhill rides up to this point, but this was the most exciting and thrilling because of the speed I was traveling and because my legs began to feel a little uncomfortable because I wasn't sitting on my saddle. I was riding my bicycle like a jockey does a horse and used my legs as shock absorbers. My bicycle computer recorded a top speed of 57 miles per hour at one point on my descent.

Upon our arrival in Salida, some of us decided to stop for lunch where we encountered a group cycling from the East Coast to the West Coast. They appeared exhausted and somewhat disillusioned with their journey. They shared with us that the company they had hired for their adventure had only supplied them with maps for navigation. Their journey involved camping out every night, regardless of the weather conditions, which necessitated them to carry additional equipment like pots, pans, and cooking utensils alongside their standard cycling gear. The challenge of maintaining personal hygiene was evident, as showering opportunities were sporadic at best. The thought of not being able to shower daily, a routine I sometimes indulged in twice a day, was unimaginable to me. They expected their cross-country ride to last 100 days. Hearing their story, I couldn't help but feel sympathy for their situation, especially knowing the comfort of a hotel with clean sheets and a warm shower awaited me every night.

The most challenging day of my cross-country ride unfolded in Missouri, amidst a backdrop of cold, relentless rain. The trouble began with my front derailleur malfunctioning, causing the chain to frequently slip between the two front chainrings. This led to my legs spinning uncontrollably whenever the chain missed its mark, which, after several hours, resulted in significant pain in my legs and knees.

An unexpected moment of respite came when I stopped to help a small goat entangled in a barbed wire fence. Assisting the animal momentarily alleviated my discomfort, but the relief was short-lived. As the day progressed, not only did the physical pain intensify, but a deep fatigue set in, compounded by hunger. Then, a familiar foe surfaced: anger. It was startling how quickly frustration took hold, reaching a peak when I aggressively maneuvered my bicycle as if leaping over a curb. At that moment, I was so overwhelmed with anger that had my shoes come unclipped from the pedals, I might have abandoned my bicycle in a field and ended my journey then and there. Fortunately, my shoes remained secure, and I managed to reach the hotel, albeit well past dinner time.

Recognizing my anger, I reminded myself of the importance of self-control—a virtue necessary for someone of my mature, almost "seasoned citizen" age. The source of my frustration was clear: the malfunctioning bicycle chain. I faced a choice: succumb to my anger or seek solutions. Choosing the latter, I opted to transform my mindset and attitude. Instead of dwelling on my frustrations, I focused my energy on finding a solution, reaching out to the TREK bicycle company and locating a bike shop that could address the mechanical issues.

The shift in approach not only helped me manage my anger but also reinforced the value of focusing on solutions rather than being overwhelmed by problems. It was a lesson in resilience and the power of a positive attitude, even in the face of unexpected challenges. With my bicycle still experiencing gear shifting issues, I went ahead with the ride planned for the next day. I found myself having to pay extra attention to the gear shifts, mindful of the malfunction, especially given it would be several days before we could reach a repair shop.

On July 4th, 2007, Independence Day brought a festive spirit to our ride. Many of my fellow riders and I decorated our bicycles with American flags and streamers to celebrate. That joyous morning was a sight to behold, with riders and bikes adorned in vibrant decorations. However, this day was set to be different because until now, our journey had been free of any injuries. The weather was as beautiful as ever, and we made numerous stops along our route. Our support and gear or SAG crew were stationed at various patriotic locations along the way. At each stop, I vividly recall indulging in at least two giant peanut butter and jelly sandwiches versus the normal one sandwich I had on other days. In a light-hearted spirit, I felt that eating these sandwiches in abundance was my playful contribution to the national holiday.

In the afternoon, upon reaching the hotel, I sat outside with several others, waiting for the remainder of the riders to arrive. It had become a daily routine to hear about others' experiences, such as stopping to take pictures of the scenery or meeting interesting people along the route. I enjoyed listening to their stories, and many days I took on the role of riding sweep or being the very last rider, ensuring that everyone arrived safely. That day our hotel was located on a busy street, and our approach involved riding downhill on a side road next to the hotel. This required merging onto the main street and maneuvering past a large storm drain cover with a slight bump while at the same time going around the corner at a relatively fast speed.

As the last group of riders was arriving and riding over the storm drain cover, a fellow rider, who happened to be a grandmother, had her camera hanging from her handlebars. Unfortunately, as she bounced over the drainage cover, the camera became dislodged and dropped between her front wheel and fork. Her front wheel came to an abrupt stop, causing her to go flying over the handlebars. She landed face-first on the pavement. My friend, a physician from Gettysburg, and I rushed over to her. The doctor quickly assessed her condition to determine the urgency and nature of her injuries. He presented her with treatment options, and she decided to have him stitch her wounds and provide pain medication. We lifted her up and carried her to her room. The doctor stayed with her throughout the evening and later informed us that she was fortunate to have avoided any broken bones.

As per the contract with America by Bicycle, if a participant is injured or falls ill, they are required to stop their ride. This meant that she would have to halt her journey. Several of us appealed to the ride leaders, requesting that she be allowed to continue and ride in one of the support vans for a few days. This way, they could monitor her progress and determine when it would be safe for her to ride again. Thankfully, they agreed, understanding that this may be her only opportunity to fulfill a lifelong dream. Within three days, her stitches were removed, and most of her bruises were fading. By the end of the first week, she was back on her bicycle. For the next few days, I rode with her, engaging in conversations about our families and her grandchildren. Fortunately, on one of those days, we had our shortest riding distance, a road was closed because of construction, and we were only able to ride 38 miles that day.

My chainring issues continued making it difficult to ride nevertheless I was determined to find a bicycle repair shop the day we rode into Champaign Illinois. There I found a TREK bicycle repair shop that was about to close at five o'clock on a Saturday. The mechanic was the owner who was very gracious when he said bring it in and let's take a look at it. The owner could have sold me a complete front derailleur but said it was too expensive when he heard I was fundraising for the Fisher House Foundation. He spent the next five hours diagnosing and repairing my bicycle. It was 10 p.m. when he finally finished. The problem was that the front derailleur had warped somehow allowing the chain to miss a chainring and fall between the front two chainrings. He installed a new wider chain and adjusted the chainrings. He was certain the repairs would last until I finished my ride. The bill in my opinion was too low. Another bike shop in the Washington, D.C., area would have charged four times as much. To compensate for the difference, I doubled the payment. This was another example of the compassion and benevolence I experienced on my ride. With my bicycle now operating much more smoothly, I was able to resume our regular cycling schedule.

After Champaign and before Crawfordsville, Indiana I had the privilege to meet and ride with then Captain John Snyder of the U.S. Army, who was stationed in Indianapolis. John wanted to ride to Crawfordsville and then onto Indianapolis with me because he couldn't take much time away from work. We rode together stopping in Crawfordsville, IN to visit Wabash College and Brownsburg to visit the Roark bicycle manufacturing facility. We watched Roark build handmade custom titanium bicycles. Each bicycle is built one at a time with the same precision and technology they used to create aerospace components. Each finished bicycle had the purchaser's name etched into the frame, along with the serial number. It was an interesting process, and the precise manufacturing was magnificent to watch. The finished bicycles were beautiful pieces of art, responsive to ride, and very light weight.

During our ride John and I discussed our time in the Army and how he entered the Army right out of high school then went to the First Gulf War, "Operation Iraqi Freedom." After leaving the Army John attended college and took Reserve Officer Training Corps classes to become a commissioned officer. After graduation he returned to the Army as an officer. We also talked about our time at Fort Bragg and the similarities in our career paths were amazing. We continued our friendship after I completed my ride. On at least one occasion John visited and had dinner with Cathy and me while he was visiting the Pentagon. After retirement he moved back to Washington State and has a successful career in technology security.

Indianapolis was a rest day city and Cathy flew from Maryland to spend the two days with me. This was a special time for me because the day before on July 8th I celebrated my 59th birthday riding my bicycle from Crawfordsville. It was so wonderful to have Cathy visit with me on a rest day and be with me to celebrate my birthday. Many of my fellow riders wanted to visit the Major Taylor Velodrome. It's an outdoor concrete arena for track cycling named for the 1899 world champion cyclist Major Taylor. He was an African American professional cyclist and could be considered the greatest American bicycle sprinter of all time by today's standards. He had a great racing career in and outside of the United States and died of a heart attack in 1932 at the age of 53. Several of my fellow riders and John Synder rode over to the velodrome for pictures and to see if we could ride

Cathy at the Indianapolis Motor Speedway near the Brickyard

around the track. It was open to the public and my lovely wife Cathy was able to see me and others zip around the race course while she took pictures.

While at the Velodrome, we met several locals who were practicing. I remember one racer in his mid to late 30s who had his family with him. It was obvious that he was a bicycle racer by the size of his developed legs. His son had a small bicycle as well. We enjoyed watching as this little boy whizzed around the banked concrete track. Then it was time to watch his father take to the track and practice. WOW! He was fast! I knew I was way past my prime to even think about going out with him for a lap or two like two of my fellow riders tried. I had a blast on that track creating my best times. Being a technologist, I briefly considered how technology had changed over the years, and the knowledge of bicycle physics especially from the book I'd been reading opened many possible advancements in equipment and training since Major Taylor raced.

One of my fellow cyclists had a personal connection with the manager of the Indianapolis 500 racetrack. Thanks to this friendship, we received special permission to cycle around the track the following day. We arrived early, explored the motor speedway museum, and even sat in some of the historic winning cars. The museum was so rich in history that we would have needed days to fully appreciate everything.

Me at Major Taylor's Velodrome in Indianapolis

On the day of our ride, Cathy came along to take photos as I completed four laps of the 2.5-mile track, totaling 10 miles. The track is named the Brickyard because it was originally constructed with red brick. Over time, asphalt replaced the bricks for a smoother ride, leaving only the finish line with its iconic bricks. Crossing the historic "Brickyard" finish line left me breathless.

Our two days in Indianapolis flew by, filled with sightseeing and the highlights of the area. The best part was spending time with Cathy, sharing stories of my journey, the people I met, and the places I saw. My fellow cyclists and Cathy shared their stories too, including Cathy's college shopping trip with Casey in Wyoming and Colorado. While I wished I could have joined them, I recognized it as a special bonding time for them.

We had been typically covering 80 miles a day, however, on July 14, 2007, I experienced my longest day of cycling across the United States. Leading up to this date, I had already completed several consecutive days of riding, each exceeding 100 miles. Riding these long distances in the western states did not present problems. Because I found joy in the conversations, stunning scenery, photography, and interactions with the people I encountered along the way. Prior to this transcontinental journey, my longest bike ride had been a 185-mile race from Baltimore to Ocean City, Maryland. Yet, during this cross-country adventure, I believe my most extended day of cycling occurred while we were in Indiana.

On one picturesque day, as I rode carefully following my route map to avoid getting lost, I passed by a beautifully decorated and well-maintained home. It was July, and I noticed a brightly yellow-painted bicycle in the front yard, likely a tribute to the ongoing Tour de France, which typically happens in the first half of the month of July.

Unfortunately, on this day, I made an unusual and dangerous mistake. As I cycled, my focus drifted away from the road. I began reminiscing about the years I spent watching the Tour de France with Cathy. This tradition began after we were married, and we continued every July after our daughter Casey was born. Lost in those memories, as well as memories of my own bike racing experiences before marrying Cathy, I missed a crucial left turn and unintentionally rode thirty additional miles. It was only when I tried to find the street to make the required left turn that I realized I had veered off the designated route. Eventually, I had to ask for directions, which led to riding an additional thirty miles just to get back to the street I was supposed to turn left on. By the end of that day, due to my distraction and failure to follow the cue sheet, I mistakenly had ridden over 160 miles.

Upon reaching Indianapolis, the change from the arid West to the humid Eastern United States was striking. The increased humidity each morning marked our entry into a more densely populated area with heavier traffic, requiring us to be extra cautious on even rural roads.

On a particularly memorable day, we were cycling on the back roads on the southern outskirts of Cleveland. The challenge here wasn't just the amount of traffic but also how fast it was moving. Particularly the dump trucks, which would speed past us at alarming rates, often going over the speed limit. It felt like we were on a racetrack.

The most intense moment came when several dump trucks passed by extremely close and at such high speeds that I was amazed I wasn't hit. One truck even lifted its tires off the ground while taking a curve, something I had never seen before. Despite these harrowing experiences, we were fortunate that no accidents happened, and I came through it all without a scratch.

After seeing the concerning driving behavior, I decided to take a lunch break. While eating, I saw two police officers also getting lunch. I took this chance to ask them what they thought about the local driving habits. To my surprise, they confirmed that the majority of drivers were indeed reckless and mentioned they often handed out traffic tickets for such behavior. They advised me to be careful while cycling on those roads. This conversation with the police officers made me even more relieved to be moving on from the Cleveland area!

Continuing my journey, I pedaled onto Highway 5, following the scenic route along Lake Erie's shoreline. I passed through charming coastal towns like Erie and Presque Isle, PA each with its distinct allure and attractions. During lunch at a restaurant near the Erie Port Authority, I enjoyed a distant view of the stunning sandy beaches at Presque Isle State Park, adding to the day's breathtaking picturesque experiences.

The Lake Erie Wine Country region, with its rolling vineyards and picturesque wineries, was a beautiful visual treat. I was tempted to sample the local wines, but I decided against drinking alcohol while cycling. Nonetheless, my ride along Highway 5 offered an incredible opportunity to witness and appreciate Lake Erie's beauty and explore the charming places along its shores. The stunning lake vistas, quaint towns, and natural wonders enhanced my appreciation for the diverse landscapes and hidden gems of this part of the United States.

As I pedaled through the scenic landscapes of this region, I relished every moment, savoring the breathtaking views, the tranquil sounds, and the peaceful atmosphere that enveloped Lake Erie and its surroundings. It was another remarkable episode in my cross-country bicycle adventure, adding yet another captivating memory of the natural beauty of the United States.

On our final rest day, my riding buddy Andrew suggested we rent a car and drive to Niagara Falls and I agreed. Neither of us had been to Niagara Falls and to help reduce our costs Andrew asked several riders if they wanted to go. Because there were eight of us going, Andrew rented a large Lincoln Town Car. It was a fun ride packed in that car like a can of sardines. It was well worth it because Niagara Falls is one of the world's most iconic and breathtaking natural wonders. Located on the border between the United States and Canada, with its beautiful and powerful waterfalls and scenic vistas.

402

As we approached the area, we could hear the thunderous roar of the cascading water, building up anticipation for our visit. Upon arriving at Niagara Falls State Park, we found several panoramic views of the falls from various observation points. The sheer power and beauty of the three waterfalls was a spectacular visual experience. We only had a few hours for a visit because of our drive to and from, plus we had to return the rental car. Due to our limited time, we were unable to participate in many of the exciting activities at the Falls. One of the most popular ones that I would have liked to have experienced was the Maid of the Mist boat tour. This boat tour goes right up to the base of the falls, providing an up-close and personal view of the fall's power and beauty. There were waiting lines and the only boat tour available was midafternoon.

We decided to walk around and visit the Cave of the Winds instead. After purchasing our tickets, we were provided ponchos and small umbrellas. I wondered why all the rain gear. The water cannot be that heavy. But I put my poncho on and took an umbrella. The Cave of the Winds tour took us down a series of wooden walkways to the base of the Bridal Veil Falls. Along the way we began to feel the mist blowing up to the entrance of the tunnel. At the bottom of the Cave of the Winds observation decks,

Me with Niagara Falls in the background

we were able to get within 20 feet of the thundering Niagara Falls. Now I realized why we needed ponchos because the experience reminded me of being in those heavy monsoon storms in Vietnam. The torrents of water cascading down and the extreme winds blowing us all over the observation deck reminded me of videos I had seen of hurricanes hitting our gulf coast states. That powerful experience gave me a true sense of the strength and power of the water cascading over the falls. Afterwards we had a group photograph taken with Niagara Falls in the background.

Then it was time to depart because of the sun setting, but as we left the area we were bathed in a fascinating array of colors, creating a beautiful scenic departing landscape. It was a perfect ending to our Niagara Falls experience. I'm sure all of us cherished every moment we spent at Niagara Falls because we could experience one of the most incredible natural wonders of the world. The sheer size, power, and grandeur of the falls left an indelible impression on me, serving as a testament to the awe-inspiring beauty of nature we continued to see throughout our ride across America.

My bicycle journey across the United States was not only a physical and scenic adventure but also a heartwarming experience of meeting kind and generous people along the way. Those encounters added a special touch to my cross-country trip and created cherished memories that would stay with me forever. It's kind of a cliche, but it's also totally accurate. Stopping to meet individuals along the ride took time and effort. It did not happen every day, but it did occur often. It was so special to have a conversation with another person who took time from their daily routines and my taking time from riding to talk. Those beautiful moments with people made my bicycle ride across the United States a life-altering and positive experience!

Throughout my journey, I encountered people from different walks of life who went out of their way to offer assistance, support, and genuine kindness. Whether it was a couple doing yard work, a small-town resident, a person in a restaurant, or a passerby, the generosity I experienced left a lasting impact on me.

In some towns, I was greeted by locals who engaged in conversations that made me feel welcomed as I passed through on my bicycle. I also encountered kind strangers who once they heard I was fund raising for The Fisher House Foundation and wounded veterans offered their financial assistance. I provided a link to my web page so they could make their donations. They served as constant reminders of the goodness in people's hearts.

My bicycle was always a great conversation starter. People saw me as somewhere between a little crazy and a complete idiot because I actually chose to travel across the country by bicycle in the 21st century. Because of the bike, they found me harmless and thought I wouldn't mind a little chit chat. If they saw me with a couple of my riding buddies with our bicycles outside a restaurant, convenience store, or hotel, they most often asked the following questions:

Where are you headed?

Where did you start?

How many miles do you ride every day?

What do you eat?

At some point in the conversation, I'd get a chance to ask them, "Are you from around here?" Meeting people this way happens a lot less when we are traveling inside a gas-powered, climate-controlled 2,000-pound-plus

Gifford's in New York State, just one of our many great lunch stops along the way

vehicle. As I traveled on my bicycle, I briefly conversed with Walmart greeters, café waitstaff, car ferry employees, convenience-store clerks, and fellow restaurant patrons.

The genuine warmth and friendliness I encountered in my interactions with people enriched my journey. Whether it was a cheerful greeting from a passing driver, a smile from a pedestrian, or a conversation with a curious local, these simple gestures were always appreciated. These encounters reminded me that despite differences in backgrounds, cultures, and beliefs, there is a common thread of compassion that unites the citizens of the United States. It was a testament to the inherent goodness and willingness to help others that exists within individuals across the United States.

On any given day, I also found happiness when I discovered my power to push myself to wherever I was headed during my ride. Bicycle riding across the United States is no small feat, and I was fortunate to find happiness and inspiration along the way. There were many times I thought of a new phrase or saying. This one I like best: "We should look closely at the life we live because it should look identical to the future life we want to live." Those words stayed with me the entire ride and were a constant reminder of what a wonderful experience I was having by riding my bicycle across the United States.

That phrase also emphasized the importance of self-reflection and aligning my present actions with my desired future. By reflection and examination of our current choices, behaviors, and attitudes, we can assess whether they are in line with the life we envision for ourselves. During my ride, those words served as a constant reminder to be mindful of my actions and decisions, ensuring they were in harmony with the future I wanted to continue to create. Riding over 4,000 miles across diverse landscapes and experiencing the vastness and diversity of the United States provided a unique perspective. Because of the challenges I faced along the way, they continued to strengthen and teach me additional valuable lessons about flexibility, determination, resilience, and the beauty of the world around me. Similar to the lessons learned in the Army and the Vietnam War.

Because of my continued self-reflection, I felt we were going too fast as we completed each day's miles. Looking back on that time, maybe I did not want that special journey to end. It would have been nice to have taken more time to explore and talk with additional people along the way. What an incredible opportunity and life experience to have the ability to complete a ride like this and to see so much of the United States! I was grateful and blessed to have had the opportunity to take two months off work to accomplish such a life-changing achievement. However, I was still committed to being at a designated location at the end of each day. A hotel with clean sheets and a shower awaited me like those in New York's Finger Lake region.

On the morning of my journey through the Finger Lakes area, it had been raining all night, and the rain persisted as I set out on my bike in the morning. Despite the challenging conditions, the rain added a touch of mystique and beauty to the landscape, but it also required extra caution while riding to ensure our safety. Although I had experience riding in the rain before, this day felt different. As I made my way through the traffic and wet roads, the rain continued to pour, creating a serene yet challenging atmosphere. The lush greenery of the Finger Lakes region appeared even more enchanting in the rain, but it also made the roads slippery, posing a potential hazard for me and my fellow cyclists.

Fate took an unexpected turn when I turned my head left in response to someone I thought was yelling at me. At that moment, I missed noticing a small, one-inch-high curb covered in water to the right of my path. The heavy rain made the road surface slick, and when I inadvertently hit the small curb, I lost my balance and fell. Thanks to the cushioning effect of the water, the impact of my fall was significantly softened.

An ambulance heading in the opposite direction observed my fall and immediately stopped to assist. I was part of a small group and they stopped as well. I was laying on this rain-soaked road embarrassed and laughing at how I had just fallen. I couldn't believe that such a small curb had brought me down so quickly. The EMTs and my fellow riders were over me instantly. When an EMT asked if I was hurt, I said no but asked if my teeth were okay while smiling ear-to-ear. Everyone had a good laugh and they helped me up and made sure I was able to continue to ride. Fortunately, I didn't suffer any injuries or even tears in my riding clothing.

After I quickly regained my composure, I was thankful that the road's unique rain-soaked condition had provided protection during the mishap. It only took a few moments before we cleared the road so traffic could continue. Once again, we were on our journey again in the rain, but everyone was a little more cautious and alert to the road's conditions. The rain gradually subsided, allowing everyone to appreciate the beauty of the Finger Lakes region despite the minor earlier delay.

That unexpected incident served as a reminder of the unpredictable nature of outdoor adventures and the importance of adapting to changing circumstances. My fall and subsequent realization of the road's water cushion acted as a testament to the role that nature or providence can sometimes play in our safety, even in unexpected ways.

With my renewed sense of resilience and a deeper appreciation for the journey, I continued riding through the beautiful Finger Lakes region. Like all life experiences, I possessed a renewed sense of embracing both the challenges and the unexpected moments that made my bicycle adventure even more memorable.

On the final day of my ride, I reached Portsmouth, New Hampshire, where Cathy awaited me at the Atlantic Ocean beach. This spot marked the official end of my journey—and the special tradition of dipping my front wheel in the Atlantic Ocean. Before this important event, Cathy had called and informed Charles and Martha Robinson, who were spending their

Me with Charles and Martha Robinson at Portsmouth, NH, with a fellow rider

summer at their vacation home in Maine, about my nearing completion of the ride. They kindly joined Cathy at the beach in Portsmouth to celebrate this moment with me.

The arrival at the end of my ride was made incredibly heartwarming and memorable by the presence of Cathy, Charles, Martha, and our wonderful neighbors from Lutherville. They spent their summer in Maine each year and helped us with Casey when she was a baby. Their support added a beautiful touch to the end of my journey. Additionally, being welcomed by hundreds of relatives and friends of everyone who completed the ride made the occasion even more special. Their presence not only showed their pride and joy in our achievement but also fostered a sense of community and shared celebration. The challenge we undertook was more than a personal endeavor; it was a collective journey supported by the encouragement of everyone involved. We all helped each other through the highs and lows, except for one individual who preferred to ride alone despite my attempts to join him. Drawing from my early Army days, I believe in the power of teamwork to overcome any challenge, but he chose to continue solo and eventually left the ride in the last week, missing the shared experiences of triumph and struggle. Perhaps a year or so later he completed the last portion to finally complete his ride across the United States.

Dipping my front wheel into the Atlantic Ocean marked the culmination of my cross-country bicycle journey, a deeply symbolic action to celebrate completing my bicycle ride across America. This act was bittersweet; while part of me yearned to continue the adventure, another part eagerly anticipated returning to my family and the life I loved and cherished. This moment was not just about reaching a geographical endpoint; it represented the peak of my physical and mental endurance, a testament to unwavering determination and perseverance.

As I celebrated this milestone, I was reminded of the profound significance of connection and support from loved ones. These relationships, and the shared experiences they foster, fill our accomplishments with deeper meaning. Standing before the ocean, its vastness and strength mirrored the magnitude of my journey, providing a fitting backdrop for reflecting on this significant accomplishment of my life.

A bittersweet moment after completing 4,286 miles across America. In a way, I didn't want it to end, but I also wanted to return to my family and life I loved so much.

After the wheel dunking ceremony, Cathy and I followed Charles and Martha to their summer home in Maine. We spent the night with them and enjoyed visiting while I answered their many questions about my ride. The following morning, we departed and began our drive home.

Being with Cathy as she drove the eight hours to return home, I realized how much I missed her over those two months of bicycle riding. We talked the entire drive home. Cathy told me about life around the house without Bob. How she and Casey had managed maintenance tasks like replacing our water heater. We discussed Allanwood Place and whether there were any changes or issues with our neighborhood and families during my time away.

When I arrived home and pulled into the garage, I was really tired and just wanted to sleep. However, my plans took an unexpected turn when our neighbors dropped by. They were eager to hear about my experiences cycling across the United States. What started as a simple visit turned into an impromptu and lively Allanwood party that went on until 2am. Finally, everyone left, and I could finally go to bed.

410

The next morning, at 5:00 a.m. I got up after having slept just three hours. I was still feeling exhausted, but I was determined to work on my bicycle and get it ready for racing. Despite the fatigue, I was in excellent shape after completing my ride. I felt confident about returning to bicycle racing, even competing with the younger cyclists in my club.

It had been over two months since I last rode my beautiful red BMW K1200RS motorcycle. After enjoying breakfast this morning, I decided it was time to take it out again. I rode to Damascus to visit the bicycle shop that had previously helped me prepare for my cross-country ride. My goal for today's visit was to buy several components to reconfigure my bicycle for racing.

At the bike shop, I had a pleasant chat about my ride with the owner while purchasing the new components. Once done, I headed back home on my motorcycle. While riding through Damascus, two young boys asked me to go fast on my flashy "Arrest Me" red motorcycle. I indulged them and accelerated quickly from a traffic light. After covering three blocks, I realized I should be more cautious as I was feeling exhausted. So, for the rest of the journey back home, I made sure to ride within the speed limit. Once I finally arrived at home, I planned to take a much-needed nap.

Finally, arriving home from my motorcycle ride to Damascus I pulled up to the open garage behind our cars, I turned off the motorcycle and placed my feet close to the motorcycle on the ground as I had for the past two months while riding my bicycle. I was not wearing my motorcycle shoes, only running shoes because they were more comfortable. My feet were too close to the motorcycle, and I didn't have the needed leg leverage over the motorcycle's weight. The motorcycle weighed 625 pounds, 600 pounds more than my 25-pound bicycle. The motorcycle began to lean toward the left. I pulled hard right, and it snapped right. I had hoped it would straighten so I could lean it on the side stand. Instead, I was so exhausted and didn't react fast enough and couldn't stop the motorcycle's tilting motion toward the right. Instead, I was so exhausted and didn't react fast enough and couldn't stop the motorcycle's tilting motion toward the right. It continued falling, with me still straddling it. The motorcycle landed on the inside of right foot. OUCH!

With my right foot trapped and injured, I realized the severity of the situation when I couldn't free it from beneath the 650-pound machine. Despite my attempts to call for help, Cathy couldn't hear me from inside the house.

My beautiful red BMW K1200RS motorcycle

The engine fairing pressing down on my foot made it clear I was hurt, especially since my foot was compressed to about two inches. Unable to lift the motorcycle on my own, I took several deep breaths and managed to pull my foot out, experiencing intense pain and the sound of bones breaking.

I made it inside without immediately revealing the extent of my injuries to Cathy, even as my foot began to swell rapidly. Together, we managed to upright the motorcycle using a strap and my car, after which I resorted to taking pain medication to manage the worsening discomfort.

The next day, a visit to the emergency room confirmed eight broken bones in my right foot, including a particularly painful split in the metatarsal bone. The doctor advised and I agreed for natural healing over surgery, I chose to wear a boot, avoiding the discomfort of metal pins and screws in the future.

The injury was a stark contrast to my previous physical fitness, leading to months of recovery and a slow return to activities. This experience taught me to appreciate each moment, even in injury, as an opportunity for growth and humility. It underscored the importance of resting and listening to my body, especially as I embrace the "seasoned citizen" phase of my life.

4,000 miles and 20 years—
The Journey and Jubilation

Sometimes life offers the perfect canvas on which to paint our dreams. For me, the canvas was 4,286 miles long, stretching across the United States on two wheels. My trusty bicycle and I, together, made a pilgrimage that was as much about self-discovery as it was about the scenic beauty of the America I'd always wanted to intimately know. Every turn of the pedal was a stroke of paint on my life's canvas, each mile an indelible ink in the diary of my existence.

As much as the ride was a lone endeavor, it was underpinned by a supporting community of loved ones, cheering from afar. There were phone calls and messages from friends and family that kept me going. And most importantly, there was the abiding love and support of my wonderful wife Cathy, the cornerstone of the other journey I've been on for 20-years—our marriage.

This brings me to Allanwood Place in Maryland, the setting for a celebration as significant as the journey itself. The ride across America culminated in a different kind of adventure—a 20th-anniversary party we held in our home. With about 100 people packed into the rooms throughout our home and our ski chalet basement, the air was filled with joy and nostalgia.

Guests arrived with wide smiles and stories, some having been with us since the first chapter of our marital journey. The walls of our home, usually quiet observers, seemed to come alive with laughter and chatter, the windows reflecting twinkling eyes and heartfelt hugs. The food was a feast for the soul, each dish a reflection of the years and experiences we've shared— laboriously prepared by Cathy, close friends and relatives.

As I looked around our home that evening, I felt the same triumphant surge I had felt at the end of each day's ride. It was a realization that we had covered countless miles, both literally and metaphorically, and had arrived at a beautiful destination each time.

If the 4,286-mile bike ride taught me the power of personal endurance, the 20-year marriage filled with love and the celebration that followed taught me the enduring power of love. That juncture in my life, that incredible milestone marked by a tire dipping into the Atlantic Ocean and the clinking of champagne glasses at Allanwood Place, was a testament to two parallel journeys. One through diverse terrains and the other through the varied landscapes of marital life filled with love. And so, standing at that intersection of milestones, I could only think of one phrase to sum it all up—Another Lucky Day Lived. A toast—Here's to the miles we've covered and the miles yet to come. Onward, always.

Returning to Work after Retirement the First Time

The story of retiring the first time in 2005 started when our family went on a vacation to California, where we visited my dear friend Bob McLaughlin, a fellow Vietnam veteran. During our visit, I had a realization that the time since our service in Vietnam felt like it was just yesterday, and it hit me that our lives were passing by rapidly.

This realization became the primary reason for my decision to retire from the Federal Reserve Board of Governors. Eventually, I chose to return to work in the technology field but in a different role. It was a profound moment of contemplating mortality and the finite nature of our lives, which acted as a powerful catalyst for reevaluating my priorities and seeking a more fulfilling path.

The truth is, we all have a limited amount of time on this Earth, and what's even more bewildering is that none of us knows exactly how much time we have. It can all be taken away in an instant, which is why making the most of our time becomes crucial for our meaningful journey through life. As I reflected on my own mortality, I realized that my priorities had shifted, and I started contemplating what I truly desired to do with my remaining time. Witnessing how people spent their time in the corporate world over my career further solidified my desire for something different. I came to appreciate that I wanted to pursue a different path while I still had the opportunity.

After retiring from my position at the Board of Governors of the Federal Reserve System, I found myself unsure about returning to a corporate environment and uncertain about my career path. However, my passion for technology remained strong, and I wanted to explore opportunities in that field. I knew I needed time to carefully consider my options before committing to any work-related decision. During this period, various organizations approached me with enticing offers, prompting me to seek advice from our trusted friend and neighbor, John Meyer. He was knowledgeable about the employment landscape in the D.C. area. Over the course of four months, I sought John's guidance and valued his insights on companies in the region.

One afternoon, John called me unexpectedly and asked if we could discuss job offers in person. I immediately agreed, and we sat down over a glass of wine in our newly remodeled basement, designed to resemble a cozy ski lodge. To my surprise, our conversation veered away from previous offers, as John expressed his intention to offer me a position at Computer Sciences Corporation (CSC), where he worked. He provided a detailed description of the job, explaining that I would be involved in writing proposals for government technology projects. It was an ideal opportunity since I would have the necessary tools, including a computer and cell phone, and the added benefit of working from home. The position aligned perfectly with my interests, and the prospect of working remotely enhanced its appeal.

Transitioning into this new role at CSC allowed me not only to continue my work with technology but also granted me the flexibility and autonomy that suited my priorities and lifestyle at that stage of my life. It was absolutely wonderful to find an opportunity that aligned so well with my desires and aspirations. My journey with CSC, along with subsequent experiences in the technology field, brought me a sense of fulfillment, personal growth, and a renewed sense of purpose.

CSC Lends Name to Bike Racing

In the 1980s, the Denmark subsidiary of CSC took a significant step into the world of sports by becoming the sponsor of Bjarne Riis' Team CSC, a road bicycle racing team. This move marked the beginning of a journey filled with remarkable achievements and formidable challenges. Over the years, Team CSC distinguished itself as a formidable contender in the cycling world, consistently competing in and finishing the globe's most prestigious endurance races. The team's dedication, skill, and strategy propelled them to the forefront of professional cycling, earning them accolades and respect within the cycling community.

However, the team's journey was not without its trials. The shadow of doping allegations loomed over their accomplishments when a rider tested positive for banned performance-enhancing substances. This incident cast a pall over the team's achievements, reflecting the broader challenges faced by the sport of cycling during that era. The doping scandal underscored the intense pressure athletes often faced to perform at the highest levels and the ethical dilemmas that could arise in the pursuit of victory.

About a year and half after my cross-country ride and subsequent broken foot, I had the opportunity to participate in a training ride before one of the East Coast's premier bicycle races in Northern Virginia was an experience I'll never forget. Despite the injury, I had dedicated myself to training, believing that I had regained my racing form. However, as I would soon discover, I was far from reaching the peak condition necessary for competitive bicycle racing. I learned to pace myself and respect my limits, a lesson that came with the acceptance of aging and prioritizing personal well-being over competition. This mindset shift allowed me to live a more enriching life, focusing on personal growth and fulfillment, embracing each season of life with contentment and gratitude.

Nevertheless, the corporate officers at CSC wanted me to join the team for this ride to demonstrate the competitive spirit and commitment of CSC staff outside of the workplace. The training ride spanned forty miles—a distance I had previously tackled with ease and confidence. Yet, this time, the context was vastly different. My riding companions were young, vibrant cyclists in their early 20s, while I had recently celebrated my 61st birthday. The generational gap was palpable, not just in years but in the raw energy and speed these young riders brought to the road. Throughout the ride, there were moments when I doubted my ability to keep pace. The youthful exuberance of my companions translated into a relentless tempo, as they seemed determined to outperform me, turning the training ride into an impromptu race.

Despite the challenges, and perhaps a stroke of luck as several of the young Team CSC riders encountered flat tires, I managed to complete the ride alongside them. This accomplishment was also a testament to the enduring spirit of determination. It underscored a valuable lesson: the essence of competition and camaraderie in cycling transcends age. Finishing that forty-mile journey, winded but undeterred, I was reminded of the importance of pushing one's limits and the sheer joy of participating, regardless of the outcome. It was a poignant reminder that, in the realm of sports and

Me with the Tour de France Team CSC out for a training ride or RACE!

life, it's not always about finishing first but about the courage to continue and the resolve to finish what we start.

About four years later, in the early 2000s, as CSC's senior executives began to contemplate the sale of the corporation, decisions regarding the future of the bicycle racing franchise became a focal point. Ultimately, the decision was made to sell the bicycle racing franchise to a European racing team. This transition marked the end of an era for CSC's involvement in professional cycling but also opened a new chapter for the team under new ownership. The legacy of Team CSC, characterized by both its sporting successes and the challenges it faced, remains a significant chapter in the history of professional road bicycle racing.

CSC Background

Let me provide some background about Computer Sciences Corporation and its beginning. The company was formed in the 1950s when the infant technology industry created new developments in computing. One of CSC's founders, Robert Patrick, had built targeting systems for U.S. Government intercontinental ballistic missile programs. The other CSC founder, Fletcher

Jones, who was working at North American Aviation at the time brought most of its earliest engineering recruits from North American Aviation to join CSC. It had closed its intercontinental ballistic missile and fighter plane programs to develop space missions. Together Patrick and Jones formed CSC and won its first government contract with NASA in 1961 to work on the Apollo moon landings, the Space Shuttle missions, and the Hubble Space Telescope. Large government projects became a trademark of CSC success. Most of those technology projects were at the core of my profession and hobbies. Because of technology's vast ubiquity, very little of life today is not affected by technology in some way, shape, or form.

When I began working at CSC, it was struggling to recover from several years of lagging financial performance due to significant delivery and implementation problems with large customers such as NASA, the IRS, and the Department of Homeland Security (DHS). To reduce overhead costs and become more cost-effective CSC began using less expensive offshore resources to make its outsourcing deals competitive and attractive to customers. The presence of non-citizen offshore resources working on government projects that required high-level security clearances posed significantly higher potential national security risks. One of my primary tasks was to prepare proposal responses to government solicitations that could win contracts. I believed there were ways of offering services and staffing without utilizing less expensive and less qualified offshore resources. On several of the proposals I completed, the client appreciated that CSC offered American onshore resources and facilities instead of offshore services. But this would change because CSC would eventually buy foreign companies to provide staffing and resources.

Using my experience in proposing United States resources, CSC won several contracts. It wasn't long before resource management was reassigned to me. There were many other problems and issues within resource management that needed to be solved as well. In addition to resource management, I was requested to help with data center improvement projects. These were fun projects where a significant amount of my experience could be applied. One contract stands out as the most enjoyable. CSC was awarded a contract to modernize the National Institute of Health (NIH) data centers. I especially enjoyed the National Library of Medicine (NLM) data center project within

418

NIH the most because I observed medicine and its use of cutting-edge technology advances in treatment. Each day I would walk past male and female cadavers with their veins filled with a solid color liquid displaying the body's blood vessels. Other cadavers' organs were sliced into extremely thin pieces to provide different views of research for treatment options. It reminded me of graduate school when a friend who worked at NIH gave me a tour that demonstrated how technology was being used in medicine. Little did I know that this medical technology would directly impact me later.

Because of the success with business proposals, it wasn't long before other CSC business components began asking me to attend client meetings and help in their development of business proposals. My work plate overflowed. Most of my time was spent at client sites or working from home. Working from home at first was lots of fun because I would wake up at 5 a.m., make coffee, shower, get dressed, check emails by 6am, and then go to work without having to commute. Initially, while working from home, my workday would end at 5 p.m., but over time, my workday began to extend well beyond 5 p.m. Yet becoming thoroughly engrossed in my work, I overlooked the amount of time spent performing it. I often worked overnight and into the following day. I enjoyed the work thoroughly because I was doing what I loved to do.

2010 Census Technology

In 2000, CSC was awarded a contract by the Department of Commerce to conduct the national census for that year. It was a successful venture, giving CSC valuable experience in handling such projects. When the preparation for the 2010 census began, the Department of Commerce requested proposals, and CSC submitted one that highlighted its successful experiences with census operations and management. Nevertheless, Lockheed Martin ultimately won the contract to handle data collection and standardization for the 2010 census, with an estimated projected value of $12 billion. A significant portion of this cost was allocated to information technology, which included the use of hand-held computing devices with GPS capability for data collection—a first for a census.

Recognizing the complexity of the project, Lockheed Martin sought an experienced partner and decided to bring CSC on board as a subcontractor due to its substantial experience in conducting previous censuses.

I was personally asked to participate in the 2010 Census project but this time, I had the option to decline the request because of my then existing workload. However, after understanding the responsibilities of the role, I found this technology assignment could be extremely exciting and decided to accept it. Before delving into the project, I was given a refresher on the history of the census, dating back to the first decennial census conducted in 1790, which was mandated by the Constitution to allocate US Representatives based on the population count every ten years.

My specific duties involved managing the acquisition and installation of various equipment required to complete the census, such as computers, phones, and processing equipment. Additionally, I had to oversee physical and technical security measures, especially the level of security required for two large warehouse facilities in Baltimore and Phoenix, each spanning the size of seven football fields. To navigate within these massive facilities, many staff members used bicycles, but I opted to walk to observe the equipment operation more closely and effectively.

At those facilities, it was amazing to see mail trucks delivering pallets filled with boxes of completed census documents. The facilities equipment operators would then move these pallets inside, where the boxes were unpacked, and the forms taken to workstations for processing. The completed census forms were processed using optical reading equipment, and it was nice to see the smooth functioning of the workflow operations we had previously diagrammed before the project began.

To ensure efficiency, the facilities operated in three shifts, seven days a week, with hundreds of employees working at each location. The information collectors who utilized the new hand-held computing devices faced operational challenges, particularly in rural areas with inadequate internet services for data transmission to and from the devices. These same devices required nightly updates, further complicating the gathering and processing of census data. Because of these problems and issues the hand-held devices were ultimately abandoned and the paper forms became the primary data collection medium.

I split my time between the Phoenix and Baltimore facilities. Walking into one of the facilities a person would see row after row of workstations throughout with employees processing paper forms. After the facilities became operational, I thought of each facility as a paper form processing factory. Also, after the forms were processed, they were shredded and recycled after the information was collected and stored electronically.

The Baltimore location was an easy drive from home with only minor stop-and-go traffic. Most days, I would ride my BMW motorcycle and travel on Interstate 95 and through the Harbor Tunnel toll road to Essex.

Phoenix was completely different than Baltimore because of the extreme heat. On several occasions, when I left the processing facility the temperature would be above 105 degrees. Those extreme temperatures amazed me. I often thought, who would want to live here throughout the year? One person commented about the heat by saying we should be thankful it's a dry heat. I responded, "Yes, it's a dry heat, but it's still like sticking one's head into a hot oven." Being extremely dry and hot, I used moisturizers to avoid skin damage. I was also cautioned about grabbing the metal portion of the seat belt in cars because the metal could burn my hand if I had left my rental car in the sunlight. After work in the evenings, I would go to spinning classes and then return to my hotel near 10 p.m. At that time of night, the temperature was still over 100 degrees.

Most of the time while at the facilities everyone would continually check and make sure the equipment was operating properly. Technology and process problems became a priority, solving these problems was critical to the success of the census. If a piece of equipment failed it could adversely affect the entire day's operation. For example, when one of our Phoenix data transmission lines began to drop data, I caught the next flight to Phoenix to troubleshoot why this was occurring. It wasn't long before the problem was discovered and to my amazement, the data line had been installed too close to the hot roof by a contractor. The heat wasn't allowing the data to be transmitted which caused portions of the data to be lost. Having the contractor return and properly reinstalling the wire resolved the problem immediately.

Another issue I faced was organizations or persons constantly trying to hack into our systems at the Baltimore facility. What was puzzling to me was this wasn't a problem for the Phoenix location. I continually monitored and reviewed security reports daily and changed our operating procedures weekly at the Baltimore facility. One morning as I arrived, an unauthorized individual or organization had just successfully surpassed our security and accessed the facility's timekeeping system. The system was designed to stop working if the software was inappropriately accessed or an operating error occurred. We had to stop all electronic communications in and out of the facility then reinstalled the software. After the application was back up and running and we had finished diagnosing how the system was violated it was discovered that whoever had hacked the system could only obtain titles of reports. I realized we had dodged a major problem, and we further strengthened our security procedures to deny further access to any census data or information. We were also able to discover the intruder's personal identifying information and promptly reported this information to the local police and security agencies for immediate follow-up.

At the end of the 2010 census, more than 308 million people were counted at the contract cost of $12 billion. The results of this effort provided essential data to Congress to guide apportionment and redistricting of local congressional districts.

Finally Retiring—Maybe

As this project was winding down, I talked with Cathy about the possibility of resigning and finally retiring. We talked about it at some length because I loved technology and wasn't sure what I'd do in retirement. Eventually we agreed that I would provide a resignation letter to the corporate headquarters and finally retire.

On the day I hand-delivered my resignation letter, something unexpected happened. I was invited into the executive conference room where they asked me not to retire but to consider working on a contract they believed would be a perfect fit for me and where I could make a difference. This contract happened to be the most significant and profitable one in CSC's history. However, during the in-depth briefing on the contract, I learned that it had been awarded three years prior but had failed to deliver any of the required deliverables.

After hearing this, I requested some time to think about the opportunity. That evening, Cathy and I discussed the pros and cons of this potential assignment. Eventually, we decided that I should accept the offer and move to this program. The next day, I called the CEO's office to let them know that I would stay on and move to this program.

Later that day, the Chief Operating Officer provided me with a detailed briefing on CSC's experience with this contract up to that point. The way the briefing was presented suggested that the issues were mainly caused by the contracting organization, the Department of Homeland Security.

However, I quickly discovered that this program had more issues than initially presented.

Let me provide background and perspective about this financially significant program. In July 2008, CSC won a billion-dollar contract to consolidate 22 data centers for the Department of Homeland Security (DHS). It was called The DHS Data Center Consolidation program and it aimed to streamline the department's information technology infrastructure, optimize resource allocation, enhance security, and reduce operational costs. However, the complexity of this endeavor demanded specialized knowledge and skills to overcome various technical, operational, and organizational hurdles. Some of the program's complexity resulted from the Department of Homeland Security being created from the most extensive federal government reorganization since 1948 when the Department of Defense was created. Nevertheless, CSC realized that a crucial success factor would be having individuals with successful data center experience. CSC could draw upon their experiences and industry insights to better manage a large-scale data center consolidation like this.

The contract required the establishment of two mega data centers. The primary data center would be where all DHS data centers would be moved and consolidated. All like technology assets would be consolidated allowing for efficient collaboration and data sharing across all DHS organizations. The primary data center was located within a World War II bomb-making facility and there was also a backup data center. During the briefing I received at corporate everything seemed straightforward and not overwhelming. Moving data centers is an extremely complicated process, but by using proven methodologies, it can be accomplished without much disruption. The complexities of merging data centers with diverse legacy systems while ensuring uninterrupted service delivery and addressing security was the top priority for DHS. When I arrived on the program late in 2010, three years after the contract had been awarded, CSC hadn't completed a single data center move/consolidation. A vice president had been assigned to run this program after the contract was awarded in 2008.

423

From all indications, the program's main priority was to generate as many task orders as possible for additional work. Unfortunately, this focus led to overlooking several other important priorities. For instance, one of the hiring requirements for the DHS contract was that each individual working on any aspect of the contract had to possess at least a college degree. However, this requirement was not consistently met, as some individuals without the necessary qualifications were hired.

Moreover, there were issues with recruiting individuals lacking expertise in critical areas such as data center operations, network architecture, hardware infrastructure, virtualization, and disaster recovery planning. These areas were crucial for the successful execution of the contract, as they enabled the team to effectively handle challenges like system integration, capacity planning, and business continuity.

To address these concerns and ensure a more successful outcome, I recognized the need to hire a resource manager. The resource manager's role was essential in rectifying past oversights and ensuring compliance with all contract hiring requirements. With the right team members onboard, we could now move forward with greater confidence in achieving our goals.

Almost immediately I discovered that there were no formal industry standards or processes, including project management, being utilized for such a significant project. This is despite CSC's emphasis on using industry technology standards and processes for customers. I was disappointed with this decision by the original management team, but believed we could still succeed by turning this around and implementing formal industry standards and procedures. My first priority was to transition the project into using the CSC industry standards and processes. The same standards and processes that were cited in every proposal for new work. Fortunately, the project managers were receptive to the idea as they realized the benefits of defined processes and procedures.

Besides the technical challenges in the data centers consolidation effort, there were operational and organizational obstacles within CSC and DHS. Resistance to change, coordination among diverse stakeholders, and minimizing disruptions to ongoing operations were some of the issues. To effectively manage and resolve these challenges, I had to collaborate with others throughout CSC.

424

Over the next two years, I dedicated myself to improving the operations of this program to ensure CSC didn't lose the contract. I successfully consolidated two large DHS data centers into the primary site. To foster a team environment and encourage cooperation among project managers, I initiated Wednesday conference calls where they could discuss their weekly successes and issues. These calls were mandatory and provided valuable input for our Thursday status presentations with DHS executive management.

To enhance communication, I designed a quadrant report in PowerPoint, and implemented it helping each project manager present their project's critical areas. DHS management found this new weekly briefing format helpful, gaining better insight into the challenges being faced and resolved. Through these efforts, we were able to significantly improve the program's operations and maintain the contract.

I provided weekly briefings to CSC executive management, summarizing the lessons learned from the DHS Data Center Consolidation program. Along with these briefings, I offered written documents and procedures outlining best practices for managing similar initiatives. Emphasizing the importance of involving experienced professionals from the project's beginning, conducting thorough planning and risk assessments, maintaining open communication channels, and adopting an iterative implementation approach.

The success of the DHS Data Center Consolidation program heavily relied on the expertise and experience of individuals with a deep understanding of data centers. They played a critical role in navigating the technical, operational, and organizational complexities of the consolidation effort. By sharing and applying the lessons learned, we paved the way for future contracts and initiatives to achieve successful outcomes.

After two years of managing the challenging and complex DHS Data Center Consolidation contract, I decided it was time to retire from the corporate setting. This second retirement would mark a significant milestone, presenting a unique opportunity for exploration, personal growth, and fulfillment. With our careful consideration of financial planning, health and wellness, lifelong learning, community engagement, and personal aspirations, Cathy and I aimed to chart a successful course toward a rewarding and purposeful retirement.

Years ago, I realized that endings can often be painful, as they pave the way for new beginnings. Beginnings and endings are interconnected in various aspects of our lives, and without endings, there would be no room for fresh starts. By acknowledging the need for closure, we can avoid becoming stuck or stationary. I passionately believed that we required assistance and guidance to recognize that our current chapter needed to come to a close. Having previously sought coaches for sports and career changes, I now felt the need for a life coach. I really believed life coaching would be a collaborative partnership between us and a coach, who would help us continue our personal growth and navigate retirement effectively. This realization was the primary reason I sought the help of a life coach.

Life Coaching

Exceptional sports coaching has played a crucial role in shaping our favorite world-class athletes. Similarly, CEOs, entrepreneurs, business leaders, executives, and professionals owe a significant portion of their success to business coaching. In sports and when I was preparing to retire from the Federal Reserve Board of Governors, I realized the importance of having a coach to guide me through that transition. I approached a friend who had previously retired from the Social Security Administration and had achieved great success. Believing that he would be the perfect retirement coach for me, we began meeting regularly to discuss my goals both before and after retiring, while keeping track of my progress. As he generously offered his time for free, I wanted to make the most of our meetings by being well prepared, sharing my progress, and discussing any setbacks or delays. Drawing on his experience, he provided valuable suggestions for resolving issues and overcoming obstacles. His coaching proved instrumental in my successful transition to retirement, while also affirming the skills I had developed over the years.

While work-related coaching is well-known, the concept of life coaching is unfamiliar to many. Cathy and I were both going through career transitions. Cathy was already retired, and I was still working at CSC but looking forward to retirement. For years, we had talked about moving from Maryland after Casey graduated and we both retired. However, we felt like we weren't making any progress with those plans.

We decided to take the first step and met with our financial advisor to reevaluate our finances. Prior to my retirement from CSC, we were in a holding pattern, waiting for different elements of our lives to converge so that we could determine how to begin the next chapter of our lives. During the meeting, our advisor mentioned that he had worked with a life coach to improve his relationship with his sister. Given our situation of feeling stuck and uncertain about the future, we asked him for the contact information of his life coach.

Life coaches undergo extensive training to learn effective communication techniques and the art of asking the right questions. They acquire additional knowledge to quickly identify individual or family needs and desires.

At first, Cathy was hesitant and preferred to adopt a wait-and-see approach. Drawing from my positive experiences with other forms of coaching, I believed that seeking assistance would be beneficial. We were in a situation where we needed help to move forward, balancing our current life in the Washington, D.C., area with retirement plans and supporting Casey through graduate school.

I had faith that a life coach could assist us in setting goals with actionable steps and provide valuable tips, tools, and strategies to propel us forward. While friends and family could offer advice and lend an ear, a life coach would objectively help us determine what truly mattered, and guide us to our new goals and objectives. She offered us perspective, support, and numerous tools that proved invaluable.

Our life coach played a pivotal role in helping us unlock our full potential, which enabled us to achieve our desired goals in our journey toward retirement and our move from Maryland. Acting as a supportive friend and trusted advisor, she pushed us to clarify our goals and aspirations, while holding us accountable for our actions and encouraging personal growth.

We met with our life coach weekly for eight weeks. She provided exercises, recommended books to read, had conversations, and experimented with new approaches so we could further discover ourselves. We discovered more about each other than we had known or realized before. We learned new aspects about each other after 20-plus years of marriage. Our life coach was about our age and I believed she was dealing with many of the same issues as Cathy and me. The process was fun. She worked with us to identify and focus on the most important aspects of our life together. I believe we brought out her passion because we were curious and ready to grow and excited about gaining new insights. We didn't want to settle for where we were, but where we could go successfully.

Over my life I learned that life is about transition as it required me to change and grow. I realized this when I transitioned from the Army and war to civilian life. I read several books about transitions during that period, and discovered they could offer opportunities for self-reflection and growth. A transition can provide opportunities for redefining our aspirations and sometimes our identities. I had to deal with a very unexpected transition during and after a divorce that required me to adjust and navigate through an unanticipated emotional low and betrayal period. I knew I had to embrace life's curveballs with openness and curiosity. Because of that my heart was open to meeting the best partner a guy could ever hope to share life with. I wanted to ensure neither Cathy nor me were resisting change. Her continued participation was necessary to ensure our next transition would be a success.

My second half of life has been more in tune with living and family and not just focused on education and career. The changes in life's second half offered an exceptional opportunity to break with the social conditioning that has carried us this far and to do something new and different. I think this transition began many years ago when I would wake early and contemplate life while creating a deeper introspection of my life. I thought about how I had lived as a human yesterday, and how I would live the wonderful day that God had blessed me with that new day. Cathy and I faced the "unknown" of our future, and I realized we had all new days ahead of us. The process with a life coach helped me realize that aging isn't just a downward slope but a unique and extraordinary transitional journey upward. Our time with the life coach prompted us to move forward. We made the decision to look for a new place to call home. I developed a thorough list of criteria for what we both wanted for our new location, work, home, and lifestyle to be. This way we were now moving forward instead of being in-between and undecided. Cathy and my life's journey have taken us to many places. It's been a winding road with detours, roadblocks, clear sailing, and discovery. But we are now more robust and energetic as we travel on beautiful roads of discovery that brighten our daily lives.

IX. Fayetteville, Arkansas

Moving to Arkansas and Building Our Home in Fayetteville

The first time Cathy and I visited Fayetteville, Arkansas was in 1987. She wanted to take me on a tour of the University of Arkansas and was driving her parents' car from Hot Springs Village. Fayetteville struck me as a charming and small university town. When we later considered relocating, it became one of our top three choices, alongside Evergreen, Colorado, and Boone/Blowing Rock, North Carolina.

While we were deciding which place to choose in 2012, Cathy's father developed a severe skin illness. Initially planning a consultation at the Mayo Clinic, he took a turn for the worse and was rushed to the emergency room in Hot Springs. That same afternoon, Cathy and Casey flew to Arkansas to be by Cathy's fathers' side.

Coincidentally, we had recently listed our home for sale, expecting it could take up to a year to sell. However, it sold in just five days. The anxious new owners wanted to move in within 20 days, a timeline further complicated by the emergency with Cathy's father's illness. With our real estate agent's assistance, we negotiated for more time. I stayed back in Maryland to arrange storage for our belongings and look for temporary housing.

Prior to these events, Cathy had been enjoying her retirement by volunteering at the Sandy Spring Museum and serving as a docent for the Montgomery County Historical Society. Just the previous year, she had accepted the contractural role of Interim Executive Director at the Sandy

Spring Museum. However, given the sudden sale of our home and her father's health crisis, she chose to resign as Interim Executive Director at the Sandy Spring Museum. This turned out to be a timely decision because it allowed her to focus entirely on supporting her father and stepmother. Upon arriving in Hot Springs, Cathy and Casey quickly realized the severity of the situation. Cathy's father soon slipped into a coma and passed away early the following Monday from septic shock, the same cause that had claimed my mother.

The week that followed was a whirlwind. As we grappled with the loss of Cathy's father we were also dealing with and managing all the aspects of the closing of our house sale. I took charge of the overall house sale process then and worked on securing a moving company, eventually settling on a local Montgomery County firm. This turned out to be an excellent choice because the company employees knew Northwest Arkansas well because they had moved families to and from the Walmart headquarters. Cathy, in the meantime, was busy arranging all the details relating to her father's funeral and Church service, which was in itself a daunting effort. During all this, we hadn't yet decided where we would move to next, leaving us in a state of uncertainty. We believed we would have more time to decide between the three locations we were considering. It's fair to say Cathy and I were in agreement that Evergreen, Colorado, was number one on our list. Number two was the Boone/Blowing Rock area of North Carolina, and number three was Fayetteville, Arkansas.

After Cathy and Casey returned, we began packing. The family who bought our home loved our furnishings. They purchased most of our furniture and several of our cherished rugs, making the move slightly easier. Moving has its emotional costs, but it also signals a new chapter in life. Selling a home is often a poignant experience, made more complicated for us due to the family emergency. For Casey, it was particularly difficult as she had spent her entire life in that home. Over the past months, I've found myself reflecting on what our home meant to us—more than just a physical space, it was a repository of memories and shared experiences.

Over these many months writing this autobiography, I've reflected on our journey and the weight of leaving our Allanwood home has settled in. The move was more than a change of address; it was also leaving behind a rich grouping of friendships and a huge tapestry of memories of our daily life. From dinner parties to shared laughter, our Allanwood home was a silent witness to years of our lives. While the walls of our previous residence might be mere structures, the memories built there are everlasting.

New Hometown

We decided to try Fayetteville for a short period because it was the ideal location to drive to Hot Springs Village to settle Cathy's parents' estate. I searched for a temporary place to live in Fayetteville but only found a house or two in Bella Vista, a former retirement community, approximately 45 minutes from Fayetteville. Cathy would say if we want to live in Fayetteville and get to know the area, why not live there? I continued to look and eventually located a 2-bedroom, 2-bath furnished apartment. The rent was very reasonable even with our two dogs, Binker and Stormy. We signed the lease agreement without seeing it in person. We only had pictures from the internet.

Shortly after arriving in Fayetteville, Cathy and I celebrated our 25th wedding anniversary. We had dinner at Theo's restaurant, which is known for its excellent reputation and for being one of the better restaurants in the area. It was a wonderful way to celebrate our anniversary! Even today we reminisce about that special evening dining together to commemorate such a milestone in our relationship and a great way to create lasting memories.

We were adapting well to our new apartment living life. Along with it being fully furnished, we also had a washer and dryer, making life easier for us. We embarked on a serious house-finding mission. We were constantly looking for the right home in the right neighborhood. We worked with several real estate agents, but the properties they showed us never met our requirements. We didn't want to live in a house that was a step down in quality from our home in Maryland. We just had to keep looking.

After being disappointed many times with the homes the agents showed us, we began to think we should build a new home. We had our as-built plans from our home in Maryland and loved the layout of that home. We began to discuss what we would change or add to our previous home's design if we were to build a house. Having created a list of items, we began to look for building lots while still looking for existing homes.

We discovered a lovely, wooded neighborhood called Dogwood Canyon with only six custom-built homes and several very nice building lots for sale.

One two-acre corner lot had a sizable for sale sign on it. I called the number listed on the sign and spoke briefly about purchasing the lot. I inquired about the asking price, and the voice on the other end said, "Make me an offer." I wasn't comfortable with the conversation, so I said thanks and concluded the call.

We continued to look for building lots and homes for sale in the 3,200 square-foot range. I believed several building lots on the east side of Fayetteville would be great for building a house, mainly because they were flat and wouldn't need to be graded or filled in, thereby reducing construction costs.

But Cathy wanted to return to the two-acre lot in Dogwood Canyon and walk around it again. The lot was excellent and somewhat flat, and the neighborhood had curbs and wide streets. I could see only one problem, the rear of the lot declined into a very steep canyon. While on this visit, I again called the number on the sign, hoping to learn more about the lot and the selling price. I learned through my research it was in foreclosure, but I had no idea of the original selling price or the appraisal. When the bank employee again said, make me an offer, I spouted out a number and there were a few seconds of silence. I thought he might hang up on me but said, let me check on that price. I'll call you tomorrow with an answer. We weren't disappointed because he called back the following day and said the bank accepted our verbal offer.

Purchasing the building lot was easy, and we closed on it quickly. The person we worked with to acquire the lot also assisted with obtaining a building loan. When the time came, he and his loan officer provided names of insurance agents and contacts in the city government for utilities. I found a person who could create a detailed set of building plans based on our requirements and our as-built plans from our home in Maryland.

I contacted the Northwest AR Home Builders Association and obtained their list of builders. I reviewed the 86 names and made initial inquiry calls. I began whittling the list down to six builders. We met with those six builders and reviewed our plans and requirements documents with each builder. After the interviews, we decided to eliminate two builders because we believed they didn't fully understand the type of home we wanted built.

We continued to create our list of requirements into must-haves, essentials, and nice-to-haves until we had a complete package. I then sent the plans and requirements with a spreadsheet to each builder electronically. I developed a spreadsheet so we could perform a side-by-side comparison for the final evaluation of the builders' responses and costs.

When all the building proposals were returned, we began a detailed review of each proposal. In the past, when I would conduct solicitations, I would eliminate the lowest and highest bidders. But I didn't this time because I wanted to determine other qualities beyond costs. We conducted reference checks and looked at the builders' latest projects. This was the primary influencer for our selection because the prices were higher than planned or anticipated. Cathy and I believed the builder who I initially believed would be best was ultimately the winner. We created and sent a letter to each builder who hadn't been selected. I wanted to professionally close the loop with each builder who took the time and energy to submit a bid.

We arranged a meeting with the chosen builder at our building lot to discuss the placement of our new house. The architect who designed our house and created the plans had visited the lot numerous times, carefully considering the location and elevation for our home. During the meeting, we brought up the builder's initial estimate of a 9-month construction period and inquired whether this timeline was still accurate. Based on my understanding of Maryland's building codes and the requirements for licenses and permits, I had anticipated a more conservative 12-month timeframe. To our surprise, the builder confirmed that the 9-month schedule was indeed feasible. This revelation made me realize that I had underestimated how smoothly and swiftly a building project could proceed outside the bustling D.C. area.

The builder said the groundbreaking would begin the following day, and shortly after that, the footers and foundation would be created. The week when the framing started, we once again met with the builder to discuss additional specifics of the building project. During our conversation, Cathy asked the builder if he could do a specific task. He replied yes, but he couldn't begin until the following week when his best carpenter was finished with another job. Immediately Cathy said, that would be great. Then suddenly, she blurted out you can use Bob, he likes working with his hands and is good at this work. Before responding, he turned to me and asked if I could be at the job site the following morning by 7 a.m. Because I had already been volunteered, I said yes. That was the beginning of my third career as a carpenter's helper. I would be in training for the next seven months.

I believed my new job as a carpenter's helper would be somewhat dull and tedious at the time. But I immediately discovered how much fun it was. Over the next seven months, I learned much about home construction and woodworking. I had seven of the most wonderful and enjoyable months of my life. I worked from 7 a.m. to after 7 p.m. every day and half a day or more on Saturdays. Cathy was also engaged and spent many hours on the job site. Building a 4,100-square-foot house involves several steps and considerations. Hiring experienced professionals, such as contractors, architects, and subcontractors, is crucial to ensure a smooth and successful construction journey. The builder we selected had his own group of contractors who had worked with him for years. Because of that we believe our project went smoothly compared to the many other home building projects we had heard about.

Our construction project began by getting the lot ready, which included the first step of lot clearing. There was only one small tree removed in the middle of our lot. I felt terrible about taking down that little tree, but considering we were building on the edge of a canyon with many trees, one wasn't too much. We did replant several other hardwood trees around the lot in its memory. The lot was mostly level, and we didn't have to do much leveling before the trenches were dug for our foundation and support piers as well as water, electricity, septic lines and other utilities.

In those early days, Cathy and I would visit the job site to see the progress of our building project. We both watched as the concrete was poured for the footers and foundations. There was ample room for a crawl space, and I talked about adding a basement, as we had in our other two homes. But common sense prevailed, and I thought, why would we need the additional space for just Cathy and me, not to mention the added construction costs?

The pouring of footers and foundation was completed in a flash. Then the framing began. The men who did the framing were excellent because they had hardly any waste. They used what little scrap lumber that was left to make several closets larger and to build window seats in the upstairs bedrooms. The builder proposed using a whole-house wrap to protect the house

436

from moisture, heat, and cold. It was fun to watch the installation process as the crew measured, cut the wrap and installed the material.

After our house was under roof, and the windows and doors were installed, we had a more comfortable work environment. The home's major systems began to be installed, including plumbing and pipes, electrical wiring, switches and outlets, heating and cooling units, and related ducts.

During this stage of construction, there was so much work it wasn't easy to follow the separate individual tasks. I wanted to ensure tasks were completed according to the building plans and specifications. At the same time, I learned how to create all the custom molding used in our house. I would ride my motorcycle to the job site and open the house each morning. I would walk around cleaning up material or trash I had missed picking up the evening before. After the construction crew arrived and began working, I would drive to the builder's "gimongous" workshop, which was filled with every imaginable woodworking tool available. Each day he would review with me the steps for making the moldings. After I had begun to successfully operate the equipment, he would drive to our construction site, which was five minutes away.

I usually worked at the builder's workshop until noon, and someone would drive over and pick up the moldings I had made that morning. Returning to the job site, I would assist in installing the moldings. I enjoyed every minute of this manual labor. I learned so much about woodworking, carpentry work, and many other tasks related to building a home. I was learning how to craft, shape, and join many types of wood to create functional and aesthetically pleasing parts for our house. I was learning a new wide range of techniques, such as cutting, planing, joining, and finishing. These new woodworking skills allowed me to create custom pieces tailored specifically to the various parts of the house.

After walls had been constructed using two-by-six studs, it was time to insulate the exterior and interior walls. I didn't know what insulation would be used because I hadn't specified a type or rating. I believed the builder would install the traditional insulation with the aluminum backing. To my surprise, the builder had already decided to use cellulose. Not knowing much about cellulose insulation, I wasn't aware of its capabilities or benefits. The builder educated me on this type of insulation by explaining how its qualities were much better than the others. The floor joists and walls below the house were insulated using traditional aluminum-backed spun fiberglass insulation. The insulation was the last to be installed after the electrical, security, and internet wiring.

The builder and I would meet at the job site on Saturdays and usually work up to six hours. On one Saturday, as we talked while working, I asked what it was like to operate a Bobcat. I wanted to know if it was like driving a tank or an armored personnel carrier[46] (APC). He wasn't sure but when he explained the operation, they sounded very similar. There were two large trenches that had been created for water and sewer and electrical lines that needed the dirt moved back to cover all the utilities. He handed me the keys and said, "Why don't you go out and use the Bobcat to fill those trenches with dirt." It took only five minutes to familiarize myself with the hand and foot pedals, and away I went. I had a blast operating the Bobcat for the next four hours. The builder took several pictures of me operating it because I was like a child with a Tonka toy playing in the dirt. What fun!

Most of the initial inside work was nearing completion. The drywall panels were hung, taped, plastered, and sprayed with additional plaster. This process was foreign to us because on the east coast sheetrock was nailed and plastered and the plastered seams were sanded smooth before being primed and painted. But our builder was adamant about spraying the walls with additional plaster to cover what he called the wall imperfections. It's just another layer of moist plaster sprayed over the sheetrock called mud. Admittedly it had to grow on me, and I'm still uncomfortable with the look because I like smooth walls. Plus, if we decide to apply wallpaper, the walls will have to be sanded, or a thick base paper that smooths the walls will need to be installed first.

Probably the most enjoyable task for me was adding all the interior finishes. I had so much fun installing the cabinet drawers, doors, baseboards, casings, window sills, stair steps, balusters, kitchen cabinets, and moldings. The plumber installed all the bathtubs, vanities, kitchen appliances, water heater, and remaining plumbing components. A talented tile crew installed the hard-surfaced flooring and tile.

---

[46] An armored personnel carrier (APC) is a broad type of armored military vehicle designed to transport personnel and equipment in combat zones. Since World War I, APCs have become a very common piece of military equipment around the world. https://en.wikipedia.org/wiki/Armoured_personnel_carrier

Bobcat Bob at work

When I arrived at the job site at 6:45 to 7 a.m. it wasn't long before Roberto the hardwood floor installation technician would come onsite. I could have watched him working for hours. Roberto would look through the stack of flooring for the correct length. He was masterful and precise in selecting and placing each piece of wood. We had purchased the large 4.25-inch boards with multiple sizes. We wanted our floor to look like the flooring we loved while visiting the western states. In the west they used wood that had many of the beautiful original imperfections, and we selected a similar darker color to enhance the flooring wood grain.

Areas inside the house were used for workstations. These workstations were used to make stairway newel posts, coffered ceiling panels, and the barn doors for our offices. The stair newel post wood had been cut in the builder's workshop. I assembled and completed each in the house. I was apprehensive as I built the first one because each piece of wood was cut, nailed, and glued separately. Those panels were beautiful even without applying any stain. I took my time attaching the wood clamps to avoid scratching or scarring the wood. The following day the builder walked me through each step to place, install and nail the molding around those handrail newel posts. What an accomplishment.

The stair newel posts had to be built prior to the stairs being installed because the builder and I agreed to work the following Saturday to install the stairs. That Saturday the builder began reviewing the mathematics for the stairs. The first step was to measure the total rise and then divide the total rise number by the typical height per step. He had performed this process many times over his career. I tried to grasp the process quickly, but he wasn't waiting for me to commit the process to memory. He took all types of measurements rapidly. I remember him calculating the correct length of the stringers to fasten each step. At times it felt like this was a test of my mathematical skills. The stairs were measured and precisely cut, as we placed and nailed each step onto the stringer.

On Monday, the handrail and balusters had to be installed. Measuring the railing was a two-person job. The builder and I did that together. He showed me how to join each section of the handrailing. It was after this that the real fun began. I asked who would be installing the balusters. He grinned and said, "You." Once again, I had never attempted a precise task like this one. Okay, maybe working on and repairing computer equipment, but some of those mistakes were covered by other hardware, and a staircase handrail would be the first thing a person saw walking into our home. The builder handed me a drill and a giant drill bit, told me the measurements, and said, "Be careful. We don't want to mess up the owner's beautiful railing."

With the stairs installed, it was time to begin constructing the coffered ceiling. First, let me provide some background about coffered ceilings and their history. I was visiting Asheville, North Carolina, in the early 1970s when I first saw coffered ceilings touring Vanderbilt's Biltmore Estate, the largest privately-owned house in the United States. The ceilings were so massive and beautiful, that they created a lasting impression on me. On our honeymoon in the British Isles, Cathy and I visited other large estates with coffered ceilings. But it was over the Christmas holidays in 2012 when we were on a cruise with Casey, that we decided our next home would have coffered ceilings. There were several cruise ship dining rooms with coffered ceilings, and we took pictures for future use. When we asked the builder if we could have a coffered ceiling in our family room he smiled and said let me think about that overnight. The following morning, he arrived at the job site with a two-by-two piece of finished plywood with a penciled design of a coffered ceiling with exact dimensions and sizes of wood. The plan also included the steps for constructing each ceiling panel.

Our builder had scheduled a mission trip to Honduras and would leave in a week. Before he left, he coached me through the entire process of constructing a coffered ceiling panel. After his instruction, he asked if I wanted to go to Honduras and do carpentry work. I was honored he had asked me to go. Smiling, I said I must finish constructing the coffered ceiling panels before the boss returned. I said maybe next year.

The following week, I constructed each coffered ceiling panel and placed the molding precisely on the panels as instructed. Installation of those panels was a two-person job because one had to hold a panel while another had to simultaneously nail the panel to the ceiling. One of the other carpenters helped me install the panels. The five lengthwise large and wide beams required two people to install. Once again the other carpenter and I installed the lengthwise beams. Our family room ceiling has approximately 600 cut pieces of molding.

The next step in our construction project was painting the entire house inside and out. Cathy and I, along with the assistance from our designer Al Glover, selected only five color variations. These color variations provided precisely the look we wanted for our interior. Neither Cathy nor I were involved with the painting, only the selection of the colors. The walls and ceiling were spray-painted in the colors specified. I do not recall a Maryland painter using a sprayer only brushes and rollers to paint homes.

In Maryland, we had become accustomed to using water-based or latex paint due to the state's restrictions on oil-based varieties. This preference led to an extensive discussion with our builder and his painter in Arkansas. Despite their preference for oil-based paint, we insisted on using latex. Our builder remarked that it might be years before Arkansas mandates the use of latex paint. Although they were initially displeased with our choice, we expected them to adapt over time.

I observed more run marks than usual in the paintwork and brought this up with the painter. His response was lighthearted yet revealing when he mentioned not charging us for the extra paint used, subtly indicating their limited experience with spraying latex paint. Latex paint is thinner than oil-based paint, making it more challenging to spray evenly. This interaction highlighted the nuances and learning curve involved in working with different types of paint.

After completing the concrete driveways and walkways, we focused on our landscaping, which Cathy primarily managed. We again created a solicitation that was sent to several landscape companies in the area. Several responded. One was so high we thought we were back in the Washington, D.C., area. In hindsight, we might have been better off in the long run if we had selected that company. The landscaping company owner we chose came to our job site and gave a personal presentation for his proposal. He was a masterful salesman and wowed us. It wasn't until his personnel arrived to perform the work that we realized the error in our selection. The short version of the story is that we had to be engaged in every aspect of our landscaping project. After they finished the initial work, we immediately terminated all remaining tasks. It took six years and several other landscapers to bring our property to our envisioned look.

Our builder had suggested participating in the yearly Parade of Homes show at the beginning of our home-building project. The Parade of Homes celebrates the great features and exciting new home projects in Northwest AR (NWA). The NWA Parade of Homes offers something for everyone. It encourages each builder member to participate and display their craft through new construction or remodeling projects. In 2013, when our home was part of the Parade of Homes, there were only three basic judging categories: 1. street/curb appeal, 2. best layout, or 3. overall best home. Today there are many additional categories.

For years the Parade of Homes occurred over Father's Day, but it has changed since our house was in the parade. Preparing our new home was crunch time for Cathy and me. We had to perform or complete so much work, not to mention the stress of waiting for many back-ordered purchased items. After completing the construction, we moved our furniture and belongings from storage and transported them to our new home. Our home builder received awards for the best curb appeal and layout. Our builder invited Cathy and me to the NWA Parade of Homes yearly dinner, where builders received their awards. We enjoyed the event and meeting the other builders and many of the judges.

Relocating and Thriving in America's Hidden Gem

Living in Fayetteville and the broader Northwest Arkansas region has been an experience for Cathy and me that has been filled with countless joys and discoveries. Nestled in the Ozark Mountains, Fayetteville offers a unique blend of natural beauty, vibrant culture, and a welcoming community spirit that makes it more than just a place to live—it's a place to thrive. The town's streets are lined with charming boutiques, diverse eateries, and cafes that invite leisurely afternoons spent with friends and family. The local farmers' markets burst with the colors and flavors of the region, showcasing the bounty of local produce and artisanal goods. Fayetteville's commitment to arts and education, exemplified by the presence of the University of Arkansas, infuses the city with a youthful energy and a passion for discovery and innovation.

The natural surroundings of Northwest Arkansas are a constant source of wonder and adventure. The region's sprawling parks, picturesque trails, and clear, flowing rivers offer endless opportunities for outdoor activities, from hiking and biking to kayaking and fishing. The changing seasons paint the landscape in vivid colors, from the lush greens of spring to the fiery hues of autumn, making every outing a memorable experience. The area's commitment to conservation and outdoor recreation is evident in its well-maintained trail systems and public green spaces, ensuring that the natural beauty that defines Northwest Arkansas will be preserved for generations to come.

Beyond the scenic beauty and cultural richness, it's the sense of community that truly sets Fayetteville and Northwest Arkansas apart. Neighbors become friends, and strangers are greeted with smiles, creating a warm and inclusive atmosphere. The region's festivals, community events, and local traditions foster a strong sense of belonging and togetherness. Whether it's cheering on the Razorbacks sports team, enjoying a concert or Broadway play at the Walton Arts Center, attending an up-close play at Theater Squared or participating in one of the many local charity events, there's an intense sense of pride and communal spirit that makes living here genuinely wonderful. In every way, Fayetteville and Northwest Arkansas represent the best of what a community can offer. The sense of belonging and community pride is a rare find, making the region not just a place to live, but a place to call home—a home where every season brings new adventures, every neighborhood has its own story, and every resident contributes to the shared tapestry of community life. A place where nature's beauty, cultural vibrancy, and a friendly community converge to create an unparalleled living experience not found in many communities across the United States.

Our Adventures in Taos and Angel Fire, New Mexico

Following the Parade of Homes and the considerable effort and stress involved in building our new home, we needed a break. So, we decided to take a trip to Taos and Angel Fire in New Mexico. Both of these towns boast attractive ski areas. I had always wanted to ski in Taos but never found the time for it. Our drive along Interstate 40 was pleasant, featuring stretches where the landscape stretched out flat and seemingly endless. Cathy had arranged for our stay in Taos at a Marriott resort. We were assigned a ground-floor room, which was convenient for storing my bicycle, walking to dinner, and enjoying the sunrise and sunset from outside.

I rode my bicycle daily in Taos, exploring much of the area, even the mountains. There was so much to see. I enjoyed getting lost and finding my way back. I would return to the hotel and tell Cathy about what I saw on my bicycle ride. Then after showering and dressing, we would drive over the route I had previously ridden by bicycle. Cathy would walk around Taos while I was biking and would show me interesting things she saw as well.

After staying in Taos, we drove to Angel Fire, New Mexico, an area I thoroughly enjoyed visiting. I would classify the Angel Fire area of New Mexico as one of the most beautiful areas I've ever visited. Every day, I would ride my bicycle, get lost in the incredible majestic beauty, and forget about time, only living in the moment of extraordinary beauty.

On one of those bicycle rides, I found the Vietnam Veterans Memorial, which Bougie Criswell had told me I must see. I had been out riding when I saw a sign providing directions. I followed the directions to the entrance and was surprised at the small mountain I had to climb to get to the memorial. The base of Angel Fire is approximately 8,600 feet above sea level. On this day, my riding was taking me to higher elevations. I stood at the bottom of the road leading up to the memorial, thinking I could do this. I locked my shoes into my pedals and began to climb that hill/mountain to the top. On several occasions, I was breathing so hard that I contemplated stopping and walking the remainder of the way, but I chose not to. I'm glad I didn't because I felt a real sense of accomplishment after climbing that small mountain.

The memorial included six large buildings at the top of a small mountain with a static Huey helicopter mounted on steel poles. A placard in the entranceway described why this memorial was constructed there in New Mexico. The memorial, initially known as the Vietnam Veterans Peace and Brotherhood Chapel, had its origins in a battle near Con Thien (Hill of Angels), South Vietnam, in which 17 men lost their lives. Con Thien was a military base located extremely close to the demilitarized zone (DMZ) that began as a U.S. Army Special Forces camp, then transitioned to a United States Marine Corps combat base in 1967.

The Battle of Con Thien occurred when the North Vietnamese PAVN (People's Army of Vietnam) besieged the U.S. Marine Corps base. First Lieutenant David Westphall, a Marine platoon leader, was killed early in the battle. His parents, Victor and Jeanne Westphall, wanted to honor his service and began constructing the memorial to honor the memory of their son and the 16 men who died with him on May 22, 1968.

It was an emotional experience as I walked among the buildings and read placards and signs about those who died during the battle. Cathy and I drove back to the memorial the next day because she wanted to see and experience it as well.

Later that day, Cathy and I rode our bicycles to the Angel Fire golf course, further into the mountains and situated beautifully among large pine trees and several streams. We did several rides together, exploring the beautiful mountain passes. At 8,600 feet above sea level, the air was fresh and sweet. The next day I went on a round trip 75-mile bicycle ride to Cimarron, New Mexico, a small town located on the eastern slope of the Sangre de Cristo Mountain range and inhabited by just over 1,000 people. On July 4th, Cathy and I drove to Cimarron, then to Ute Park and Eagle Nest Lake, where we walked around, enjoying the beauty of the surrounding mountains and valleys. The following day we decided to take Route 412 on our drive home allowing us to travel through small towns we'd never been to before. We drove for hours during one travel stretch without going through a city or town. We then wondered aloud where individuals would go for health care or groceries.

Nevertheless, we did see wind turbine farms with spinning blades that appeared to cover the entire landscape. We passed a man riding a bicycle in the middle of nowhere with a small ice chest attached to his bike. The wind was blowing our SUV all over the road. I could only imagine how difficult it was for this lonely man to ride his bicycle on that extremely hot day. To make matters worse, he was riding in regular clothes and not bicycle riding apparel.

The New Mexico trip was a wonderful respite from moving and home building. It gave us both time to relax and explore the beauty of New Mexico. It also gave us time to plan our next year's anniversary celebration.

Celebrating Our 25th Anniversary

Cathy and I postponed celebrating our 25th wedding anniversary for two years because of the move to Fayetteville and the building of our home. Planning our postponed 25th anniversary celebration, we decided to indulge ourselves and take a Viking River Cruise from Paris to Normandy and watch the end of the Tour de France in Paris. We anticipated a river cruise would be a mode of travel unlike any other we had experienced. We would be in a floating hotel and would not have to pack and unpack every day as we traveled through France. We reviewed several river cruise operators and decided on the Viking Cruise Line because of their offerings and the excellent personal reviews. Our first river cruise was fantastic; on a scale of 1 to 10, it was a 20.

We stayed in Paris three days before and three days after our river cruise. During the last three days, we watched the end of the Tour de France bicycle race in Paris. Cathy had been to Paris before we were married, and I had never been but always wanted to go. We both wanted to visit the little towns on the way to the WWII D-Day beaches in Normandy. The Paris to Normandy cruise allowed us to see towns and beaches along the way without having to drive from town to town. Viking took care of everything for us, even making the hotel arrangements before and after our river cruise.

In Paris, we spent our days walking and riding tour buses, viewing the city and the many beautiful landmarks. We strolled through the Luxembourg Gardens and the Tuileries, toured four museums, and climbed to the top of the Arc de Triomphe and the Cathedral of the Sacred Heart, the famous white church atop a hill in Montmartre. While strolling through the streets atop Montmartre, we viewed many street artists and decided to commission an artist to paint a bicycle to celebrate our trip to Paris and that year's Tour de France.

At the Louvre, we tried to see the Mona Lisa painting from maybe 100 feet away. The room was filled with tourists trying to take pictures with their phones and tablet computers. This made viewing the Mona Lisa difficult at best. I thought the famous painting would be huge, but instead, it was tiny, measuring maybe 30 by 20 inches. We learned from the literature that the image portrays Lisa Gherardini, the wife of a Florentine cloth merchant, and is significantly smaller than standard poster copies.

While walking through the Louvre, Cathy and I became separated. To make matters worse, she had my wallet, passport, and even the hotel keys with her. I walked around for over an hour, trying to find her. I would have tried calling her by cell phone but our cell phones weren't working in France as we had originally planned. After several text messages to Cathy, she responded. It wasn't easy to hear the message alerts with so many people and the loud hum of activity within the Louvre. That afternoon while walking back to our hotel, we laughed about being separated and lost in a sea of people.

The next day we toured the Palace of Versailles, an enchanting and impressive castle where art and nature combine perfectly. King Louis XIV created this unique palace, away from Paris to protect the monarchy from the conspiracies of the capital. The palace symbolizes power. The most important figures of the kingdom, princes, courtiers, and ministers lived with the King at Versailles. Everything about the palace is one-of-a-kind opulence, extravagance, balance, and symmetry, conveying power over the ordinary citizen.

The Palace of Versailles is where the phrase "let them eat cake" originated. We toured the palace with a Viking tour guide, who explained the phrase supposedly said by Marie Antoinette in 1789 during one of the famines in France during the reign of her husband, King Louis XVI. But it was not attributed to her until half a century later. Discovering that anti-monarchists never cited the anecdote during the French Revolution was fascinating. Instead, it acquired great symbolic importance in subsequent historical accounts when pro-revolutionary commentators employed the phrase to denounce the extremely greedy ancient upper ruling classes as oblivious to France's citizens' needs during that period. Based on that information and history, we learned much and could understand why the French Revolution occurred.

Years earlier we would read to our daughter Casey about art and artists. I believe it introduced her to art and exposed her to different forms of creativity. She fell in love with the water lilies paintings and they piqued her interest and appreciation of the beauty of Monet's art. Cathy and I helped foster her love for his artwork and instilled in her a passion for the arts by reading books about artists to her and taking her to visit Monet's art exhibits.

Visiting Giverny and seeing Monet's gardens and home in person was a wonderful personal experience. It allowed us to witness the actual source of inspiration for Monet's masterpieces. Walking through and observing the gardens, surrounded by the vibrant colors and serene landscapes that Monet himself once admired and painted was an awesome experience. This experience had the power to deepen our understanding and appreciation of art, as well as create cherished memories we still talk about years later. The fact that we actually had the opportunity to visit Giverny and Monet's home, having previously nurtured Casey's love for his paintings, added an extra layer of significance and personal meaning to our experience that day.

Back on the river boat after the tour, we signed up for watercolor painting lessons after being inspired by Monet. Our art instructor was also the tour guide for Giverny. She had moved to Giverny to study art. She sparked my interest in watercolor painting. When we returned to Fayetteville, Cathy and I took additional watercolor painting lessons and thoroughly enjoyed creating our own paintings. Cathy has purchased all the supplies to begin a regular Bob and Cathy class, but I'd like to finish this book first before embarking on a new project.

After our visit to Giverny, our river cruise continued to Rouen, France—a historically significant city with a rich heritage and charming streets. Once we disembarked, we set out to explore the city, which was currently undergoing updates and improvements to make the walking surfaces larger and safer to walk on.

Our first stop was the magnificent Rouen Cathedral, a Gothic masterpiece that captivated us with its intricate architecture and towering spires.

We took our time admiring the stunning facade and ventured inside to marvel at the beautiful stained-glass windows and grand interior.

Next, we strolled through the picturesque streets of Rouen, lined with half-timbered houses and charming cafes. The city had a unique charm, with its well-preserved medieval architecture and narrow winding alleys. We couldn't resist stopping at a local bakery to indulge in some delicious pastries and coffee, savoring the flavors of France.

Rouen is also known for its association with Joan of Arc, the legendary French heroine. We visited the famously historic Place du Vieux-Marché, where Joan of Arc was executed. The square is now home to a memorial and a modern church dedicated to her. Standing there, we couldn't help but feel a sense of awe and reflect on the remarkable history that had unfolded in this very place.

As we strolled along, we came across several streets with metal stanchions guiding pedestrians to the other side. There was also a small alleyway where stanchions blocked our path. I decided to cross it anyway with Cathy in tow since it was just a short distance. I was carrying our rain coats in my messenger bag, which looked like a pillow on my side.

As we passed by one of the buildings, I greeted a gentleman standing and smoking nearby. He acknowledged my greeting, but as I tried to step over one of the stanchions, I lost my balance and fell on my right side. Thankfully, the messenger bag acted as a cushion protecting my upper body from hitting the ground, but unfortunately, the jagged metal edge of the broken stanchion cut my neck maybe a half inch deep. I was very lucky that morning, because the jagged stanchion missed hitting my carotid artery.

Witnessing the incident, the man smoking the cigarette quickly rushed to our aid, shouting words in French we couldn't understand. He had paper napkins on hand and promptly placed them on the wound to stop the bleeding. Cathy also removed several paper towels from my messenger bag to replace the soaked napkins. We were fortunate to be only two blocks away from the river boat. We walked back immediately for additional first aid. After cleaning the wound and applying a fresh bandage, we were ready to enjoy a delightful dinner on board without any additional excitement. The cruise offered a fantastic dining experience, with exquisite French cuisine and a selection of fine wines. We relished every bite and raised a glass to toast our memorable journey.

As we retired to our cabin for the night, we felt grateful that I hadn't been injured more severely. We were also thankful for the opportunity to explore Rouen and immerse ourselves in its rich culture and history.

The following morning, having arrived at Normandy, we boarded tour buses to visit the Normandy beaches and The Normandy American Cemetery and Memorial. We also stopped at several German artillery emplacements along the way. At the Normandy American Cemetery and Memorial, we were struck by its immaculate beauty and meticulous maintenance. The grounds were impeccably cared for, adding to the solemnity and reverence of the site. It was clear that every detail had been thoughtfully designed, from the memorial to the visitor center.

Walking through the cemetery, we were met by the overwhelming sight of over 9,000 white cross gravesites stretching across the vast landscape. The sheer number of fallen soldiers was a humbling reminder of the sacrifice and loss experienced during World War II. Each cross represented a young life cut short, a poignant reminder of the price paid for freedom.

For some of us, visiting The Normandy American Cemetery and Memorial brought our personal histories to the forefront. Memories of past conflicts, such as my time in the Vietnam War, resurfaced, emphasizing the gratitude and sense of fortune for having survived and lived blessed lives. The contrast between the rows of crosses and our own lives became stark, reminding us of the preciousness of every day and the responsibility to honor those who never had the chance to experience the fullness of life.

The efforts of the French staff who worked at The Normandy American Cemetery and Memorial to honor the fallen and acknowledge the sacrifices made during D-Day were profoundly moving and significant. Their organization of a special ceremony showcased their deep respect and gratitude for the historic importance of D-Day and the immense sacrifices of the soldiers involved. This thoughtful gesture highlights the enduring appreciation and recognition of the bravery and selflessness that played a crucial role in shaping history.

At The Normandy American Cemetery and Memorial, the gesture of giving each visiting person a rose to be placed randomly on the graves was a beautiful tribute. It symbolized not only remembrance but also a personal connection and act of gratitude towards the individual soldiers buried there.

Placing the rose given to me on a random grave allowed me to take a moment of reflection for the soldier who gave his life for the cause of freedom.

As I walked down the steps of the main monument, what I saw was a sea of numbers. These numbers, however, were not numbers. They were men and many were boys who had lived with hopes, dreams and fears. Sometimes these monuments represented letters that had been hand-delivered by a solemn man dressed in uniform. All these men and boys represented here were the countless lives with potential that ended too short and often in loneliness. I walked down countless rows of white crosses and Stars of David. My sadness grew heavier the further I walked. What struck me incredibly hard were the countless graves dedicated to unidentified soldiers. The gravity of a nameless grave deprives the soldier of proper remembrance and leaves the family with a painful lack of closure. I wanted to pay my respects to each one of these, but I don't think all the time in the world would have been enough for me.

It took 614 steps, almost seven minutes, to walk from the last grave row back to the first. I was surprised at the size of the cemetery. Seven mi-

Me laying flowers at the cemetery in Normandy, France

nutes of markers and seven minutes of lost lives. The 9,400-war dead, and 1,600 names of those missing on that day of June 6, 1944. That experience had a profound impact on both Cathy and me. That special and emotional day has stayed with me long after returning home. It was the significance of the ceremony that left a lasting impression on both of us. The collective energy of placing a rose on a grave and the shared moments of reflection left an impression that is the true testament to the power of remembrance.

The following day we began our river cruise back to Paris to watch the end of the Tour de France. Paris is indeed a city that captivates one with its rich history, stunning architecture, and artistic treasures. We spent the following days creating delightful and memorable experiences exploring the city. We set out on a self-guided walking tour of the Marais, the Jewish quarter, which was a fascinating way to discover the neighborhood's unique character. The combination of mansions and designer shops created an interesting contrast and showcases the area's diverse influences and vibrant atmosphere.

Visiting the Musee de L'Orangerie to see Monet's "Water Lilies" is a true treat for art enthusiasts. Monet's masterpiece, along with other impressionist artworks, offered a chance to immerse ourselves in the beauty and creativity of this renowned art movement. It's an experience that allowed us to appreciate the talent and vision of these remarkable artists.

Watching the Eiffel Tower light up at night was a magical sight. The flashing lights that illuminate the iconic landmark create a stunning spectacle that adds to the city's romantic ambiance. That night as Cathy and I walked along the Seine River and seeing the Eiffel Tower lit up with all those lights created a moment that was imprinted in our memories.

Visiting Napoleon's Tomb was another opportunity to delve into the history of France. The grandeur of the tomb and the significance of Napoleon's legacy provided a glimpse into the country's past and its influential figures.

Strolling by the vendor kiosks on the Left Bank we immersed ourselves in the lively artistic atmosphere of Paris. The combination of sidewalk vendors, inviting cafes, incredible outdoor sculptures, beautiful architecture, and ornate bridges adorned with love locks added to the city's charm and romance. There was a bridge that connected the left bank with the right bank and was full of closed locks. They are called love locks and are a Paris tradition where couples etch their names or initials on a padlock, attach it to a bridge and discard the key, symbolically sealing their love forever. Cathy and I saw this on several Parisian bridges we walked over. The Pont des Arts, a footbridge spanning the Seine River from the Left Bank to the Louvre, and the Pont de l'Archevêché, nestled near the illustrious Notre Dame Cathedral, were adorned with these locks as well.

The best was yet to come, the ending of the 2014 Tour de France on the Champs Elysees. This ending of the race was the 101st edition of the race, one of cycling's Grand Tours. The almost 2,300-mile race included 21 stages. We purchased seating tickets precisely at the finish line and experienced a day-long fun filled party environment for the city residents as well as foreign spectators such as us. Food and drink were everywhere. The French Air Force even flew fighter jets overhead with colored smoke billowing from the aircraft.

Since I started following the Tour de France in the 1970s, I was only occasionally able to watch the women's race. They race first and the focus is on the men's race, which has always been disappointing to me. I believe there are many excellent and talented women world-class racers that I'd like to watch. Because of this I was thrilled to watch the women finish before the men this time. These athletes were exceptional; their skill as bicycle racers was evident as they crossed the finish line. The men's team was due to arrive about 90 minutes later.

I left my seat to find the perfect vantage point for capturing the finish on camera. On TV, they replay the finish multiple times to see any of the details missed at the finish. This time, I was ready to record every moment as the riders crossed the finish line. However, I was caught off guard by their incredible finishing speed. Before I knew it, they had zoomed past my lens in a blurred swoosh, swoosh, swoosh. Cathy, who watched from her seat, was equally amazed by the racers' velocity.

After the last racers crossed the line and the awards ceremony concluded, Cathy and I strolled back to our hotel. Our route took us down the world-famous Champs-Élysées. We indulged in some window shopping and even paused at a few cafes to sample French wine. Three days before the race, the finishing course had been set up. Now, as we walked back, we watched as the barriers and lane dividers were swiftly disassembled. The process was so well-coordinated, it felt like watching a ballet. By the time we reached our hotel, the boulevard had returned to its regular, bustling self.

As we boarded the plane at Charles de Gaulle Airport, escorted by the attentive Viking staff, we carried with us the lingering romance of our river cruise through Paris and Normandy. The trip had been a second honeymoon, a celebration of love and history wrapped in the gentle embrace of the French countryside. But as the plane ascended, leaving behind the elegance of Europe, my mind began to shift gears. Our next adventure would swap the cobblestone streets for rugged canyon walls, the serene riverbanks for the roaring rapids of the Colorado River.

The Grand Canyon awaited us—a stark contrast to the refined landscapes of France and the beaches of Normandy. The transition from the historic charm of France to the raw, untamed beauty of the American Southwest was more than just a change of scenery; it was a leap from one world to another. As the memory of our anniversary cruise faded into the background, a new excitement took hold. This time, we would trade the luxury of a river cruise for the thrill of navigating the wild waters of the Colorado River, primitive camping under a sky full of stars, and forging new bonds in the heart of the canyon.

Our journey was about to take a turn toward the unexpected, the adventurous, and the truly unforgettable.

Grand Canyon River Rafting and Camping Out Under the Stars Adventure of 2014

Our Grand Canyon Colorado River rafting trip was an experience like no other. It was a journey that tested our resilience, strengthened our bonds, and left us with memories that will last a lifetime. It was shortly after our Viking River cruise from Paris to Normandy and our thrilling Tour de France finale. The contrast between the historical significance of Normandy and the natural wonder of the Grand Canyon was extremely striking. Both experiences left us with a deep sense of appreciation for life's adventures.

Our diverse group of Grand Canyon adventurers, including friends from Maryland and those we met for the first time as we boarded the rafts, came from all walks of life. I was in awe of how quickly we connected with one another. We shared a passion for nature and an eagerness to explore the wilderness. From the very first day, it felt like we were a close-knit family embarking on a grand adventure together. Camping each night under the stars was a surreal experience. The breathtaking beauty of the canyon under the night sky filled our hearts with wonder and humility. The camaraderie around the campfire, as we sat in a circle with our chairs, enjoying adult beverages, and sharing stories of the day's adventures, created a warm and inclusive atmosphere.

Our makeshift porta potties were undoubtedly one of the most unique aspects of the trip. Converting WWII ammunition cans into practical porta potties was both resourceful and environmentally conscious. It was a reminder of the importance of minimizing our impact on the pristine wilderness we were privileged to explore and visit. The gourmet-like meals prepared by our guides were a delightful surprise. Despite being in the heart of wilderness and nature, we enjoyed dishes that could rival any five-star restaurant. The flavors added a touch of luxury to our rustic camping experience. I appreciated the effort put into providing us with nourishing and delicious food.

Setting up the tent with Cathy during the first three nights proved to be a comical challenge. As someone new to camping, she embraced the experience with enthusiasm, even in the face of tent poles that seemed determined to thwart us. Our shared laughter and determination to overcome these obstacles strengthened our love, making each successful tent setup even more rewarding.

As the days passed, we found ourselves growing closer to our fellow adventurers. The trip brought us face-to-face with nature's raw beauty, but it also revealed the beauty within each person we encountered. We learned from one another, celebrated our differences, and discovered how similar our dreams and aspirations truly were.

Towards the end of our adventure, we were whisked away in a Bell Jet Ranger helicopter to a nearby ranch. The refreshing shower and brief respite from camping were a reminder of the harmony between adventure and comfort. It gave us a chance to reflect on the incredible experiences we had shared and prepare for the return to our everyday lives.

The Grand Canyon Colorado River rafting trip was a journey of growth, connection, and embracing the unknown. Cathy and I left with hearts full of gratitude for the privilege of exploring such a magnificent wonder of nature with a group of exceptional individuals. It was a week that had forever changed us, and I knew that these memories would be cherished for the rest of our lives. With a sense of wonder and gratitude I will remember that time as a blessing and an opportunity to reflect on the many gifts I have been given in life.

Retirement, My Final Frontier

Retirement, a transformative phase in life, marked the beginning of a new and uncharted frontier for me. It symbolized a profound transition from the rigors of my work I loved to a realm of freedom, self-discovery, and relaxation. I must admit, as I embarked on this journey, I was filled with a mix of anticipation, curiosity, and a hint of trepidation.

For years, my life had been dictated by schedules, deadlines, and professional responsibilities. The concept of retirement, once a distant notion, stood before me as the ultimate frontier. A vast expanse of time and possibilities waiting to be explored. It offered an opportunity to redefine my purpose, pursue forgotten passions, and reconnect with the people and activities that bring me joy.

Yet, amidst the excitement, there was a sense of uncertainty. Retirement allowed for the creation of a profound change in routine and identity. The structured days of work gave way to a blank canvas, ready to be painted with the colors of my choosing. It required a shift in mindset, as I began to navigate the uncharted waters of leisure and self-directed pursuits.

Retirement was not merely a cessation of work for me but rather an invitation to embrace a lifestyle characterized by freedom and personal fulfillment. It allowed me the chance to indulge in hobbies, travel with Cathy to many beautiful destinations, immerse myself in nature, engage in lifelong learning and teaching, and spend more time with those who I want to spend time with. It's a chapter in my life where I can prioritize my well-being, nurture relationships, and savor the simple pleasures that often eluded me during my busy working years.

Like any frontier, retirement also presented challenges. The absence of a structured routine initially felt disorienting, so I continued going to bed and awaking at the same time as I had while working. Armed with resilience, adaptability, and a willingness to embrace change, I was confident in my ability to navigate these uncharted territories and craft a retirement with Cathy that was filled with love, purpose, and fulfillment.

When I cannot be sure how many days there are left in life, every day becomes as essential as a year. I have and continue to try not to waste a minute wishing my life could be lived again. Instead, I fill each day as high as I can without spilling over because I have so much left to do in this life! Therefore, I am constantly making to-do lists so nothing is overlooked, missed, or forgotten.

I realized that I am facing what is essentially the last major transition of my life, retirement. I've lived my life in routines. The benefits of routines were taught to me by my parents and the Army. I occasionally thought about what it would be like to live in retirement, and even talked with retired friends and listened to their experiences. Cathy and I engaged a life coach to assist us in this significant transition. We believed nurturing social relationships and self-actualization was essential in our future.

In retrospect, people can rationalize their life or retirement decisions and experiences to suit themselves. I would venture to state that perhaps some retirees are reluctant to paint anything other than a beautiful rosy retirement picture. I didn't want to be one of them because my decision to retire held no guarantee of my expected outcomes for retirement happiness. I considered there would always be wild cards that could shape retirement in unexpected and undesirable ways or directions. For example, moving to an unfamiliar location such as Fayetteville, AR. Or the absence of friends from former social networks available in Maryland and the Washington, D.C., areas. The 2008 stock market crash substantially affected our portfolio of investments negatively, as did the 2022 recession. Presently there is much talk and forecasts of additional trouble around the corner. Add to this the loss of continuity, meaning, and identity in my familiar roles, which constituted my work/life structure. These were some of the topics considered before and after retiring because of their potential impact on our lives.

Since we retired, I have attempted to categorize all my activities as projects. I became a Toastmaster. Writing and giving speeches were projects. Even riding my bicycle for 60 miles would be a project because I would define my goal and objective of 60 miles, thinking through the best route, ensuring the bike was prepared for such a ride, and the speed needed to finish by a specific time of day, etc. I believe that projects keep my mind off all the negativity in today's chaotic and politicized world. Therefore, I thought big and small projects would keep the gray matter inside my cranium in good working order while generating positive daily moods.

Projects in Retirement

In my retirement, I've dedicated myself to various crafts, finding solace and therapy in working with my hands. This hands-on approach has been more than just a hobby; it's a form of meditation that diverts my focus from personal and life challenges, fostering a positive mindset. The act of crafting is a universal language, transforming the spark of an idea into tangible beauty without the need for words. The term "craft" derives from the Old English "craeft" and the German "kraft," both implying "strength" or "power." To me, crafting is the power to create something unique, utilizing both mental and physical skills to bring unseen wonders to life.

An example of this is the rug, pillows, and juice can lamps I made after my time in Vietnam, using nothing but my imagination, inspiration, hands, skills, and vision. This creative alchemy, when focused upon, unveils the true essence of skill and craft, which can manifest in various forms, from writing an autobiography to crafting a pine cone Christmas tree, a glass-covered cork top side table, or an outdoor coffee table combining aluminum, wood, corks, and glass. My involvement in teaching classes at the Osher Lifelong Learning Institute at the University of Arkansas has further enriched my experience, blending social engagement with creativity and thought.

These retirement activities have not only provided joy and fulfillment but also, I believe, contribute significantly to successful aging and cognitive health by incorporating social interaction, physical movement, creativity, and intellectual stimulation.

Along with our cognitive health, Cathy and I created a Salon of the Mind two years prior to the COVID-19 pandemic. The essence of The Salon's mission was simple yet powerful: to facilitate conversations and foster the exchange of diverse ideas. It encouraged participants to question thoughts and concepts openly, creating an intellectually stimulating environment that nurtured growth and enlightenment. It was a wonderful experience for all who participated. The Salon created an enduring commitment to fostering meaningful conversations and nurturing a more compassionate, connected environment in the Fayetteville area. Research all seasoned citizens who have lived past 100 years and see what they did in retirement. I'd bet they were active both mentally and physically.

X. Heart Matters

Life-Changing Event

Following my completion of a ride across the United States, I initially had no desire to embark on such a demanding journey again, spanning over 4,000 miles on a bicycle. While I continued to ride my bicycle, I avoided undertaking excessively long rides. However, as time passed, my thoughts began to drift back to the previous ride, reminiscing about the incredible experience it had been. Eventually, the idea took hold that I should undertake the same adventure on the 10th anniversary of my initial cross-country ride. This notion became a regular occurrence in my mind over time.

Upon relocating to Arkansas, I realized the potential for substantial fundraising opportunities from generous corporate donors in Northwest AR. In 2014, I made the decision to organize another fundraising ride in support of The Fisher House Foundation and wounded veterans. As 2016 approached, I gradually increased the distance of my daily training rides. I committed myself to consistently riding 45 to 60 miles per day on a weekly basis. Let me briefly digress and mention that during my first ride across the United States, I had no significant physical or cycling problems. As I previously wrote, I only experienced a single fall, which occurred during a major rainstorm in upper New York State. Luckily, the abundance of water on the road cushioned my fall, and I emerged unscathed without any damage to my clothing or even a bruise. Throughout the over 4,000-mile journey, I encountered only one flat tire, and that happened within the first few miles on the very first day. I didn't face any physical or psychological issues throughout that entire bicycle ride.

It wasn't until several years after completing the first ride, following our move to Arkansas, that I began experiencing heart rhythm problems on a regular basis. Initially, I would feel my heart flutter or palpitate irregularly. As I continued to ride for both enjoyment and training, my abnormal heart rhythm became more noticeable.

Upon relocating to Northwest AR, I discovered that it was a cyclist's paradise. The entire area aligned with my vision of ideal biking conditions. Within minutes of beginning my rides, I could find myself on well-maintained country roads with minimal automobile traffic. The region's roads featured short but steep hills with gradients ranging from 12 to 14 percent, offering an excellent opportunity to develop strong leg muscles for climbing. While I enjoyed the challenge of conquering these hills, I could not help but question why I should have to exert so much effort, considering my age. To make the struggle of climbing these hills more manageable, I decided to modify my bicycle's rear derailleur, opting for a mountain bike gearing setup. This choice seemed logical since mountain bikes equipped with suitable gear ratios can navigate dirt hills more easily than standard bikes.

I was thrilled with the new gearing setup, which allowed me to conquer many challenging hills. With my sights set on the upcoming 10th-anniversary cross-country bicycle ride, I aimed to increase my mileage and training intensity. My goal was to ride between 400 to 450 miles per week, just as I had done in the past. This high-mileage training was crucial for preparing myself to tackle mountains and endure consecutive rides of 100 miles or more.

August 2, 2016, marked a significant turning point in my life. After attending a meeting with Cathy in Fayetteville, we returned home around noon. I swiftly changed into my cycling gear to embark on a hill training ride to Lincoln, Arkansas. The route to Lincoln featured two scenic and challenging climbs, making it an ideal 40 to 60-mile training ride for a 68 year old.

After kissing Cathy goodbye, she left to play cards and I hopped on my bicycle and headed towards Lincoln. Unfortunately, my ride took an unexpected turn merely two miles into the journey. As I encountered a slight incline with a gradient of around five to six percent, my heart began to palpitate. Despite feeling this irregularity, I continued riding, assuming that my heart would return to its normal rhythm once I reached level ground. To my dismay, that wasn't the case. Instead, my heart started beating at a significantly faster rate. At that moment, I was on North Rupple Road, heading towards Wedington Road. Glancing down at my bicycle computer, which also served as a heart rate monitor, I was astounded to see my heart rate reading at 255 beats per minute.

This experience with my heart palpitations and the sensation of a large tuna fish bouncing inside my chest was the most severe episode I had ever encountered. Prior to this, while at home I had already consumed a bottle of Pedialyte and stopped at a nearby Shell gas station/convenience store to buy and drink a bottle of Gatorade, hoping it would help slow down my heart rate and restore normalcy. Interestingly, there was a large fire station with EMTs located just across the street and a couple of doors down from the gas station. While I briefly considered walking my bike to the fire station for assistance, I held onto the hope that my heart rate would naturally return to normal.

Additionally, there was an unknown individual lingering around me, seemingly interested in my bicycle and the computer mounted on the handlebars. Given my heightened tension and the rush of adrenaline, I didn't want to deal with the potential complications of confronting someone who might have had ill intentions toward my bike, the bicycle computer, or me. Eventually, the individual walked away, and I finished my Gatorade.

As my heart continued to beat rapidly and erratically, I made the decision to ride back home, while monitoring my pulse rate on the computer as I pedaled. Surprisingly, it began to slow down, but now it was beating at an alarmingly low rate of 26 to 28 bpm. "It was at that crucial moment, as I pedaled my way home, that a stark realization hit me: I was in serious trouble. This harrowing experience underscored the vital importance of always being acutely aware of my surroundings and the conditions. So many negative thoughts I had never experienced before began to flow through my mind, but I continued onward to return home. I really wasn't prepared mentally for this because it was a serious unexpected challenge. As I pedaled back home, the seriousness of this weighed heavily upon me. I continued to question how my heart could be feeling this way as I had taken great care of it over the years in my physical exercise and competitions. As I continued to pedal home my thoughts were reminiscent of those in Vietnam when all was lost. I asked God how this could be such a potentially dangerous or unpredictable situation. Once I arrived home, I grabbed a bottle of Pedialyte from the refrigerator and found myself drenched in heavy perspiration. I hastily grabbed a handful of paper towels and wiped the sweat off my head and face. Growing increasingly concerned, I found my car keys and rushed to the emergency room at Washington Regional Hospital. To my amazement, there was an available parking space right in front of the emergency room doors.

I hurried inside the emergency room, showing the nurses behind the desk my bicycle computer. I expressed my uncertainty about what was happening to my heart. I questioned whether it could be a heart attack given my heart rate exceeding 255 bpm. One of the nurses promptly went to the room located behind the emergency room desk and turned on the lights, while the other nurse asked me to sign in. I then called Cathy and told her that I was in Washington Regional's emergency room. Initially, she laughed, assuming it was a joke. I assured her that I wasn't kidding. At that moment, one of the nurses instructed me to accompany her. I shared with Cathy what was transpiring, expressed my love, and said goodbye. I was then placed onto a gurney, and the nurses quickly conducted an EKG, both expressing their astonishment at the peculiar pattern they observed. Later, I discovered that the type of EKG they witnessed is commonly referred to as a Tombstone EKG, and the reason for the name can easily be inferred.

As I was swiftly transported down the corridor, it felt like a scene from a movie, with the camera capturing the ceiling lights whizzing by overhead. Looking down the hallway, I noticed a group of 15 to 20 individuals waiting for me outside a treatment room. This was a team led by a young emergency room physician named Hunter Henry. Upon reaching the designated area, Dr. Henry's team removed my cycling gear, including shoes and jersey, (they didn't cut any of my garments off like on television) and proceeded to connect me to various instruments and IV needles. I was filled with anxiety, unsure of what to expect or what would come next. I sensed that many members of Dr. Henry's team shared the same sentiments. How would they restore my heart rhythm to normal? To quell my anxiety and hopefully theirs, I engaged each person in conversation, asking about their motivations for entering the medical field. By focusing on their responses, I diverted my attention from their actions and any lingering thoughts about my unknown condition.

Within an hour, they successfully lowered my heart rate without any drastic measures, such as getting shocked. I was then transported to an upstairs room with a bed. The entire experience, from the moment of arrival at the hospital, remains etched in my memory. The staff at Washington Regional Hospital treated both Cathy and me with genuine care and friendliness. After approximately an hour of further processing and gathering additional information about my medical history, I was taken to the cardiac catheterization (Cath) lab. Though the staff provided a detailed explanation of the procedure, I was unable to fully absorb the specifics. Perhaps I was in a state of disbelief or shock about what was unfolding. By that point, my body had received a substantial amount of fluids, and the temperature in the Cath lab felt unbearably cold. It felt like it was a bone-chilling minus 40 degrees Fahrenheit. I began to shiver uncontrollably, despite my efforts to mentally stop the shivering and trembling. It was an unprecedented level of coldness that I had never experienced before. Even when I requested warm blankets in a trembling voice, the warm blankets failed to provide relief from the cold. The medical personnel began moving swiftly, and I was still shaking when a staff member in the Cath lab injected me with something that instantly relieved the extreme cold sensation. Shortly thereafter, I was further sedated, and I lost consciousness.

After approximately two hours, I began to regain consciousness and found myself in the presence of cardiologist Dr. Ramaswamy, who was completing the catheterization procedure on my heart. In my groggy state, I could observe the screens and see what she was doing. Witnessing the inside of my own heart in real-time was a fascinating experience, and I hoped that I didn't accidentally utter any expletives in my awe. As Dr. Ramaswamy concluded the procedure, I watched her perform the final angioplasty[47] on one of my arteries. Soon after, I drifted back into unconsciousness, wondering if my momentary excitement had prompted her desire for a quiet working environment.

Following the procedure, I was transported back to my room, where the nursing staff kept a close eye on my condition. Not long after settling into my room, two physicians and three nurses visited me, eager to understand what had transpired.

---

[47] Angioplasty is a procedure used to open clogged heart arteries. Angioplasty uses a tiny balloon catheter that is inserted in a blocked blood vessel to help widen it and improve blood flow to the heart.

I recounted my entire journey, from my initial ride across the United States to my relocation to Arkansas and the training for my 10th-anniversary ride. I mentioned that I had retired and moved from Washington, D.C. One of the physicians seemed astounded that I hadn't lost consciousness despite the extreme fluctuations in my heart rate. They explained that my heart had been in a state of ventricular tachycardia (V-tach) for over an hour. It was at that moment that I truly realized how fortunate I was to be alive, when they described the condition and what happens to those who experience it.

The first night in the hospital proved to be exciting. Cathy was with me until close to midnight. It was then that she was told to go home and get her rest. The medical staff would monitor me over the rest of the night. After Cathy left, I began to relax and settle into the hospital environment, drifting off to sleep, alarms suddenly went off, prompting a rush of nurses and physicians into my room. The cause of the alarms was my heart rate dropping once again, this time to 26 bpm. Once my heart rate returned to over 40 beats per minute, the medical professionals departed, with the exception of one nurse who was assigned to stay with me for the next two hours, ensuring that my heart rate remained stable. She was a young nurse from Texas, pursuing her Ph.D. in nursing. During those two hours, we engaged in a delightful conversation about her education and discussed my experiences working in Washington, D.C., as well as the reasons behind our decision to move to Northwest AR.

The first night in the hospital was filled with challenges, as my repeatedly dropping heart rate made it difficult to sleep. The nursing staff diligently monitored my condition, taking my blood and vital signs every two hours and recording the information on my medical chart. The night was also emotionally charged, as I overheard physicians outside my room reviewing my records and making comments. Their remarks, of surprise at my survival after being in ventricular tachycardia (V-tach) for over an hour, stirred up a range of emotions within me. I felt incredibly blessed to be alive but also grappled with questions about why this had happened to me. It was a time of deep reflection, contemplating my past close calls and wondering why I had been spared.

As I struggled to sleep, my thoughts turned to the possible causes of my heart condition. None of my immediate family members had ever been diagnosed with heart issues, and my yearly physical examinations and checkups always showed normal cholesterol levels and no heart issues. Over the previous ten years I had two Nuclear Stress tests and an MRI of my heart before my first ride across America. Some of my Army friends and family members speculated that my current heart problem might be a latent result of exposure to chemicals during my time in Vietnam, Laos, and Cambodia. One physician even mentioned that those chemicals could lay dormant in my body's cell sub structure.

Finally, morning arrived, bringing with it a new day and a renewed sense of hope. I was grateful to still be alive and hoped for this positive trend to continue. The electrophysiologist[48] who would be performing the electrophysiology study on my heart explained that the test would record the electrical activity and pathways of my heart. Also, this study would determine the best treatment for my abnormal heart rhythm. He believed that my heart was traumatized and decided to wait for two days before proceeding with the study.

After two days of waiting, the electrophysiologist performed a procedure on my heart to identify the source of the issues. Following the procedure, the electrophysiologist informed me that I needed a pacemaker due to my low heart rate. This is not uncommon for individuals who are active in exercise and sports. He recommended a combination unit pacemaker and defibrillator, which would help regulate my heart rate and deliver shocks if necessary. Two days later, the device was implanted under my skin, resting on top of my pectoral muscle just below my left collarbone.

I shared this information with my friend Bob McLaughlin from Fresno, California, who provided me with numerous peer-reviewed research articles discussing the effects of chemicals we were exposed to in Vietnam. While I sought answers from the cardiologists about why this happened to me, they could not provide a specific diagnosis and attributed it to bad luck. They did however express interest in staying informed about any research I found on the connection between the chemicals used in Vietnam and ischemic heart disease.

---

[48] An electrophysiologist, also known as a cardiac electrophysiologist or cardiac EP, is a cardiologist who focuses on testing for and treating problems involving irregular heart rhythms, also known as arrhythmias.

My 70th Birthday

On July 8, 2018, I celebrated my 70th birthday, another significant milestone in my life. It was a moment that made me reflect on how I had arrived at this age. I still felt young at heart, mentally and sometimes even physically. Throughout history, many people haven't had the privilege of reaching 70 years of age. My father, siblings, and loved ones had all passed away before reaching this age. This made this milestone all the more meaningful for me.

As I navigated the journey of aging, I encountered various challenges and surprises along the way. The most significant one occurred two years earlier at age 68 when I experienced ventricular tachycardia. This health scare served as a wake-up call and a reminder of the fragility of life. However, despite the obstacles, growing older has been a positive experience overall. I didn't conform to societal expectations or live by predefined notions of how I should feel at my age. Instead, I embraced life on my own terms.

I have come to the realization that there is no universal formula for aging gracefully. Each person's experience is unique, with individual responses to the inner and outer transformations that come with age. What mattered most to me was maintaining a sense of fluidity and adaptability. I have learned to constantly shift gears, embracing the changes that came my way while focusing on what I could and wanted to do. Life has taught me the importance of staying flexible and open to new possibilities, regardless of age.

As my 70th birthday approached, I was unaware of the surprise that awaited me. Unbeknownst to me, Cathy and Casey had been diligently planning a special celebration for over two months. It was a testament to their love and thoughtfulness. I was about to be pleasantly surprised.

A few weeks before Casey's visit, I had casually mentioned to Cathy that it would be fun to go bowling or play a game of putt-putt golf. It was a simple suggestion, a way to enjoy some quality time together as a family. Little did I know that this innocent remark had sparked an idea in Cathy's mind.

Cathy proposed that we go bowling after Casey's arrival and try out the laser bowling alley in Rogers. I thought it was a fantastic idea and eagerly looked forward to the activity, reminiscing about the times I had gone bowling with my mother during my childhood. However, little did I know that Cathy and Casey had something more elaborate planned for my 70th birthday.

On the day of my birthday, as we arrived at the bowling alley, I noticed a sense of excitement in the air. It was not just an ordinary bowling outing—it turned out to be a surprise birthday party organized by Cathy and Casey. The staff at the bowling alley were experienced in creating parties for children. My birthday party was modeled after a child's event with all the fun and excitement. I was overwhelmed with joy and gratitude as friends and family gathered to celebrate this milestone of my life in such a setting.

The bowling alley was transformed into a festive space adorned with decorations, balloons, and a beautifully decorated cake. The room resonated with laughter, hugs, and well-wishes from loved ones and friends who had gathered to honor this special occasion. It was a heartwarming reminder of the love and care that surrounded me.

As I blew out the candles on my birthday cake, I couldn't help but reflect on the wisdom I had gained throughout my life. I realized that aging involves not just the passing of time but also the relationships and memories we create along the way. This surprise celebration was a testament to the connections I had fostered, and the meaningful experiences shared with those I cherished.

I felt a renewed sense of purpose and gratitude as I embraced the future with resilience. My 70th birthday marked not only a milestone in my life but also a reminder to continue living on my own terms, cherishing every moment that came my way. The love and thoughtfulness that Cathy and Casey had poured into planning this surprise celebration touched me deeply, reinforcing the importance of family, love, and connection.

The planning for my 70th birthday celebration was meticulous and thoughtful. Cathy and Casey started by having invitations printed three months in advance, ensuring that my Arkansas friends could mark their calendars and join in the festivities. They chose a bowling alley as the venue, recognizing its suitability for hosting a fun and lively party.

The day of my birthday began with lunch at our favorite little eatery, the Briar Rose. We enjoyed delicious food, setting the tone for a joyous celebration. The highlight of the evening was a giant birthday cake, specially baked to commemorate the occasion from Briar Rose. It was a delightful way to kick off the festivities and indulge in sweet treats.

As the evening unfolded, I laughed and bowled and everyone had the chance to participate in various activities beyond bowling itself, such as laser tag, putt-putt, and pinball. We also engaged in exhilarating games of indoor laser tag, enjoyed child-size motorcycle and race car rides, and explored the many other attractions the facility had to offer. Each person received tokens to play games and rides, ensuring that everyone could join in the fun.

Cathy and Casey went above and beyond to make the celebration personal and memorable for me. They focused on creating an experience that celebrated me as an individual rather than simply emphasizing my age. They intentionally avoided clichés and jokes often associated with milestone birthdays, instead aiming to make me feel loved, appreciated, and young at heart.

As a special touch, each guest received a goody bag filled with thoughtful items. From Fisher's popcorn from Ocean City, MD, to Baltimore baked cookies, model airplanes, cars, motorcycles, and even a helicopter. Every detail was carefully chosen to bring joy and delight.

Celebrating my 70th birthday on July 8, 2018, was a blessing and a milestone that prompted deep reflection on my journey to this age. Despite losing family members before they reached 70, the significance of achieving this milestone was not lost on me, especially after overcoming health challenges like ventricular tachycardia at 68. Embracing aging on my own terms, I cherished the flexibility and openness to new possibilities life offered. The surprise birthday celebration organized by Cathy and Casey, filled with thoughtful touches and based on a casual remark I made about bowling, deeply moved me. The presence of dear friends from Northwest Arkansas added to the joy of the occasion. This celebration not only commemorated a personal milestone but also reinforced the value of family, love, and connection in my life, encouraging me to look forward to the future with gratitude, resilience, also a renewed enthusiasm and appreciation for the journey ahead.

A Shocking Event—Thursday, December 19, 2019

On December 19, 2019, Cathy and I were busy preparing our home for Christmas, following our family tradition. Our daughter Casey was planning to visit us for Christmas, bringing along her two dogs, Penny and Roscoe. We had been decorating the house for the past three days and were almost done. Deciding to take a break, we had dinner and planned to finish up the remaining decorations the next day. After cleaning up from dinner, we relaxed by watching television until around 10 p.m. when we both went to bed, feeling satisfied with our Christmas preparations.

At 11:30 p.m. I suddenly sat up in bed and told Cathy that I had just been shocked. Initially, I thought she might have felt the electric shock as well by lying next to me. But she was concerned because my body shook like those of TV shows who get shocked with a defibrillator before I sat up, which startled her. Despite feeling fine, I proceeded to transmit data from my pacemaker/defibrillator to Washington Regional Hospital. After completing the transmission, I called the Walker Heart Clinic to speak with the physician on call, but instead I talked with the cardiologist nurse, whom I had woken from sleep. Since I didn't feel unwell, she advised me to call back at 7:30 a.m. the next day so they could review the transmitted data.

Upon reviewing the data, the only significant finding was that my heart rate had gone above 200 bpm for over 10 seconds, triggering the defibrillator shock. The electrophysiologist physician determined that modification in my medications was needed. As a precaution when prescribing more potent medications, the cardiologist suggested I stay in the hospital for three days for heart monitoring while starting the new medication. This hospital stay is a standard practice in the medical industry to ensure patients can tolerate the new medication and its dosage. I packed some clothes, my computer, and a new book for my hospital stay and called Casey to let her know what had happened. We could tell immediately that our call was upsetting her. Months later, when we talked about my hospital stay, she said she believed this would be the last Christmas with Dad. I can only imagine what was going through her mind as she drove to Fayetteville from Nashville. We wanted to be honest and upfront with Casey because years earlier, we promised to tell her the truth about any medical issues that could impact us as a family. Over the years, we have kept that promise. Emerging from a three-day hospital stay, I finally breathed in the sweet air of freedom as I returned home. The familiar embrace of Cathy, Casey, and our lively quartet of pets embraced me with warmth.

Grace and Liberty, our loving little Schnoodles, wasted no time in accepting their newfound cousins, Penny and Roscoe, into their home. However, what truly caught my attention was their synchronized symphony of loud barking. At the slightest hint of one dog's vocal outburst, the rest would join in a harmonious chorus that echoed throughout the house and made our ears ring. And when the urge to go outside struck one, the entire pack, wanted to go with wagging tails and eager eyes, rallied to the door. It was a fun sight to see, the lightning-fast formation of this merry band of mischievous loving companions, created a memory in my heart and mind that would forever bring a smile to my face.

Double the Love: How Two Schnoodle Puppies Stole Our Hearts

Grace and Liberty, our darling little furry companions, entered our lives following the heartbreaking loss of our previous pets Binker and Stormy. Determined to find loving companions, I went in search of adopting another female pup, hoping for the same unbreakable bond our previous Schnoodle Stormy shared with Cathy. The memory of our charming Stormy, always by Cathy's side, created in my heart the desire for another female companion for her. I contacted the original breeder but unfortunately, they didn't have pups nor were they expecting any liters in the foreseeable future.

Thus, my search began for a new furry four-legged family member. Ultimately, I found a reputable breeder in Libertytown, Maryland. I called to inquire if there were any pups available for adoption, but none were available at that time. But the breeder did say she was expecting a litter near Christmas. On Thanksgiving Day, I received an email from the breeder in Libertytown that she just had a litter born with two females and one male. She sent pictures of the two females because the male had already found a home in Rockville, Maryland. I must be honest, when I read the email and opened the attached pictures of those two precious females and upon seeing them, I was instantly in love. They were just so cute and precious. I printed the pictures and showed them to Cathy to determine if she was ready to take on the responsibility of adopting a pet again. But those pictures created an immediate smile on Cathy's face. She said she wanted to think about it overnight. The next morning at breakfast we talked about it and still Cathy wanted to consider the responsibility of being a pet parent again. I called the breeder and mentioned that we were interested but weren't sure which pup to adopt and would call again in a day or so with our decision. It was obvious to me that Cathy wanted the presence of another loving dog in our home, but her heart was still aching from the loss of Stormy. Stormy was with her everyday wherever she would go in the house and losing Stormy had hurt Cathy deeply.

Realizing this, we talked about the love that Binker and Stormy provided in our lives and all the fond memories we had with them. We made the decision to welcome both females into our lives and home. We traveled to Maryland in late January from Northwest Arkansas Regional Airport (XNA) directly to Washington Reagan Airport. Once we obtained a car, a Chrysler Minivan with three rows of seats, we drove to Frederick, MD, and checked into the hotel. Afterward, we then drove to Liberty Schnoodles Kennels to see our little pups. Once we arrived, we were greeted by the owner and allowed to hold our little girls for the first time. They were so tiny and cute. After making the arrangements to return the following day we drove back to Frederick for the night.

The following morning the temperature was dropping into the mid-teens and snow was in the forecast. Because of the changing weather conditions, we decided to check out early and drive back to Liberty Schnoodles. On the drive it began to flurry and by the time we arrived the roads were covered with snow. Completing the adoption paperwork process, we loaded our new adoptees into the minivan and headed for Washington, D.C., in a major winter storm.

We stopped in Frederick for coffee and purchased play toys for our little girls. Before I left, I lowered each row of seats creating one big floor area for the puppies to play. When I returned with several small toys, I found Cathy on the floor at the back of the minivan playing with the puppies. It was a beautiful scene. I could tell Cathy was absolutely loving the opportunity to play with the adorable bundles of joy. This was what I had hoped for when we decided to bring dogs into our home again.

The drive to Washington, D.C., was longer than expected due to the snow falling and the worsening road conditions. When we finally arrived at Washington Reagan Airport, we placed the tiny puppies into a small carrier and returned to the minivan. The airport had a dog walking area outside underneath the elevated subway tracks. We decided that it was time for a puppy potty break. The area was covered with stones that were larger than the puppies and they had difficulty finding a place to do their business. I joked with Cathy about who was the colder, the girls or us, and which of us wanted to get back to the warmth of the indoors the quickest. The wait for the flight departure was uneventful and our cute little puppies never barked or cried. I believe they wanted us to hold them on the plane ride to Northwest Arkansas but they never made any noise. We held the carrier on our laps and would occasionally talk to them through the sides to reassure them.

After we arrived in Northwest Arkansas, we wanted to take the puppies outside for another potty break. Much to our surprise there was an indoor pet facility. It had indoor/outdoor carpeting with a small water hose to wash the carpet. I could go into great detail describing how nice this little facility was but let me say I was really surprised at the completeness and appointments of the room. On the drive home we continued our conversation about names for our new family additions. Finally, we decided to name one Grace because it was a testament to their Thanksgiving Day birth. The other, a joyful reminder of their origin, we affectionately named Liberty, in honor of the place where they first opened their eyes to the world, Liberty Kennels, located within the town of Libertytown, MD. That's how our two little Schnoodles became Grace and Liberty.

Grace and Liberty

The addition of Grace and Liberty into our home following the loss of our beloved Binker and Stormy has brought an immense amount of love and joy into our lives. Despite initial uncertainties about adopting again, the sight of Grace and Liberty's pictures instantly warmed our hearts and led to the decision to welcome both into our family. This decision was driven by the cherished memories and love provided by our previous pets, recognizing the unique comfort and companionship that dogs bring into our lives.

Our trip to Maryland amidst winter's chill to meet and adopt Grace and Liberty was filled with moments of anticipation, joy, and a sense of renewal. From the first embrace at Liberty Schnoodles Kennels to the playful and tender moments shared in a snow-covered parking lot, these puppies quickly became much more than pets; they became family. Their names, Grace and Liberty, symbolize the gratitude and freedom their arrival has brought into our lives, serving as a reminder of the serendipitous journey that led them to us.

Now, Grace and Liberty infuse every day with their spirited presence, enriching our home with boundless love and constant companionship. Their arrival has woven a new tapestry of memories and joy into the fabric of our lives. They stand as a testament to the love and joy that pets bring, transforming our home into a place of warmth, laughter, and unconditional love.

While Grace and Liberty brought immense joy and comfort to our lives, my health journey continued to present its own challenges. Following a significant heart event on December 19, 2019, I faced a critical decision regarding my treatment.

A Cardiac Ablation on March 16, 2020

After my heart was shocked by my defibrillator on December 19th, 2019, I had a three-day hospital stay to change my medication regimen and ensure it was well-tolerated without complications. Cathy and Casey joined me for a crucial follow-up appointment with the cardiologist. During this visit, I had the chance to discuss a topic that had been on my mind for a while: should I consider a heart ablation procedure?

In fact, my curiosity about ablations began in 2016, prior to the insertion of the pacemaker/defibrillator. Because my friend Bob McLaughlin had suggested I should have the procedure. He had the procedure performed on his heart several years earlier, and it was successful in resolving his heart's electrical issues. I asked my cardiologist about the feasibility of performing this procedure prior to the placement of my pacemaker/defibrillator. Much to my surprise, his response had been firm and unequivocal. He said ablations were fraught with danger, and he advised against pursuing them. At that time, I had placed my trust in his judgment, convinced that he knew what was best for my heart.

However, at this recent appointment, armed with my own research on heart ablations, I approached the cardiologist with newfound knowledge and steadfastness. My research had yielded no evidence or peer reviewed studies suggesting that ablation procedures were inherently dangerous. Quite the contrary, they had become standard practices within the cardiology community over many years. With an air of reluctance, the cardiologist begrudgingly acknowledged the relative safety of ablations. He then suggested that his partner, a fellow practitioner, perform the ablation procedure. He also suggested we meet with his partner to discuss the ablation with him present to interpret and decipher his partner's responses to my questions and concerns. This was a very odd dynamic that left us perplexed and uncertain about the true intentions behind his statement.

As we exited the office, Casey, with a look of concern on her face, expressed her deepest misgivings. "Dad," she said, "I do not want you to undergo this procedure at this hospital. Allow me to take charge of researching the country's top specialists in ventricular tachycardia ablation. I will compile a comprehensive list of the top five cardiologists ensuring you receive the absolute best care and expertise."

Her words resonated deep within me, underscoring the love and dedication that pervaded our family's unwavering support. We knew we had embarked on a journey filled with uncertainties and difficult decisions. Together, armed with knowledge and a shared commitment to finding the finest medical expertise, we set forth on a quest for answers.

Her list of ablation specialists contained the name of the cardiologist who initiated this specific procedure in 1987 and had been recruited by Vanderbilt University Medical Center in Nashville, TN. I scheduled an initial consultation with Dr. Stevenson and several of his staff members and fellows for mid-February 2020 at the Vanderbilt Medical Center. During the consultation, Dr. Stevenson thoroughly discussed my condition and some technical aspects of my condition. Dr. Stevenson believed my heart problems were within the electrical pathways of my heart. Think of it as a beltway around a major city, and the cars on the beltway are the electrical signals traveling in one direction. All of a sudden one or more cars (electrical signals) hit a bump in the road and veer off the beltway to an offramp, and then cause an accident. The accident is an extra beat or a skipped beat. This is my generalization definition.

Dr. Stevenson said he had reviewed the cardiologist's diagnosis from Fayetteville. Based on that diagnosis, this ablation would be a routine procedure requiring at most two hours to complete. He even drew a heart diagram identifying the problem area based on the diagnosis. He answered each of my questions, addressed my concerns, and spent time with Cathy and Casey, answering their questions and concerns as well.

But the best question came from Cathy when she asked, "Can you give me my Bob back, please?" I took this to mean her Bob who was always physically active. But because of the shocks I slowed down. He looked at each of us and said: "Yes, I believe I can get Bob back to being Bob." The decision to proceed was made. Dr. Stevenson and his team would perform the ablation on March 16th, 2020.

Fast forward to Sunday, March 15, 2020 we arrived in Nashville just days before the COVID-19 pandemic lockdowns. I was at the hospital at 6am on Monday, March 16th. After the admissions process, I was taken to the cardiology unit. It wasn't long before I was prepped for surgery in the catheterization laboratory. The last thing I remember saying to someone was that this was a routine procedure, and I would be able to return home that afternoon. Then the lights went out.

Cathy and Casey had to wait well beyond two hours. Finally, a staff member explained that it was more complicated than anticipated but didn't explain why. I can't imagine the anxiety and worry they must have been going through. Every hour, another staff member would provide an update. This continued for seven long hours when, finally, Dr. Stevenson came out to Cathy and Casey to explain that the original diagnosis was incorrect. He had to spend much of the procedure looking for the areas the Fayetteville cardiologist identified as the problem. Because he didn't find the issues in the areas of the original diagnosis, he had to perform a complete electrophysiology (EP) study[49] again on my heart several times.

---

[49] Electrophysiology studies (EPS) are tests that help doctors understand the nature of abnormal heart rhythms (arrhythmias). Electrophysiologic testing uses catheters inserted into the heart to find out where abnormal heartbeats are coming from.

During the EP study, Dr. Stevenson and his team inserted small, thin wire electrodes into a vein on both sides of my groin and veins on both wrists. He or a team member threaded the wire electrodes through the vein and into my heart. To accomplish this, they used a particular type of X-ray procedure called fluoroscopy. Once in my heart, the electrodes measured my heart's electrical signals. Electrical signals were also sent through the electrodes to stimulate my heart tissue to cause my abnormal heart rhythms to return so they could precisely determine the cell area that was the source of the problem.

Based on the original diagnosis, the area to be ablated should have been in the lower left chamber close to the septum. But when Dr. Stevenson looked there, no abnormal electrical signals were detected. He then performed the EP study and discovered the problems were in the lower right chamber and on the outside of the right exterior portion of the heart. I learned that an outside-of-the-heart ablation is called epicardial ablation. At the end of the procedure, Dr. Stevenson and his team had to perform two ablations on my heart, one on the inside and the other on the outside. This procedure took over seven hours to complete.

Dr. Stevenson used a long needle to access my heart. The surgical needle was inserted through the skin in the upper portion of my stomach and advanced through the lining of the fluid-filled sack (pericardium) surrounding my heart. A tube (sheath) was then inserted, and catheters were passed through the tube to access the outside surface of the heart. Dr. Stevenson had to perform some very delicate procedures to ablate this area. The wall of my heart was punctured, and it began to bleed into the pericardium. That required a tube to be inserted from the outside of my belly into the stomach to drain the blood.

Because of the length of the procedure, I was intubated, with a breathing tube connected to a ventilator to assist in my breathing. Another catheter was inserted to prevent me from relieving myself on the surgery table. I can only imagine how I looked to Cathy and Casey when they entered my intensive care unit room. I had a tube sticking out of my mouth and another out of my upper stomach, a catheter, and holes and needles in both sides of my groin and arms.

I spent the next two days in the hospital recovering. I was given a powerful narcotic twice to manage pain, but its effects were frightening. When the nurse wanted to administer another, I declined because of concern of long-term dependency.

The pain was excruciating, and I believed I could manage it, drawing on my experiences as a 20-year-old. This particular combination of pains was unique and unfamiliar to me. In hindsight, I should have communicated with the physician assigned to provide pain medication and requested something less potent. I also developed a persistent cough from the breathing tube. On the second day, I managed to get out of bed and walked to another part of the hospital for an ultrasound test on my heart.

Due to the COVID-19 pandemic, Vanderbilt Medical Center, like many other organizations, was preparing to close to the public due to the crisis. Aware of this situation, Dr. Stevenson understood my reluctance to stay in the hospital without Cathy. Uncertain of how long the shutdown would last, I requested discharge before the lockdown was in place, and Dr. Stevenson agreed that I could leave before the pandemic restrictions took effect. After reviewing my previous tests, it didn't take long for me to be released from the hospital.

Once discharged, we went back to our hotel with the intention of catching the one-hour-long flight back home. Unfortunately, luck was not on our side as the flight got canceled due to the nationwide shutdown caused by the COVID-19 pandemic. The entire country was undergoing a shutdown, leading to the cancellation of our planned return flight.

During that time, Cathy was busy arranging for a rental car while I was dealing with a fever and chills, bundled up in bed in an attempt to keep warm. Despite my worsening condition, I made the ill-advised decision not to return to the hospital. I convinced myself that I would start feeling better soon and didn't want to be alone in Vanderbilt Hospital if I got locked in due to the pandemic restrictions. Looking back, it was the worst choice I could have made, as I should have immediately returned to the hospital and received medical treatment for the symptoms I was experiencing.

Despite the circumstances, we proceeded with our plan to rent a car, and Cathy took on the challenging task of driving us back home, covering a grueling journey of eight and a half hours. To make matters worse, we encountered a severe thunderstorm lasting approximately six hours after crossing into Arkansas from Tennessee. Cathy navigated through the storm using the high-beam headlights and the car's emergency flashers to ensure visibility for other drivers. The conditions were treacherous, and she did an excellent job of driving us safely home.

By the weekend, I was genuinely surprised by the deteriorating state of my health. My fever skyrocketed to 104 degrees, intensifying the severity of my cough. My nose seemed determined to participate in a non-stop marathon, incessantly running and causing increased discomfort. At this point, every inch of my body throbbed, as if I had been struck not once, but twice, by a fully loaded dump truck. The combination of these symptoms was deeply distressing and raised significant alarm for Cathy.

After receiving a negative result from my COVID-19 test, the physician who conducted the test advised me to contact my primary care physician at the VA hospital and inform them of my condition. This particular physician had prior experience at the VA and was familiar with my primary care physician. Sensing the urgency, I wasted no time and called my primary care physician as soon as I arrived home. However, I was instructed to head straight to the VA emergency room instead of scheduling a routine appointment.

Following an afternoon spent in the emergency room, I received a diagnosis of pneumonia and a partially collapsed lung, likely stemming from the earlier intubation. It became evident that if I had stayed at Vanderbilt, my condition might not have deteriorated to such an extent. The VA emergency room physician prescribed three different antibiotics and provided medication to ease my cough. What truly stood out was the exceptional level of care displayed by the physician. This physician even gave me his personal cell phone number and encouraged me to reach out over the weekend if my condition worsened or if I had any questions.

Throughout the weekend, we exchanged numerous text messages as the physician promptly responded to my inquiries and questions. When I called on Monday, I expressed my deep appreciation for his and the VA's kindness and generosity in addressing my concerns. To my surprise, the physician responded with a lighthearted tone, mentioning that they found our discussions enjoyable. He said he rarely had the opportunity to engage in such detailed medical conversations and answer questions like mine.

This experience was a testament to the physician's unwavering dedication and willingness to go above and beyond, making me feel supported and cared for throughout my recovery process.

June 16, 2020, Another Shock Riding My Bicycle

Yesterday is history, and tomorrow is a Mystery.
Today is a gift; that's why it's called The Present!

Three months after my ablation procedure, I asked Dr. Stevenson and his team about the possibility of discontinuing the medications. While they were reluctant but agreed to let me gradually stop the medications. I was overjoyed by this decision, feeling a sense of relief and happiness. Not following recommendations, the next morning, I made the impulsive decision to abruptly halt all medications at once and went for a short bicycle ride. It felt exhilarating, and the initial days were filled with excitement and positivity. I felt invincible, as if riding my bike could magically cure my heart's electrical issue.

I started with 10-mile rides, then gradually increased the distance by two miles over each ride. This pattern of a two-mile increase per ride continued over the following weeks, eventually allowing me to complete rides of approximately 26 miles. Embarking on my next ride my goal was to complete 28 miles. When I reached the University of Arkansas's agriculture center, everything seemed fine. I stood up on the pedals, putting more energy into crossing the road. It felt exhilarating to rise from the saddle and generate a burst of energy to make my way across the street.

I maintained that position for approximately another 10 yards, enjoying the ride. When I suddenly felt a tingling sensation in my legs and then began to feel lightheaded. In an instant, it happened, BANG! My defibrillator delivered an extremely powerful shock to my heart, comparable to the dramatic scenes we often witness on television when doctors use paddles to revive patients.

The entire episode unfolded rapidly, lasting no more than two seconds. I continued pedaling for another 20 additional feet before managing to stop. I unclipped my feet from the pedals and began cursing. To any bystanders,

I must have appeared like a person with mental disorders, walking around and cursing at the bicycle computer I held in my hand.

The young men working at the University Agriculture Center had witnessed the entire episode, including my cursing, and yelling to myself. One of the young men rushed over immediately, displaying genuine concern and offered his assistance. After assuring the young man numerous times that I was okay, he eventually returned to his work. I then walked my bicycle to the side of a concrete wall, sat down against it, and called Cathy to transport me home.

My next call was to Vanderbilt Hospital to inform Dr. Stevenson and his team about what had transpired. I also contacted Washington Regional Hospital. Once I arrived home, I transmitted the data from my pacemaker/defibrillator Washington Regional for their review and forwarding to Dr. Stevenson.

Later that afternoon, upon speaking with Dr. Stevenson's team at Vanderbilt, they advised me to return to their hospital in Nashville for a thorough examination of my heart. After reviewing the data from my pacemaker/defibrillator, Dr. Stevenson wisely reiterated that I should have tapered the reduction of my medications. He also reminded me about the severity of the recent seven-hour ablation. Looking back, I realize that it was my emotions driving those feelings of joy. In hindsight, it would have been wiser to gradually reduce the medications, starting with one pill a day, then half a pill, and eventually stopping altogether, while closely monitoring my well-being.

As I left Dr. Stevenson's office, contemplating the advice given and the importance of caution in my journey toward recovery, I couldn't help but reflect on the larger arc of my life. Health scares have a way of making us pause, not just to consider our next steps but to reflect on all the steps we've already taken. That afternoon marked yet another lesson in a life filled with triumphs and challenges.

Closing Thoughts

Life is not about finding yourself.
Life is about creating yourself.
— George Bernard Shaw

As I reflect upon the pages of my life's journey, it is hard to believe how swiftly the years have passed. It feels like just yesterday when I embarked on this adventure alongside my beloved wife, full of youthful optimism and boundless dreams. Yet, as I stand at the threshold of my winter years, I am filled with wonderment at the relentless passage of time.

The images of my past flicker before my eyes, providing glimpses of the person I once was, and the aspirations that fueled my spirit. And now, here I am, confronted with the reality of aging, caught off guard by the swiftness of this transformation. How did the years slip away so effortlessly? Where did the exuberance of my youth vanish?

I recall observing older individuals as I traversed the various stages of life, perceiving them as beings who existed in a distant realm, far removed from my own. The concept of my winter season seemed incomprehensible, an abstract notion beyond my grasp. And yet, here I stand, surrounded by retired friends whose hair has turned gray or white and whose steps have grown slower. The vibrant souls I once knew, including myself, now bear the unmistakable marks of time. We have become the elders we once glimpsed, never anticipating that this would be our fate.

It is a humbling realization, a testament to the transient nature of life itself. As I witness the changes etched upon our faces and bodies, I understand that we are part of an endless cycle, passing the torch from one generation to the next. We are the torchbearers now, entrusted with the wisdom and experience we have gained along the way.

I find solace in the shared experience of aging. We are not alone in our journey. Together, we navigate the complexities of growing older, cherishing the memories that shaped us and embracing the evolving seasons of life. As I bid farewell to the days gone by, I welcome the future with open arms, eager to explore the mysteries that still lie ahead, knowing that the stories etched in the pages of my autobiography are merely a prelude to the grander narrative still unfolding.

Every passing day, I find myself reveling in simple pleasures, such as the soothing touch of water during my showers. Taking a nap has shifted from being a treat to a necessary respite, lest I doze off while reading a book or watching TV with my dear Cathy. Unprepared as I am for the inevitable aches, pains, and the gradual loss of strength, I embark upon this new season of life.

Winter has arrived, and though I cannot foresee its duration, I know it extends beyond earthly bounds. A new adventure awaits beyond the horizon. While I do harbor a few regrets, they are but fleeting moments in the grand tapestry of my existence. For there are countless accomplishments and experiences that I am proud to have woven into the fabric of my being. It is the essence of a lifetime, a testament to my journey.

To those who have yet to face their own winter, let me impart a gentle reminder that it will arrive sooner than expected. Whatever dreams and aspirations stir within you, pursue them with urgency. Do not delay, for life rushes past at an extraordinary pace. Today is your canvas, and there is no guarantee of witnessing all the seasons of your life. Live in the present, express your love, and ensure your loved ones know the depth of your affection. May they recognize and cherish the years of devotion you have dedicated to them.

As I contemplate the remaining chapters of my existence, a tempered optimism envelops me. My experiences and memories have been etched in diverse narratives, painted strokes that depict the odyssey of my life. It is my hope that these stories become a shared heritage, a corpus that celebrates my triumphs, adventures, and reflections. A unified tale that illuminates the evolution of my character, shaping not only my own life but also the collective fabric of our family's legacy.

My desire to create a lasting legacy for our daughter and the Rodweller family remains steadfast. Through the chronological organization of my life's story, blending flashbacks and short-framing stories, I have sought to convey not just a narrative but an Ethical Will—a collection of personal accounts, philosophical musings, and the values and goals that have shaped my existence. It is my hope that this compilation provides a profound understanding and meaning of my life, love, and interrelationships.

In this pursuit, I have strived to capture my memories in a clear and unbiased manner, satisfying my yearning for symbolic immortality. Symbolic immortality, to me, signifies the memories of my life history, philosophy, deeds, and spirit, perpetuated and remembered long after I am gone. It is within these memories that my legacy resides, offering guidance, inspiration, and a connection to future generations.

Vietnam ignited within me a greater appreciation for the brevity and fragility of life. It served as a wake-up call, a reminder that eternity eludes us, and that each second, we live is a precious gift. Like stars shimmering in the night sky, a fleeting raindrop or a snowflake melting away, these miraculous seconds urge us to seize the present, to embrace life's wonders and never squander a single moment.

My legacy, as I have come to understand, transcends financial wealth. Cathy and I have intentionally cultivated a family environment centered not on material riches, but on the essence of life itself. We recognize that no amount of money can replace the treasured memories we create together. When disaster befalls a couple, their most profound regret often lies in losing the precious pictures that encapsulate cherished family moments. Through my words, I endeavored to paint mental pictures, weaving vivid imagery that creates lasting impressions in the hearts and minds of those who read this book.

As I conclude this chapter of my life, I ask you to reflect on the importance of creating a meaningful legacy for your own family. Embrace the fleeting nature of our existence, for it is in this recognition that we find the motivation to live purposefully and to forge lasting connections. Cherish the moments, nurture the bonds, and impart your values and wisdom upon future generations. May the memories we create and the lessons we pass down become the foundation of a legacy that echoes through time, a testament to a life well-lived, filled with love, compassion, and an unwavering appreciation for the miraculous seconds we are granted.

Humility, a virtue both hard-earned and gracefully received through the winding journey of my life, stands as a cornerstone of character and holds great significance. It is through the rich tapestry of experiences we gather along our path in life—each with its own profound cost—that humility gains its depth, urging us to value and cherish each day as a precious gift and to embrace joy in the very act of living. Our existence unfolds not as a mere dress rehearsal, but

Cathy and I continue to make loving memories.

as the actual grand performance of life itself, urging and compelling us to seize every moment, every second with intention and gratitude.

Contemplating the mysteries of life and the afterlife, I have sought answers from spiritual leaders, questioning the nature of death, consciousness, and what lies beyond. While the certainty of these answers eludes me, I have come to the realization that living a virtuous life rooted in humility is of utmost importance. If a just and compassionate God exists, they would value the essence of who I am, the virtues I have embraced, and the humility I have cultivated, rather than mere devotion. Conversely, if God were unjust, it would be unworthy to worship them. And if God were nonexistent, I would find solace in knowing that my honorable and noble life will endure through my legacy and the loving memories of those I hold dear.

I've attempted to give my definition of humility that I believe underscores its role in our lives not just as a personal attribute, but as a guiding principle for living a meaningful, virtuous life. It highlights humility's power to enrich our lives, shape our interactions with others, and anchor us in a sense of purpose that transcends the material world, offering a path to true fulfillment and peace.

As I stand at this juncture in my life, I am aware that there are still countless opportunities and adventures awaiting me. I am reminded of Paul S. McElroy's words in "New Beginnings" to move forward with hope, focusing on what can be accomplished rather than being hindered by what is beyond our reach.

Regardless of our position in the cycle of life, we should always treasure our relationships, find value in our meaningful work, and appreciate our place in the world. Our legacy is not merely about the material possessions we leave behind but the impact we have on the lives of others. I hold onto the hope of heaven, but even if it does not exist, I take solace in the fact that I have led a good life, treating everyone with respect and justice, as any benevolent God would desire.

As I stand on the precipice of this new chapter of my life, I am filled not with fear or trepidation but with a deep sense of gratitude. Gratitude for the love that has sustained me, for the challenges that have sharpened my resolve, and for the moments of beauty that have left their mark on my soul. My life has been a mosaic of experiences, each piece adding its unique color and shape to the whole. And as I look at the masterpiece I have created, I am grateful and proud.

There is an inherent beauty in the unknown—the new adventures, the opportunities for growth, and the unexpected joys that await. Life continues to surprise me, and I have learned to embrace these surprises with an open heart. For in every season, there is wonder to be found, and in every ending, there is the promise of a new beginning. So, as I turn the page to whatever lies ahead, I do so with the same optimism and boundless dreams that carried me through all these years. The adventure is far from over.

Life itself is a precious gift, and how we choose to live it becomes our gift to future generations. Let us make it extraordinary, embracing each day with enthusiasm, finding enjoyment, and spreading happiness. May we embark on new adventures, seeking the wonders that each day unveils.

May my story serve as a testament to the power of perseverance, the beauty of human connection, and the infinite possibilities that lie within each of us. Remember, dear reader, that your story is still being written, and every choice you make has the potential to redefine your narrative. Embrace your uniqueness, chase your dreams with unwavering passion, and leave an indelible mark on the world. Go forth with confidence and prosperity, knowing that each new day offers limitless possibilities for growth and fulfillment.

About the Author

Robert **Kennedy Rodweller** is an experienced IT professional whose career has spanned a wide range of sectors—from government and law, to manufacturing, to healthcare and finance. He has held key positions as a senior technology expert, effectively leading major organizations and overseeing complex national technological projects to ensure their successful execution and timely completion. He has managed multi-million-dollar budgets and built an excellent track record in team development and profit-and-loss management. His leadership skills also allowed him to play a pivotal role in guiding technology research and development initiatives.

His autobiography chronicles a personal narrative of the significant events, challenges, and successes that have shaped his life. Through personal reflections, he offers detailed insights into his thoughts, feelings, and motivations.

Now retired, he and his wife, Cathy, live in Fayetteville, Arkansas, with Grace and Liberty, their two Schnoodle dogs.

Milton Keynes UK
Ingram Content Group UK Ltd.
UKHW052142311024
450402UK00017B/126/J